Visit America's Be

Open Days
Directory 2018
opendaysprogram.org

MW01170848

Special thanks to:
The Kayne Foundation
The Leon Levy Foundation
The Ruettgers Family Charitable Organization

Publisher's Cataloging-in-Publication
(provided by Quality Books, Inc.)
The Garden Conservancy's Open Days Directory:
Visit America's Best Private Gardens, 2018 ed., 23rd ed.
   p. cm.
   Includes index.
   ISSN: 1087-7738
   ISBN – 13: 978-1-893424-03-6
   ISBN – 10: 1-893424-03-0
1. Gardens—United States—Directories.
2. Botanical gardens—United States—Directories.
3. Arboretums—United States—Directories.
   I. Garden Conservancy
   II. Title: Open Days Directory
   SB466.U65G37 2010   712'.07473
                QBI00-836

Published and distributed by
The Garden Conservancy
P.O. Box 608, Garrison, NY 10524

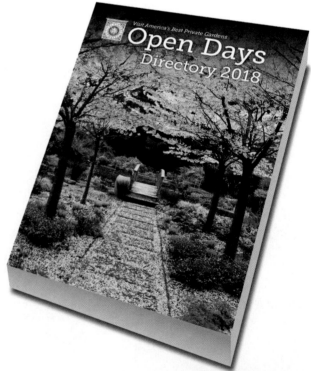

Cover: Weissman Garden, Bainbridge Island, WA
Photo: Eric Weissman

www.opendaysprogram.org

Open Days
Directory 2018

Cultivating Place

An award winning public radio program and podcast on gardening and natural history **mynspr.org**

cultivatingplace.com

Get out, get inspired, and stay curious.

That's what Open Days is all about!

Thanks so much for participating in the Garden Conservancy's award-winning Open Days program and helping us fuel America's passion for gardens and gardening. While our mission is educational, we also think Open Days is lots of fun. We hope you agree, and that you'll explore Open Days gardens near and far to help make the 2018 season our most exciting yet.

Your free admission ticket is on the page before the back cover.

Happy garden visiting!

Open Days 2018
ONE ADMISSION
(where admission tickets are accepted. Restrictions apply.)

Name _____

Address _____

City _____ State ____ Zip code _____

Email _____

Please provide your email address for reminders about Open Days and special events in your area. We protect your privacy and will not share with third parties.

PHOTOCOPIES OF THIS CARD WILL NOT BE ACCEPTED

SEIBERT & RICE

FINE ITALIAN TERRA COTTA

www.seibert-rice.com
(973) 467.8266

In this book...

Gardens by Date
Gardens are listed by date, then by state, county, and city, beginning on page 23.

Gardens by Location
Gardens are listed by state, then by county, city, and date beginning on page 32.

Digging Deeper Programs by Date
A complete listing of all of our Open Days special programs begins on page 39. Program full descriptions are in the corresponding state section.

Full Descriptions by State
Detailed descriptions of the 2018 Open Days season begin on page 44 and are organized alphabetically by state. Within each state section, Open Days gardens are listed by date, then by county, then town, then garden name. Garden and event descriptions, hours, and travel directions are included.

Information and directions for each private garden is submitted by the individual owner. We make every effort to ensure accuracy, but there will inevitably be last-minute changes and corrections. Please check **www.opendaysprogram.org** for any changes, and to sign up for email reminders, changes, and special events invitations. We promise to never share your email address and you may opt out at any time.

Public Gardens
At the end of each state section, there is a partial listing of public gardens in that state that are connected to our Open Days program.

Symbols

♿ Parts of the garden are handicapped accessible

NEW Garden opening for the first time

2014 The most recent year this garden was open

📷 Photographs are permitted

🏷PLANT SALES

Be the BEST garden guest

Open Days are special invitations into private gardens. Please reward the generosity of our garden hosts by following these simple garden-visiting rules:

SIGN IN
Please sign in at the admissions table. Our volunteer Garden Greeters would love to welcome you.

HANDS OFF
Plants and their parts must remain in the garden: no picking, pinching, or removing of plant pieces of any kind.

GREET THE HOST
Many Garden Hosts can be found in the gardens during their Open Day, identified by their "Garden Host" button. Please say hello! And let them know how much you enjoyed their garden.

BE THE BEST GUEST
- Take it with you—do not leave litter in the garden, and please do not smoke!
- Stay on designated paths (and out of people's houses!)
- Follow any posted signs or directions.
- Bring a friend, but not your furry friend. Sorry, no pets or therapy animals allowed.
- Children are very welcome at Open Days, and must be supervised at all times.
- Park your car so others can enter and leave the parking area easily.
- Respect the owner's preference for photographs. See garden listing or ask at entry. Tripods are not permitted.
- Restrooms are not available, even if "It's an emergency!" Please go before you arrive, or ask at the admissions table for directions to the nearest public facilities.
- Most gardens featured on Open Days are private and not normally open to the public. Please respect the privacy of these Garden Hosts and only visit their gardens on the dates and times posted.
- Respect the privacy of our Garden Hosts by not contacting them directly outside of the Open Day.

Plan your garden visits

Open Days are self-guided tours that take place *rain or shine*. Simply observe the dates and times the gardens are open and plan your visit.

Where possible, we have scheduled gardens to be within a reasonable driving distance of each other. (Occasionally we find a garden that simply must be included, despite being off the beaten path.) We do our best to make sure published garden directions are accurate. Always check directions before you leave home; bring a map or GPS system along with garden addresses.

Admission to Gardens
Admission to Open Days gardens begin at $7 per person, children 12 and under are free. You may pay in cash or check or redeem Open Days admission tickets at the entrance of each garden. Save on admission by purchasing Open Days admission ticket booklets in advance. Booklets include six tickets for the price of five. That's one free garden visit per booklet. When buying ticket booklets in advance, our members enjoy 50% off!

Order Your Tickets
Online at **opendaysprogram.org**
By calling 1 (888) 842-2442 toll free, M – F, 9 – 5 ET
Advanced tickets are mailed USPS, please allow at least 10 business days for delivery.

Members Discount
We save the best deals for Garden Conservancy members, who may purchase ticket booklets in advance at 50% off. Interested? Learn more about membership at gardenconservancy.org

Digging Deeper Programs
We keep adding special programs to our Open Days. Certain Digging Deeper programs may require additional fees and advance registration through **opendaysprogram.org** or by calling our toll-free order line, 1 (888) 842-2442, 9 – 5 ET.

The admission card in the image reads:

Open Days 2018
ONE ADMISSION
(where admission tickets are accepted. Restrictions apply.)
Name
Address   State   Zip code
City
Email
Please provide your email address for reminders about Open Days and special events in your area. We protect your privacy and will not share with third parties.

Support our partners

Our nursery and retail partners bring their choice selections of plants and garden-related merchandise to Open Days. We hope you enjoy browsing their wares and taking a part of Open Days home to your own garden.

Adams Fairacre Farms, Poughkeepsie, NY
www.adamsfarms.com

Avant Gardens, North Dartmouth, MA
www.avantgardensne.com

Broken Arrow Nursery, Hamden, CT
www.brokenarrownursery.com

Cricket Hill Garden, Thomaston, CT
www.treepeony.com

Digging Dog Nursery, Albion, CA
www.diggingdog.com

Garden Fever! Portland, OR
www.gardenfever.com

Hortus Conclusus, Stone Ridge, NY
www.hortus.biz

Landcraft Environments, Mattituck, NY
www.landcraftenvironment.com

Long Creek Nursery, Frederick, MD
www.ecologiadesign.com

Northwest Garden Nursery, Eugene, OR
www.northwestgardennursery.com

Opus Plants, Little Compton, RI
www.opusplants.com

Paxson Hill Farm, Bucks County, PA
www.paxsonhillfarm.com

Peckham's Greenhouse, Little Compton, RI
www.peckhamsgreenhouse.com

Pixie Perennials, Wilton, CT
www.pixieperennials.com

Pondside Nursery, Hudson, NY
www.pondsidenursery.com

Rare Find Nursery, Jackson, NJ
www.rarefindnursery.com

Shades of Green, Charlton, NY
www.lotsahosta.com

Surreybrooke Nursery, Middletown, MD
www.surreybrooke.com

White Flower Farm, Morris, CT
www.whiteflowerfarm.com

Thank you to the garden businesses and public gardens that support this nation-wide education program through their advertising and participation.

We are so grateful to the following organizations who partner with us to bring Open Days to their communities:

Charleston Horticultural Society, Charleston, SC
The Cummer Museum of Art & Gardens, Jacksonville, FL
Evergreen Foundation, Goffstown, NH
Hardy Plant Society of Oregon, Portland, OR
Hollister House Garden, Washington, CT
Innisfree Garden, Millbrook, NY
The Marin Art & Garden Center, Ross, CA
Mary M.B. Wakefield Charitable Trust, Milton, MA
Peckerwood Garden Conservation Foundation, Hempstead, TX
Spoleto Festival USA, Charleston, SC
Tompkins County Community Beautification Program, Ithaca, NY
Williamette Valley Hardy Plant Group, Eugene, OR

Ernie & Marietta O'Byrne's Garden, Eugene, OR
The O'Byrne garden returns to our Open Days program in 2018. It showcases an astonishing array of choice plants, many of them grown from seed.
Photo by Marion Brenner

Overview and mission

Through all of our programs and outreach, we champion the vital role that gardens play in our history, our culture, and our quality of life.

Since 1989, when the Garden Conservancy was founded by renowned plantsman Frank Cabot, we have helped more than 80 outstanding American gardens survive and prosper. Every year since 1995, our signature education program, Open Days, has been opening the gates to hundreds of private gardens across the country, allowing thousands of visitors to explore beautiful spaces not normally open to the public.

> *The mission of the nonprofit Garden Conservancy is to* **save** *and* **share** *outstanding American gardens for the education and inspiration of the public.*

SAVING

In partnership with garden owners, gardeners, communities, horticulturists, garden designers, and historians, we work to preserve outstanding gardens across America. We help new and emerging public gardens become community-based public resources by drawing upon the expertise from our own dedicated staff as well as that of our network of experts in all aspects of garden design, management, and restoration. We also contribute to the welfare of existing public gardens, helping them manage both natural and manmade challenges to their survival. Many of the gardens we work with are National Historic Landmarks or on the National Register of Historic Places.

SHARING

The best way to learn about gardening, garden design, and the transformative power of gardens is to experience gardens in person. Since 1995, some 3,000 private gardens have participated in our signature Open Days program, welcoming more than one million visitors in states across the country.

Our garden-study tours and wide-ranging education programs further the sharing of ideas as well as distinctive gardens.

JOIN US!
Call (845) 424-6500, M – F, 9 – 5 ET
Email membership@gardenconservancy.org
Visit gardenconservancy.org/membership

The Gardens of Alcatraz. San Francisco Bay, CA
The Garden Conservancy ten-year partnership with the Golden Gate National Parks
Conservancy and the National Park Service successfully rehabilitated the historic gar-
dens at this National Historic Landmark.
Photo by Marion Brenner

Become a member!

Join a community of committed supporters — help us save and share outstanding American gardens.

You are passionate about the important role gardens play in our communities and in our lives. Help preserve the artistic, historic, and cultural legacy of American gardens by becoming a member of the Garden Conservancy today!

Membership not only supports our preservation work and Open Days program; it puts you at the center of all we do. Join the conversation — through our lectures and symposia, publications, and Digging Deeper events, you can learn and exchange information about gardening, sustainability, design, and preservation.

As a member, you receive exclusive benefits including:

- FREE copy of our *Open Days Directory*
- 50% discount on Open Days tickets
- Subscription to our print and electronic newsletters
- Invitations and discounted admission to Conservancy-sponsored lectures and Digging Deeper events
- Participation in our Member Discount Club
- Subscription to *Better Homes & Gardens* or *Martha Stewart Living*

Never has there been a better time to be a member!
Call (845) 424-6500, M - F, 9 - 5 ET
Email membership@gardenconservancy.org
Visit gardenconservancy.org/ membership

Saving Outstanding American Gardens for Future Generations

Since 1989, preservation has been at the core of the Garden Conservancy's mission to save and share outstanding American gardens for the education and inspiration of the public. We have helped dozens of gardens across the country make the transition from private paradise to public resource. We also help to rescue gardens after natural disasters and to rehabilitate historic gardens so that they preserve their cultural relevance and, where possible, recover the brilliance of their design.

Our preservation staff forges partnerships with garden owners and community organizations in order to help gardens become independent, sustainable entities open to the public.

Our garden preservation work is done in varied settings from coast to coast. The broad range of garden types reflects an equally wide range of challenges they face. Together, our more than eighty different preservation projects illustrate the many ways we help gardens survive and thrive, to inspire us today and future generations tomorrow.

For more information about our preservation program, visit gardenconservancy.org/preservation.

Organizational Development

Garden Conservancy assistance at Gaiety Hollow in Salem, OR, helped preserve the home office and garden of pioneering American landscape architects Elizabeth Lord and Edith Schryver. We helped structure a board of directors and provided guidance on a cultural landscape report and a marketing plan.

Historic Rehabilitation

The rehabilitation of Blithewood Garden in Annandale-on-Hudson, NY, is the Conservancy's latest preservation project. Our partnership with Bard College includes facilitating project management and exploring treatment options for this 115-year-old Beaux Arts gem.

Preserving Horticultural Collections

Peckerwood Garden in Hempstead, TX, has a an important collection of over 3,000 species from Texas, Mexico, and Asia. We helped form a conservation foundation, guided strategic planning and collections management initiatives, and hold a conservation easement.

Garden Rescue

The Garden Conservancy provided a grant to **Swan House Garden** at the Atlanta History Center for the removal of non-historic trees to preserve this Country Place Era garden designed by Trammell Shutze.

Documentation

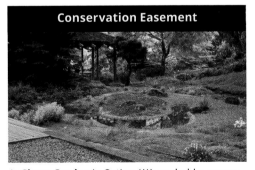

Our documentation program will preserve important American gardens through an online encapsulation of the "spirit of the place." Preserving the archives that tell the story of **Rocky Hills**, in Mt. Kisco, NY, will preserve the legacy of the garden and its creator.

Conservation Easement

At **Chase Garden** in Orting, WA, we hold a conservation easement to protect this iconic, mid-century Pacific Northwest landscape in perpetuity. The easement will safeguard the garden's horticultural and design attributes, and annual public access.

Ingredients for Successful Preservation Planning

Garden preservation is central to the mission of the Garden Conservancy. Since 1989, we have worked with more than 80 gardens from coast to coast on various aspects of preservation, from on-the-ground rehabilitation projects to helping to create organizational structure.

In our work with emerging public gardens, we have observed that the ingredients essential to successfully transitioning a garden to operate as a viable, independent entity fall into three categories: **Legacy**, **Resources**, and **Context**. Assessing a garden by these criteria will reveal important strengths — or weaknesses that will affect a garden's potential to thrive.

Not all important gardens can be preserved as public gardens. This realization challenges all of us who value their cultural importance to create new techniques to preserve the spirit and history of our most significant gardens. The Garden Conservancy is doing this through our documentation program and by the use of conservation easements.

The Ruth Bancroft Garden illustrates how these "ingredients for success" translate into real-life garden preservation planning.

Ruth Bancroft (1908-2017)
Creator of the Ruth Bancroft
Garden, Walnut Creek, CA

LEGACY
How is the garden or its creator significant? Does it have a unique or iconic design or important plant collection? Does the site or the creator have historic and/or cultural importance?

The Ruth Bancroft Garden is significant for its remarkable collection of water-conserving plantings, as well as its inspiring and forward-thinking creator. Over more than 50 years, Ruth assembled thousands of plants that are able to thrive in the dry, Mediterranean climate of California's interior valley areas. The garden inspired our founder, Frank Cabot, to create the Garden Conservancy, so that special gardens like Ruth's could be preserved for public enjoyment.

RESOURCES
Both human and financial resources are necessary for the ongoing success of a public garden. Are there dedicated, energetic staff, volunteers, and board members with relevant experience and skills? Is there an endowment or donor base in place, or the potential for one? Other viable sources of revenue — programming, sales, and visitation?

Groundbreaking for the new Visitor and Education Center at the Ruth Bancroft Garden

The Ruth Bancroft Garden has benefited from the energy and dedication of a board that has nonprofit and fundraising experience, as well as the gardening expertise of paid staff and volunteers who tend the garden and advance Ruth's horticultural vision. The Ruth Bancroft Garden, Inc. has had good success raising funds needed and their nursery's plant sales have also produced reliable revenue.

CONTEXT

The context of a garden includes its physical location as well as various cultural and demographic characteristics. Is there sufficient population density to support the garden? Easy access by public transportation and adequate parking? Potential for partnerships with other cultural institutions? Community support for cultural resources?

The Ruth Bancroft Garden is located in Walnut Creek, CA, a populous suburb in the San Francisco Bay Area. There are many educational and cultural institutions nearby, and a long tradition of support for cultural arts. The garden is easily accessible by public transportation, bicycle, or foot; and will soon have expanded on-site visitor parking.

Photo: Marion Brenner

Montrose
Hillsborough, North Carolina

Montrose evokes the landscape and layout of a nineteenth-century Southern country estate. It is listed on the National Register of Historic Places.

Working with the bones of the original garden, Nancy and Craufurd Goodwin transformed a neglected 61-acre historic estate, creating a garden filled with plants that grow well in the area's clay loam soil, arranged by color and form. Nancy Goodwin is a noted plantswoman and garden writer who has dedicated herself to making Montrose a cultural and horticultural resource for all.

The gardens include venerable trees, sunny perennial gardens with dazzling displays, and a rock garden planted with heirloom bulbs. Elsewhere on the property, a profusion of native plants create a carpet beneath the trees.

"This place is my life and its gardens my obsession."
- Nancy Goodwin

Montrose: Life in a Garden (Duke University Press, 2005) chronicles a year in Nancy Goodwin's garden.

Several seminars, two open days, and a snowdrop walk are planned for 2018, weather permitting. Reservations are requested. For notification of opening dates and times, please send an email requesting to be put on the Montrose email list.

montrosegdn@embarqmail.com
Address: 320 St. Marys Road, Hillsborough, NC 27278
Telephone: 919.732.7787

Garden Conservancy Northwest Network

The Garden Conservancy Northwest Network (GCNN) promotes communication, networking, and resource sharing for member gardens and horticultural organizations in Oregon, Washington, and British Columbia. Its mission is to further the shared goals of advancing horticultural education, and preserving and opening exceptional gardens for public enjoyment and edification.

The GCNN hosts two professional workshops annually. The first 2018 GCNN workshop will be held on Saturday, February 24, at Dunn Gardens in Seattle, WA, and will explore the topic of building a strong board of directors. A second workshop will be held in the fall at a date to be determined.

The GCNN is open to advocates of garden preservation representing public gardens, horticultural organizations, and gardens in transition from private to nonprofit or public ownership. For more information, please visit the Preservation section of www.gardenconservancy.org or send an email to Tanya DeMarsh-Dodson, Network Coordinator, at tddodson@gmail.com.

Current GCNN members include:

Albers Vista Gardens
Bellevue Botanical Garden
Bloedel Reserve
Cottage Lake Gardens
E. B. Dunn Historic Garden Trust
Friends of Rogerson Clematis Collection
Friends of the Moore-Turner Heritage
    Gardens
Hardy Plant Society Oregon
Highline SeaTac Botanical Garden,
Kruckeberg Botanic Garden
Lakewold Gardens
Leach Botanical Garden
Lord & Schryver Conservancy
Meerkerk Gardens
Elisabeth C. Miller Botanical Garden
Milner Gardens & Woodland
Ohme Gardens
Peninsula Park Rose Garden
Powellswood Garden Foundation
Rhododendron Species Foundation
Seattle Chinese Garden
Soos Creek Botanical Garden
South Seattle Community College
    Arboretum
Streissguth Gardens
Yakima Area Arboretum

Photo: Marion Brenner

Sharing Gardens

Preserving gardens, that most fragile art form, is always a challenge and will never happen in a vacuum. By nurturing and expanding a garden culture, the Garden Conservancy is also growing a culture of garden stewards, people who care enough to preserve gardens. Sharing gardens and garden ideas is critical, for this is where the passion for gardens begins.

Since 1989, the Conservancy has been sharing gardens and cross-pollinating ideas in many ways, including offering public educational programs in cities across the country, private events and garden-study tours for participants in our Society of Fellows, and Open Days, our best-known educational and garden-visiting program.

Lectures, Symposia, and Other Public Programs

The Garden Conservancy presents and co-sponsors numerous other educational programs across the country. In 2018, the Garden Conservancy is presenting our first national series of lectures, film screenings, and author talks: twenty programs in eight cities. They offer a number of ways for our members and the general public to stay engaged with issues related to the design, history, preservation, and cultural significance of gardens, with a particular emphasis on American gardens.

The Garden Conservancy is the only national organization in the United States that focuses on the evolving practice of preserving gardens. With that in mind, we have gathered a diverse group of practitioners to discuss the peculiar challenges of, and creative approaches to, garden preservation. They range from an artist who records his ephemeral garden on porcelain plates, to a landscape architect who had to destroy one historic garden to re-create another.

For the latest details on educational programs we present or co-sponsor, please visit gardenconservancy.org.

Society of Fellows Tours and Special Events

Each year, members of the Garden Conservancy's Society of Fellows travel to domestic and international destinations to explore outstanding gardens and historic landscapes. In appreciation of their annual support, Fellows are invited to participate in garden-study tours and other special educational programs. In 2018, the Society of Fellows will travel to Dallas and Fort Worth, Texas; Highlands and the Southern Appalachians in North Carolina; Nantucket, Martha's Vineyard, and Great Island, Massachusetts; and Portugal.

For information about joining our Society of Fellows and becoming eligible for these garden-study tours, please contact Bridget Connors at (845) 424-6500, M - F, 9 - 5 ET.

Open Days
The Garden Conservancy's signature education program

www.opendaysprogram.org

booklets of six tickets for twenty-one dollars — to order more, visit *www.gardenconservancy.org/store.*

We've also enclosed information about our Member Discount Club. We hope you partake in this great benefits which offers you discounts at nurseries and other garden-related businesses.

If you have any questions about your membership or its benefits, please feel free to contact us at 845-424-6500 or membership@gardenconservancy.org.

Sincerely,

Claire Briguglio
Development Associate

Enjoy!

THE GARDEN CONSERVANCY

20 NAZARETH WAY I PO BOX 608, GARRISON, NY 10524 I 845.424.6500/6501FAX I GARDENCONSERVANCY.ORG

Ms. Barbara K. Jones
271 Argyle Rd
Orange, CT 06477-2915

Dear Ms. Jones,

Thank you for your commitment to the Garden Conservancy as an Individual member! We are grateful for your support which makes it possible for us to save and share outstanding American gardens for the education and inspiration of the public.

As a member, you are entitled to a complimentary copy of the **Open Days Directory** and **one complimentary Open Days admission ticket,** enclosed here. As a special summer promotion and to thank you for joining, we're also including an additional pack of four Open Days admission tickets! Tickets are valid for two years and can be used during the 2018 or 2019 season. Members also receive a 50% discount on advance purchases of additional Open Days garden admission ticket booklets. Member tickets are sold in

The Garden Conservancy Member Discount Club

We are delighted to have you as a member and thank you for joining our group of dedicated garden enthusiasts!

One of your exclusive member benefits includes access to our Member Discount Club entitling you to discounts at participating nurseries, public gardens, and other garden-related businesses around the country.

Brighter Blooms Nursery
www.brighterblooms.com
10% off your order
online code: gcmember2018

Bard College Arboretum
www.bard.edu/arboretum
10% off group tours
Contact 845-752-LEAF or email arboretum@bard.edu

Cobrahead LLC
www.cobrahead.com
10% off your order
online code: gcmember2018

Ruth Bancroft Garden
www.ruthbancroftgarden.org
free admission

Johnny's Selected Seeds
www.johnnyseeds.com
5% off your order
online code: 18-1783

White Flower Farm
www.whiteflowerfarm.com
20% off your order
You should have received a discount code card with your acknowledgment letter. If not, contact membership@gardenconservancy.org

Womanswork
www.womanswork.com
15% off your order
online code: gcmember2018

To redeem discounts from these retailers and organizations, present your Garden Conservancy Membership Card at the time of purchase. For online shopping, please use the special codes listed above for Garden Conservancy member use only.

Visit **www.gardenconservancy.org/discount-codes** for more information.

Open Days Program

Fueling America's passion for gardens and gardening, Open Days is fundamentally a nationwide community of gardeners teaching and inspiring each other. From expert to novice, we think there is no better way to improve as a gardener than by experiencing a diverse range of gardens first hand and talking shop, so to speak, with fellow gardeners.

Since 1995, Open Days has welcomed more than one million visitors into thousands of inspired private landscapes – from urban rooftops to organic farms, historic estates to innovative suburban lots – in forty-one states.

This incredible annual program is produced almost entirely by volunteers, hundreds of individuals who help us showcase regional horticultural and stylistic expressions in a national context, celebrating the rich diversity in American gardens. Find out how you can join this dynamic team of Open Days volunteers by emailing us at opendays@gardenconservancy.org.

[What] the Garden Conservancy has...launched is an institution, and if my hunch is right, [Open Days] could do more for horticultural cross-fertilization than anything to hit the American garden scene since, well, the bumblebee.

—Michael Pollan
"The Garden Path," *Vogue*, April 1997

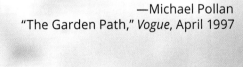

Inspired by the rich informal conversations that typify Open Days, special, site-specific programs were added to enhance the Open Days roster in 2015. In these **Digging Deeper** events, small groups of visitors come together for informative yet informal talks, tours, and demonstrations with experts from every facet of the garden world: landscape architects, garden writers, plant collectors, artists, and more.

In 2017, we further enriched Open Days by adding fun, family-oriented activities, events that spark curiosity and wonder in gardeners of all ages.

In 2018, Open Days is hosting some fifty special Digging Deeper programs. While many are free, most require advance registration or pre-purchase of a special ticket. These fill up quickly, so be sure to reserve your place early!

Gardens by Date

Saturday, March 24

New York, Tompkins County
Trumansburg
• Hitch Lyman's Garden, 11 to 3

Saturday, April 14

Florida, Duval County
Jacksonville
• Ann & John Baker Garden, 12 to 4
• The Cummer Museum of Art & Gardens, 10 to 4
• Garden of Mr. & Mrs. Preston Haskell, 12 to 4
• Garden of Ann & David Hicks, 12 to 4
• Garden of Mr. & Mrs. William H. Morris, 12 to 4

Sunday, April 15

New Jersey, Essex County
Nutley
• The Mountsier Garden, 10 to 4

Sunday, April 22

California, Los Angeles County
Pasadena
• Eriksson Garden, 10 to 4
• The Erskine Garden, 10 to 4
• La Casita del Arroyo Garden, 9:30 to 3:30
• Penner Garden, 10 to 4
• Sill Garden, 10 to 4
San Marino
• The Garden on Coniston Place, 10 to 4
South Pasadena
• Hermosa Hillside Garden, 10 to 4
New York, Putnam County
Cold Spring
• Stonecrop Gardens, 10 to 5

Saturday, April 28

Texas, Harris County
Houston
• Itchy Acres, 10 to 4
• Heights Pollinator Café and Shade Garden, 10 to 4
• Steve Stelzer and Kathleen English, 10 to 4
• Selia Qynn's Garden Habitat, 10 to 4

Sunday, April 29

New York, Westchester County
Lewisboro
The White Garden, 10 to 3

Saturday, May 5

California, Mendocino County
Gualala
• Mullins' Mendocino Stonezone, 10 to 4
Mendocino
• The Gardens at Harmony Woods, 10 to 4
New Jersey, Essex County
East Orange
• The Secret Garden @ 377—The Gotelli Garden at Harrison Park Towers, 10 to 4
Short Hills
• Greenwood Gardens, 10 to 5
Morris County
Chatham
• Jack Lagos, 10 to 4
Somerset County
Far Hills
• The Hay Honey Farm, 10 to 5
• Stone House Garden, 10 to 4
New York, Columbia County
Copake Falls
• Margaret Roach, 10 to 4

Sunday, May 6

California, Los Angeles County
Los Angeles
• Arden Garden, 10 to 4
• The Chung Garden, 10 to 4
• Fischer Garden, 10 to 4
• Garden of Kathleen Losey ,10 to 4
• Lombard Simon Garden, 10 to 4
• Marlborough School, 9:30 to 3:30
• Villa Abbondanza, 10 to 4
Connecticut, Fairfield County
Greenwich
• 12 Bayberry Lane, 10 to 4
• Sleepy Cat Farm, 10 to 4

Wilton
• Pixie Perennials, 10 to 4
New York, Suffolk County
Old Field
• Two Grey Achers, 10 to 4

Saturday, May 12
California, Alameda County
Albany
• Keeyla Meadows, 10 to 4
Oakland
• Casa de Sueños, 10 to 4
• Leianne's Garden, 10 to 4
• Order and Exuberance in a Hillside Garden, 10 to 4
Connecticut, Litchfield County
Sharon
• Cobble Pond Farm, 1 to 4
Warren
• Covered Bridge Gardens, 10 to 4
New York, Dutchess County
Amenia
• Broccoli Hall—Maxine Paetro, 10 to 4
Suffolk County
East Hampton
• Biercuk & Luckey Garden, 10 to 4
• Glade Garden—Abby Jane Brody, 10 to 4
• Levy-Barnett Garden, 10 to 2

Sunday, May 13
New York, Putnam County
Cold Spring
• Stonecrop Gardens, 10 to 5

Saturday, May 19
California, Santa Cruz County
Santa Cruz
• "Tropics" of Santa Cruz, 10 to 4
• Tom Karwin's Garden, 10 to 4
Soquel
• Odonata, 10 to 4
New York, Westchester County
Bedford Hills
• Phillis Warden, 10 to 4
Chappaqua
• Shobha Vanchiswar & Murali Mani, 10 to 4
Katonah
• Clementine Close, 10 to 4

Mount Kisco
• Rocky Hills, 10 to 4

Sunday, May 20
New York, Nassau County
Locust Valley
• Carol & Jim Large's Garden, 10 to 4
Old Westbury
• Howard Phipps Jr. Estate, 10 to 4

Saturday, May 26
New York, Suffolk County
East Hampton
• Chip Rae & Chuck Schwarz, 10 to 4
• Edwina von Gal—Marsh House, 10 to 4
• The Garden of Dianne B., 10 to 2
• Previti/Gumpel Garden, 10 to 4
Pennsylvania, Bucks County
Gardenville
• Twin Silo Farm, 10 to 4
New Hope
• Gardens at Half Moon, 10 to 4
• Paxson Hill Farm, 10 to 4
Rhode Island, Newport County
Little Compton
• Sakonnet, 9:30 to 6
South Carolina, Charleston County
Charleston
• Eight private gardens located within walking distance in the historic district, 10 to 4. More information at gardenconservancy.org/open-days/charleston

Sunday, May 27
Rhode Island, Newport County
Little Compton
• Sakonnet, 9:30 to 6

Saturday, June 2
California, Marin County
Mill Valley
• Beauty by the Bay, 10 to 4
• Mediterranean Marin, 10 to 4
Ross
• Marin Art & Garden Center, 10 to 4
Tiburon
• 15 Seafirth Place, 10 to 4
• Tiburon Hillside Garden, 10 to 4

Mendocino County
Boonville
• Meadow Watch, 10 to 4
Hopland
• Frey Gardens, 10 to 4
Connecticut, Fairfield County
Redding
• Horsefeathers, 10 to 4
Ridgefield
• The Barlow Mountain Garden of Helen Dimos & Benjamin Oko, 10 to 4
• Garden of Ken & Margaret Uhle, 10 to 4
• Ken Eisold's Garden, 10 to 4
Wilton
• Pixie Perennials, 10 to 4
Litchfield County
Litchfield
• Glenn Hillman, 2 to 6
Roxbury
• Japanese Gardens at Cedar Hill, 10 to 4
Washington
• Hollister House Garden, 10 to 4
West Cornwall
• Michael Trapp, 10 to 4
Maryland, Frederick County
Frederick
• Basford Family Garden, 10 to 4
• High Glen Gardens, 10 to 4
• Long Creek Homestead, 10 to 4
• Rausch Woodland Gardens, 10 to 4
Middletown
• Surreybrooke, 10 to 4
Myersville
• Edgewood Garden, 10 to 4
New York, Suffolk County
Cutchogue
• Arnold & Karen Blair, 10 to 4
Flanders
• Garden of Valerie M. Ansalone, 10 to 4
South Carolina, Charleston County
Charleston
• Eight private gardens located within walking distance in the historic district, 10 to 4. More information at gardenconservancy.org/open-days/charleston

Sunday, June 3
Connecticut, Fairfield County
Fairfield
• Garden of Kathryn Herman, 10 to 4
Westport
• Green Isle, 11 to 4
• The Blau Gardens, 10 to 4
Massachusetts, Bristol County
Rehoboth
• McIlwain Garden, 10 to 4
Seekonk
• Landscape Designer Andrew Grossman's Display Gardens, 10 to 4
New York, Nassau County
Glen Cove
• Kippen Hill, 10 to 4
Great Neck
• Fairview Cottage Garden, 10 to 4
Sands Point
• Fern's Glade, 10 to 4

Saturday, June 9
Connecticut, Hartford County
Burlington
• The Salsedo Family Garden, 10 to 4
Canton
• Sudden Delight, 10 to 4
Collinsville
• Small Pleasures—A. Walter Kendra, 10 to 4
Massachusetts, Norfolk County
Canton
• Eleanor Cabot Bradley Estate, 10 to 4
Milton
• The Former "Mrs. Holden McGinley Garden" Designed by Ellen Biddle Shipman, 10 to 4
• The Roberts Garden—Formerly the "Helen Gilbert Estate" Designed by Fletcher Steele, 10 to 4
• Mary M. B. Wakefield Estate, 10 to 4
Suffolk County
West Roxbury
• Dustman-Ryan Garden, 10 to 4
New York, Columbia County
Claverack
• Ketay Garden, 10 to 4
• Peter Bevacqua & Stephen King, 10 to 4

Hudson
• Versailles on Hudson, 10 to 4
West Taghkanic
• Arcadia—Ronald Wagner & Timothy Van Dam, 10 to 4

Sunday, June 10

District of Columbia
Georgetown
• 1228 30th Street NW Garden, 10 to 4
• Georgetown Garden—Nancy Gray Pyne, 10 to 4
Maryland, Montgomery County
Chevy Chase
• Everett Garden Designs Home Garden, 10 to 4
Silver Spring
• GreenHeart Garden, 10 to 4
New York, Livingston County
Pavilion
• Linwood Gardens, 10 to 4
Putnam County
Cold Spring
• Stonecrop Gardens, 10 to 5
Garrison
• Ross Gardens, 10 to 4

Saturday, June 16

Connecticut, Hartford County
Glastonbury
• The Murray Gardens, 10 to 4
Litchfield County
Falls Village
• Bunny Williams, 10 to 4
Washington
• Brush Hill Gardens—Charles Raskob Robinson & Barbara Paul Robinson, 10 to 4
• Highmeadows—Linda Allard, 10 to 4
• Hollister House Garden, 10 to 4
New Haven County
Stony Creek
• Uptop—Garden of Fred Bland, 10 to 4
Wallingford
• Wintergreen Garden, 10 to 4
Missouri, St. Louis County
Kirkwood
• The MP Garden, 10 to 4

Ladue
• Far Meadows, 10 to 4
St. Louis
• Secret Garden, 10 to 4
• One Terry Hill Lane, 10 to 4
New Hampshire, Cheshire County
Dublin
• Robertson Garden, 10 to 4
Jaffery
• Thoron Gardens, 10 to 4
Hillsborough County
Hancock
• Eleanor Briggs' Garden, 10 to 4
• May Place Gardens of Bill and Eileen Elliott, 10 to 4
Peterborough
• Michael & Betsy Gordon, 10 to 4
New Jersey, Essex County
Montclair
• Claire Ciliotta, 10 to 4
New York, Dutchess County
Amenia
• Broccoli Hall—Maxine Paetro, 10 to 4
Washington, Kitsap County
Bainbridge Island
• Garden of Gayle Bard, 10 to 4
• Ravenswold II, 10 to 4
• The Skyler Garden, 10 to 4
• Weissman Garden,10 to 4
Indianola
• Sam & Karen Brindley's Garden, 10 to 4
• Windcliff, 10 to 4

Sunday, June 17

New York, Westchester County
Bedford
• High and Low Farm, 10 to 4
Bedford Hills
• Phillis Warden, 10 to 4
Katonah
• Barbara & Tom Israel, 10 to 4
Yorktown
• Barbara & John Schumacher, 10 to 4
Vermont, Windham County
Westminster West
• Gordon & Mary Hayward's Garden, 10 to 4

Windsor County
Hartland
• Brian Stroffolino's HeartLand Farms & Sylvia Davatz's Garden, 10 to 4
Windsor
• Cider Hill Gardens & Art Gallery—Sarah & Gary Milek, 10 to 4

Saturday, June 23

California, Mendocino County
Albion
• The Gardens Surrounding Digging Dog Nursery and the Private Gardens of Deborah Whigham & Gary Ratway, 10 to 5:30
Mendocino
• The Garden of Cherie Christiansen & Franz Arner, 10 to 4
• Moss Garden, 10 to 4
Connecticut, Litchfield County
Kent
• Mica Quarry Estate—Garden of Monika & Buddy Nixon, 10 to 4
Illinois, Cook County
Winnetka
• Gothic Victorian Garden, 10 to 4
New Jersey, Bergen County
Allendale
• Monfried Garden, 10 to 4
Mahwah
• Sisko Gardens, 10 to 4
Oakland
• Les Bois Des Chiens (The Dogs' Woods), 10 to 4
River Edge
• Anthony "Bud" & Virginia Korteweg, 8:30 to 4
River Vale
• Cupid's Garden—Audrey Linstrom Maihack, 10 to 4
New York, Dutchess County
Millbrook
• Squirrel Hall, 10 to 4
• Innisfree Garden, 11 to 5

Poughkeepsie
• Alice Pond, 10 to 4
• Frank & Lois Van Zanten, 10 to 4
• Dappled Berms—The Garden of Scott VanderHamm, 10 to 4
Stanfordville
• Zibby & Jim Tozer, 10 to 2
Saratoga County, Charlton
• Shades of Green, 10 to 4
Middle Grove
• Dalton Garden, 10 to 4
Saratoga Springs
• Collins Garden, 10 to 4
• Sarah Patterson's Garden, 10 to 4
Schuylerville
• Fiddle-i-fee-Farm, 10 to 4
Vermont, Bennington County
East Arlington
• Rogerland, 10 to 4
Manchester
• Turkey Hill Farm, 10 to 4
Manchester Village
• A Cook's Garden, 10 to 4

Sunday, June 24

Illinois, Cook County
Evanston
• Evanston Lakefront Garden, 10 to 4
Winnetka
• The Robb Garden, 10 to 4
Lake County
Lake Forest
• Suzanne's Gardens, 10 to 4
Massachusetts, Berkshire County
Sheffield
• 1391 Barnum Street, 10 to 4
New York, Columbia County
Craryville
Rabbit Hill, 10 to 5
Hillsdale
• Texas Hill, 10 to 4
Millerton
• Helen Bodian, 10 to 4
Spencertown
• Landscape of Linda B. Horn, 10 to 2

Ulster County
Highland
• Teri Condon—Gardensmith Design, 12 to 4
Kingston
• Garden of Peggy & Frank Almquist, 10 to 4
New Paltz
• Springtown Farmden, 1 to 4:30

Saturday, June 30
Connecticut, Fairfield County
Sherman
• Peter's Opus, 10 to 4
New York, Dutchess County
Pawling
• Scherer Garden, 11 to 4
Suffolk County
Mt. Sinai
• Tranquility, 10 to 4

Saturday, July 7
New York, Dutchess County
Amenia
• Jade Hill—Paul Arcario & Don Walker, 10 to 4
Millerton
• Barbara Agren's Smithfield Cottage, 10 to 4
Putnam County
Cold Spring
• Stonecrop Gardens, 10 to 5
Suffolk County
Jamesport
• Winds Way Farm, 10 to 4
Mattituck
• Dennis Schrader & Bill Smith, 10 to 4
Shelter Island Heights
• Birdhouse Garden, 10 to 4
Tioga County
Spencer
• Myers Gardens, 10 to 4
Tompkins County
Freeville
• Manzano Garden, 10 to 4
Ithaca
• Shelia and Louis Out's Garden, 10 to 4
Lansing
• Lion Garden, 10 to 4
Oregon, Lane County

Eugene
• Enright Garden, 12 to 4
• Laurelwood Garden, 12 to 4
• Northwest Garden Nursery, 12 to 6
• Buell Steelman & Rebecca Sams, 12 to 4

Thursday, July 12
Massachusetts, Nantucket County
Nantucket
• House in the Woods, 10 to 4
• The Garden at 7 Pocomo, 10 to 4
• Garden of Gale H. Arnold, 10 to 4
• Blueberry Hill—Douglass and Caroline Ellis, 10 to 4
• Morash Victory Garden, 10 to 4

Saturday, July 14
Colorado, Pitkin County
Aspen
• Gratia, 10 to 4
Basalt
• The Feathered Nest, 10 to 4
Woody Creek
• Woody Creek Artist's Garden, 10 to 4
Connecticut, Litchfield County
Bridgewater
• Maywood Gardens, 10 to 4
Falls Village
• Bunny Williams, 10 to 4
Lakeville
• Juniper Ledge, 10 to 4
Warren
• Mulla Garden, 10 to 2
Washington
• Hollister House Garden, 10 to 4
New London County
Stonington
• Kentford Farm, 10 to 4
New Hampshire, Hillsborough County
Goffstown
• Evergreen, 10 to 5
• Oak Hill Garden, 10 to 4
Merrimack County
Epsom
• Wells Corner, 10 to 5

New Jersey, Hunterdon County
Stockton
• Bellsflower Garden, 10 to 4
• The Gorrell-Schucker Garden, 10 to 4
• The Garden at Federal Twist, 10 to 6
Morris County
Chatham
• Jack Lagos, 10 to 4
New York, Suffolk County
Bridgehampton
• Entwood Garden, 10 to 4
• Pamela Harwood & Peter Feder, 10 to 4
East Hampton
• Yugen, 10 to 4
• Garden of Arlene Bujese, 10 to 2
• Edwina von Gal—Marsh House, 10 to 4
Oregon, Multnomah County
Portland
• Ediger Garden, 10 to 4
• Ferrante Garden, 10 to 4
• Nancyland, 10 to 4
Pennsylvania, Bucks County
Carversville
• The Vicarage, 10 to 4
New Hope
• Paxson Hill Farm, 10 to 4

Sunday, July 15
New Hampshire. Hillsborough County
Goffstown
• Evergreen, 10 to 5
• Oak Hill Garden, 10 to 4
Merrimack County
Epsom
• Wells Corner, 10 to 5

Saturday, July 21
Connecticut, Litchfield County
Sharon
• Lee Link, 10 to 4
Massachusetts, Berkshire County
Ashley Falls
• **Steele Garden, 10 to 4**
New Jersey, Monmouth County
Little Silver
• Garden of Diana Landreth, 10 to 4

Locust
• Nancy & Dan Crabbe's Garden on the Navesink River, 10 to 4
• Still Waters, 10 to 4
Rumson
• Cousins' Garden, 10 to 4
• King & Leigh Sorensen, 10 to 4
New York, Dutchess County
Millbrook
• Innisfree Garden, 11 to 5
Millerton
• Hyland/Wente Garden, 10 to 4
Stanfordville
• Ellen & Eric Petersen, 10 to 4
Jefferson County
Chaumont
• Lakeside Quarry Garden, 10 to 4
Watertown
• The Walton Garden, 10 to 4
Westchester County
Cortlandt Manor
• **Vivian & Ed Merrin, 10 to 2**
Mt. Kisco
• The Greneker Retreat, 10 to 4

Sunday, July 22
Connecticut, Hartford County
Glastonbury
• The Murray Gardens, 10 to 4
New Haven County
Meriden
• George Trecina, 10 to 4
Wallingford
• Wintergreen Garden, 10 to 4
Illinois, Lake County
Highland Park
• Highland Park Residence, 10 to 4
Lake Forest
• The Gardens at 900, 10 to 4
Mettawa
• Mettawa Manor, 10 to 4

Sunday, July 29
New York, Columbia County
Austerlitz
• Steepletop—Poet Edna St. Vincent Millay's Garden, 10 to 4:30

Canaan
• Rockland Farm, 10 to 4
Chatham Center
• Polemis Garden, 10 to 4
Westchester County
Bedford Hills
• Phillis Warden, 10 to 4
Pound Ridge
• James and Ellen Best's Sara Stein Garden, 10 to 4
South Salem
• Garden of Bernard Marquez & Tim Fish, 10 to 6

Saturday, August 4
New Jersey, Hunterdon County
Stockton
• Pretty Bird Farm, 10 to 4
New York, Greene County
Catskill
• Abeel House Prairie, 10 to 4
• High Falls, 1 to 7
Pennsylvania, Bucks County
New Hope
• Paxson Hill Farm, 10 to 4

Sunday, August 5
Illinois, Du Page County
West Chicago
• The Gardens at Ball, 10 to 4

Saturday, August 11
New York, Columbia County
Hudson
• Livingston House Garden, 10 to 4
• Red Gate Farm, 10 to 4

Sunday, August 12
New York, Putnam County
Cold Spring
• Stonecrop Gardens, 10 to 5

Saturday, August 18
Connecticut, Fairfield County
Redding
• **InSitu, 10 to 4**
New York, Columbia County
Copake Falls
• Margaret Roach, 10 to 4

Spencertown
• Landscape of Linda B. Horn, 10 to 2

Saturday, August 25
Connecticut, New London County
Stonington
• Stone Acres Farm, 10 to 2
Rhode Island, Washington County
Hopkinton
• Garden of Louis Raymond & Richard Ericson, 10 to 3

Sunday, August 26
Connecticut, Litchfield County
Cornwall
• Something to Crow About Dahlias, 10 to 4
Roxbury
• Japanese Gardens at Cedar Hill, 10 to 4
West Cornwall
• Roxana Robinson—Treetop, 10 to 4

Sunday, September 2
New York, Putnam County
Cold Spring
• Stonecrop Gardens, 10 to 5

Saturday, September 8
Connecticut, New Haven County
Meriden
• George Trecina, 10 to 4
Northford
• Reeds Gap West Residence, 10 to 4
New Jersey, Essex County
Nutley
• The Mountsier Garden, 10 to 4
Short Hills
• Greenwood Gardens, 10 to 5
Morris County
Flanders
• Sterling Garden, 10 to 4
Somerset County
Far Hills
• The Hay Honey Farm, 10 to 5
• Stone House Garden, 10 to 4

Sunday, September 9
Connecticut, Fairfield County
Wilton
• The Harris Garden, 10 to 4

Litchfield County
Washington
• Highmeadows—Linda Allard, 10 to 4
• Hollister House Garden, 10 to 4
• The Rocks, 10 to 4
Washington Depot
• Appledore, 10 to 4
New Jersey, Hunterdon County
Pottersville
• Jardin de Buis, 10 to 4
New York, Westchester County
South Salem
• Garden of Bernard Marquez & Tim Fish, 10 to 6
Waccabuc
• James & Susan Henry, 10 to 4

Sunday, September 16
Connecticut, Fairfield County
Greenwich
• Sleepy Cat Farm, 10 to 4
Wilton
• Pixie Perennials, 10 to 4

Saturday, September 22
New York, Dutchess County
Dover Plains
• Copperheads, 10 to 4
Millbrook
• Clove Brook Farm—Christopher Spitzmiller, 10 to 4
• Innisfree Garden, 11 to 5
• Katie Ridder and Peter Pennoyer, 10 to 4
Stanfordville
• Bear Creek Farm, 10 to 4

Sunday, September 23
New York, Ulster County
Accord
• Eric Stewart and Dr. Michael Sheran, 10 to 4
• Hollengold Farm, 10 to 4
Olivebridge
• James Dinsmore Garden, 10 to 4
Stone Ridge
• Hortus Conclusus, 10 to 4

Sunday, October 7
New York, Putnam County
Cold Spring
• Stonecrop Gardens, 10 to 5

Saturday, October 13
New York, Dutchess County
Pawling
• The Brine Garden—Duncan & Julia Brine, 12 to 6

Gardens by Location

California

ALAMEDA COUNTY

Albany
•Keeyla Meadows, Saturday, May 12
Oakland
•Casa de Sueños, Saturday, May 12
•Leianne's Garden, Saturday, May 12
•Order and Exuberance in a Hillside Garden, Saturday, May 12

LOS ANGELES COUNTY

Los Angeles
•Arden Garden, Sunday, May 6
•The Chung Garden, Sunday, May 6
•Fischer Garden, Sunday, May 6
•Garden of Kathleen Losey, Sunday, May 6
•Marlborough School, Sunday, May 6
•Lombard Simon Garden, Sunday, May 6
•Villa Abbondanza, Sunday, May 6

Pasadena
•Eriksson Garden, Sunday, April 22
•The Erskine Garden, Sunday, April 22
•La Casita del Arroyo Garden, Sunday, April 22
•Penner Garden, Sunday, April 22
•Sill Garden, Sunday, April 22
San Marino
•The Garden on Coniston Place, Sunday, April 22

South Pasadena
•Hermosa Hillside Garden, Sunday, April 22

MARIN COUNTY

Mill Valley
•Beauty by the Bay, Saturday, June 2
•Mediterranean Marin, Saturday, June 2
Ross
•Marin Art & Garden Center, Saturday, June 2

Tiburon
•15 Seafirth Place, Saturday, June 2
•Tiburon Hillside Garden, Saturday, June 2

MENDOCINO COUNTY

Albion
•The Gardens Surrounding Digging Dog Nursery and the Private Gardens of Deb-orah Whigham & Gary Ratway, Saturday, June 23

Boonville
•Meadow Watch, Saturday, June 2

Gualala
•Mullins' Mendocino Stonezone, Saturday, May 5

Hopland
•Frey Gardens, Saturday, June 2

Mendocino
•The Garden of Cherie Christiansen & Franz Arner, Saturday, June 23
•The Gardens at Harmony Woods, Saturday, May 5
•Moss Garden, Saturday, June 23

SANTA CRUZ COUNTY

Santa Cruz
•Tom Karwin's Garden, Saturday, May 19
•"Tropics" of Santa Cruz, Saturday, May 19
Soquel
•Odonata, Saturday, May 19

Colorado

PITKIN COUNTY

Aspen
•Gratia, Saturday, July 14

Basalt
•The Feathered Nest, Saturday, July 14
Woody Creek
•Woody Creek Artist's Garden, Saturday, July 14

Connecticut

FAIRFIELD COUNTY

Fairfield
•Garden of Kathryn Herman, Sunday, June 3

Greenwich
•12 Bayberry Lane, Sunday, May 6
•Sleepy Cat Farm, Sunday, May 6; Sunday, September 16

Redding
•Horsefeathers, Saturday, June 2
•InSitu, Saturday, August 18

Ridgefield
•The Barlow Mountain Garden of Helen Dimos & Benjamin Oko, Saturday, June 2

•Garden of Ken & Margaret Uhle, Saturday,-
June 2
•Ken Eisold's Garden, Saturday, June 2
Sherman
•Peter's Opus, Saturday, June 30
Westport
•The Blau Gardens, Sunday, June 3
•Green Isle, Sunday, June 3
Wilton
•The Harris Garden, Sunday, September 9
•Pixie Perennials, Sunday, May 6; Saturday,
June 2; Sunday, September 16
HARTFORD COUNTY
Burlington
•The Salsedo Family Garden, Saturday, June
9
Canton
•Sudden Delight, Saturday, June 9
Collinsville
•Small Pleasures—A. Walter Kendra, Satur-
day, June 9
Glastonbury
•The Murray Gardens, Saturday, June 16;
Sunday, July 22
LITCHFIELD COUNTY
Bridgewater
•Maywood Gardens, Saturday, July 14
Cornwall
•Something to Crow About Dahlias, Sunday,
August 26
Falls Village
•Bunny Williams, Saturday, June 16; Satur-
day, July 14
Kent
•Mica Quarry Estate—Garden of Monika &
Buddy Nixon, Saturday, June 23
Lakeville
•Juniper Ledge, Saturday, July 14
Litchfield
•Glenn Hillman, Saturday, June 2
Roxbury
•Japanese Gardens at Cedar Hill, Saturday,
June 2; Sunday, August 26
Sharon
•Cobble Pond Farm, Saturday, May 12
•Lee Link, Saturday, July 21
Warren

•Covered Bridge Gardens, Saturday, May 12
•Mulla Garden, Saturday, July 14
Washington
•Brush Hill Gardens—Charles Raskob Rob-
inson & Barbara Paul Robinson, Saturday,
June 16
•Highmeadows—Linda Allard, Saturday,
June 16; Sunday, September 9
•Hollister House Gardens, Saturday, June 2;
Saturday, June 16; Saturday, July 14; Sun-
day, September 9
•The Rocks, Sunday, September 9
Washington Depot
•Appledore, Sunday, September 9
West Cornwall
•Roxana Robinson—Treetop, Sunday, Au-
gust 26
•Michael Trapp, Saturday, June 2
NEW HAVEN COUNTY
Meriden
•George Trecina, Sunday, July 22; Saturday,
September 8
Northford
•Reeds Gap West Residence, Saturday, Sep-
tember 8
Stony Creek
•Uptop—Garden of Fred Bland, Saturday,
June 16
Wallingford
•Wintergreen Garden, Saturday, June 16;
Sunday, July 22
NEW LONDON COUNTY
Stonington
•Kentford Farm, Saturday, July 14
•Stone Acres Farm, Saturday, August 25
District of Columbia
DISTRICT OF COLUMBIA
Georgetown
•Georgetown Garden—Nancy Gray Pyne,
Sunday, June 10
•1228 30th Street NW Garden, Sunday, June
10
Florida
DUVAL COUNTY
Jacksonville
•Ann & John Baker Garden, Saturday, April 14

- The Cummer Museum of Art & Gardens, Saturday, April 14
- Garden of Mr. & Mrs. Preston Haskell, Saturday, April 14
- Garden of Ann & David Hicks, Saturday, April 14
- Garden of Mr. & Mrs. William H. Morris, Saturday, April 14

Illinois
COOK COUNTY
Evanston
- Evanston Lakefront Garden, Sunday, June 24

Winnetka
- Gothic Victorian Garden, Saturday, June 23
- The Robb Garden, Sunday, June 24

DU PAGE COUNTY
West Chicago
- The Gardens at Ball, Sunday, August 5

LAKE COUNTY
Highland Park
- Highland Park Residence, Sunday, July 22

Lake Forest
- The Gardens at 900, Sunday, July 22
- Suzanne's Gardens, Sunday, June 24

Mettawa
- Mettawa Manor, Sunday, July 22

Massachusetts
BERKSHIRE COUNTY
Ashley Falls
- Steele Garden, Saturday, July 21

Sheffield
- 1391 Barnum Street, Sunday, June 24

BRISTOL COUNTY
Rehoboth
- McIlwain Garden, Sunday, June 3

SeEkonk
- Landscape Designer Andrew Grossman's Display Gardens, Sunday, June 3

NANTUCKET COUNTY
Nantucket
- Garden of Gale H. Arnold, Thursday, July 12
- The Garden at 7 Pocomo, Thursday, July 12
- House in the Woods, Thursday, July 12
- Blueberry Hill—Douglass & Caroline Ellis, Thursday, July 12

- Morash Victory Garden, Thursday, July 12

NORFOLK COUNTY
Canton
- Eleanor Cabot Bradley Estate, Saturday, June 9

Milton
- The Former "Mrs. Holden McGinley Garden" Designed by Ellen Biddle Shipman, Saturday, June 9
- Mary M. B. Wakefield Estate, Saturday, June 9
- The Roberts Garden—Formerly the "Helen Gilbert Estate" Designed by Fletcher Steele, Saturday, June 9

SUFFOLK COUNTY
West Roxbury
- Dustman-Ryan Garden, Saturday, June 9

Maryland
FREDERICK COUNTY
Frederick
- Basford Family Garden, Saturday, June 2
- High Glen Gardens, Saturday, June 2
- Long Creek Homestead, Saturday, June 2
- Rausch Woodland Gardens, Saturday, June 2

Middletown
- Surreybrooke, Saturday, June 2

Myersville
- Edgewood Garden, Saturday, June 2

MONTGOMERY COUNTY
Chevy Chase
- Everett Garden Designs Home Garden, Sunday, June 10

Silver Spring
- GreenHeart Garden, Sunday, June 10

Missouri
ST. LOUIS COUNTY
Kirkwood
- Far Meadows, Saturday, June 16
- The MP Garden, Saturday, June 16

St. Louis
- One Terry Hill Lane, Saturday, June 16
- Secret Garden, Saturday, June 16

New Hampshire
CHESHIRE COUNTY
Dublin
- Robertson Garden, Saturday, June 16

Jaffery
•Thoron Gardens, Saturday, June 16
HILLSBOROUGH COUNTY
Goffstown
•Evergreen, Saturday, July 14; Sunday, July 15
•Oak Hill Garden, Saturday, July 14; Sunday, July 15
Hancock
•Eleanor Briggs' Garden, Saturday, June 16
•May Place Gardens of Bill & Eileen Elliott, Saturday, June 16
Peterborough
•Michael & Betsy Gordon, Saturday, June 16
MERRIMACK COUNTY
Epsom
•Wells Corner, Saturday, July 14; Sunday, July 15

New Jersey

BERGEN COUNTY
Allendale
•Monfried Garden, Saturday, June 23
Mahwah
•Sisko Gardens, Saturday, June 23
Oakland
•Les Bois Des Chiens (The Dogs' Woods), Saturday, June 23
River Edge
•Anthony "Bud" & Virginia Korteweg, Saturday, June 23
River Vale
•Cupid's Garden—Audrey Linstrom Maihack, Saturday, June 23
ESSEX COUNTY
East Orange
•The Secret Garden @ 377—The Gotelli Garden at Harrison Park Towers, Saturday, May 5
Montclair
•Claire Ciliotta, Saturday, June 16
Nutley
•The Mountsier Garden, Sunday, April 15; Saturday, September 8
Short Hills
•Greenwood Gardens, Saturday, May 5; Saturday, September 8
HUNTERDON COUNTY

Pottersville
•Jardin de Buis, Sunday, September 9
Stockton
•Bellsflower Garden, Saturday, July 14
•The Garden at Federal Twist, Saturday, July 14
•The Gorrell-Schucker Garden, Saturday, July 14
•Pretty Bird Farm, Saturday, August 4
MONMOUTH COUNTY
Little Silver
•Garden of Diana Landreth, Saturday, July 21
Locust
•Nancy & Dan Crabbe's Garden on the Navesink River, Saturday, July 21
•Still Waters, Saturday, July 21
Rumson
•Cousins' Garden, Saturday, July 21
•King & Leigh Sorensen, Saturday, July 21
MORRIS COUNTY
Chatham
•Jack Lagos, Saturday, May 5, Saturday, July 14
Flanders
•Sterling Garden, Saturday, September 8
SOMERSET COUNTY
Far Hills
•The Hay Honey Farm, Saturday, May 5; Saturday, September 8
•Stone House Garden, Saturday, May 5; Saturday, September 8

New York

COLUMBIA COUNTY
Austerlitz
•Steepletop—Poet Edna St. Vincent Millay's Garden, Sunday, July 29
Canaan
•Rockland Farm, Sunday, July 29
Chatham Center
•Polemis Garden, Sunday, July 29
Claverack
•Ketay Garden, Saturday, June 9
•Peter Bevacqua & Stephen King, Saturday, June 9
Copake Falls

•Margaret Roach, Saturday, May 5; Saturday, August 18
Craryville
Rabbit Hill, Sunday, June 24
Hillsdale
•Texas Hill, Sunday, June 24
Hudson
•Livingston House Garden, Saturday, August 11
•Red Gate Farm, Saturday, August 11
•Versailles on Hudson, Saturday, June 9
Millerton
•Helen Bodian, Sunday, June 24
Spencertown
•Landscape of Linda B. Horn, Sunday, June 24; Saturday, August 18
West Taghkanic
•Arcadia—Ronald Wagner & Timothy Van Dam, Saturday, June 9

DUTCHESS COUNTY
Amenia
•Broccoli Hall—Maxine Paetro, Saturday, May 12; Saturday, June 16
•Jade Hill—Paul Arcario & Don Walker, Saturday, July 7
Dover Plains
•Copperheads, Saturday, September 22
Millbrook
•Clove Brook Farm—Christopher Spitzmiller, Saturday, September 22
•Innisfree Garden, Saturday, June 23; Saturday, July 21; Saturday, September 22
•Katie Ridder & Peter Pennoyer, Saturday, September 22
•Squirrel Hall, Saturday, June 23
Millerton
•Barbara Agren's Smithfield Cottage, Saturday, July 7
•Hyland/Wente Garden, Saturday, July 21
Pawling
•The Brine Garden—Duncan & Julia Brine, Saturday, October 13
•Scherer Garden, Saturday, June 30
Poughkeepsie
•Alice Pond, Saturday, June 23
•Dappled Berms—The Garden of Scott VanderHamm, Saturday, June 23

•Frank & Lois Van Zanten, Saturday, June 23
Stanfordville
•Bear Creek Farm, Saturday, September 22
•Ellen & Eric Petersen, Saturday, July 21
•Zibby & Jim Tozer, Saturday, June 23

GREENE COUNTY
Catskill
•Abeel House Prairie, Saturday, August 4
•High Falls, Saturday, August 4

JEFFERSON COUNTY
Chaumont
•Lakeside Quarry Garden, Saturday, July 21
Watertown
•The Walton Garden, Saturday, July 21

LIVINGSTON COUNTY
Pavilion
•Linwood Gardens, Sunday, June 10

NASSAU COUNTY
Glen Cove
•Kippen Hill, Sunday, June 3
Great Neck
•Fairview Cottage Garden, Sunday, June 3
Locust Valley
•Carol & Jim Large's Garden, Sunday, May 20
Old Westbury
•Howard Phipps Jr. Estate, Sunday, May 20
Sands Point
•Fern's Glade, Sunday, June 3

PUTNAM COUNTY
Cold Spring
•Stonecrop Gardens, Sunday, April 22; Sunday, May 13; Sunday, June 10; Sunday, July 8; Sunday, August 12; Sunday, September 2; Sunday, October 7
Garrison
•Ross Gardens, Sunday, June 10

SARATOGA COUNTY
Charlton
•Shades of Green, Saturday, June 23
Middle Grove
•Dalton Garden, Saturday, June 23
Saratoga Springs
•Collins Garden, Saturday, June 23
•Sarah Patterson's Garden, Saturday, June 23
Schuylerville

•Fiddle-i-fee-Farm, Saturday, June 23

SUFFOLK COUNTY
Bridgehampton
•Entwood Garden, Saturday, July 14
•Pamela Harwood & Peter Feder, Saturday, July 14
Cutchogue
•Arnold & Karen Blair, Saturday, June 2
East Hampton
•Chip Rae & Chuck Schwarz, Saturday, May 26
•Biercuk & Luckey Garden, Saturday, May 12
•Edwina von Gal—Marsh House, Saturday, May 26; Saturday, July 14
•Garden of Arlene Bujese, Saturday, July 14
•The Garden of Dianne B., Saturday, May 26
•Glade Garden—Abby Jane Brody, Saturday, May 12
•Levy-Barnett Garden, Saturday, May 12
•Previti/Gumpel Garden, Saturday, May 26
•Yugen, Saturday, July 14
Flanders
•Garden of Valerie M. Ansalone, Saturday, June 2,
Jamesport
•Winds Way Farm, Saturday, July 7
Mattituck
•Dennis Schrader & Bill Smith, Saturday, July 7
Mt. Sinai
•Tranquility, Saturday, June 30
Old Field
•Two Grey Achers, Sunday, May 6
Shelter Island Heights
•Birdhouse Garden, Saturday, July 7
TIOGA COUNTY
Spencer
•Myers Gardens, Saturday, July 7
TOMPKINS COUNTY
Freeville
•Manzano Garden, Saturday, July 7
Ithaca
•Shelia & Louis Out's Garden, Saturday, July 7
Lansing
•Lion Garden, Saturday, July 7
Trumansburg
•Hitch Lyman's Garden, Saturday, March 24

ULSTER COUNTY
Accord
•Eric Stewart & Dr. Michael Sheran, Sunday, September 23
•Hollengold Farm, Sunday, September 23
Highland
•Teri Condon—Gardensmith Design, Sunday, June 24
Kingston
•Garden of Peggy & Frank Almquist, Sunday, June 24
New Paltz
•Springtown Farmden, Sunday, June 24
Olivebridge
•James Dinsmore Garden, Sunday, September 23
Stone Ridge
•Hortus Conclusus, Sunday, September 23
WESTCHESTER COUNTY
Bedford
•High and Low Farm, Sunday, June 17
Bedford Hills
•Phillis Warden, Saturday, May 19; Sunday, June 17; Sunday, July 29
Chappaqua
•Shobha Vanchiswar & Murali Mani, Saturday, May 19
Cortlandt Manor
•Vivian & Ed Merrin, Saturday, July 21
Katonah
•Barbara & Tom Israel, Sunday, June 17
•Clementine Close, Saturday, May 19
Lewisboro
•The White Garden, Sunday, April 29
Mount Kisco
•Rocky Hills, Saturday, May 19
•The Greneker Retreat, Saturday, July 21
Pound Ridge
•James & Ellen Best's Sara Stein Garden, Sunday, July 29
South Salem
•Garden of Bernard Marquez & Tim Fish, Sunday, July 29; Sunday, September 09
Waccabuc
•James & Susan Henry, Sunday, September 9

Yorktown
•Barbara & John Schumacher, Sunday, June 17

Oregon
LANE COUNTY
Eugene
•Buell Steelman & Rebecca Sams, Saturday, July 7
•Enright Garden, Saturday, July 7
•Laurelwood Garden, Saturday, July 7
•Northwest Garden Nursery, Saturday, July 7
MULTNOMAH COUNTY
Portland
•Ediger Garden, Saturday, July 14
•Ferrante Garden, Saturday, July 14
•Nancyland, Saturday, July 14

Pennsylvania
BUCKS COUNTY
Carversville
•The Vicarage, Saturday, July 14
Gardenville
•Twin Silo Farm, Saturday, May 26
New Hope
•Gardens at Half Moon, Saturday, May 26
•Paxson Hill Farm, Saturday, May 26; Saturday, July 14; Saturday, August 04

Rhode Island
NEWPORT COUNTY
Little Compton
•Sakonnet, Saturday, May 26; Sunday, May 27
WASHINGTON COUNTY
Hopkinton
•Garden of Louis Raymond & Richard Ericson, Saturday, August 25

Texas
HARRIS COUNTY
Houston
•Heights Pollinator Café and Shade Garden, Saturday, April 28
•Itchy Acres, Saturday, April 28
•Selia Qynn's Garden Habitat, Saturday, April 28
•Steve Stelzer & Kathleen English, Saturday, April 28

Vermont
BENNINGTON COUNTY
East Arlington
•Rogerland, Saturday, June 23
Manchester
•Turkey Hill Farm, Saturday, June 23
Manchester Village
•A Cook's Garden, Saturday, June 23
WINDHAM COUNTY
Westminster West
•Gordon & Mary Hayward's Garden, Sunday, June 17
WINDSOR COUNTY
Hartland
•Brian Stroffolino's HeartLand Farms & Sylvia Davatz's Garden, Sunday, June 17
Windsor
•Cider Hill Gardens & Art Gallery—Sarah & Gary Milek, Sunday, June 17

Washington
KITSAP COUNTY
Bainbridge Island
•Garden of Gayle Bard, Saturday, June 16
•Ravenswold II, Saturday, June 16
•The Skyler Garden, Saturday, June 16
•Weissman Garden, Saturday, June 16
Indianola
•Sam & Karen Brindley's Garden, Saturday, June 16
•Windcliff, Saturday, June 16

Digging Deeper Programs by Date

Saturday, March 24
New York, Dutchess County
Millbrook
• Plant, Therefore, I Am—Stories from a Connecticut Kitchen Garden with Pamela Page; at Cary Institute of Ecosystem Studies. 2 PM

Saturday, April 14
New York, Dutchess County
Millbrook
• The Budget-Wise Gardener with Kerry Ann Mendez; at Cary Institute of Ecosystem Studies. 11 AM

Saturday, April 28
New York, Dutchess County
Millbrook
• The Garden in Every Sense and Season—A Bootcamp for the Senses with Tovah Martin; at Cary Institute of Ecosystem Studies. 11 AM

Sunday, April 29
New York, Westchester County
Lewisboro
• The Magic of Making More Plants: A Workshop for Kids; at The White Garden. 10 AM & 2 PM

Saturday, May 5
New Jersey, Somerset County
Far Hills
• Sharpening Your Garden Tools with Michael Clayton; at The Hay Honey Farm. 10 AM to 5 PM
California, Mendocino County
Gualala
At the Mullins' Mendocino Stonezone:
• Stone work demonstrations and Q & A. 10 AM to 4 PM
• A bonsai styling and presentation with expert Bob Shimon. 2 PM
At the Gualala Arts Center:
• Stone work demonstrations and Q & A. 10 AM to 4 PM

• Tours of the Global Harmony Sculpture Garden. 1 PM

Sunday, May 6
Connecticut, Fairfield County
Greenwich
• The Spring Vegetable Garden To Do List with Alan Gorkin; at Sleepy Cat Farm. 11 AM & 1 PM
• Family Scavenger Hunt; at Sleepy Cat Farm. 10 AM to 4 PM

Saturday, May 12
Connecticut, Litchfield County
Sharon
• Spring Beauties—An Early Season Garden Workshop with Lynden Miller in her garden. 10:30 AM
New York, Suffolk County
East Hampton
• An Evocative Vision—The Designers' Country Place with Peter van Hattum; at Hertenhof. 10 AM

Saturday, May 19,
California, Santa Cruz County
Santa Cruz
• Thematic Garden Planning with Tom Karwin in his garden. 4 PM
New York, Westchester County
Mount Kisco
• Tovah Martin's Bootcamp for the Senses; at Rocky Hills. 2 PM

Sunday, May 20
Illinois, Cook County,
Glencoe
• Visions of Nature—the gardens of Nicole Williams and Larry Becker. 3 PM to 5 PM
New York, Nassau County
Westbury
• Looking for Little Epiphanies with George Woodard; at Howard Phipps Jr., Estate. 10:30 AM

Sunday, May 26
Pennsylvania, Bucks County
Point Pleasant
• Drama and Drainage—The Gardens at Mill Fleurs. 4 PM
New York, Suffolk County
East Hampton
At Edwina von Gal's Marsh House:
• Tea for Two, the Soil and You! 10:30 AM to 4 PM
• Guided Garden Tours. 11 AM and 3 PM
• Perfect Earth Seed Bomb Workshop. 2 PM

Saturday, June 2
Connecticut , Fairfield County
Redding
• Elements of Historical Garden Design—Bringing Ideas of the Past into Gardens of Today; at Horsefeathers. 11 AM and 3 PM
Connecticut, Litchfield County
Litchfield
• Ornamental Herbs—Savory and Stunning with Tovah Martin; at the Garden of Glen Hillman. 3 PM
California, Mendocino County
Gualala
• Tours of the Global Harmony Sculpture Garden; at the Gualala Arts Center. 1 PM
Maryland, Frederick County
Frederick
• Hourly guided tours; at High Glen Gardens. 10 AM to 4 PM
• Guided Garden Tours; at Surreybrooke. 10 AM to 4 PM
• Edible Landscaping with a Permaculture Twist with Michael Judd; at Long Creek Homestead. 3 PM

Saturday, June 9
Connecticut , Hartford County
Burlington
• Guided garden tours; at the Salsedo Family Garden. 10 AM to 4 PM

Sunday, June 10
Washington, DC
At Georgetown Garden of Nancy Gray Pyne or Andrea Filippone & Eric T. Fleischer:

• Boxwood for the Future. 12 PM
• Compost Tea for Healthy Soil and Healthy Gardens. 1 PM

Saturday, June 16
New Hampshire, Hillsborough County
Peterborough
• Succession Planting for Mere Mortals with Michael Gordon; at Michael & Betsy Gordon's Garden. 4 PM

Sunday, June 17
New York, Westchester County
Katonah
• Skillful or Showy—Placing Ornament in the Garden with Barbara Israel in her garden. 11 AM
Vermont, Windham County
Putney
• A Walking Design Workshop with Gordon & Mary Hayward's Garden in their garden. 4 PM

Saturday, June 23
California, Mendocino County
Albion
At Digging Dog Nursery:
• Guided tour of the private gardens of Deborah Whigham & Gary Ratway. 1 PM
• Japanese Maple Container Garden Demonstration. 3 PM
New York, Saratoga County
Charlton
• Shades of Green—The Lush Beauty of a Shady Garden with Wynne Trowbridge; at Shades of Green Garden. 2:30 PM

Sunday, June 24
Illinois, Lake County
Lake Forest
• Garden Enchantment—An Afternoon at Camp Rosemary. 3 PM to 5 PM
New York, Columbia County
Spencertown
• A Meadow Restoration Through the Seasons—Late Spring at the Garden of Linda Horn. 10 AM to 4 PM

Saturday, July 7

Oregon, Lane County
Eugene
• A Tapestry Garden—The Art of Weaving Plants and Place with Ernie & Marietta O'Byrne; at Northwest Garden Nursery. 10 AM

Saturday, July 14

New York, Suffolk County
East Hampton
• Subtle and Mysterious Beauty—Exotic Plants and Asian Ideas in a Hamptons Garden; at Yugen. 9:30 AM to 11:30 AM
Bridgehampton
• Rocks, Ponds, Waterfalls, and Exotic Trees—A Strolling Garden to Soothe and Stimulate; at Entwood Gardens. 2 PM
Colorado, Pitkin County
Basalt
• Guided garden tour of Rock Bottom Ranch. 11 AM
New York, Suffolk County
East Hampton
At Edwina von Gal's Marsh House:
• Tea for Two, the Soil and You! 10:30 AM to 4 PM
• Guided Garden Tours. 11 AM
• The Dirt on Soil Health. 1 PM to 3 PM
Oregon, Multnomah County
Portland
• Book signing with Amy Campion and Paul Bonine, authors of *Gardening in the Pacific Northwest*; at St. John Garden. 10 AM to 4 PM
• Book signing with Donald Olson, author of *The Pacific Northwest Garden Tour* and *The California Garden Tour*; at Eastman Griffin Garden. 10 AM to 4 PM

Sunday, July 22

Illinois, Lake County
Lake Forest
• Garden Enchantment—An Afternoon at Camp Rosemary. 3 PM to 5 PM
Mettawa
At Mettawa Manor:
• A Day-Long Garden Celebration with Bill Kurtis and Donna LaPietra. 10 AM to 4 PM
• Beekeeper demonstration. 1 PM

Saturday, August 4

New York, Greene County
Catskill
• Confessions of a Prairie Plant Addict; at Abeel House Prairie. 10 AM

Saturday, August 11

New York, Columbia County
Claverack
• Creative Pragmatism—An Innovative Approach to Reclaiming Land and Developing a "Nearly Native Garden;" at Peter Bevacqua & Stephen King's Garden. 4 PM

Saturday, August 18

New York, Columbia County
Spencertown
• A Meadow Restoration Through the Seasons—High Summer; at the Garden of Linda Horn. 10 AM to 4 PM

Saturday, August 25

Rhode Island, Washington County
Hopkinton
• Natural is for Wimps—Training Plants into Extraordinary Shapes; at the Garden of Louis Raymond & Richard Ericson. 3:30 PM & 5 PM
Connecticut, New London County
Stonington
• Ellen Shipman book signing with Judith Tankard; at Stone Acres Farm. 11 AM to 1 PM

Sunday, September 9

New Jersey, Hunterdon County
Pottersville
At Jardin de Buis: Andrea Filippone & Eric T. Fleischer
• Boxwood for the Future. 12 PM
• Compost Tea for Healthy Soil and Healthy Gardens. 1 PM
Connecticut, Fairfield County
Wilton
• Art and Science in the Garden; at the Harris Garden. 3 PM

Sunday, September 16

Connecticut, Fairfield County
Greenwich
• Garden Bounty with Chef Seen Lippert; at Sleepy Cat Farm. 4 PM to 5:30 PM

Saturday, September 22

New York, Dutchess County
Dover Plains
• Amazing Annuals—Usual, Unusual, and Where to Find Them; at Copperheads. 10 AM
Millbrook
• Made By Hand—Ceramist Christopher Spitzmiller's Garden and Art; at his Clove Brook Farm. 2 PM

Sunday, September 23

New York, Ulster County
Stone Ridge
• Unusual Edibles—Treasures for Garden and Table; at Hortus Conclusus. 1 PM

Saturday, October 13

Connecticut, Litchfield County
Washington
• An Autumn Afternoon with Linda Allard; at Highmeadows. 1 PM to 3 PM

Sunday, November 4

California, Los Angeles County
Santa Monica
• In the Pink—Autumn in a California Garden; at The Marek/Bernatz Garden. 4 PM

CALIFORNIA
Pasadena
Sunday, April 22

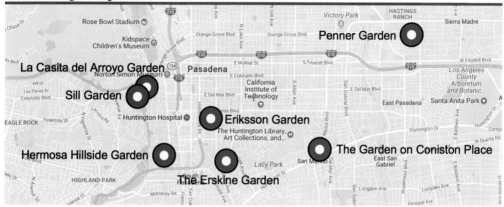

★ Start your day at La Casita del Arroyo, 177 South Arroyo Boulevard, Pasadena, 9:30 a.m. to 3:30 p.m.

Maps and discounted admission tickets will be available there. Admission: free.

Los Angeles County
PASADENA
ERIKSSON GARDEN
3790 Shadow Grove Road, Pasadena
Hours: 10 a.m. to 4 p.m.
📷 | NEW

Part laboratory, part sanctuary, the gardens surrounding landscape architect Nord Eriksson's Pasadena home bring together a lifetime of influences. The 1949 ranch-style home won over Nord, Cynthia, and their two sons six years ago, offering the chance to develop artful garden rooms on the 18,000-square-foot lot. Largely a blank slate, the grounds beckoned for something new. Six years later, hints of Nord's appreciation of Scandinavian, Japanese, and Mediterranean design can be found in the remade gardens. The gently sloping land, anchored by a magnificent native Englemann oak, was terraced to create interest, retain rainwater, and create a variety of spaces for family life and entertaining. A tapestry of textural paving weaves throughout; concrete, brick, slate, gravel, and pebble are crafted into a soulful mix. Walls of arroyo cobble and concrete block trace lines in the garden, originally laid out by pioneering landscape architect Edward Huntsman-Trout. A sojourn to Spain and Mallorca allowed Nord to study resilient landscapes and influenced his design of the lap pool and plantings of the rear gardens. In the front yard, ivy has been replaced by a mix of grasses and salvias with accents of *Agave* and *Aloe*. Today, the garden grows, teaches lessons, and brings deep satisfaction. It's a joy to come home to...and a gift to share.

DIRECTIONS—Located off Manzanita Avenue, 7 blocks north of Foothill Boulevard in the Lower Hastings Ranch neighborhood of Pasadena.

THE ERSKINE GARDEN
1410 Lomita Road, Pasadena
Hours: 10 a.m. to 4 p.m.
 | NEW

Fifty-seven years ago, in 1961, owner Georgiana and husband Paul Erskine bought their Colonial-style home built in 1937 by Morris Miller, a noted Pasadena plantsman. Here they raised three children, and over the years the garden evolved into a series with great structure and style. Georgiana, a Smith College history and art history major, resolved early on to travel and study historical gardens. She felt strongly that the original garden was visible at once, giving the garden "no sense of mystery." Her continuing studies took her to the Sorbonne and the École du Louvre for graduate study, and gave her the opportunity to do further research with visits to noted European gardens. The genesis of her eventual garden design plan was a visit to the classic Moorish gardens at the Alhambra, and a visit to Italy where the emphasis on axial design became the design focus. As the property is a peculiar triangle, adjustments were made to the axis to accommodate the shape, giving the impression now that the garden is a rectangle... [Read full description online]

DIRECTIONS—From the 210 Freeway, take Exit 26/Lake Street in Pasadena and head south for 0.7 miles. Turn right on Del Mar Boulevard for 0.3 miles. Turn left on South El Molino Drive for 1.3 miles. Go through traffic circle. Turn right on Woodland Road for 381 feet. Turn left on Lomita Drive for 364 feet. Destination is on the right.

—From the 110 Freeway, take to the north end and turn right on Glenarm Street. Turn right on South Oakland Street, through traffic circle for 0.4 miles. Turn slight left on Lomita Drive, destination is on the left.
—From the 10 Freeway, take Atlantic Boulevard/Exit 23A-238 North toward Pasadena for 2.5 miles. Continue north as road name changes to Los Robles Avenue 1.0 miles. Turn right onto South Oakland Avenue, 479 feet. Sharp right onto Lomita Drive, destination will be on the left.

PENNER GARDEN
220 South San Rafael Avenue, Pasadena
Hours: 10 a.m. to 4 p.m.
 | NEW

In 1963, Smith & Williams designed this single-story mid-century home on the banks of the Arroyo River. Sited to best take advantage of the views, the post-and-beam residence provides walls of glass and a seamless transition to the outdoors and vistas beyond. During the renovation of all the outdoor spaces, the current owners wanted to maximize the outdoor entertaining space, as well as create a more natural connection, utilizing Southern California indigenous plants. Nord Erickson designed a landscape vocabulary that both leveraged the architectural lines of the home and maximized visual attention to the existing palm, oak, and olive trees on the property. As for plants, the focus was to utilize drought-tolerant specimens and citrus as much as possible. An outdoor kitchen was built, with an herb and vegetable garden integrated into the surrounding wall. The infinity pool is anchored by a band of grass above and seating area below.

DIRECTIONS—From # 134, go east toward Pasadena and exit at San Rafael. Turn

right and immediately right again at the light (Colorado Boulevard). Take the first immediate left onto South San Rafael and proceed approximately 0.25 mile to 220 South San Rafael Avenue.
—From the 210, reverse the directions: east to South San Rafael; left and then right on Colorado to South San Rafael; left to 220 South San Rafael.
—From the 110 coming from Los Angeles, travel east toward Pasadena to the Orange Grove Boulevard exit. Turn left and take South Orange Grove to California Boulevard (4th light). Turn left down to Arroyo Boulevard. Turn left on Arroyo Boulevard and turn right at the La Loma Bridge. Take La Loma to South San Rafael, turn right and travel to #220, approximately 0.3 mile.

SILL GARDEN
709 South Euclid Avenue, Pasadena
Hours: 10 a.m. to 4 p.m.
📷 | ♿ | **NEW**

Located in the Madison Heights section of Pasadena, this home displays an interesting combination of elements drawn from the Craftsman and Prairie styles. The house next door to the north (Montessori school) was built in 1908. Julia Child attended school there as a young child. The current owners have lived in this home since 1991. In 1996, the owners hired landscape architect Sally Farnum of S.E. Farnum Associates. At that time, in the northwest corner of the yard was a concrete slab, which served as a badminton court. Ms. Farnum recommended breaking up the concrete and using the remnants to create an elevated garden.

New additions included redwood trees, jasmine, *Coleonema pulchellum,* and *Euphorbia characias*. The middle south part of the yard by the *Cedrus deodara* was covered with ivy, which was removed and replaced with the walking path and featured acanthus, *Ligularia*, angel's trumpet, *Viburnum, Clivia*, 'Iceberg' roses, and a trumpet vine. In 2012, the owners removed 600 square feet of overgrowth that was nearly a century old and replaced it with a formal garden featuring decomposed granite, roses, citrus trees, *Podacarpus*, and Carolina cherry trees.

DIRECTIONS—From the 210 or 134 Freeway, take the Lake Avenue exit and head south. Turn right on California Boulevard and then left on Euclid Avenue.
—From the 110 Freeway, when the freeway ends, continue straight. Turn right on California Boulevard, then right on Euclid Avenue.

SAN MARINO
THE GARDEN ON CONISTON PLACE
2410 Coniston Place, San Marino
Hours: 10 a.m. to 4 p.m.
📷 | ♿PARTIAL | **NEW |**

When this house with its three tall towers was designed in 1927, I think the towers were meant to reflect the San Marino city logo, which shows the ancient city walls and towers of the Republic of San Marino, on the Italian peninsula. My home is commonly called "the Coniston Castle." It was purchased forty-six years ago, and the various projects to fix, fix, fix and then sell turned the house and especially the garden into a real "love affair." Owen Peters, FASLA, designed a complete renovation of the entire property, including hardscape and plantings. Walls were built around the corner for privacy. Soil was moved, holes were dug, beds prepared and planted, and outdoor tiles laid. We worked on this "labor of love" over an entire winter while watching our neighbors leave to enjoy fun activities. Many of the original plantings have been changed.

Ten years ago the west side's patio was enlarged and is now surrounded by hydrangeas and 'Iceberg' roses. Then the drought came and, encouraged by the State of California, we removed the grass in the parkways and replaced it with more drought-tolerant plants...[Read full description online]

DIRECTIONS—Just 2 blocks north of Huntington Drive, turn north on Kenilworth Avenue and go to the intersection with Coniston Place.

—From the 210 Freeway, take Sierra Madre Boulevard and drive south to Kenilworth Avenue, turn left, and proceed to the intersection with Coniston Place. The mountains are to the north.

SOUTH PASADENA
HERMOSA HILLSIDE GARDEN
255 Hillside Road, South Pasadena
Hours: 10 a.m. to 4 p.m.
📷 | ♿PARTIAL | **NEW**

Hermosa Hillside Garden is on corner of Hillside Road and Hermosa Street. The residence is known as the C.F. Paxton House, after the rancher who commissioned it in 1919, and his wife, Renelje Schenck, created the original landscape. It is listed on the City of South Pasadena Inventory

of Historic Resources. The architect was the famous Reginald D. Johnson, his award-winning structure was called a "sunny house in the Spanish style." "In drawing up this design, Mr. Johnson concentrated his efforts on providing a type of architecture suitable to Southern California, but showing the architectural work one finds along the Mediterranean." (*Pasadena Star-News*: May 14, 1921). Shortly after it was built it won a gold medal, first prize, for having the best design of residential architecture in a competition with 569 others from all parts of the United States. It has been called the quintessential California home. Over the years, the landscaping suffered from deferred maintenance, rusting wire fence, crumbling stacked walls, dying oleanders, and overgrown hedges causing unsightly and unusable space between the house and the street. [Read full description online]

DIRECTIONS—Take the 110 Freeway East and exit at Orange Grove Boulevard. Go north on Orange Grove Boulevard to Columbia Street, go left, and left again on Hermosa Street. Park on Hermosa Street where it intersects with Hillside Road.

—From the 134 Freeway, take Orange Grove Boulevard exit, go south on Orange Grove Boulevard to Columbia Street, go right, and then left on Hermosa Street. Park as signs indicate.

PUBLIC GARDEN PARTNER

Los Angeles County
PASADENA
LA CASITA DEL ARROYO GARDEN
177 South Arroyo Boulevard, Pasadena
Lacasitadelarroyo.org.
Hours: Year round, daily, dawn to dusk
Admission: Free

★ Start your tour here on Sunday, April 22 between 9:30 a.m. and 3:30 p.m. Tickets and maps to all of the Pasadena area gardens will be available.

La Casita del Arroyo (The Little House

on the Arroyo) was built as a community meeting house in 1933, a joint venture by the Pasadena Garden Club and the City of Pasadena. Natural materials from the Arroyo were combined with recycled materials from the velodrome built for the 1932 Olympics as a work project during the Great Depression. In 1988, the Pasadena Garden Club in conjunction with noted landscape architects Isabel Greene and Yosh Befu designed and installed a water demonstration garden intended as an educational resource for the greater Pasadena community, that promoted plants suitable for a Mediterranean climate as well as water-saving irrigation systems.

In 2010, the Pasadena Garden Club redesigned the Butterfly Garden, which leads from the Arroyo up to the main garden and the Casita. As a joint venture with the City, the building may be rented to non-profit groups, weddings, and receptions by applying to the City of Pasadena. The gardens, maintained by the Pasadena Garden Club, are open year round as a self-guided tour during daylight hours only. Visitors may park on the street adjacent to La Casita or come up through the trails in the Arroyo.

DIRECTIONS—From I-210 in Pasadena, exit south onto Orange Grove Boulevard. Turn right onto Arbor Street to Arroyo Boulevard. Turn right and #177 is on left.
—From I-110, continue from end of freeway north on Arroyo Parkway. Turn left onto California Boulevard which dead ends at Arroyo Boulevard. Turn right and continue to #177.
—From Highway 101 east, exit at Orange Grove Boulevard, just before the I-210 junction. Turn right onto California Boulevard which dead ends at Arroyo Boulevard. Turn right and continue to #177.

What our Garden Hosts recommend in Pasadena

San Gabriel Nursery
632 S San Gabriel Blvd,
San Gabriel, CA 91776
(626) 286-3782
www.sgnurserynews.com

B-Man's Teriyaki & Burgers
3007 Huntington Dr #102
Pasadena, CA 91107
(626) 568-0386
www.bmans.com

Belle Fontaine Nursery
838 S. Fair Oaks Ave, Pasadena CA
(626) 796-0747
www.bellefontainenursery.com

Gales Restaurant
452 Fair Oaks Ave, Pasadena, CA 91105
(626) 432-6705
www.galesrestaurant.com

Mendocino County
Saturday, May 5

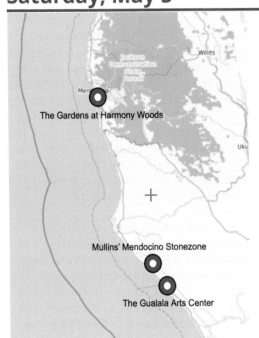

The Gardens at Harmony Woods

Mullins' Mendocino Stonezone

The Gualala Arts Center

pebbled flagstone paths as well as undulating patterned-granite terraces provide a setting for serene contemplation and deep musings. A full-scale traditional Irish tower rises to provide visitors with a spectacular view of the ocean. Come ready to ask questions and discover the various principles that hardscape artisans follow to complement and enhance natural features of the landscape and garden.

Mullins' Mendocino Stonezone
DIGGING DEEPER
**Stone work demonstrations and Q & A
Free with garden admission**

Come ready to ask questions and discover the various principles that traditional hardscape artisans use to complement and enhance natural features of the landscape and garden with stone installations.

Mendocino County
GUALALA
MULLINS' MENDOCINO STONEZONE
44600 Fish Rock Road, Gualala
Hours: 10 a.m. to 4 p.m.
📷 | 2017

This is a special opportunity to visit the private garden estate of Peter Mullins. Situated among the magnificent redwoods of Northern California, this scenic coastal property allows visitors to explore a myriad of whimsical stone structures, garden follies, and sculptural installations, all tucked tastefully into the landscape. This large forested property imparts that wonderful sense of place that can only be created with time and patience. Walls and trees, patios, standing stones, floral "sculptures," and

Lead project craftsmen, John Shaw-Rimmington from Port Hope, Canada, Kevin Carman from Art City in Ventura, California, and John Fisher of Fort Bragg, California, have contributed to the stone work at the Gualala Arts Center and the Mullins property, and there will be much new work to be seen.

Mullins' Mendocino Stonezone

DIGGING DEEPER
2 PM
Bonsai styling
Presentation and display
Free with garden admission

Award-winning bonsai expert Bob Shimon of Gualala, California, will discuss styling bonsai. Examples of his bonsai will be on display throughout the day.

DIRECTIONS —From Highway 1, head east on Fish Rock Road for 2.2 miles. Main property is on left, secondary property on right. Parking is available near the house and along the road. Please be respectful of space, traffic, and neighbors.

MENDOCINO
THE GARDENS AT HARMONY WOODS
44380 Gordon Lane, Mendocino
Hours: 10 a.m. to 4 p.m.
📷 | ♿PARTIAL | **2014**

The Gardens at Harmony Woods, nestled into a cathedral of redwoods, reflect a penchant for collecting an enormous range of unusual and beautiful plants. The emphasis is on rhododendrons and conifers, with more than 300 specimens of each, but they are a small part of a vast array of plant material gracing the beds. Education through research, cataloguing, and labeling is an integral part of the owners' collecting and a way of sharing their knowledge. The gardens were created over twenty-five years ago and continue to evolve. Waterfalls and a stone bridge add the timeless magic of age. Rusted artifacts that complement the redwood bark are situated throughout the beds. Gently falling waters, ever-changing colors, and contrasting textures delight and nourish every day. The Gardens at Harmony Woods has been accepted into the Smithsonian Institution's Archives of American Gardens.

DIRECTIONS —GPS does not work here! Gordon Lane is halfway between Van Damme State Park to the south and the village of Mendocino to the north on Highway 1. Turn east onto Gordon Lane and continue to the end of the paved road. Turn left onto the dirt road and go to the end and through the redwood gate. Number 44380 is on the left gatepost. Enter the property and continue straight ahead to park in the dressage ring.

PUBLIC GARDEN PARTNER

Mendocino County
GUALALA
THE GUALALA ARTS CENTER
46501 Old State Highway, Gualala
Hours: Monday to Friday, 10 a.m. to 4 p.m. and Saturday to Sunday, noon to 4 p.m. Grounds are always open to the public. Garden looks best March through November, although redwood forest and paths are lovely year round.
Admission: Free
(707) 884-1138
gualalaarts.org

Gualala Arts Center is a 15,000-square-foot visual and performing arts venue on eleven acres of redwood forest that sits one-quarter mile from the Pacific Ocean on the Mendocino Coast. This jewel of the Redwood Coast is tucked into the redwood forest next to the Gualala River and includes a Haiku garden path, a Redwood Grove Events Area adorned with hand-built stone walls, multiple walkways, large bronze sculptures, large boulders, unique garden art, outdoor areas that invite you to pause and reflect, and a Meditation Grove of old growth redwoods that stand tall among large ferns and lush greenery. Patios and outdoor event areas are home to many annual and perennial plants and flowers native to the Mendocino-Sonoma coastal area. Sculptures and outdoor artwork complement the forested grounds and gardens at every turn. Indoor galleries change monthly and Gualala Arts hosts many festivals and events throughout the year. Gualala Arts is thrilled to team up with the Stone Foundation and Peter Mullins' Mendocino Stonezone for the open garden tours. Many of the stone masons have created one-of-a-kind sculptures that remain on the grounds of Gualala Arts for all to admire. The newly remodeled redwood grove is a legacy build by the Stone Foundation and is a great place to stop for a picnic lunch amongst the towering redwoods, surrounded by the ancient art of stone masonry.

Gualala Arts Center
46501 Old State Highway, Gualala

DIGGING DEEPER
10 AM – 4 PM
Stone Work Demonstrations

Stone Foundation members/artists Kevin Carman and John Shaw-Rimmiton will answer questions about their stone installations at the Gualala Arts Center throughout the day, when the grounds and the 15,000 square-foot visual and performing arts center will be open for self-guided tours.

Gualala Arts Center
DIGGING DEEPER
1 PM
Guided Garden Tours — Free

Executive Director, David "Sus" Susalla will give tours of the Global Harmony Sculpture Garden with highlights of the first Serge installed in the United States (a gift from the Yakut people of Sakha Republic), the Haiku Stone Path in honor and memory of artists Jane and Werner Reichhold, the Torii Gate (traditional wood archway), and the Meditation Grove in the Redwood Grove Event Area, newly-remodeled by the Stone Foundation.

DIRECTIONS—From San Francisco, take Hwy 101 to Petaluma. Take Bodega Avenue north along the Sonoma Coast. Continue north until crossing the county line that is the Gualala River. Take the first right, Old Stage Road. After 0.25 mile, turn right onto Old State Highway. The Gualala Arts Center will be on your right at 46501 Old Stat Highway.

What our Garden Hosts recommend in Mendocino County

Trinks
39140 CA-1, Gualala, CA 95445
(707) 884-1713
www.trinkscafe.com

Frannie's Cup & Saucer
213 Main Street, Point Arena, CA 95468
(707) 882-2500
www.frannyscupandsaucer.com

215 Main
215 Main Street, Point Arena, CA
(707) 882-3215

Los Angeles
Sunday, May 6

★ Start your day at the Marlborough School, 250 South Rossmore Avenue, Los Angeles, 9:30 a.m. to 3:30 p.m. Enter through the 3rd Street security kiosk into the parking lot on the southeast corner of the property; please do not park along Arden Boulevard. Maps and discounted admission tickets will be available there. Admission: free.

Los Angeles County
LOS ANGELES
ARDEN GARDEN
456 South Arden Boulevard, Los Angeles
Hours: 10 a.m. to 4 p.m.
📷 | 2009

Since its last appearance on Open Days in 2009, the Arden Garden has matured and undergone a few changes. Under the continuing guidance of landscape architect Joseph Marek, who designed the gardens

in 2003, the plantings in the front garden have been pared down to green *Pittosporum* balls and *Ligustrum* shrubs with a few flourishes of color coming from drifts of lavender and 'Golden Celebration' roses. Privet cones at the front door and Italian cypress sentinels punctuate the architecture of this stately Windsor Square home. The King palms and olive tree in the back garden have reached majestic proportions, providing shade to the spa garden and to the kitchen terrace. The vines atop the pergola covering the living and dining spaces are laced out semiannually to provide welcome sun in winter and spring and cooling shade in the warmer months, which often stretch through the fall holidays. The small central lawn, or *tapis vert*, surrounded by a new hedge of *Rhaphiolepis umbellata* 'Minor', has been further reduced and is now a mere "throw rug." It still serves however as a green counterpoint to the Sweetwater sandstone "floors" and pool coping and to the gravel paving throughout the garden. Please visit again or for the first time!

DIRECTIONS—From Wilshire Boulevard, turn north onto Arden Boulevard. The garden is at the northeast corner of South Arden and 5th Street. Park on either street.

THE CHUNG GARDEN
61 Fremont Place, Los Angeles
Hours: 10 a.m. to 4 p.m.
NEW

This Fremont Place garden is a treasure trove of rare and exotic plants. Precisely and artfully planted, the garden is a horticulturalist's dream with unique varieties of roses, succulents, palms, and fruiting and flowering trees. The front garden is planted with a variety of fragrant plumerias intermixed with succulents and roses. Individual irrigation systems have been installed to provide the right amount of water for the various types of plants. Mrs. Chaney Chung and plant expert and designer Youn Kim have carefully replanted the entire property in miniature vignettes, with plants suited to each room of the garden, surrounding one of the most historic homes on Fremont Place. Built in 1924, the home was designed by Myron Hunt, a prominent architect of the era. The new garden, installed last year, provides a wonderful new setting for this architectural classic.

DIRECTIONS—From the Santa Monica 10 Freeway, exit at Crenshaw Boulevard north to Wilshire Boulevard, then left at Wilshire. Turn left at the light at Fremont Place and Wilshire Boulevard.
—From the Hollywood 101 Freeway, exit at Vine Street, go south to Wilshire Boulevard. Vine Street becomes Rossmore Avenue. Cross Wilshire Boulevard and enter Fremont Place. The gate will admit any Garden Conservancy visitors. Turn left after the gate, then right on East Fremont Place. The Chung Garden will be on your right at 61 Fremont Place, the Lombard Simon Garden will be in the next block on your left, at 78 Fremont Place.

FISCHER GARDEN
354 South Windsor Boulevard, Los Angeles
Hours: 10 a.m. to 4 p.m.
 | &PARTIAL | **NEW**

This Colonial Revival home in historic Windsor Square was designed by architects Hunt and Burns in 1915, with a library addition by Robert Farquhar. The property was recently redesigned to be more drought-tolerant by reducing expansive lawns and to accommodate both intimate and large-scale entertaining. It is divided into rooms tied together by patterned-brick and bluestone paving as well as boxwood hedges. An allée of Holly Oak trees occupies much of the front garden. The back garden includes pergolas, terraces, a fire pit area, rose and raised vegetable gardens, Japanese maples for shade, and a pool with cabana.

DIRECTIONS—From Hollywood and Vine Street, proceed south on Vine Street (becomes Rossmore Boulevard) to 4th Street. Turn left on 4th Street to Windsor Boulevard. The house is located at the northeast corner of 4th Street and Windsor Boulevard.

GARDEN OF KATHLEEN LOSEY
526 South Norton Avenue, Los Angeles
Hours: 10 a.m. to 4 p.m.
 | &PARTIAL | **NEW**

I moved into my home in November of 2012 and proceeded to do a major change of the landscape over a two-year period. The front was mostly decomposed granite, succulents, drought-tolerant plants, and a large pepper berry tree, all of which I removed. Of course, I kept the three wonderful *Arbutus* trees. I also transplanted the *Ligustrum* hedge from the lower yard and added more, to line the inside of the wall for privacy. On the walkway (where the *Arbutus* are), I planted a small hedge of 'Little Ollie' and filled in with lavender, geranium, and other smaller plants. Last year my daughter moved away, so I incorporated her large boxwoods in terra-cotta pots into the scheme. I wanted a "patch of grass," so added the Marathon II lawn as you see it now. I also extended the small front patio by three feet, making it usable for hosting cocktails and watching my Standard Poodle and Pomeranian play at the end of the day. I also planted two climbing roses (Cl. 'Royal Sunset' and 'Dream Weaver'), which only seem to get better with each passing year. I transplanted small hydrangeas, oakleaf hydrangeas, and 'Iceberg' roses from my previous garden and was fortunate that the boxwoods were able to be re-transplanted when the work was done. The vintage patio furniture is from my parents' home in Altadena, and the "arbor seating bench" was brought over, again, from my previous garden...[Read full description online]

DIRECTIONS—Garden is on South Norton—1.5 blocks north of Wilshire and 2.5 blocks south of Third Street—between Bronson Avenue and Van Ness Boulevard.
—From the 10 Freeway, exit at Crenshaw Boulevard north to Wilshire Boulevard and turn right. Turn left onto South Norton Avenue.
—From the 101 Freeway, exit at Sunset Boulevard south. Go south on Van Ness Boulevard to Third Street and turn right. Turn left onto South Norton Avenue.

LOMBARD SIMON GARDEN
78 Fremont Place, Los Angeles
Hours: 10 a.m. to 4 p.m.
&PARTIAL | **NEW**

We did the front garden soon after we bought this traditional 1937 house in the early 1990s. It is a shady grove of California live oaks surrounded by majestic Italian cypresses. The path to the front door is flanked by boxwood parterres. A garden maze next to one side of the front door was designed for our oldest daughter, then three years old. The back garden is on two levels. In the far back, the lower (originally a paddle tennis court) became a play space surrounded by California sycamores and *Podocarpus* trees. Later we renovated the court space to become a sports court with basketball hoop. In 2004, after we added on to the back of the house, Judy Horton designed the gardens and courtyard on the upper level. She clad the two-story house with purple wisteria and yellow Lady Banks roses, shaded the terrace with a Chinese elm, and filled the beds with Mediterranean shrubs. Four years ago, after the guesthouse was remodeled for elderly parents, Judy created gardens around the guesthouse and redid the motor court...[Read full description online]

DIRECTIONS—From the Santa Monica 10 Freeway, exit at Crenshaw Boulevard north to Wilshire Blvd, then turn left at Wilshire. Turn left again at the light at Fremont Place and Wilshire Boulevard.
—From the Hollywood 101 Freeway exit at Vine Street, go south to Wilshire Boulevard. Vine becomes Rossmore. Cross Wilshire and enter Fremont Place. The gate will admit all Garden Conservancy visitors. Turn left after the gate, then right on East Fremont Place. The Chung Garden will be on your right at 61 Fremont. The Lombard Simon Garden will be in the next block on your left at 78 Fremont.

VILLA ABBONDANZA
535 South Norton Avenue, Los Angeles
Hours: 10 a.m. to 4 p.m.
📷 | **2010**

Our garden was one of the first front-yard gardens in Windsor Square. We bought our 1920s Italianate-style house in 1986 and began renovations in 1989. We replaced a weedy front lawn with a garden. We ripped out dead rose bushes to make room for a swimming pool. We built high stucco walls to enclose the new pool and created a rear courtyard with an outdoor fireplace. The olive and guava trees, along with the hardscape and the climbing roses, are all that remain from experiments with a mostly native garden in the 1980s and a garden of roses and flowering perennials in the 1990s. Today, our low-maintenance garden is filled with *Aloe*, *Agave*, assorted other succulents, and Mediterranean perennials. The ground is covered in Yosemite pebbles. The rear courtyard garden is full of potted trees and shrubs with colorful foliage. There is a wall of vintage plant hangers filled with succulents. Blue-flowering *Petrea volubilis* covers the walls. The new courtyard and the original loggia are paved in concrete tiles with slate accents.

DIRECTIONS—Garden is on South Norton—1.5 blocks north of Wilshire and 2.5 blocks south of Third Street—between Bronson Avenue and Van Ness Boulevard.
—From the 10 Freeway, exit at Crenshaw Boulevard north to Wilshire Boulevard and turn right. Turn left onto South Norton Avenue.
—From the 101 Freeway, exit at Sunset Boulevard south. Go south on Van Ness Boulevard to Third Street and turn right. Turn left onto South Norton Avenue.

What our Garden Hosts recommend in Los Angeles County

Roast Deli and Market
147 S Barrington Ave, Los Angeles, CA 90049
(310) 476-1100
www.roastdelimarket.com

Le Petit Greek
127 N Larchmont Boulevard, Los Angeles
(323) 464-5160
www.lepetitgreek.com

Armstrong Garden Center
3226 Wilshire Blvd., Santa Monica, CA
(310) 829-6766
www.armstronggarden.com

Santa Monica
Sunday, November 4

The Marek/Bernatz Garden

DIGGING DEEPER
4 PM
In the Pink—Autumn in a California Garden
REGISTRATION: $40 Garden Conservancy Members / $50 general

Joseph Marek and his partner, John Bernatz, have been gardening this spot in Santa Monica for twenty years and have explored many different design and planting ideas and schemes over that time. Joseph is a landscape architect and has been a plant lover his whole life. His particular passion is for roses and rose hybridizing. While the garden has been a favorite since its first appearance on Open Days in 2003 and is great to visit in spring when the roses are in full bloom, the garden is rarely seen by visitors in fall—often the most beautiful time to see California gardens. Aloes in the garden burst into bloom in shades of lime green, buttery gold, tangerine, and coral in autumn, with early November being the best time to see them here. The back garden holds a special surprise with an abundant profusion of magenta blossoms of *Hypoestes aristata*—originally a gift as a cutting from another plant friend—that has now naturalized and provides masses of unmatched color every fall. There's never a day that goes by without an orchid of some sort or variety blooming in the garden, so be sure to keep your eyes open. We'll have a tour through the gardens and share our thoughts on how it has changed and matured—like us—over the years. Join us for a glass of wine and if we are really lucky we'll be graced with one of our perfect pink autumn sunsets. Joseph Marek is a plant nut. His plant collections range from aloes to tillandsias and from epiphyllums to orchids. He enjoys trying out new plants and building new plant collections. John Bernatz enjoys keeping all the plants (and Joseph!) in check.

Registration required — space limited
Go to opendaysprogram.org
or call 1 (888) 842-2442

San Francisco East Bay
Saturday, May 12

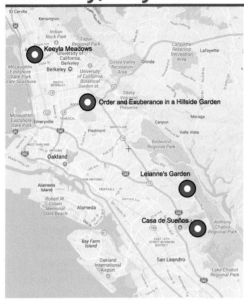

brilliantly colorful plantings. You will find images of Keeyla's garden in her book, *Fearless Color Gardens*. Some of Keeyla's handmade pots and garden sculptures will be offered for sale.

DIRECTIONS—From I-80, take the Gilman Street exit east about 1 mile to San Pablo Boulevard (large street with a traffic light). Go 2 blocks past San Pablo Boulevard. Turn left onto Stannage Avenue. Go 1 block. Garden is on east side of street.

OAKLAND
CASA DE SUEÑOS
11110 Lochard Street, Oakland
Hours: 10 a.m. to 4 p.m.
📷 | ♿PARTIAL | **2016**

In the beginning, this was a full acre covered with giant eucalyptus, juniper, and ivy. It has been transformed into a garden paradise. My son, a landscape designer, worked continually with our crew to build stone walls, patios, pathways, a large koi pond, arbors, a shade house, and a nursery. My travels have inspired me to create lush and interesting plantings...graced with many friends' art, including that of Keeyla Meadows, Marcia Donahue, and Vickie Jo Sowell.

DIRECTIONS—Take I-580 to the Golf Links Road exit. Turn left uphill past Oakland Zoo and go 1.5 miles. Turn right onto Caloden, then right onto Malcolm, and left onto Lochard Street. Garden is 1.5 blocks on left. Park on street and please do not block neighbors' driveways.

Alameda County
ALBANY
KEEYLA MEADOWS
1137 Stannage Avenue, Albany
Hours: 10 a.m. to 4 p.m.
📷 | ♿PARTIAL | **2016**

Keeyla Meadows is a painter, sculptor, and garden designer who makes gardens that are full-scale works of art you can walk into and be a part of. Her own garden is a living painting of vibrant colors. Keeyla is known as a pioneer in making artistic gardens more adaptable to small-scale gardens where color means filling the garden "frame" with attention to detail. Much of the color is provided by flowers. The garden is an invitation to local pollinators: "hummers," bees, and butterflies. Many materials are incorporated into the garden work: painterly pavings, wavy walls, mosaic benches, bronze sculptures, and

LEIANNE'S GARDEN
13971 Skyline Boulevard, Oakland
Hours: 10 a.m. to 4 p.m.
📷 | ♿PARTIAL | **2017**

Enjoy panoramic views of the San Francisco Bay from the ample seating in this hillside garden. Walls, patios, and paths are built almost completely from recycled materials. Featuring an eclectic and unusual plant collection, the garden spaces—now growing in after eight years—include shade gardens under redwoods and cedars, a cactus and succulent hillside, a grape arbor patio with bay view, and a twelve-foot elephant topiary watching over a shady terrace bordered by tree ferns. There are hillside gardens with aloes, proteas, Epi cacti, orchids, bromeliads, carnivorous plants, fruit trees, and Australian plants, and fountains. It is home to hummingbirds, chickens, koi, and more.

DIRECTIONS—In Oakland, take I-580 to the Keller Avenue exit. Go east (uphill) on Keller Avenue. When Keller ends at Skyline Boulevard, turn left onto Skyline Boulevard, which has a median strip at this point. Go 0.9 mile and make a U-turn at Hansom. Proceed to 13971 Skyline (blue house on bay side of street). Street parking is available and plentiful.

ORDER AND EXUBERANCE IN A HILLSIDE GARDEN
6055 Manchester Drive, Oakland
Hours: 10 a.m. to 4 p.m.
📷 | **2013**

After restoring a 1926 house, we decided to complement the house with a large Mediterranean-inspired garden. The Oakland Hills fire of 1991 had left a few of the original trees and roses, which we incorporated into our plan. With some assistance from landscape designers, we selected plant species well suited to the dry climate of the Bay Area and designed granite walls and curving pathways to promote good drainage. While the emphasis is on low-maintenance, drought-resistant plants, there is an exuberant abundance of colorful, blooming varieties planted in drifts, creating form and pattern in the garden. The tall *Podocarpus* hedge conceals neighboring houses while preserving breathtaking panoramic views from the terrace above. The koi pond and gentle splash of the waterfall offer a place for meditative retreat and attract various birds and wildlife.

DIRECTIONS—From San Francisco, take the Oakland Bay Bridge East and follow signs for Route 580 East to Oakland. Then take Highway 24 eastbound to the Broadway exit. After exiting, get in the right lane and turn right onto Broadway. Almost immediately, you will turn left on the first street, Ocean View, at the crest of the hill. Wind your way up Ocean View and take the second right, at Manchester Drive. Number 6055 Manchester is the third house on the right, a Mediterranean with a circular driveway.
—From the South Bay, take Route 880 northbound and follow signs to Route 980 and Highway 24 East toward Walnut Creek. Exit Highway 24 at the Broadway exit. After exiting, get in the right lane and turn right onto Broadway. Proceed as directed above.
—From the North Bay, take Route 580 eastbound and merge onto I-80 westbound. Continue past Berkeley and Emeryville onto Route 580 East toward downtown Oakland and Hayward. Take Highway 24 East toward Walnut Creek and take the Broadway exit. After exiting, get in the right lane and turn right onto Broadway. Proceed as above. Park on the street.

What our Garden Hosts recommend in San Francisco East Bay

Pollinate Farm & Garden
2727 Fruitvale Ave, Oakland, CA 94601
(510) 686-3493
www.sgnurserynews.com

Sequoia Diner
3719 MacArthur Blvd, Oakland, CA, 94619
(510) 482-3719
www.sequoiadiner.com

Sparky's Giant Burgers
4120 Redwood Rd, Oakland, CA 94619
(510) 531-5617

Sushi Go Go
3535 Pierson St, Oakland, CA 94619
(510) 532-9999
www.sushigogooakland.com

Phnom Penh House
3912 MacArthur Boulevard,
Oakland, CA 94619
(510) 482-8989
www.phnompenhhouse.com

Santa Cruz
Saturday, May 19

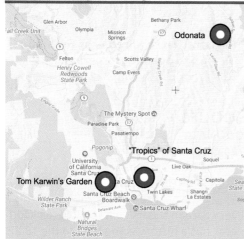

Santa Cruz County
SANTA CRUZ
"TROPICS" OF SANTA CRUZ
119 Effey Street, Santa Cruz
Hours: 10 a.m. to 4 p.m.
📷 | ♿PARTIAL | **NEW**

Serious subtropical: palms, tree ferns, and all else semi-tropical. Much has been in the ground for twenty to thirty years. A boulder-strewn pond, surrounded by long sequentially blooming temperate perennials, provides much more va-va-va-voom color than most subtropical, foliage dominant gardens. A Victorian-style greenhouse contains a wide variety of plants, from xerophytic to tropical. All squeezed in on a sixty- by-220-foot lot, providing numerous ideas for the home gardener.

DIRECTIONS—Highway 17-880 drops you off on Ocean Street. Proceed south to the Soquel Avenue signal and turn left. Turn right at the Seabright Avenue signal. Proceed a few blocks to Effey Street, turn right. Garden is a half-block on the right. Look for the palms.

TOM KARWIN'S GARDEN
121 Easterby Avenue, Santa Cruz
Hours: 10 a.m. to 4 p.m.
📷 | ♿PARTIAL | **NEW**

The entire yard (100-feet by 170-feet) has been developed with plantings from the five Mediterranean climate zones. Additional beds are used for roses, salvias, irises, Japanese perennials, agaves, *Echeverias*, South African succulents, and a very small orchard. In addition, there are a ten-foot-by-twelve-foot greenhouse, a central patio with a small aboveground pond, and a small sitting area in the back of the garden. There are a house and garage as well. There is no vegetable garden, but there are four dwarf apple trees, a lemon tree, a large fig tree, and a California native grapevine that is trying to take over the garden. The garden is in a continuous state of revision, unlike some gardens that feature many mature plants. (There are several large trees on the property, to be sure). The garden's overall theme might be "small-scale botanical garden."

DIRECTIONS—Enter Santa Cruz on Highway 1, which is Mission Street. On the west side of the city, at a traffic light, turn northwest off Mission Street on to Walnut Avenue. Turn left on the fourth street, which is Easterby Avenue. Go to 121 Easterby, is the middle of this one-block street, on the downhill side.

Tom Karwin's Garden

DIGGING DEEPER

4 PM
Thematic Garden Planning
with Tom Karwin
REGISTRATION: $30 Garden
Conservancy Members / $35 general

Tom Karwin's talk with revolve around the rewards and challenges of organizing the garden around a theme or—more likely—a series of themes, the differences between themes and styles in landscape design, and will include an overview of relevant online resources. There will be an opportunity for participants to describe their own experiences with thematic garden planning.

Tom is a lifetime Master Gardener (certified in 1999–2009), and garden writer with a weekly garden column for two newspapers in California's Monterey Bay area (2001 to present—sixteen years!). His columns are archived on http://ongardening.com. He is current president of the Monterey Bay Area Cactus & Succulent Society, past president of the University of California–Santa Cruz Arboretum, past president of the Monterey Bay Iris Society, and member of several garden related local and statewide groups. He is retired from staff positions at University of California–Los Angeles and UC–Santa Cruz.

Registration required — space limited
Go to opendaysprogram.org
or call 1 (888) 842-2442

SOQUEL
ODONATA
720 Olson Road, Soquel
Hours: 10 a.m. to 4 p.m.
📷 | ♿PARTIAL | **NEW**

Every garden has its own story to tell. Odonata* has a history going back to the 1800s when a lumberman named Olson cleared the forest and built a pleasure garden with ponds and stone paths. Although the original garden had been derelict for many decades when Sherry Austin bought the property, she wanted to honor the garden's past, creating stone walls and other features that speak to an era gone by. As a plant collector, she arrived twenty years ago with more than 350 rare and unusual plants obtained from arboretum sales and mail-order sources and set about planning a garden. Magnolias, dogwoods, rare conifers, and spring-flowering trees were planted for spring bloom, fall color, and winter interest. Woody plants and perennials were added for fragrance and foliage contrast. There are more than fifty varieties of both old and modern roses, and a plethora of variegated plants. It was the siren song of bearded irises, however, that lured Sherry into amassing over 800 varieties, which are scattered about the property, both in dedicated beds and mixed in with other plantings. Like plot twists in a novel, there is no end to this garden story. It continues to evolve with each new chapter.

*The name Odonata is the scientific order that includes dragonflies, which have become the garden's talisman.

DIRECTIONS—From San Francisco Peninsula: From Highway 17, take the Summit Road exit and cross back over the freeway to the right. Make a left turn onto Summit Road. Drive 3.8 miles to Old San Jose Road (aka Soquel-San Jose Road) and turn right (0.25 mile past the Summit Store on the left). Follow Old San Jose Road 4.1 miles to Olson Road, slow down, and turn right. (Olson Road is at the bottom of a long downhill straightaway and just before a sharp curve to the left. It is nearly a hairpin right.) Continue down the middle of Olson Road. It is a one-lane road, so you may need to use turnouts to let oncoming traffic go by. Drive about 0.7 mile on Olson Road and look for Sherry's mailbox, #720. Curve off to the right and turn into the second driveway, at the dragonfly gate.
—From Santa Cruz area: From Highway 1, take the Porter Street/ Bay Avenue exit (Exit 437) and turn toward the mountains. Freeway to Olson Road is about 6 miles up Old San Jose Road to Olson Road. Turn left on Olson Road (you'll see "5614" and "EV" on beige cement wall). Continue down the middle of Olson Road. It is a single-lane road, so you may need to use turnouts to let oncoming traffic go by. Drive about 0.7 mile on Olson Road, and look for Sherry's mailbox, #720. Curve off to the right and turn into the second driveway, at the dragonfly gate.

What our Garden Hosts recommend in Santa Cruz

The Garden Company
2218 Mission Street, Santa Cruz
(831) 429-8424
www.thegardenco.com

Hidden Gardens
7765 Soquel Dr. #A, Aptos, CA 95003
(831) 688-7011
www.aptoshiddengardens.com

Marin County
Saturday, June 2

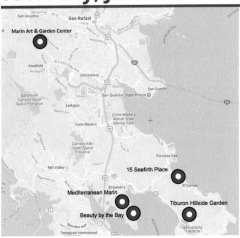

★ Start your day at Marin Art & Garden Center, 30 Sir Francis Drive Boulevard, Ross. Maps and discounted admission tickets will be available there. Admission: free.

OUR PARTNER IN MARIN COUNTY

MARIN ART & GARDEN CENTER

Located on eleven serene acres in the heart of the Ross Valley, the Marin Art & Garden Center's vision is to preserve and share its beautiful historic site, while enriching the community through exploration and discovery in the arts and the natural environment. MAGC is an independent non-profit organization that is open to the public from dawn to dusk. Thousands visit each year to experience MAGC's unique gardens, stroll through the grounds, and attend engaging programs.

Marin County
MILL VALLEY
BEAUTY BY THE BAY
25 Egret Way, Mill Valley
Hours: 10 a.m. to 4 p.m.
NEW

This secret and sophisticated Mediterranean-style garden is elegant in its simplicity and dramatic in the planting. A gracious terrace decorated with choice garden ornaments looks out on a broad vista of the Bay. Mature olive trees frame the entry, and a spectacular lemon allée crowns a side garden.

DIRECTIONS—From Highway 101, take Tiburon Boulevard for 1.5 miles until you get to East Strawberry Drive. Turn right and continue for a mile before turning left onto Weatherly Drive.
At the fork, turn left to stay on Weatherly Drive and then take the first left onto Egret Way. #25 will be toward the end of the street, on your right.

MEDITERRANEAN MARIN
313 Reed Boulevard, Mill Valley
Hours: 10 a.m. to 4 p.m.
📷 | 2012

This multi-level Mediterranean-style garden is terraced down a hillside overlooking Richardson Bay and a wildlife preserve, with San Francisco in the distance. The visitor discovers a series of different spaces, led by gravel paths, flights of stone stairs, and low stone walls. Among the spaces are a waterfall garden, pear trees espaliered over an arbor, and a long, descending walkway with a unique cascade that captures run-off water. A "shed" has been added as a retreat in a quiet corner of the garden. All terraces have seating for taking in the views and diverse garden treatments, many with their own water features. A series of mature cypresses punctuate the relaxed setting. Finally, a large Canary Island palm frames these views from a curved terrace; it sets the tone for the property. Plantings include olive trees, swaths of mature *Aeonia, Agave*, bromeliads, citrus, roses, wisteria, and more.

DIRECTIONS—From Highway 101, take the East Blithedale Avenue exit. Turn left onto Tiburon Boulevard/CA-131 East. Turn right onto East Strawberry Drive and immediately right onto Belvedere Drive. Take the first left onto Ricardo Road. Turn left onto Reed Boulevard, and #313 will be on your left. Street parking is available on Reed Drive. Additional parking is available at The Seminary at Strawberry, located at the end of Reed Boulevard (at Storer Drive), just a short (but steep) walk from the garden.

TIBURON

15 SEAFIRTH PLACE
15 Seafirth Place, Tiburon
Hours: 10 a.m. to 4 p.m.
NEW

Tranquility and beauty abound at this Tiburon bayside home. Get lost exploring meandering walkways draped in oak and acacia and enjoy spectacular views of the Bay. Follow a seasonal brook lined with towering redwoods, as it makes its way past citrus and fig trees to a quiet beach. The 2008 garden redesign by landscape architect Rich Sharp creates an outdoor living space with many different rooms: a spa area, fire pit, dining area, a bridge over the creek, an aviary section, and a

secret hillside patio. Bluestone is used for the patios and stone walls. Existing native and Mediterranean trees, plants ideally suited for our coastal climate, create a lush abundance of vegetation bordered by the formal landscaped patios, seating areas, and rose garden.

DIRECTIONS—From Highway 101, take Tiburon Boulevard just past Blackie's Pasture and turn left onto Trestle Glen Boulevard. At the end of the road, take a right onto Paradise Drive. Go approximately 0.5 mile and turn left onto Seafirth Road, then take the first left onto Seafirth Place. #15 will be on the left.

TIBURON HILLSIDE GARDEN
55 Spring Lane, Tiburon
Hours: 10 a.m. to 4 p.m.
📷 | 2004

My three-quarter-acre garden is located on a southwest-facing hillside overlooking San Francisco Bay. You will wind your way down to the pool through magnificent old oak trees on many small paths packed with specimen plants. The succulent garden contains an unusual collection of *Euphorbia, Kalanchoe, Aloe,* and *Echeveria.* In the shade gardens are collections of ferns and hydrangeas. Throughout the garden, you will see many of my ceramic sculptures as well as other examples of our sculpture collection.

DIRECTIONS—From Highway 101 take the Tiburon Boulevard exit. Drive approximately 4 miles to a 3-way light, which is at Lyford Drive. Turn left on Lyford Drive, left on Roundhill Road, left on Spring Lane, and left again on Spring Lane. We are #55 Spring Lane. Please park on street.

PUBLIC GARDEN PARTNER

Marin County
ROSS
MARIN ART & GARDEN CENTER
30 Sir Francis Drake Boulevard, Ross
(415) 455-5260
magc.org
Hours: Year round, daily, dawn to dusk
Admission: Free, guided tours of grounds
offered regularly

★ Start your tour here on Saturday, June 2.
Tickets and maps to all of the Marin County
gardens will be available.

Marin Art & Garden Center's eleven acres
have a rich history of inspiring artists, gardeners, and conservationists. Founded in
1945 on a former estate property, MAGC is
a lively center for learning, cultural programs, and celebrations. It is a hidden jewel in the heart of Marin County. Majestic
specimen trees highlight a landscape rich
in flowering shrubs and seasonal plantings.
The Edible Garden and Habitat Garden are
the setting for hands-on workshops, and
summer concerts take place on the lawns.
Lectures, classes, and performances are
held year round. Resident groups include
the Ross Valley Players, an acclaimed
community theater group; Laurel House
Antiques, a popular shopping destination;
and the Moya Library-Ross Historical Society, a valuable resource for local history.
Pixie Park, designed by Robert Royston
in the 1950s, is a beloved playground for
local families on the MAGC campus.

DIRECTIONS—From 101 North, take the
Sir Francis Drake Boulevard exit. Keep
right at the fork and continue west for ten
to fifteen minutes, depending on traffic.
The Marin Art & Garden Center is on right,
directly across from the Lagunitas Bridge.
Turn into the main entry and park in the lot.
—From 101 South, take Exit 450B toward
San Anselmo, which merges onto Sir Francis Drake Boulevard. Continue west for ten
to fifteen minutes, depending on traffic.
The Marin Art & Garden Center is on right,
directly across from the Lagunitas Bridge.
Turn into the main entry and park in the lot.
Please note: If you enter the above address
into Google Maps or another other online
map service, please be sure to specify that
the address is in Ross. Otherwise, you
could end up in another town, as there is
more than one 30 Sir Francis Drake.

Mendocino County
Saturday, June 2

Mendocino County
BOONVILLE
MEADOW WATCH
13020 Ornbaun Road, Boonville
Hours: 10 a.m. to 4 p.m.
📷 | ♿ | 2017

When we bought the eighteen-acre rural property, there was no garden. Now we have a house, barn, a one-acre pond, gardens, two rescue horses, and barn cats. Initially, when we decided to have a garden, we had no fencing. We started with an herb garden, which the deer wouldn't be attracted to, then later fenced it in to include other types of plants. We have roses and many different kinds of lavender all over, especially concentrated along both sides of a corridor that leads to the pond. The garden contains a number of sculptures by local artist Rebecca Johnson. Densely planted areas include a small vegetable garden with raised beds; a section that attracts butterflies and bees; mixed beds of flowering shrubs, perennials, and bulbs; a small orchard of mixed persimmon, peach, pear, plum, and very old apple trees; a rust collection of assorted wheels; bamboo in a horse trough; Russian sage; and naturalized *Gaura* and bearded iris.

The back garden parallels the barn, with its newly built bedroom and bath and outdoor shower. Xeriscaping is the whole point of the garden and, although a watering system exists, in times of drought it is hand-watered by our dedicated caretaker. Fir, pine, and redwood provide an evergreen backdrop.

DIRECTIONS—From the south, take US 101 North. Take Exit 522 for CA-128 West toward Fort Bragg/Mendocino. Go approximately 29 miles and turn left onto Mountain View Road/Mountain View 510 Road. Turn right onto Ornbaun Road. Driveway is on the left through a white wooden fence. —From Fort Bragg take Highway 1 South. Turn left onto Comptche-Ukiah Road and continue to CA-128 East. Turn left onto CA-128 East. Turn right onto Mountain View Road/Mountain View 510 Road and right again onto Ornbaun Road. Driveway is 0.6 mile on the left through a white wooden fence.

HOPLAND
FREY GARDENS
300 Ralph Bettcher Drive, Hopland
Hours: 10 a.m. to 4 p.m.
📷 | 2017

Frey Gardens is a one-acre sustainable, colorful, and profuse habitat garden. The garden is seven years old and is composed of a naturalistic mix of native plants and others that attract and support a wide variety of insects and birds. There is a small vegetable garden in addition to many rustic structures such as benches, a hermit's hut, chicken coop, bar, and whimsical gate posts.

DIRECTIONS—The garden is 100 miles from San Francisco and Berkeley if you go directly north on Highway 101. It is 1 hour north of Santa Rosa, 30 minutes north of Healdsburg, and 15 minutes north of Cloverdale. In Hopland, take the first left at Mountain House Road. Immediately after the bridge behind the gas station on Highway 101, turn right onto MacMilan. Make an immediate left onto Ralph Bettcher Drive. Garden is at #300, the second house on right. Look for signs. Park anywhere along the road or at the closed elementary school across the street. Watch out for ditch on left side of road.

—From the north, Hopland is approximately 15 to 20 minutes south of Ukiah on Highway 101. Turn right onto Mountain House Road on the south end of Hopland. Immediately AFTER the bridge behind the gas station, turn right onto MacMilan. Make an immediate left onto Ralph Bettcher Drive. Garden is the second house on the right, #300. Look for signs. Park anywhere along the road or at the closed school across the street. Watch out for the ditch on the left side of the road. Garden is 2-3 minutes from Highway 101.

PUBLIC GARDEN PARTNER

Mendocino County
GUALALA
THE GUALALA ARTS CENTER

46501 Old State Highway, Gualala
(707) 884-1138
gualalaarts.org
Hours: Garden looks best March through November, although redwood forest and paths are lovely year round. Arts center open Monday to Friday, 10 a.m. to 4 p.m. and Saturday to Sunday, noon to 4 p.m. Grounds are always open to the public.
Admission: Free

Gualala Arts Center is a 15,000-square-foot visual and performing arts venue on eleven acres of redwood forest that sits one-quarter mile from the Pacific Ocean on the Mendocino Coast. This jewel of the Redwood Coast is tucked into the redwood forest next to the Gualala River and includes a Haiku garden path, a Redwood Grove Events Area adorned with hand-built stone walls, multiple walkways, large bronze sculptures, large boulders, unique garden art, outdoor areas that invite you to pause and reflect, and a Meditation Grove of old growth redwoods that stand tall among large ferns and lush greenery. Patios and outdoor event areas are home to many annual and perennial plants and flowers native to the Mendocino-Sonoma coastal area. Sculptures and outdoor artwork complement the forested grounds and gardens at every turn. Indoor galleries change monthly and Gualala Arts hosts many festivals and events throughout the year. Gualala Arts is thrilled to team up with the Stone Foundation and Peter Mullins' Mendocino Stonezone for the open garden tours. Many of the stone masons have created one-of-a-kind sculptures that remain on the grounds of Gualala Arts for all to admire. The newly remodeled redwood grove is a legacy build by the Stone Foundation and is a great place to stop for a picnic lunch amongst the towering redwoods, surrounded by the ancient art of stone masonry.

DIRECTIONS—From San Francisco, take Hwy 101 to Petaluma. Take Bodega Avenue north along the Sonoma Coast. Continue north until crossing the county line that is the Gualala River. Take the first right, Old Stage Road. After 0.25 mile, turn right onto Old State Highway. The Gualala Arts Center will be on your right at 46501 Old State Highway.

Gualala Arts Center
DIGGING DEEPER
1 PM
Guided garden tour
Free

Executive Director, David "Sus" Susalla will give tours of the Global Harmony Sculpture Garden with highlights of the first Serge installed in the United States (a gift from the Yakut people of Sakha Republic), the Haiku Stone Path in honor and memory of artists Jane and Werner Reichhold, the Torii Gate (traditional wood archway), and the Meditation Grove in the Redwood Grove Event Area, newly-remodeled by the Stone Foundation. Grounds and the 15,000 square-foot visual and performing arts center will be open for self-guided tours from 10 AM to 4 PM.

Mendocino County
Saturday, June 23

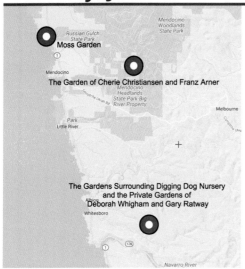

Mendocino County
ALBION
THE GARDENS SURROUNDING DIGGING DOG NURSERY
THE PRIVATE GARDENS OF DEBORAH WHIGHAM AND GARY RATWAY
31101 Middle Ridge Road, Albion
Hours: 10 a.m. to 5:30 p.m.
📷 | ♿ | **2016** | 🏷 PLANT SALES

Nestled among towering redwoods atop a rural ridge, Digging Dog Nursery and its elaborately planted grounds cover approximately two acres. A verdant backdrop of clipped evergreen and deciduous hedges sculpt distinctly separate spaces, thresholds, and views beckoning with anticipation. Inspired by old-style tradition and emphasizing year-round appeal, the garden offers dramatic perennial borders, some more than 150-feet-long, which are threaded together by pathways and tree-lined trails. This structured layout juxtaposes ebullient plantings, which feature a diverse collection of unusual plants and favored mainstays. Digging Dog Nursery is a mail-order and retail nursery featuring hard-to-find perennials, ornamental grasses, shrubs, trees, and vines that flourish in a variety of garden settings throughout the country. Plants will be available for sale.

DIRECTIONS—From the south on Highway 1, turn right onto Albion Ridge Road; from the north on Highway 1, turn left. Go 4 miles east on Albion Ridge Road. Turn right onto Middle Ridge Road (right turn only; this is a 3-way intersection). Go 0.3 mile on Middle Ridge Road. You will see a cluster of mailboxes on right and then, directly ahead on left, our driveway and a tree with a Digging Dog Nursery sign on it. Turn left into driveway, and shortly turn right into parking lot. A green sign on left reads Nursery Parking. Once you pull into the parking lot you will see the farm gates and our welcome sign. Parking lot is small; more parking along roadside. If you need additional directions, please call (707) 937-1130.

Digging Dog Nursery
and the Private Gardens of Deborah
Whigham and Gary Ratway
DIGGING DEEPER
1 PM
**Guided garden tour
Free with garden admission**

Join renowned specialty growers and garden designers, Deborah Whigham and Gary Ratway, for a guided tour of their home garden. Featured in the Garden Conservancy's book, Outstanding American Gardens, their private oasis is not regularly open to those visiting their adjacent Digging Dog Nursery and its fabled display gardens.

Marion Brenner

DIGGING DEEPER
3 PM
**Japanese Maple
Container Garden Demonstration
Free with garden admission**

Join Deborah Whigham, co-owner of Digging Dog Nursery, and Patricia Smyth, Japanese maple expert and owner of Essence of the Tree, for a demonstration on selecting the perfect Japanese maple and companion plants for a container that will look beautiful through the changing seasons, plus caring for your tree so it will last for decades. Digging Dog Nursery will be selling plants throughout the Open Day, and Essence of the Tree will start selling plants at noon. Learn more at www.diggingdog.com and www.essenceofthetree.com.

MENDOCINO
MOSS GARDEN
45145 Brest Road, Mendocino
Hours: 10 a.m. to 4 p.m.
📷 | ♿PARTIAL | **2016**

The surrounding tree-studded state park and coastal headlands of the Pacific Ocean lend an isolated feeling to the Moss Garden. Set back from the strong breezes of the bluff's edge, the house provides a sheltered garden setting, while an ocean view beckons. The charming redwood residence, enhanced with Northern European details, inspired the garden's layout and many of its architectural elements. Aligned with the house, the sunken garden required substantial excavation to lower it beyond the reach of harsh winds, thus creating a suitable microclimate for an array of unexpected plants. The leftover soil became the main component in the construction of the rammed earth walls, which retain and partition garden rooms and impart a classic time-worn appeal. Leeward of the house, the protected orchard garden brims with blooms, conveying a blousy exuberance. In contrast, the heather garden features mounding forms in an exposed wind-contoured tapestry of texture and color.

DIRECTIONS—About 1 mile north of the town of Mendocino, turn west off Highway 1 at entry point of Russian Gulch State Park and Point Cabrillo Drive. Continue directly west onto Brest Road. Go about 0.25 mile to a gate that reads "Moss, 45145." Proceed through the gate and park in the indicated area.

THE GARDEN OF CHERIE CHRISTIANSEN AND FRANZ ARNER
8085 Outlaw Springs Road, Mendocino
Hours: 10 a.m. to 4 p.m.
📷 | ♿ | **NEW**

Our sculpture garden surrounds our sculpture studio in the woods. We carve our pieces under a large crane, and the finished sculptures are displayed along an inviting path in a woodland setting. Our main feature is a large water sculpture set in a pond with a white granite background. As many of our pieces are stone-and-water sculptures, experiencing this garden is much like being in a beautiful river setting. About half of the sculptures have reticulating water moving over them. The sound this movement makes over stone combines with the abstract / architectural and natural forms to create a unique garden-art moment.

Our sculptures are surrounded by clumping Himalayan bamboos, rare rhododendrons, camellias, diverse water plants, and many other woodland plants, which promote a healing and renewing involvement with our art. Our sculpture garden is part of an extensive plan that includes a semi-formal herb garden, vegetable garden, rock garden, pond with waterfall, and rose and cutting gardens. More than fifty rare rhododendrons and more than sixty rare camellias provide color against the beautiful redwoods from November to June. Then perennials, continuously flowering bulbs, and a large dahlia collection bloom to November. For more information and photos, please visit our website: www.christiansenarnersculpture.com.

DIRECTIONS—From the single stoplight on Highway 1 in the village of Mendocino, turn east onto Little Lake Road and go exactly 4 miles to the 4-mile marker. Turn right onto Outlaw Springs Road and go up the hill 0.25 mile to a big fat "Y." Turn left at the big "Y." Ours is the second driveway on the left, where there is a 8085 sign on a tree. Follow that driveway on around past a large stand of bamboo and take the first left (follow signs), which will take you to the sculpture garden. (Do not pay attention to the numbers coming up Outlaw Springs Road, as they are not consecutive.)

PUBLIC GARDENS

Contra Costa County
WALNUT CREEK
THE RUTH BANCROFT GARDEN
1552 Bancroft Road, Walnut Creek
(925) 944-9352
www.ruthbancroftgarden.org

The three-and-one-half-acre Ruth Bancroft Garden is filled with hundreds of stunning succulents. The Ruth Bancroft Garden, Inc. is a 501(c)(3) nonprofit which owns the Garden and raises funds for its preservation. The Garden is an outstanding example of a water-conserving garden and houses important collections of aloes, agaves, yuccas, and echeverias.
Hours: Tuesday through Sunday, 10 a.m. to 4 p.m. Closed for July 4, Thanksgiving day, the Friday after Thanksgiving, Christmas day, and New Year's day. Guided tours with admission are offered on Saturdays and Sundays at 11 a.m. throughout the year, and Fridays through Sundays from April through October.
Admission: $10 general, $8 seniors and students. Free for members, children under 12, Garden Conservancy and American Horticulture Society Reciprocal Admissions Program members.

DIRECTIONS— From San Francisco or Oakland drive east on Highway 24, and continue onto I-680 North. Exit Treat Boulevard and turn right. Go about 1 mile, then turn right onto Bancroft Road. Make a U-turn at Stratton Road. The Ruth Bancroft Garden will be on your right.
—From Sacramento drive west on I-80 and exit onto I-680 South. Exit at Treat Boulevard and turn left from the off ramp onto North Main Street. Make the next left onto Treat Boulevard. Go about 1 mile, then turn right onto Bancroft Road. Make a U-turn at Stratton Road. The Ruth Bancroft Garden will be on your right.
—From San Jose, drive north on I-680. Exit onto Treat Boulevard and turn right. Go about 1 mile, then turn right onto Bancroft Road. Make a U-turn at Stratton Road. The Ruth Bancroft Garden will be on your right.

San Francisco County
SAN FRANCISCO
GARDENS OF ALCATRAZ
Alcatraz Island, San Francisco
(415) 561-4900
www.alcatrazgardens.org
Hours: Year round, daily. Closed Thanksgiving, Christmas, and New Year's day. Admission: Free docent-led garden tours, Fridays and Sundays, 9:30 a.m. from the Alcatraz dock. Wednesdays an Open Garden viewing called "Ask the Gardener" from 11 a.m. to 2 p.m.
Admission: There is no entrance fee to visit Alcatraz Island. However there is a charge for the ferry service to and from the island, which is supplied by a private company under contract with the National Park Service. For additional information on schedules, prices, and to purchase tickets in advance (tickets are made available about ninety days in advance) please visit www.alcatrazcruises.com or call (415) 981-7625. Alcatraz frequently sells out, as much as a week in advance, in summer and near holidays.

The gardens were created by inmates, officers, and the families who lived and gardened on Alcatraz Island over its long history as a military fortification and prison, and in its later role as a federal prison. The Garden Conservancy, in partnership with the National Park Service and the Golden Gate National Parks Conservancy, led a ten-year project to rehabilitate the garden starting in 2003. With the help of numerous volunteers, overgrowth has been removed and many of the gardens have been restored to the former beauty of the military and prison eras. More than one million visitors that visit the island every year can now see how the beautiful, well-tended gardens provided the power to transform both a harsh environment and to nourish the human spirit.

Mendocino County
FORT BRAGG
MENDOCINO COAST BOTANICAL GARDENS

18220 North Highway One, Fort Bragg
(707) 964-4352
www.gardenbythesea.org
Hours: The Garden Store and Nursery on the Plaza are open year round. Rhody's Garden Café is open April–September. There is no admission fee to visit the store, nursery, or café. March to October, 9 a.m. to 5 p.m.; November to February, 9 a.m. to 4 p.m. Closed the Saturday after Labor Day, Thanksgiving day, and Christmas day.
Admission: $15 general (15 and older); $12 seniors (65 and older); $8 juniors (aged 6 to 14); children aged 5 and under are free; $10 MCRPD resident (Gualala to Westport); $12/person for groups of 12 or more; members are free; $10 member's guests; free to American Horticulture Society Reciprocal Admissions Program members.

Mendocino Coast Botanical Gardens is a unique natural treasure located at 18220 North Highway 1, just two miles south of Fort Bragg and seven miles north of Mendocino. Our mission is to engage and enrich lives by displaying and conserving plants in harmony with our northern California coastal ecosystems. This magnificent forty-seven-acre site is one of the few public gardens located directly on the ocean's shore. The unique environment on the Mendocino Coast makes the Gardens a wonder year round; each changing season brings new flora and fauna. We welcome visitors and our local community to experience the rugged beauty of the Mendocino Coast mixed with the peaceful tranquility of our garden by the sea. For more information, visit www.gardenbythesea.org.

DIRECTIONS—Mendocino Coast Botanical Gardens is located on the west side of State Highway 1 at 18220 North Highway 1 near Fort Bragg, California. From Fort Bragg and points north: located 1 mile south of Highways 1 and 20 intersection. If you are staying in downtown Fort Bragg, travel south on Highway 1 for 2 miles to our address. We are a 0.5 mile south of the roundabout.
—From Mendocino and points south: approximately 7 miles north of the quaint town of Mendocino. Travel north on Highway 1 to our address on the west side of Highway 1. If you reach the roundabout at Simpson Lane, you are 0.5 mile too far north.

COLORADO
Aspen Area
Saturday, July 14

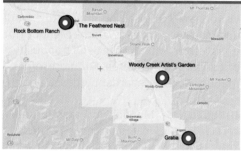

Pitkin County
ASPEN

GRATIA

284 Northstar Drive, Aspen
Hours: 10 a.m. to 4 p.m.
📷 | NEW

This award-winning garden emphasizes the greater landscape through Asian-influenced design concepts that accentuate unsurpassed views of the mountains. The site's natural amenities are exemplified and interpreted as themes throughout the design. Stone, water, and topography are manipulated to create interest while blending into the mountain context. Water, texture, and a simple black- and-white palette are key elements of the site. Water is found at the spa, stream, and pool that tie upper and lower topographic benches. The site's contouring accentuates the outdoors, captures long views, and creates interesting forms that act as a backdrop to the family's changing lives. Low stone walls meander throughout, directing views, creating outdoor rooms, and defining the great lawn. Although invisible, such sustainable systems as geothermal heating and cooling and saline purification of the pool reduce the project's footprint on the Earth and significantly reduce the home's operating and maintenance costs.

DIRECTIONS—From Aspen, take Main Street/Highway 82 up valley toward Independence Pass. Turn right onto Northstar Drive. Drive past the gatehouse and veer to the right onto Northstar Circle. Veer to the left back onto Northstar Drive and continue to the end. Park along street and walk to the driveway, marked with the address.

BASALT

THE FEATHERED NEST

1890 Hooks Spur, Basalt
Hours: 10 a.m. to 4 p.m.
NEW

Enclosed by a transparent vegetative screen, this not-so-secret "secret garden" resulted from a collaborative design effort between the owner and English garden designer Robin Williams to create a sense of intimacy within the larger landscape. Experience a dynamic ever-changing view as you stroll the curving paths of the inviting "Big Boomer" perennial garden. Farther afield, a series of ponds gives way to a sparkling stream whose wonderful sounds you will hear echoing throughout the garden. Visit the owner in her studio and learn how she transforms the beauty of her garden into art.

DIRECTIONS—Driving directions from Aspen: Just past Basalt, turn left off Highway 82 at the Willits Lane stoplight. Turn left onto Hooks Lane (cross the Roaring Fork River). After the bridge, take an immediate right onto Hooks Spur Road. Our driveway is on the right just before the entrance gate to Rock Bottom Ranch.
—Driving directions from Carbondale: Just past El Jebel, turn right off Highway 82 onto Willits Lane. Turn right onto Hooks Lane to cross the Roaring Fork River. After bridge, take an immediate right onto Hooks Spur Road. Our driveway is on the right just before the entrance gate to Rock Bottom Ranch.

WOODY CREEK
WOODY CREEK ARTIST'S GARDEN
1225 Little Woody Creek Road
Woody Creek
Hours: 10 a.m. to 4 p.m.
NEW

A garden at the end of the road that gratefully accommodates the drift of seeds from the wilderness beyond, this artist's garden is a constant work in progress, a shifting composition that changes from season to season and year to year. Awash in the color of perennials, native shrubs, and grasses, it offers a year-round cornucopia of edible treasures for birds and local wildlife. A well-tended vegetable garden offers a glimpse into the challenges of growing produce at 8,000 feet. Studio tours with the owner/artist will be available.

DIRECTIONS—From Aspen, drive west on Highway 82 approximately 5.5 miles. Go 0.8 mile past the turnoff to Snowmass Village, turn right onto Smith Way. Go 0.3 mile, turn left onto Upper River Road. Go 1.5 miles, take a sharp right turn onto Woody Creek Road. Go 0.7 mile, turn left onto Little Woody Creek Road. Follow Little Woody Creek Road to the end of the pavement. The driveway veers up the hill on the left.
—From Basalt, drive east on Highway 82 approximately 11 miles. Turn left on Smith Way. Go 0.3 mile, turn left onto Upper River Road. Go 1.5 miles, take a sharp right turn onto Woody Creek Road. Go 0.7 miles, turn left onto Little Woody Creek Road. Follow Little Woody Creek Road to the end of the pavement. The driveway veers up the hill on the left.

PUBLIC GARDEN PARTNER

Pitkin County
BASALT
ROCK BOTTOM RANCH
2001 Hooks Spur Road, Basalt
(970) 927-6760
aspennature.org
Hours: Special Garden Conservancy Open Day tour, July 14, 11 a.m. Otherwise, Monday to Friday, 9 a.m. to 5 p.m., plus Saturday, 9 a.m. to 1 p.m. in the summer.
Admission: Free; $10 suggested donation

A property of the Aspen Center for Environmental Studies, Rock Bottom Ranch is a hub for environmental education, wildlands preservation, and sustainable agriculture. The 113-acre wildlife preserve and educational ranch sits between the Roaring Fork River and the Crown of Mount Sopris, and is conveniently located midway between Basalt and Carbondale on the Rio Grande Trail. Its acreage includes wetlands, spring-fed ponds, a braid of the Roaring Fork River, cottonwood bottomlands, a view of piñon-juniper woodlands on adjacent public land, teaching farmyards, pasturelands, and gardens. The Ranch is western Colorado's "school" for teaching people of all ages how to grow healthy, local, sustainable food. This means farming using principles of ecology and natural biological cycles to satisfy human food needs while enhancing and protecting water, land, and climate resources. The Ranch is also home to in-school environmental science education programs for Aspen, Basalt, and Carbondale Elementary Schools as well as field programs for more than fifty regional schools. A conservation easement on the property ensures that it will always offer winter range and unobstructed river access for resident herds of elk and mule deer. Heron, hawk and owl nesting grounds exist at the Ranch, and its wildlands provide habitat to wildlife including bear, coyote, bobcat, weasel, and beaver.

while learning the science behind RBR's vegetable production and livestock rotational grazing system. In addition, you are free to explore the nature trail and grounds including beautiful vistas, verdant wetlands, cottonwood galleries, and more. You may see heron, red-winged blackbirds, elk, mule deer, and other local bird and wildlife. Visitors are welcome to purchase RBR products including eggs, pork, lamb, chicken, vegetables, and cut flowers.

DIRECTIONS—From Aspen: Just past Basalt, turn left at the Willits Lane stoplight off of Highway 82. Turn left onto Hooks Lane (cross the Roaring Fork River). After the bridge, take an immediate right onto Hooks Spur Road. Hooks Spur Road (approximately 2 miles) dead ends at Rock Bottom Ranch. Park in the lot, only handicapped vehicles may drive to the end of the road.

—From Carbondale: Just past El Jebel, turn right off of Highway 82 onto Willits Lane. Turn right onto Hooks Lane to cross the Roaring Fork River. After bridge, take an immediate right onto Hooks Spur Road. Hooks Spur Road (approximately 2 miles) dead ends at Rock Bottom Ranch. Park in the lot, only handicapped vehicles may drive to the end of the road.

Rock Bottom Ranch

DIGGING DEEPER

11 AM
Free guided tours of
Rock Bottom Ranch

Join Rock Bottom Ranch staff and educators to explore the Ranch, animal paddocks, hoop houses, and gardens

CONNECTICUT
Fairfield County
Sunday, May 6

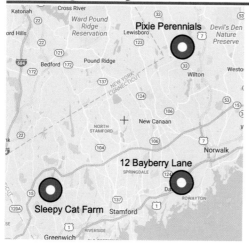

Fairfield County
GREENWICH
12 BAYBERRY LANE

12 Bayberry Lane, Greenwich
Hours: 10 a.m. to 4 p.m.
📷 | **2017**

The owner of this three-and-one-half-acre property is a hands-on gardener who designed the garden herself, often using her backhoe to make her ideas a reality. There is an eighty-foot long mixed border as well as beds of choice and unusual shade-loving varieties, a vegetable/flower garden, more than 100 peonies for cutting, a greenhouse, and many raised beds used for propagation and experimentation. Add to these an extensive compost area and beehives.

DIRECTIONS—From the Merritt Parkway Round Hill Road exit, head north and take the second right-hand turn. That is Cherry Valley Road. Then take the second street to the left, which is Bayberry Lane. We are the last house on the left, #12. Please park on the left side of the road.

SLEEPY CAT FARM
146 Clapboard Ridge Road, Greenwich
Hours: 10 a.m. to 4 p.m.
📷 | **2017**| 🏷 BROKEN ARROW NURSERY

The thirteen acres of Sleepy Cat Farm have evolved over the last twenty five years through a close collaboration between the present owner and Virginia based landscape architect Charles J. Stick. The landscape bordering Lake Avenue includes an extensive greenhouse and *potager*. The "Barn," distinguished by its half-timbered French Normandy vocabulary is surrounded by thyme-covered terraces providing an elegant stage set for a fine collection of garden ornament, sculpture and boxwood topiary. The visitor's experience of the garden unfolds as pathways lead from garden room to garden room in a carefully orchestrated series of discoveries. The central portion of the garden is distinguished by two parallel garden spaces; the first is dominated by a long reflecting pool, terminated on the north end by a wisteria-covered arbor, and on the south end by a pebble mosaic terrace and fountain basin. One of the great surprises of the tour is the adjacent garden space. Bordered by a precisely clipped hornbeam hedge, the green architecture of this room is meant to frame the view to the Chinese pavilion (Ting dynasty), positioned on a small island

in the middle of a pond teeming with koi...
[Read full description online]

Sleepy Cat Farm
DIGGING DEEPER
11 AM & 1 PM
The Spring Vegetable Garden
To Do List with Alan Gorkin
A shuttle will be provided
to the garden.
REGISTRATION: $35 Garden
Conservancy Members / $45 general

Go behind the scenes at Sleepy Cat Farm with horticulturist Alan Gorkin for spring tips to make the most of your own garden through the season. Follow Alan through the vegetable garden, where he will discuss getting the garden ready for planting. Planting demonstrations, proper use of garden tools, hardening off transplants, seeding, and soil amendments will be covered as well. Visit the greenhouse, filled with organically grown vegetable and flower seedlings ready to be hardened off and planted. Heirloom tomato plants and other choice items will be for sale. Questions are welcome!

Registration required — space limited
Go to opendaysprogram.org
or call 1 (888) 842-2442

Sleepy Cat Farm
DIGGING DEEPER
Family Time 10 AM – 4 PM
Family Scavenger Hunt
A shuttle will be provided
to the garden.
Free with garden admission

Explore the garden with family members and friends of all ages, and try the scavenger hunt to see how good you are at really looking! Each child who participates will be given a free plant with growing instructions. Children must be accompanied by an adult at all times.

DIRECTIONS—For safety reasons, there is no parking this year along Clapboard Ridge Road. Instead, attendees will meet at Camp Simmons, 744 Lake Avenue, Greenwich. There will be signage indicating both Camp Simmons as well as Garden Conservancy signage. Once there, guests will be directed to parking, and board a shuttle van which will take you to the gardens, as well as pickup. The shuttle will operate from 10 a.m. to 4 p.m.

WILTON
PIXIE PERENNIALS
200 Nod Hill Road, Wilton
Hours: 10 a.m. to 4 p.m.
📷 | 2017| 🏷 PLANT SALES

Terraced perennial gardens with a wide variety of unusual plants surround this 1740 homestead. Set on four acres, it overlooks a reservoir and is home to mature and specimen trees. A small rock garden tucked into the exposed ledge leads to a fishpond. A frog pond is nestled in between rows of flowers. The property features peach trees, an old leaning apple tree, fig trees, kiwi, blueberry bushes, strawberries, raspberries, and a vegetable garden. The kitchen courtyard garden room hosts such shade-loving plants as *Helleborus, Brunnera, Heuchera, Ligularia*, shaped boxwoods, and other varieties of perennials, which live nestled under a giant maple tree. Peonies border one length of the paddock fence, leading you to lilac bushes. A back garden built around exposed stones showcases tall plants that can be seen from the house. In late summer, a stand of *Perovskia* creates a blue backdrop for fall-flowering perennials. The garden is a work in progress, ever-changing from year to year. The "party barn" boasts quarter-sawn oak floors; it hosted town dances during Prohibition. Homegrown perennials and shrubs will be for sale on the back patio and adjacent areas. There will be a pop-up boutique in the barn featuring wonderful items made by local artisans.

DIRECTIONS—The property is 0.9 mile up on the right from the intersection of Route 33/Ridgefield Road and Nod Hill Road.

What our Garden Hosts recommend in Fairfield County

Broken Arrow Nursery
13 Broken Arrow Road, Hamden, CT 06518
(203) 288-1026
www.brokenarrownursery.com

Hollania Nursery
103 Old Hawleyville Rd, Bethel, CT
(203) 743-0267
www.hollandianurseries.com

Figs Wood Fired Bistro Restaurant
105 Church Hill Rd, Sandy Hook, CT 06482
(203) 426-5503
www.figswoodfiredbistro.net

Southwest Café
109 Danbury Rd, Ridgefield, CT 0687
(203) 431-3398
www.southwestcafe.com

Cellar Door
439 Main St, Ridgefield, CT 06877
(203) 438-2500

Debra Ann's Sweet Shop
381 Main Street, Ridgefield, CT
(203) 438-0065
www.deborahanns.com

Litchfield County
Saturday, May 12

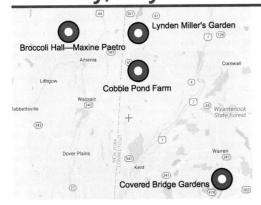

★ There is an additional garden open on this date in nearby Dutchess County, NY. See page 205.

Litchfield County
SHARON
COBBLE POND FARM
1 West Woods Road, Sharon
Hours: 1 p.m. to 4 p.m.
2017

The garden features both formal and informal herbaceous borders. Several garden rooms in pastoral settings are defined and accented by stone walls, clipped yews, sweeping lawns, mature maples, a centenary copper beech and gingko, dawn redwood (*Metasequoia*), and European birches. Unusual species have been added, which enhance the borders. Black Angus leisurely graze in nearby fields. From 1929 to 1950, the summer house, stone walls, terraces, and tree plantings were designed and overseen by Warren Manning, Percival Gallagher, and E.C. Whiting of the Olmsted firm, Chestnut Hill, Massachusetts. In spring, the borders feature lively bulb combinations. The colorful raised beds

in the vegetable garden add whimsy to the design, which continues to reflect the Olmsted plan.

DIRECTIONS—From the south, take I-84 to Route 22 North to Amenia. Turn right at the traffic light onto Route 343 and go 5 miles to Sharon's clock tower, at a 4-way stop. Turn right onto Route 41. Go 0.9 mile and turn left onto West Woods Road . Please do not turn onto Mitchelltown Road; that entrance will be closed. GPS address is 21 Mitchelltown Road.

—From the south, take Hutchinson Parkway North to I-684 North to Route 22 North (about a 45-minute drive) to Amenia, NY. Turn right onto Route 343 and drive 5 miles to Sharon. At the Clock Tower, turn right and drive 0.9 mile on Route 41 south to West Woods Road. Please do not turn onto Mitchelltown Road; that entrance will be closed. GPS address is 21 Mitchelltown Road.

WARREN
COVERED BRIDGE GARDENS
290 Lake Road (Route 45), Warren
Hours: 10 a.m. to 4 p.m.
📷 | ♿PARTIAL | **NEW**

Covered Bridge Gardens, a labor of love that has evolved over seventeen years, has perennial borders, shaded walkways, and extraordinary woodland wildflowers over a substantial part of the property. A river encircles the gardens and gives energy to the natural environment, overflowing with blue woodland phlox, campanula, hellebores, silver- painted ferns, and foam flower. A walk across the covered bridge brings you to the main cottage gardens and raised kitchen and herb beds in the front of the house. A lovely garden cottage and small pond complement the unique backdrop for the 1745 Colonial house.

DIRECTIONS—We are easily accessible from Route 202 and the center of New Preston. Turn on Route 45 toward Lake Waramaug and go straight for 2.7 miles until you see a red saltbox house on the left. Pass the house and turn left into the driveway.

The Garden of Lynden Miller, Sharon
DIGGING DEEPER
10:30 AM
Spring Beauties—An Early Season Garden Workshop with Lynden Miller
REGISTRATION: $30 Garden Conservancy Members / $35 general
Address will only be sent to registered guests

The country garden of Lynden Miller, an acclaimed public garden designer and a serious plant lover, has been her laboratory for design ideas and plant combinations since 1980. She adores early spring in her garden, particularly her woodland, and will welcome a small group to really look at what makes that work. Her site features a large mixed border backed by a curved yew hedge, a raised garden, and a cottage garden. There is a small pond and a recirculating stream, a woodland with moss paths, and many hardy hydrangeas. In 1982, Lynden Miller rescued and restored The Conservatory Garden in Central Park. Based on her belief that good public open spaces can change city life, she has since designed more than forty other gardens and parks, including Bryant Park, The New York Botanical

Garden, and Wagner Park in Battery Park City. Lynden wrote *Parks, Plants and People: Beautifying the Urban Landscape*, which won the American Horticultural Society 2010 National Book Award.

Registration required — space limited
Go to opendaysprogram.org
or call 1-888-842-2442

What our Garden Hosts recommend in Litchfield County

Kent Greenhouse and Garden
30 South Main Street Kent CT
(860) 787-5068
www.kentgreenhouse.com

The Whitehorse Country Pub
258 New Milford Turnpike, New Preston
(860) 868-1496
www.whitehorsecountrypub.com

The Pantry
5 Titus Road Washington Depot, CT
(860) 868-0258
www.thepantryct.com

Hidden Valley Eatery
88 Bee Brook Rd. Washington, CT 06794
(860) 619-0660
www.hiddenvalleyeatery.com

Women's Support Services proudly presents

TRADE SECRETS®

a beautiful gathering for a great cause

MAY 19 & 20, 2018

SATURDAY
Rare Plant & Garden Antiques Sale
LionRock Farm, Sharon CT

SUNDAY
Tour of Three Splendid Gardens
in the Litchfield Hills and the
Hudson Valley

A fundraiser for Women's Support Services -
Domestic Violence Intervention, Prevention, and Education
wssdv.org

TICKETS & INFORMATION:
TradeSecretsCT.com
or (860) 364-1080

Fairfield County
Saturday, June 2

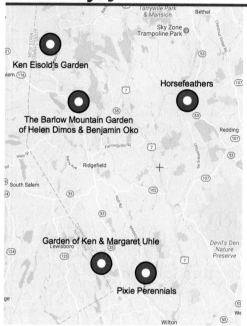

Fairfield County
REDDING
HORSEFEATHERS
313 Umpawaug Road, Redding
Hours: 10 a.m. to 4 p.m.
📷 | ♿PARTIAL | **2005**

Horsefeathers is known in Redding as the Aaron Barlow House and is the oldest dwelling in Redding. Joel Barlow, after whom the Redding high school is named, one of Aaron's brothers, lived here after the French Revolution. Joel, a diplomat and renowned poet, was an attaché at the U.S. Embassy in Paris at the time of Thomas Jefferson and was instrumental in the purchase of Louisiana from France. While residing in the house, he composed the epic poem *The Columbiad* (1807), his most famous work. The gardens, designed

by former owners Helen and Françoise Verglas with the assistance of garden designer and consultant Laura Tuttle Stabell, were on the Garden Conservancy tour for seven years before Dana and Connie Zangrillo purchased the property. The gardens, which surround the site of the circa 1723 home, contain strong elements of historical design influenced by French and English period gardens. The views are structured around the "reflecting pool," with French curves of *Nepeta* on the outer borders. Stone walls, boxwood, and a pergola give the garden architectural "bones" in all seasons...[Read full description online]

Horsefeathers
DIGGING DEEPER
11 AM & 3 PM
Elements of Historical Garden Design—Bringing Ideas of the Past into Gardens of Today
Free with garden admission

Horsefeathers was designed with many historical elements: topiary, espalier, parterres, tuteurs, a pergola, a solarium terrace, even a mini ha ha. The vegetable beds are laid out in a geometric pattern, while thyme and catmint buzz with bees. A fountain splashes in the center of a more formal area near the home. In the days before television, a stroll garden—a place to walk and talk with company after dinner—preferably with gravel walks so ladies skirts would stay clean, was a common feature, following European modes. There was an underlying need in European design to have a sense of order, of man's hand against the natural. Colonial Americans brought with them European ideals of garden design, but the American sense of practicality and the natural edge of the wilderness crept in. A looser cottage garden form emerged. Farmsteads and their gardens were carved out of the wilderness and built from locally sourced materials. What the American homesteads lacked in sophistication, they made up with creativity, simplicity, and comfort. Landscape gardener Laura Stabell will talk about how these same elements and ideas can be incorporated into the landscapes of today, whether in traditional or modern landscapes.

DIRECTIONS—From Route 7 North, take Route 107 at Georgetown for 1.7 miles, to Umpawaug Road. Continue on Umpawaug for 3.5 miles to Horsefeathers; sign on left. Look for parking signs on right.

RIDGEFIELD
GARDEN OF KEN & MARGARET UHLE
54 Silver Spring Road, Ridgefield
Hours: 10 a.m. to 4 p.m.
📷 | 2017

This one-acre garden has been designed in a woodland setting among large glacially deposited rocks. A prominent feature of the garden is its man-made winding brook, which connects two small lily ponds bordered with blue flag irises, rushes, and other marginal plants. Woodchip paths meander through the garden, characterized by mature oak trees and more than 600 varieties of perennials, shrubs, and understory trees. In another location, a lawn area is surrounded by small groupings of bald cypress, dawn redwood, and flowering trees. Informal stone steps lead down to a seventy-foot plank boardwalk through plantings of cypress and tupelo. This garden has been designed, installed, and maintained by the owner, a landscape architect, and is a good example of what can be accomplished on a relatively small property.

DIRECTIONS—From Westchester County, New York, take Route 35 east toward Ridgefield. Turn right onto Peter Parley Drive. (Peter Parley Drive is a very short diagonal street adjacent to a small red schoolhouse. It is located approximately 10 miles east of the intersection of Route 35 with I-684 and the Saw Mill Parkway). When you are on Peter Parley Drive, bear to the left and stop at the stop sign. Continue straight across the road (which is not marked) up a small incline and immediately turn right onto Silver Spring Road. Note that after 1.5 miles Silver Spring Road joins with St. John's Road at a "T" intersection. At this point turn right and continue on Silver Spring Road. Number 54 is on the left and faces a shared driveway. Please park on Silver Spring Road and walk down the shared driveway. Number 54 is the first house on the right, a one-story light green ranch. —From northern Fairfield County, take Route 35 west toward New York. Turn left onto West Lane. Make an immediate left onto Silver Spring Road. Note that after

88   Connecticut

1.5 miles Silver Spring Road joins with St. John's Road at a "T" intersection. At this point turn right and continue on Silver Spring Road. Number 54 is on the left and faces a shared driveway. Please park on Silver Spring Road and walk down the shared driveway. Number 54 is the first house on the right, a one-story light green ranch. From southern Fairfield County take Route 33 east toward Ridgefield. Turn left onto Scarlet Oak Drive. At the end of Scarlet Oak, make a right onto Silver Spring Road. Number 54 is on the right and faces a shared driveway. Please park on Silver Spring Road and walk down the shared driveway. Number 54 is the first house on the right, a one-story light green ranch.

KEN EISOLD'S GARDEN
18 Chestnut Hill Road, Ridgefield
Hours: 10 a.m. to 4 p.m.
📷 | ♿PARTIAL | 2017

This extensive garden on four acres is designed to enhance the features of the landscape: a large open field, a stream, and woodlands. The garden includes a perennial border, a woodland path with two rustic bridges, a shrub border, a grass garden, and a grove of conifers. A gazebo, pergola, several terraces, and a sculpture provide focal points.

DIRECTIONS—Five miles from the center of Ridgefield (on the south), 2 miles from I-84 (on the north).
—From Ridgefield, go north 3 miles on Route 116 to Ridgebury Road, turn right. Then go 2 miles to Chestnut Hill Road and turn left.
—From I-84, take Exit 1/Saw Mill Road. Go 2 miles south to Ridgebury Road (at intersection with George Washington Highway). Go 0.5 mile to Chestnut Hill Road, turn right.
—From North Salem, go 2 miles east on Route 116, to Ridgebury Road. Turn left, then go 2 miles to Chestnut Hill Road and turn left. There will be off-road parking in the field.

THE BARLOW MOUNTAIN GARDEN OF HELEN DIMOS & BENJAMIN OKO
11 Barlow Mountain Road, Ridgefield
Hours: 10 a.m. to 4 p.m.
📷 | 2017

This 1735 saltbox, house of landscape designer Helen Dimos and Dr. Benjamin Oko, is listed on the National Register of Historic Buildings. It is surrounded by perennial gardens that feature peonies, clematis, irises, and roses. Shrub borders contain boxwoods, hydrangeas, *Viburnum*, calycanthuses, and rhododendrons. Trees near the house include *Stewartia* and such native species as dogwoods, a fringetree, witch hazel, ironwoods, and elms. Farther out on the rolling lawn are the many trees planted over the last twenty years by the owner. She believes that, aside from architectural interventions, trees are the strongest elements in shaping spaces and creating distinct areas in the garden. Among these trees are white and mossy-cup (or bur) oaks, a fern leaf beech, a silver linden, and numerous conifers. Near the enclosed vegetable / cutting garden, there are magnolias. Farthest from the house, forming a backdrop at the bottom of the lawn, are a tupelo, a dawn redwood, and two Alaska cedars. There are also an ornamental grass border, a natural grass border, and a wetland edge border of mostly native shrubs. For approximately ten years, the property has been protected by an eight-foot wire deer fence.

DIRECTIONS—From the south and west, including North Salem, take Route 684 to Exit 7/Purdys/Somers. Turn right off

the ramp and, at the traffic light, turn left. Then almost immediately take the second right onto Route 116 (see sign). Follow 116 through North Salem, where Route 116 is joined briefly by Route 121. Where 116 and 121 divide, turn right (at Vox Restaurant) to stay on 116. From this point, Barlow Mountain Road is 3.1 miles away, on the left. Turn left (you will see a grass triangle in the middle of the intersection and a boat ramp sign). Number 11 is the fourth driveway on the right, across from a red mailbox.
—From southbound Route 22, take the exit for Routes 6 and 202. At the end of ramp, turn left. In a few miles, turn right onto Route 121. Turn left onto Route 116 by Vox Restaurant. Proceed as directed above. From westbound I-84, take the exit for Route 7 South. Turn right onto Route 35 toward Ridgefield. Turn right at Copps Hill Road (just before the Copps Hill Shopping Center; Shell station and brick bank building on left). Turn right again at the end of Copps Hill Road onto North Street. Go about 2 miles north. North Street runs into Barlow Mountain Road. Number 11 is on the left with mailbox on the right. There is limited parking. If the parking area at the house is full, or you are concerned about being blocked in, please continue past our house and take the first left onto Barlow Mountain Road, and then turn immediately right into the parking area for Pierrepont State Park. It is a very short walk from there to garden, but take great care to walk on right, where you are not in the lane of cars approaching over the crest of the hill.

WILTON
PIXIE PERENNIALS
200 Nod Hill Road, Wilton
Hours: 10 a.m. to 4 p.m.
📷 | 2017| 🏷 PLANT SALES

Terraced perennial gardens with a wide variety of unusual plants surround a 1740 homestead set on four acres, overlooking a reservoir and home to mature and specimen trees. A small rock garden tucked into the exposed ledge leads to a fishpond. A frog pond is nestled in between rows of flowers. The property features peach trees, an old leaning apple tree, fig trees, kiwi, blueberry bushes, strawberries, raspberries, and a vegetable garden. The kitchen courtyard garden hosts shade-loving plants: *Hellebores, Brunnera, Heuchera, Ligularia*, shaped boxwoods, and other varieties of perennials that live nestled under a giant maple tree. Peonies border one length of the paddock fence, leading you to the lilac bushes. A back garden built around exposed stones showcases tall plants that can be seen from the house. In late summer a stand of *Perovskia* creates a blue backdrop for fall-flowering perennials. The garden is a work in progress, ever-changing from year to year. The "party barn" boasts quarter-sawn oak floors, and hosted town dances during Prohibition. Homegrown perennials and shrubs will be for sale on the back patio and adjacent areas. There will be a pop-up boutique in the barn featuring wonderful items for sale by local artisans.

DIRECTIONS—It is 0.9 mile up on the right from the intersection of Route 33/Ridgefield Road and Nod Hill Road.

Litchfield County
Saturday, June 2

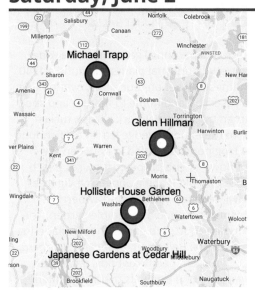

Litchfield County
LITCHFIELD
GLENN HILLMAN
179 North Street, Litchfield
Hours: 2 p.m. to 6 p.m.
📷 | ♿PARTIAL | **2008**

The garden consists of two formal parterres set against the backdrop of the
historic 1771 Lynde Lord house. The upper
garden contains a small alpine terrace set
within a formal English-style perennial
garden with a central pool and a profusion
of flowers in a subdued palette. The lower
garden is an herb garden with brick paths,
clipped box, and a small central knot
garden, with a mixture of culinary and
medicinal herbs and flowers.

DIRECTIONS—From Litchfield Green, take
Route 63 north toward Goshen. The house
is #179 and about 0.25 mile north on left.
Please park along street.

Garden of Glen Hillman
DIGGING DEEPER
3 PM
Ornamental Herbs—Savory and Stunning with Tovah Martin
Free with garden admission

Fond of all things with a past, Glenn
Hillman went one-step further than just
good taste when designing his herb garden—he found herbs that are visually
tantalizing. Working with variegated
versions and weaving together colors,
textures, and other attributes, Glenn's
garden is gorgeous—as well as being
hard working. Tovah Martin, author of
the newly published The *Garden in Every
Sense and Season*, will lead you through
the garden, engaging all your senses
for the full experience. Not only will she
share specifics about using herbs for all
their many attributes, she'll also delve
into herb garden design from ancient to
current and futuristic. Herbs have come
a long way.

ROXBURY
JAPANESE GARDENS AT CEDAR HILL
8 Bayberry Hill, Roxbury
Hours: 10 a.m. to 4 p.m.
📷 | ♿PARTIAL | **NEW**

This Japanese garden is intended to evoke a sense of serenity, as different rooms invite the visitor to pause and reflect. Stones and ledges throughout reside harmoniously with specimen trees and plantings that themselves marry color, texture, and shape. The water features induce a visual and auditory tranquility, encouraging meditation. From the teahouse, one has a commanding view of much of the garden with its borrowed Litchfield Hills landscape. Proceed through a stone garden to a series of geometrically patterned orchards and connecting footpaths.

DIRECTIONS—The property is located close to the junction of Routes 199 and 67 in Roxbury. Access is via Bayberry Hill, a small, marked private road off Route 199 that leads up the hill to the garden, where parking is available.

WEST CORNWALL
MICHAEL TRAPP
7 River Road, West Cornwall
Hours: 10 a.m. to 4 p.m.
📷 | **2017**

This intimate Old World-style garden is replete with cobbled paths, terraced gardens, raised perennial beds, and reflecting pools. Overlooking the Housatonic River, the property has a distinct French/Italian flavor.

DIRECTIONS—From Route 7, take Route 128 east through the covered bridge into West Cornwall.
—From Route 128, take second left onto River Road. House is yellow with gray trim, first on left. Please park in front or in town.

PUBLIC GARDEN PARTNER

Litchfield County
WASHINGTON
HOLLISTER HOUSE GARDEN
300 Nettleton Hollow Road, Washington
(860) 868-2200
hollisterhousegarden.org
Hours 2018: Special Garden Conservancy Open Days June 2, June 16, July 14, 10 a.m. to 4 p.m.; September 9, 9 a.m. to 4 p.m. Otherwise open every Friday, 1 p.m. to 4 p.m., and every Saturday 10 a.m. to 4 p.m., April 27 to October 6.
Admission: $5 suggested donation

Situated around an eighteenth-century farmhouse in the Litchfield Hills of northwest Connecticut, this romantic country garden features exuberant plantings set in rambling formal structure and is noted for its subtle and sometimes surprising color combinations. Reminiscent of such classic English gardens as Great Dixter and Sissinghurst, the garden is divided into a series of rooms, which open to vistas over the garden and out onto the natural landscape beyond. The garden has been a preservation project of the Garden Conservancy since 2005.

DIRECTIONS—From I-84, take Exit 15/Southbury. Take Route 6 north through Southbury and Woodbury. Turn left onto Route 47 North. Go 4 miles, past Woodbury Ski Area on left, and turn right onto

Nettleton Hollow Road. Go 1.7 miles. Garden is on right. Please park along the road or follow parking signs through the gate.

Fairfield County
Sunday, June 3

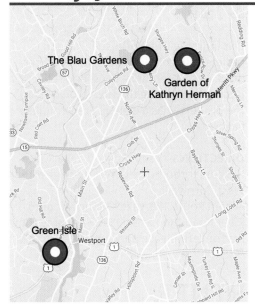

Fairfield County
FAIRFIELD
GARDEN OF KATHRYN HERMAN
10 Fence Row Drive, Fairfield
Hours: 10 a.m. to 4 p.m.
📷 | ♿ | NEW

Part of the original Pepperidge Farm estate, the gardens, created by landscape designer Kathryn Herman, surround the charming 1920s groom's cottage and chauffeur's quarters. There are a custom Alitex greenhouse with adjacent garden, an extensive vegetable garden and orchard, meadows, beehives that produce honey, a water-feature garden, and a swimming-pool garden with the original

gamecock house. A 114-foot double herbaceous perennial garden, original yew "muffins" dating back to the 1920s, sculptural evergreen plantings, and many mature deciduous trees complete the picture, all on six acres. This garden won the 2016 Stanford White Award, and the house won the 2008 Palladio Award.

DIRECTIONS—From Sturges Highway, turn onto Ridge Common. Proceed to the end of Ridge Common, and at the stop sign the driveway will be directly in front, marked with a "Private" sign. The house and property are to the left. Please park where indicated.

WESTPORT
GREEN ISLE
44 Kings Highway North, Westport
Hours: 11 a.m. to 4 p.m.
NEW

Green Isle was built in 1908; restored and renovated in 2015; and documented in Season 1 of the Emmy-nominated TV show "Life on Mar's: The Home Makeover Show," hosted by Mar Jennings and currently available on Amazon Prime. The garden design was the brainchild of Mar Jennings, who partnered with local sources and tradesmen to create an oasis that both connected to the past and reflected the modern updates to the home. He was hired for the project by the homeowner, Yvonne O'Kane. Just as any well-nurtured garden would, their relationship quickly flourished, evolving from client to best of friends. Green Isle is the first of Mar Jennings's casual luxury designs to feature both landscaping and outdoor rooms, and is not to be missed! The moment you arrive, Green Isle's native stone driveway meanders under the historic cherry trees. Boxwoods, evergreen trees, and shrubs anchor the four-season garden's design. Massive steps/rocks carved into the landscape lead you to the side garden's terrace, perfect for morning breakfast or an afternoon retreat. The rose garden and fountain await you as you pass through the back gardens into a flowering parterre with magnificent views of the in-ground pool...[Read full description online]

DIRECTIONS—Follow I-95 N to Westport. Take exit 17 from 1-95 N. From I-95, head southwest on I-95 S. Take Exit 15 for US-1 toward New Rochelle/The Pelhams. Turn left onto US-1 N/Boston Post Road/Main Street (signs for New Rochelle). Turn right to merge onto I-95 N. Take Exit 17 for CT-33 / CT-136 toward Westport/Saugatuck. Continue on CT-33 N to Kings Highway N. Turn left onto CT-33 N/Saugatuck Avenue. Turn left onto Sylvan Road. Turn right onto Post Road. Turn left onto Kings Highway N. The garden will be on the right.

THE BLAU GARDENS
8 Bayberry Ridge Road, Westport
Hours: 10 a.m. to 4 p.m.
📷 | ♿PARTIAL | **2017**

These two acres of formal and informal gardens were developed over fifty years by Barry Blau and include many mature specimens, especially rhododendron groves planted below towering oaks and surrounding a mid-century-modern house. An allée of pollarded crabapples leads to

a Neptune fountain encircled by columnar Norway spruces. Bamboo groves form a backdrop to the Asian garden, which features a large Buddha, waterfalls, a stream with water lilies and water irises, and a new area of grasses. A sunken rose garden, framed by stone retaining walls, is embellished with a boxwood parterre and fountain pools. Cherubs and Roman sculptures punctuate beds of *Geranium macrorrhizum* and *Digitalis purpurea* in summer near the entry's circular drive. A folly of terraced *Astilbe*-filled beds sports stone retaining walls and steps. Fenced-in gardens encompassed by lilacs feature roses, lilies, and other flowers and vegetables. Terraces front the house, a roof deck commands a view of the gardens, and interior plants fill a sky-lit poolroom and mezzanine. More garden elements throughout the garden are paths and walkways, benches, ornamental gates, trellises, and sculptures. Urns and planters brim with begonias in summer and mums in fall.

DIRECTIONS—Parking is very limited at this location; carpooling is suggested. Parking for the Open Day is available only at #s 9, 4, 3, and 1 Bayberry Ridge Road. There are a few spaces between #8 and #9 on the north side of Bayberry Ridge Road. Parking on Barberry Lane is not recommended.
—From Merritt Parkway/Route 15, take Exit 42/Route 57/Weston Road south. Go to 4-way stop intersection. Turn left onto Easton Road/Route 136 and go 1.8 miles. Turn right onto Bayberry Lane. Take an immediate left onto Bayberry Ridge Road (marked by a big yellow sign "no outlet" and "caution children at play"). Follow Bayberry Ridge Road all the way to the top. Number 8 is marked by two stone piers and an entry gate.
—From I-95, take Exit 18. Go north on Sher-

wood Island Connector. Turn right onto Post Road. Continue east to Maple Avenue. Turn left onto Maple Avenue. At end of Maple, turn left onto Long Lots Road. Make an immediate right onto Bayberry Lane and drive north past 4-way stop for cross highway. Continue on Bayberry Lane, past the health department and under the Merritt Parkway overpass and then down a steep winding hill. At the bottom of the hill, just before Bayberry Lane meets Easton Road/Route 136, turn right onto Bayberry Ridge Road (marked by a big yellow sign "no outlet" and "caution children at play"). Follow Bayberry Ridge Road all the way to the top. Number 8 is marked by two stone piers and an entry gate.

Hartford County
Saturday, June 9

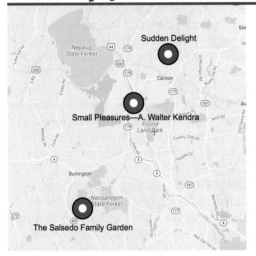

in 1995, added an expanded backyard terrace with a pool, post-and-beam gardener's tool shed, dwarf conifer collection, vegetable garden, and a collection of hardy chrysanthemums. The front yard features low-maintenance lawns punctuated by beds of native and exotic trees, shrubs, and perennials. The emphasis here is sustainability with a focus on low maintenance and minimal water requirements.

Hartford County
BURLINGTON
THE SALSEDO FAMILY GARDEN
15 Half King Drive, Burlington
Hours: 10 a.m. to 4 p.m.
📷 | ♿ | 2016

Our gardens enjoy a unique location: a hilltop, 1,000 feet above sea level, with a magnificent view of 4,000 acres of watershed and state forest. Begun in 1977, physical transformations have resulted in stone-walled terraces that render this acre-plus site usable. The last big change,

Salsedo Family Garden
DIGGING DEEPER
10 AM – 4 PM
Guided Garden tours
Free with garden admission

The Salsedo Family Garden features a yard on a hillside that has undergone a sustainable landscape transformation

since its inception in 1977. Hosts Carl and Beth Salsedo will discuss these various transformations and how-to basics of how they developed their garden landscape over a forty-year span. Dr. Carl Salsedo is an Extension Educator for Environmental and Sustainable Horticulture with the University of Connecticut UConn Extension. His work there includes developing sustainable landscaping programming, which is about reducing waste, energy, and materials—it is about thinking and observation. Its purpose is to design and create systems that imitate nature and turn problems into solutions. There are five basic tenants that every gardener can adopt in their own yard and include: sustainable organic lawn care, use of native plants, fostering a healthy environment without the use of pesticides, creating a biodiverse landscape, and practicing good ecology by recycling all the organic matter back into the landscape. This philosophy has been incorporated into Carl's *Gardening with Nature* series on Connecticut Public Television.

DIRECTIONS—Take I-84 to Exit 39 and go west on Route 4 toward Farmington. Go through Farmington about 3 miles to Unionville Center to traffic light; pass Friendly's on left. Bear right onto Route 4 (Old Masonic Hall on right, church on left). Go 1 mile along Farmington River. At light, turn left onto Route 4 and go up hill toward Burlington. Go about 1 mile and turn left onto Belden Road (fish hatchery sign is on left). At stop sign, turn right onto George Washington Turnpike and then take next left onto Cornwall. Go up hill and turn right onto Nassahegan, then take second left onto Half King Drive. Go to bottom

of cul-de-sac to middle gravel drive with granite mailbox post labeled #15. Please park in cul-de-sac.

CANTON
SUDDEN DELIGHT
148 Bahre Corner Road, Canton
Hours: 10 a.m. to 4 p.m.
📷 | ♿PARTIAL | **2017**

Through the curves of the tree-shaded pathway, up past the stately house and around the corner, you'll be surprised to find this lovely storybook garden with its richly variegated hosta hill, cedar arbor, custom chicken coop, and native perennials, all set against the backdrop of a spectacular red New England-style barn. Meander along the walking paths, stop to watch a yellow finch sip at the birdbath, spy a hummingbird flitting among the roses, or take a secret route through the various tall grasses to the barn. Sudden Delight garden welcomes you to relax and reflect.

DIRECTIONS—From I-84, take Exit 39/Farmington/Route 4 West to Route 179 to Collinsville. Turn right at stop sign and go over bridge. Follow to Route 44. Turn right at stoplight. At next light, turn left onto Lawton Road. At second stop sign, take a severe left onto Bahre Corner. The dirt driveway is opposite the black mailbox, #148. Follow driveway down, and at fork bear left. House is gray with white trim

COLLINSVILLE
SMALL PLEASURES—A. WALTER KENDRA
16 South Street, Collinsville
Hours: 10 a.m. to 4 p.m.
📷 | ♿PARTIAL | **2017**

This small village garden, located in the heart of the Collinsville historic district, is nestled under the branches of tall maples and enclosed by hemlock hedges. The garden entrance is in front of the 1858 house on Center Street; a short set of steps leads to the lower garden. Two terraces and a summer kitchen provide quiet refuge. The garden was designed and cultivated by A. Walter Kendra and the late Maxwell Shepherd, who began their shared efforts in the creation of this garden in 1971.

DIRECTIONS— From I-84, take Exit 39/ Farmington/Route 4 West about 5 miles. Pick up Route 179 North to Collinsville, about 2 more miles. At stop sign turn right. Take first right onto Main Street. Go up hill to stop sign. Turn right again, onto Center Street. Garden is at third house on right, #33-35. Use front entrance. Please park on street.

Hartford &
New Haven Counties
Saturday, June 16

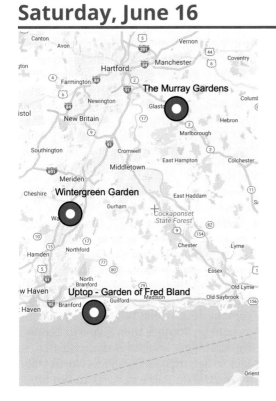

Hartford County
GLASTONBURY
THE MURRAY GARDENS
576 Thompson Street, Glastonbury
Hours: 10 a.m. to 4 p.m.
📷 | ♿ | **2017**

Our property, described in the press as the Glastonbury Botanical Gardens, is a vast, colorful collection of both perennials and annuals springing from a woodland setting of unusual and native trees. The two-acre landscaped property features three long-blooming borders and a hydrangea bed in the front. As you

enter the garden through the stone gate surrounded by unusual daylilies, you are greeted by a small pond with a sculpted copper weeping maple that gently rains all day. A journey down the front walk leads you past a weeping Norway spruce; a spectacular Kousa, or Korean, dogwood; and a sweet bay magnolia. Beyond, view a Camperdown Elm, a larch, and a *Cornus controversa* that extends horizontally over a rock pointing to a bank of carpet flower roses. Next, cross the lawn past the red buckeye and more daylily beds and enter into a naturalized woodland setting with a twisting stone path. Here you can enjoy woodland plants and sculpture surprises with soft music playing in the background. Walking through the garden gate into the backyard, you will find shade gardens built into the pool deck and a formal triangular garden containing 'Knock Out' roses and spectacular coleus and cannas inside a boxwood border...[Read full description online]

DIRECTIONS— From Hartford, take Route 2 East to Exit 10. Turn left off exit ramp onto Route 83. Take first right onto Chimney Sweep Hill. Go up hill 1.5 miles to end. Turn left onto Thompson Street. House is about 0.25 mile on right, across from farm. From east, take Route 2 West to Exit 11. Go left off exit ramp, then take second right onto Thompson Street. Garden is 1.5 miles on right. Please park on street.

New Haven County
STONY CREEK
UPTOP—GARDEN OF FRED BLAND
30-34 Wallace Road, Stony Creek
Hours: 10 a.m. to 4 p.m.
📷 | ♿PARTIAL | **2016**

This is an intensively cultivated one-acre village weekend garden created by an architect/plant collector. The garden has more than 1,400 species of plants (mostly perennials, shrubs, and small trees) arranged in many gardens: a long double border, three woodland gardens, a pool garden hidden by a rollicking serpent tapestry hedge. Many other hedges as well as rock walls (all quarried on site) add their charm. A main cottage and guest cottage with several other outbuildings are all purpose-designed to be subservient to the dominant garden. The owner is the chairman of the board of the Brooklyn Botanic Garden. The garden was published in Jane Garmey's *The Private Gardens of Connecticut*.

DIRECTIONS—Take I-95/Connecticut Turnpike to Exit 56, then turn south from the exit onto Leetes Island Road. Go about 1.5 miles to a 4-way stop sign. Continue straight through into Stony Creek Village, winding through the village on Thimble Islands Road, past the beautiful harbor and on the right. Continue past open fields, on the right and left, to the next street and turn left on Wallace Road. Wind around to the right until you find #30-34 on the left.

WALLINGFORD
WINTERGREEN GARDEN
554 North Main Street, Wallingford
Hours: 10 a.m. to 4 p.m.
NEW

This garden cradles, in its center, a 1915 Japanese-inspired Arts & Crafts home purchased and restored in the winter of 1993 by owners Tracy Alia and James Vanacore. The half-acre lot was nothing but moss, grass, and mature unkempt trees. Work started on the garden in the spring of 1994. After clearing and terracing, the real work began. Stone and brick were sought reclaimed for making patios, staircases, walls, and walkways. Specimen pines, along with a few broadleaf trees to add contrasting texture and color, were planted as the backdrop for most of the garden. The last six garden sections are interspersed with sculptures, bamboo, rhododendrons, flowering vines, arbors, perennials, succulents, and potted annuals, all to create a quiet, hidden sanctuary.

DIRECTIONS—From the north: Take I-91 south, Exit 15 to Route 68 West, left on North Main Extension, then follow to 554 North Main Street.
From the south: Take 1-91 north to Exit 13. Right on Route 5, then follow to Center Street. Go right and then left on North Main Street, then follow to 554 North Main. Or take Merritt Parkway north to Exit 64, turn right onto Quinnipiac Street, follow through town to Center Street, go to top of hill, then left on North Main Street. Follow to 554 North Main Street.

What our Garden Hosts recommend in New Haven County

Sans-Souci Restaurant
2005 N Broad St, Meriden, CT 06450
(203) 639-1779
www.sanssoucirestaurant.com

Dietrich Gardens
1818 Highland Avenue, Cheshire, CT 06410
203.271.0690
www.thegardenct.com

Litchfield County
Saturday, June 16

★ There is an additional garden open on this date in nearby Dutchess County, NY. See page 226.

Litchfield County
FALLS VILLAGE
BUNNY WILLIAMS
1 Point of Rock Road, Falls Village
Hours: 10 a.m. to 4 p.m.
📷 | **2017**

Interior designer and garden book author Bunny Williams's intensively planted fifteen-acre estate has a sunken garden with twin perennial borders surrounding a fishpond, a seasonally changing parterre garden, a year-round conservatory filled with tender plants, a large vegetable garden with flowers and herbs, a woodland garden with meandering paths, and

a pond with a waterfall. There are also a working greenhouse and an aviary with unusual chickens, an apple orchard with mature trees, a rustic Greek Revival-style pool-house folly, and a swimming pool with eighteenth-century French coping.

DIRECTIONS—From Route 7 North, go to Falls Village. Turn left at blinking traffic light onto Main Street/Route 126. Bear right (still on Route 126). Go to stop sign at Point of Rocks Road. Driveway is directly ahead. Please park in field adjacent to house.

WASHINGTON
HIGHMEADOWS—LINDA ALLARD
156 Wykeham Road, Washington
Hours: 10 a.m. to 4 p.m.
📷 | **2017**

Highmeadows sits on a hillside overlooking meadows, an apple orchard, rolling wooded hills, and fields with beautiful panoramic views of the Litchfield Hills. In the walled garden, the walls are covered with espaliered fruit trees, climbing roses, and hydrangeas. A lush rose arbor filled with pale pink and white roses interwoven with *Clematis* separates the formal garden and the *potager*. Boxwood hedges define the white formal garden. The geometric beds of the *potager* overflow with vegetables, herbs, and flowers. A woodland garden has evolved from a section of woodland trail winding through the property. Original trees and shrubs have been enriched with additional plantings of dogwoods, azaleas, *Helleborus*, ferns, spring-flowering bulbs, and woodland flowers. The courtyard garden, covered in pink and red roses mingled with *Clematis* and edged with lavender, leads to a hidden pine grove and artist's studio. The studio looks out to an old granite rock formation converted into a waterfall. A small pond is surrounded with moss, ferns, and woodland plants.

DIRECTIONS—From Washington Green at Gunn Memorial Library, turn onto Wykeham Road. Follow for about 1.5 miles until Old Litchfield Road forks left. Stay right on Wykeham for about 0.25 mile. Go up a small hill to a red barn on right. The entrance to garden is opposite barn. A sign for #156 is on a stone wall. Proceed through gate to garden.

BRUSH HILL GARDENS—CHARLES ROBINSON & BARBARA PAUL ROBINSON
55 Nettleton Hollow Road, Washington
Hours: 10 a.m. to 4 p.m.
📷 | **2017**

Take a virtual tour of Brush Hill Gardens at www.brushhillgardens.com for a preview of many different areas, including the Moon Garden planted in yellows and purples, the Rose Walk, the Peony and Wheelbarrow borders, the Serpentine Garden with its garden folly, and up through the Arch into the Woodland Walk with its series of cascading pools and rills. Each area is adorned with structures designed and built by Charles. The garden has been featured in many articles and books, including Rosemary Verey's book *The Secret Garden* and HGTV's "A Gardener's Diary." Barbara's biography, *Rosemary Verey: The Life and Lessons of a Legendary Gardener*, will be available.

DIRECTIONS—From I-84, take Exit 15 / Southbury. Take Route 6 to Route 47 and turn left. Go 4 miles, passing Woodbury Ski Area on left, and turn right onto Nettleton Hollow Road. Go 4 miles, past intersection of Wykeham and Carmel Hill roads, and watch for sign to enter parking field on left side of Nettleton Hollow Road.
—From north at intersection of Route 109 and Nettleton Hollow Road, go south on Nettleton Hollow Road for 0.3 mile, just past Clark Road. Look for signs to park in field on right.
—Brush Hill Gardens is 2 miles north of Hollister House Gardens on Nettleton Hollow Road.

PUBLIC GARDEN PARTNER

Litchfield County
WASHINGTON
HOLLISTER HOUSE GARDEN
300 Nettleton Hollow Road, Washington
(860) 868-2200
hollisterhousegarden.org

Hours 2018: Special Garden Conservancy Open Days June 2, June 16, July 14, 10 a.m. to 4 p.m.; September 9, 9 a.m. to 4 p.m. Otherwise open every Friday, 1 p.m. to 4 p.m., and every Saturday 10 a.m. to 4 p.m., April 27 to October 6.
Admission: $5 suggested donation
Situated around an eighteenth-century farmhouse in the Litchfield Hills of north-west Connecticut, this romantic country garden features exuberant plantings set in rambling formal structure and is noted for its subtle and sometimes surprising color combinations. Reminiscent of such classic English gardens as Great Dixter and Sissinghurst, the garden is divided into a series of rooms, which open to vistas over the garden and out onto the natural landscape beyond. The garden has been a preservation project of the Garden Conservancy since 2005.

DIRECTIONS—From I-84, take Exit 15/Southbury. Take Route 6 north through Southbury and Woodbury. Turn left onto Route 47 North. Go 4 miles, past Woodbury Ski Area on left, and turn right onto Nettleton Hollow Road. Go 1.7 miles. Garden is on right. Please park along the road or follow parking signs through the gate.

Litchfield County
Saturday, June 23

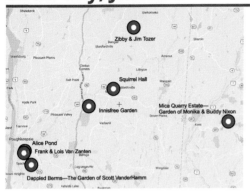

★ There are additional gardens open on this date in nearby Dutchess County, NY. See page 229.

Litchfield County
KENT
MICA QUARRY ESTATE—GARDEN OF MONIKA & BUDDY NIXON
44 Kent Hollow Road, Kent
Hours: 10 a.m. to 4 p.m.
📷 | ♿PARTIAL | **2017**

The garden reflects the owners' quest for rare, distinctive, and hard-to-find trees that can be used in borders, groupings, and open spaces, and as elements of woodlands design. Trees must not only be hardy and disease-resistant, but also have the form, texture, and foliage for year-round enjoyment. The Nixon garden is known for having one of the largest private collections of these exceptional trees in the Northeast. In this garden, there are no perennial borders or parterre-style compartments with boxwoods arranged in linear fashion. Trees have been planted along meandering stone walls and paths; they accentuate rock formations and provide shade for conversation benches and private retreats. They are identified by markers, and a plant list is given out at the entrance. The thirty-four-acre garden features extensive stonework, a koi pond, a woodlands path, trails, a massive old mica quarry, and sweeping views of Lake Waramaug. Some of the trees in the collection with a large number of cultivars are *Abies, Acer aponicum, Ceris, Fagus sylvatica, Larix, Liquidambar, Parrotia persica,* and *Sciadopitys*.

DIRECTIONS
—From Kent, take Route 341 East toward Warren and go about 6 miles. Turn right onto Kent Hollow Road and go 0.25 mile. House is on right after you pass lake on left. Watch for stone walls and two stone columns with lights. Park on road near the pond.
—From traffic light in Warren, take Route 341 West toward Kent. Go about 3 miles and turn left onto Kent Hollow Road. Go 0.25 mile. House is on right after you pass lake on left. Watch for stone walls and two stone columns with lights. Park on road near the pond.

Fairfield County
Saturday, June 30

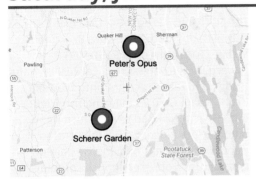

★ There is an additional garden open on this date in nearby Dutchess County, NY. See page 242.

DIRECTIONS—From the south, at the intersections of Routes 37 & 39, go north on Route 37 for 9.1 miles. Turn left onto Briggs Hill Road, then go 1.3 miles. Number 58 is on right after road becomes dirt. The house is red, and the garage gray.
—From the north and east, go south on Routes 37 and 39. Take right fork onto Route 37. Go 1 mile, then turn right onto Briggs Hill Road. Go 1.3 miles. Number 58 is on right after road becomes dirt. The house is red, and the garage gray. Please park where instructed.

Fairfield County
SHERMAN
PETER'S OPUS
58 Briggs Hill Road, Sherman
Hours: 10 a.m. to 4 p.m.
📷 | ♿PARTIAL | **2017**

This mountaintop conifer garden has been described by garden writer Tovah Martin as "astonishingly majestic and refreshingly unique." Each plant grouping is more hologram than display. Here viewers walk around the plants. Further, conifers have been placed so that window views are year-round pleasures." Conifers, with their infinite colors, sizes, and textures, do well when they are highlighted by native sedge, meadow, and lawn, and when framed by taller conifers and native deciduous trees. Many species are historic specimens, collected at the founding of the American Conifer Society.

Litchfield County
Saturday, July 14

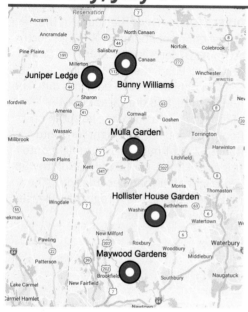

Litchfield County
BRIDGEWATER
MAYWOOD GARDENS
52 Cooper Road, Bridgewater
Hours: 10 a.m. to 4 p.m.
📷 | 2017

This private estate features a sunken perennial garden protected by ten-foot stone walls, a gazebo garden planted with flowers and shrubs to attract butterflies and hummingbirds, a rose garden planted in a French design pattern encircled by hemlocks, a woodland path populated by mature beech and cherry trees as well as *Viburnum* and rhododendrons. A ledge garden on an exposed hillside, a bed of heather, a white garden, herb garden, ornamental kitchen garden, and finally 4,000-square-foot greenhouse give visitors a richly varied tour.

DIRECTIONS—From I-84, take Exit 9 and go north on Route 25 toward Brookfield Village. Turn right onto Route 133 East toward Bridgewater. Cross Lake Lillinonah Bridge and take first right onto Wewaka Brook Road. Go 0.75 mile and turn right onto Beach Hill Road to end. Turn right onto Skyline Ridge. Go 0.5 mile and turn right onto Cooper Road. Please park on right across from greenhouse complex.

FALLS VILLAGE
BUNNY WILLIAMS
1 Point of Rock Road, Falls Village
Hours: 10 a.m. to 4 p.m.
📷 | 2017

Interior designer and garden book author Bunny Williams's intensively planted fifteen-acre estate has a sunken garden with twin perennial borders surrounding a fishpond, a seasonally changing parterre garden, a year-round conservatory filled with tender plants, a large vegetable garden with flowers and herbs, a woodland garden with meandering paths, and a pond with a waterfall. There are also a working greenhouse and an aviary with unusual chickens, an apple orchard with mature trees, a rustic Greek Revival-style pool-house folly, and a swimming pool with eighteenth-century French coping.

DIRECTIONS—From Route 7 North, go to Falls Village. Turn left at blinking traffic light onto Main Street/Route 126. Bear right (still on Route 126). Go to stop sign at Point of Rocks Road. Driveway is directly ahead. Please park in field adjacent to house.

LAKEVILLE
JUNIPER LEDGE
4 Juniper Ledge Lane, Lakeville
Hours: 10 a.m. to 4 p.m.
📷 | ♿ | **2015**

A south-facing four-acre site, once a pasture, was overgrown with Japanese honeysuckle, multiflora roses, grey dogwood, ash, and eastern juniper. The northern edge was cleared in 1958 for a Cape Cod-style house, since expanded. We left the junipers and dogwoods as found and, after installing steel deer fencing, developed a garden for strolling. Hedges, mixed shrub plantings, a three-arched arbor, decorative gates, and mixed borders guide visitors and define views of Indian Mountain and distant hills. Statues of a girl with a shell and a dancing and piping Pan are focal points. A large elm towers over mixed evergreens, and a tall pin oak shades *Hosta* and shrub junipers. There are an evergreen walk and a shade garden. Various benches and a tennis pavilion provide shaded places to rest.

DIRECTIONS—From Lakeville, go west on Route 44, the Millerton Road, to Indian Mountain Road on the left. Proceed south through the intersection with Route 112 / Lime Rock Road 0.67 mile past Indian Mountain School to Juniper Ledge Lane on the right.
—From Sharon, go toward Sharon Hospital but turn right at the firehouse onto Route 361 / Millerton Road, down the hill across a small bridge, and then right on Mudge Pond Road. Go 2 miles (it changes name to Indian Mountain Road) to Juniper Ledge Lane on the left. As you drive into Juniper Ledge Lane, parking is available in a field to your immediate right. (If it is full, proceed slowly, bearing left onto Juniper Drive until you find a place beside the road.) The entrance to the garden is across from the parking field through the wide-open white wooden gate.

WARREN
MULLA GARDEN
164 Melius Road, Warren
Hours: 10 a.m. to 2 p.m.
📷 | **NEW**

This garden sits on a clearing atop a granite outcropping overlooking a breathtaking expanse of the Shepaug Reservoir. It is unusual in its structure and content and is truly a collector's playground, consisting of a wide variety of very unusual conifers, trees, shrubs, grasses, and flowering perennials. The beds twirl and dance, creating beautiful flowing shapes and contours. The overall feel and aura are enchanting with a dueling atmosphere between the formal and informal. Don't miss the new four- square walled Persian garden, whose quadrants are planted with boxwood in the shape of balustrades from the designer's native India.

DIRECTIONS—Take Route 45 to Melius Road. Drive 1.9 miles to #164. Drive through stone walls and park on grassy area before entering second set of stone walls into garden area.

PUBLIC GARDEN PARTNER

Litchfield County
WASHINGTON
HOLLISTER HOUSE GARDEN

300 Nettleton Hollow Road, Washington
(860) 868-2200
hollisterhousegarden.org
Hours 2018: Special Garden Conservancy
Open Days June 2, June 16, July 14, 10 a.m.
to 4 p.m.; September 9, 9 a.m. to 4 p.m.
Otherwise open every Friday, 1 p.m. to 4
p.m., and every Saturday 10 a.m. to 4 p.m.,
April 27 to October 6.
Admission: $5 suggested donation

Situated around an eighteenth-century
farmhouse in the Litchfield Hills of northwest Connecticut, this romantic country
garden features exuberant plantings set in
rambling formal structure and is noted for
its subtle and sometimes surprising color
combinations. Reminiscent of such classic
English gardens as Great Dixter and Sissinghurst, the garden is divided into a series
of rooms, which open to vistas over the
garden and out onto the natural landscape
beyond. The garden has been a preservation project of the Garden Conservancy
since 2005.

DIRECTIONS—From I-84, take Exit 15/
Southbury. Take Route 6 north through
Southbury and Woodbury. Turn left onto
Route 47 North. Go 4 miles, past Wood-
bury Ski Area on left, and turn right onto
Nettleton Hollow Road. Go 1.7 miles. Gar-
den is on right. Please park along the road
or follow parking signs through the gate.

New London County
Saturday, July 14

New London County
STONINGTON
KENTFORD FARM

297 New London Turnpike, Stonington
Hours: 10 a.m. to 4 p.m.
 | ♿PARTIAL | **2017**

Kentford Farm is a perennial farm in the
making. For eighteen years, Paul Coutu
and William Turner have been creating
grass pathways and planting beds. The
farm dates back to 1727, and the previous
owner started planting in 1945. Fifty-foot
weeping cherries, a Norway spruce, copper
beech, and blue Atlas cedar, to name a few,
dot this five-acre garden. There is a walk-in
root cellar built into the hillside, and stone
walls surround the whole property. For
more information, visit www.kentfordfarm.
com.

DIRECTIONS—From New London, take
I-95 north to Exit 90/Mystic. Turn left onto
Route 27 and go to stop sign in Old Mystic
Center. Bear right and go through stop
sign, passing Old Mystic Fire Station on left.
Bear right at next fork onto North Stoning-
ton Road. Pass Clyde's Cider Mill on left. Go

to blinking light at intersection of Routes 184 & 201. Turn right onto Route 184 and go east. Kentford Farm is second driveway on left.

—From Providence, take I-95 south to Exit 90/Mystic. Turn right onto Route 27. Proceed as directed above.

—From Norwich, take Route 2 east past Foxwoods Resort Casino. Turn right onto Route 201 South toward Old Mystic. Turn left onto Route 184 East. Kentford Farm is second driveway on left.

Litchfield County
Saturday, July 21

★ There are additional gardens open on this date in nearby Berkshire County, MA (see page 159) and Dutchess County, NY (see page 254).

Litchfield County
SHARON
LEE LINK
99 White Hollow Road, Sharon
Hours: 10 a.m. to 4 p.m.
📷 | 2017

Three stone walls climb up a hillside at the top of which is a greenhouse containing a wide spectrum of succulents and tropical plants. Within the last two years, the former perennial border was replaced with a new hardscape and three Kousa, or Korean, dogwoods set off by groundcover and spring bulbs. This is an effort to minimize upkeep. One level has a fishpond, which reflects a winter conservatory attached to the house.

DIRECTIONS—From Routes 7 & 112, turn onto Route 112. Go about 2 miles to "Entrance to Lime Rock Race Track" sign. Turn left onto White Hollow Road and go 2.5 miles. Garden, #99, is on right, opposite a white fence.

—From Route 41 in Sharon, turn right onto Calkinstown Road. Take second left onto White Hollow Road. Driveway is on left opposite a white fence.

Hartford & New Haven Counties
Sunday, July 22

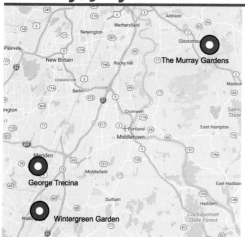

Hartford County
GLASTONBURY
THE MURRAY GARDENS
576 Thompson Street, Glastonbury
Hours: 10 a.m. to 4 p.m.
📷 | ♿ | **2017**

Our property, described in the press as the Glastonbury Botanical Gardens, is a vast, colorful collection of both perennials and annuals springing from a woodland setting of unusual and native trees. The two-acre landscaped property features three long-blooming borders and a hydrangea bed in the front. As you enter the garden through the stone gate surrounded by unusual daylilies, you are greeted by a small pond with a sculpted copper weeping maple that gently rains all day. A journey down the front walk leads you past a weeping Norway spruce; a spectacular Kousa, or Korean, dogwood; and a sweet bay magnolia. Beyond, view

a Camperdown Elm, a larch, and a *Cornus controversa* that extends horizontally over a rock pointing to a bank of carpet flower roses. Next, cross the lawn past the red buckeye and more daylily beds and enter into a naturalized woodland setting with a twisting stone path. Here you can enjoy woodland plants and sculpture surprises with soft music playing in the background. Walking through the garden gate into the backyard, you will find shade gardens built into the pool deck and a formal triangular garden containing 'Knock Out' roses and spectacular coleus and cannas inside a boxwood border...[Read full description online]

DIRECTIONS—From Hartford, take Route 2 East to Exit 10. Turn left off exit ramp onto Route 83. Take first right onto Chimney Sweep Hill. Go up hill 1.5 miles to end. Turn left onto Thompson Street. House is about 0.25 mile on right, across from farm. —From east, take Route 2 West to Exit 11. Go left off exit ramp, then take second right onto Thompson Street. Garden is 1.5 miles on right. Please park on street.

New Haven County
MERIDEN
GEORGE TRECINA
341 Spring Street, Meriden
Hours: 10 a.m. to 4 p.m.
📷 | ♿PARTIAL | **2017**

This is a thirty-year-old, one-third-acre, high-maintenance suburban garden that has been on the Garden Conservancy tour for twenty-one consecutive years. There are many varieties of trees and shrubs that form the framework for hundreds of containers of annuals and tropical plants. Every year we relocate some of the containers to create new and dramatic effects. There is a special focus on succulents, which include agave, aloe, cactus, and *Echeveria* as well as some less commonly known succulents. English latticework fencing is being added for 2018. We welcome bus tours and private showings for garden clubs.

DIRECTIONS—From I-91 North, take Exit 18/I-691 West to Exit 6/Lewis Avenue. Turn right onto Lewis Avenue (which becomes Linsley Avenue) and go to end. Turn right onto Hanover Street and go to first traffic light. Turn left onto Columbus Avenue and go to second stop sign. Turn left onto Prospect Avenue and take second right onto Spring Street. Go to fourth house on right, #341. Please park along Spring Street. Visitors with walking problems may drive up driveway.
—From I-91 South, take Exit 15/Route 68. Turn left onto Route 68 and go about 2.75 miles. Turn right onto Route 150/Main Street. Turn left onto Route 71/Old Colony Road for about 2.25 miles to third traffic light. Turn left onto Flower Street and go to end. Turn left onto New Hanover Avenue and then take first right onto Prospect Avenue. Take first left onto Spring Street.
—From I-84, take Exit 27/I-691 East to Exit 5/Route 71/Chamberlain Highway. Turn right onto Route 71 and go to end. Turn left onto West Main Street and go to first traffic light. Turn right onto Bradley Avenue and go to stop sign. Turn left onto Winthrop Terrace and go to traffic light. Go through intersection up Columbus Avenue to second stop sign. Turn left onto Prospect Avenue and then take second right onto Spring Street.

WALLINGFORD
WINTERGREEN GARDEN
554 North Main Street, Wallingford
Hours: 10 a.m. to 4 p.m.
NEW

This garden cradles, in its center, a 1915 Japanese-inspired Arts & Crafts home purchased and restored in the winter of 1993 by owners Tracy Alia and James Vanacore. The half-acre lot was nothing but moss, grass, and mature unkempt trees. Work started on the garden in the spring of 1994. After clearing and terracing, the real work began. Stone and brick were sought reclaimed for making patios, staircases, walls, and walkways. Specimen pines, along with a few broadleaf trees to add contrasting texture and color, were planted as the backdrop for most of the garden. The last six garden sections are interspersed with sculptures, bamboo, rhododendrons, flowering vines, arbors, perennials, succulents, and potted annuals, all to create a quiet, hidden sanctuary.

DIRECTIONS—From the north: Take I-91 south, Exit 15 to Route 68 West, left on North Main Extension, then follow to 554 North Main Street.
—From the south: Take 1-91 north to Exit 13. Right on Route 5, then follow to Center Street. Go right and then left on North Main Street, then follow to 554 North Main. Or take Merritt Parkway north to Exit 64, turn right onto Quinnipiac Street, follow through town to Center Street, go to top of hill, then left on North Main Street. Follow to 554 North Main Street.

Fairfield County
Saturday, August 18

Fairfield County
REDDING
INSITU

73 Diamond Hill Road, Redding
Hours: 10 a.m. to 4 p.m.
📷 | 2017

InSitu is an eight-acre sculpture garden where nature and art dramatically interact. Nestled in the rural countryside near Redding, the property is surrounded by the 312-acre Saugatuck Waterfall Natural Area, a landscape of deciduous woodlands, rocky outcroppings, and meadows, permeated by a series of small creeks that empty into the Saugatuck River. Working with a team of architects, designers, craftsmen, and artists, owner Michael Marocco has created a richly composed showcase of architecture, horticulture, and sculpture, seamlessly woven together in a series of eighteen garden rooms. InSitu's structures

were extensively renovated by New Haven-based architect Robert Orr, who drew upon their heritage as utility buildings by incorporating rustic barn beams as their framework. The house and outbuildings express the rural Connecticut vernacular spirit. Cedar shakes and deep reds and browns integrate the buildings comfortably into the landscape. The property's interior designer, New York City-based Harry Schnaper, captures Connecticut's charm and elevates it to a level of refined elegance with a palette of natural materials, richly textured fabrics, and exquisite artwork... [Read full description online]

DIRECTIONS—From the Merritt Parkway/Route 15 North, take Exit 42/Highway 57 toward Westport/Weston. Go 0.2 mile. At traffic light at end of ramp, turn right onto Highway 57/Weston Road (signs for Weston). Go 3.8 miles. Turn left onto Route 57/Georgetown Road and go 4 miles. Turn right onto Route 107/Redding Road. Go 3.9 miles. Toward the end of the reservoir, cross a small bridge. Turn left to continue on Redding Road/Route 53 North. Pass The Redding Road House and cemetery on right. At flashing light, turn left onto Diamond Hill Road. The Mark Twain Library is on left. Go about 0.25 mile. Garden is on right. Please park on upper road. *Note: The mailbox numbers are not in order.

New London County
Saturday, August 25

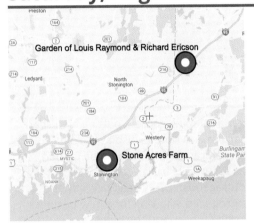

★There is an additional garden open on this date in nearby Washington County, RI. See page 301.

New London County
STONINGTON
STONE ACRES FARM
385 North Main Street, Stonington
Hours: 10 a.m. to 2 p.m.
📷 | ♿PARTIAL | **2017**

Stone Acres Farm is a small working farm situated in picturesque Stonington. The property's rolling hills, gardens, and acres of vegetable production are open to visitors on a daily basis. A century-old boxwood hedge that is one-quarter-mile long, rose arbors, and a perennial cutting garden are highlights of the historic formal garden. There are interesting old outbuildings, a carriage house, grapery, greenhouse, annual cutting garden, a ha ha, and a pond once used for ice—now home for the herons. For additional hours and visiting opportunities, see www.stoneacresfarm.com.

Stone Acres Farm
DIGGING DEEPER
11 AM – 1 PM
Ellen Shipman Book-Signing
with Judith Tankard
Free with garden admission

In the historic gardens at Stone Acres Farm, join landscape historian and Garden Conservancy Fellow Judith Tankard for a signing of her latest book, *Ellen Shipman and the American Garden.* In the 1920s and 1930s, Shipman was a famous landscape architect who designed hundreds of gardens, including sixty in Connecticut. She was known for her labor-intensive flower borders as well as charming water features and garden sculpture. Judith has also written books on Beatrix Farrand and Gertrude Jekyll. She is an Open Days Regional Representative and Garden Host on Martha's Vineyard.

(NOTE: Designed by Ellen Shipman as a series of stunning outdoor rooms, the Holden McGinley Garden in Milton, Massachusetts, can be visited during an Open Day on June 9, 2018.)

DIRECTIONS—From I-95, take Exit 91/ Stonington Borough Village. Go south to North Main Street, then turn left toward Stonington Borough. Go about 1.5 miles to #385.

—From Route 1, turn north onto North Main Street at traffic light. Number 385 is second driveway on right. Follow signs for parking.

Litchfield County
Sunday, August 26

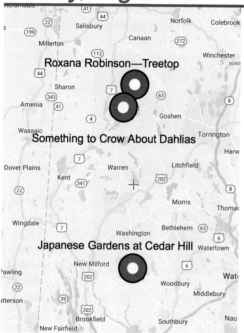

gently sloping garden, putting on a spectacular and riotous display of color. Tovah Martin recently described the garden as a "full-spectrum version of Oz, totally outrageous." Every year, new varieties are introduced, allowing for a new business selling tubers and fresh-cut stems.

DIRECTIONS—From Waterbury, take Route 8 north to Exit 44. Turn left onto Route 4 West. Go about 12 miles. The garden is on the right.
From Danbury, take Route 7 north for about 40 miles, all the way to Cornwall Bridge. At the intersection of Routes 4 and 7, bear right onto Route 4 and follow for about 3 miles. The garden is on the left side of the road.

Litchfield County
CORNWALL
SOMETHING TO CROW ABOUT DAHLIAS
34 Furnace Brook Road, Cornwall
Hours: 10 a.m. to 4 p.m.
📷 | ♿PARTIAL | **2016**

The garden has grown in the past eighteen years to include more than 2,000 plants. It showcases 175 different dahlia varieties producing countless blooms of every shape, color, and size. When in full bloom, the long rows stretch down the

ROXBURY
JAPANESE GARDENS AT CEDAR HILL
8 Bayberry Hill, Roxbury
Hours: 10 a.m. to 4 p.m.
📷 | ♿PARTIAL | **NEW**

This Japanese garden is intended to evoke a sense of serenity, where different rooms invite the visitor to pause and reflect. Stones and ledges throughout reside harmoniously with specimen trees and plantings that themselves marry color, texture, and shape. The water features induce a visual and auditory tranquility, encouraging meditation. From the teahouse, one has a commanding view of much of the garden with its borrowed Litchfield Hills landscape. Proceed through a stone garden to a series of geometrically patterned orchards and connecting footpaths.

DIRECTIONS—The property is located close to the junction of Routes 199 and 67 in Roxbury. Access is via Bayberry Hill, a small, marked private road off Route 199 that leads up the hill to the garden, where parking is available.

WEST CORNWALL
ROXANA ROBINSON—TREETOP

218 Town Street, West Cornwall
Hours: 10 a.m. to 4 p.m.
2017

On the grounds of a family Arts & Crafts house built in 1928 is an idiosyncratic hillside garden incorporating granite ledge, steep ravines, placid greensward, and a wooded slope down to a lake. The gardens themselves are separated into two areas. First the well-mannered, level terrain of "Sissinghurst," with a palette of blues, pinks, silvers, and purples; stone paths; and emerald lawn. Then "Margaritaville," a wild and rocky ravine with a riot of giant ferns; *Tithonia* in reds and oranges and yellows; and salvias and nasturtiums lending more brilliant hues. Around the gardens are deep woods full of ferns and birches.

DIRECTIONS—From West Cornwall, at the intersection of Routes 7 and 128, leave the covered bridge behind and go straight up the hill on Route 128 east for 1.19 miles. Turn left at the school onto Cream Hill Road. Continue for 1.4 miles and turn right onto Scoville Road. Go 0.7 mile to the end and a "T" intersection and turn right onto Town Street. Go 0.36 mile, down into a dip and up the hill again to Treetop. The drive-way is on the left, mailbox on the right.
—From Goshen, at the traffic circle, take Route 4 east to the blinking light, about 4 miles. At the light continue straight, up the hill, onto Route 128, about 1 mile. Turn right onto Town Street. Follow Town Street past the white church at North Cornwall to a "Y" intersection, about 1 mile. Bear left (actually stay straight) onto Town Street. Go around a curve to the right. After that big curve we are the second drive on the right. The sign at the driveway says Treetop. The mailbox is on the left and says #218.
—From the west: Take Route 112 east to Route 7. Turn left onto Route 7 north. Go about 100 yards to the traffic light just be-low Falls Village. Turn right onto tiny Lime Rock Station Road. Stay on that, bearing left at the first fork, away from River Road and onto Music Mountain Road, about 0.5 mile. Then at the next fork bear right (ac-tually stay straight) onto Cream Hill Road, going straight up the hill. Go over the top of the hill and almost all the way down on the other side, about 1 mile. Turn left onto Scoville Road. Follow to end, about 0.5 mile, and turn right onto Town Street. Go down into the dip and up the other side. Treetop is up the hill on the left, mailbox on the right #218. Driveway on right, "Treetop."
—From the north: Take Route 7 south to Route 63. Turn left onto 63 east. Follow that for about 2 miles. Turn right onto Route 43/Cornwall Hollow Road. Follow for about 2 miles. Turn right onto Lake Road. Follow that for about 1.5 miles. Turn right onto Town Street and follow it around a curve to the right. After that big curve we are the second driveway on the right. The sign at the driveway says Treetop. The mailbox is on the left and says 218. WARN-ING: Coming from the west, your GPS might try to send you up a goat trail over Music Mountain, so these directions are safer.

New Haven County
Saturday, September 8

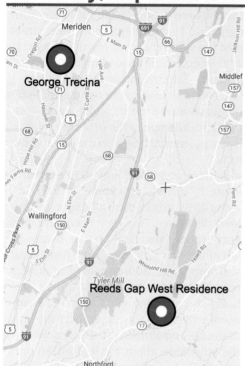

New Haven County
MERIDEN
GEORGE TRECINA

341 Spring Street, Meriden
Hours: 10 a.m. to 4 p.m.
📷 | ♿PARTIAL | **2017**

This is a thirty-year-old, one-third-acre, high-maintenance suburban garden that has been on the Garden Conservancy tour for twenty-one consecutive years. There are many varieties of trees and shrubs that form the framework for hundreds of containers of annuals and tropical plants. Every year we relocate some of the containers to create new and dramatic effects. There is a special focus on succulents, which include agave, aloe, cactus, and

Echeveria as well as some less commonly known succulents. English latticework fencing is being added for 2018. We welcome bus tours and private showings for garden clubs.

DIRECTIONS—From I-91 North, take Exit 18/I-691 West to Exit 6/Lewis Avenue. Turn right onto Lewis Avenue (which becomes Linsley Avenue) and go to end. Turn right onto Hanover Street and go to first traffic light. Turn left onto Columbus Avenue and go to second stop sign. Turn left onto Prospect Avenue and take second right onto Spring Street. Go to fourth house on right, #341. Please park along Spring Street. Visitors with walking problems may drive up driveway.
—From I-91 South, take Exit 15/Route 68. Turn left onto Route 68 and go about 2.75 miles. Turn right onto Route 150/Main Street. Turn left onto Route 71/Old Colony Road for about 2.25 miles to third traffic light. Turn left onto Flower Street and go to end. Turn left onto New Hanover Avenue and then take first right onto Prospect Avenue. Take first left onto Spring Street. From I-84, take Exit 27/I-691 East to Exit 5/Route 71/Chamberlain Highway. Turn right onto Route 71 and go to end. Turn left onto West Main Street and go to first traffic light. Turn right onto Bradley Avenue and go to stop sign. Turn left onto Winthrop Terrace and go to traffic light. Go through intersection up Columbus Avenue to second stop sign. Turn left onto Prospect Avenue and then take second right onto Spring Street.

NORTHFORD
REEDS GAP WEST RESIDENCE
325 Reeds Gap Road, Northford
Hours: 10 a.m. to 4 p.m.
📷 | **NEW**

The gardens are those of landscape designer Donna Christensen. She and her husband, David, live and work in an old apple barn on the property. They own a design/build landscape company and have collected many large specimen trees and shrubs. These have been assembled in several different gardens throughout the four acres. The front half of the property includes a two-acre pond with a gazebo, a large waterfall, and a Japanese-style garden with stone bridge. The barn home is surrounded by stone walls, terraces, pool and other water features, and flowering perennial and annual gardens.

DIRECTIONS—Turn left from Route 17 (Middletown Road) onto Reeds Gap Road west. The gardens are at 325 Reeds Gap Road. This is the 6th driveway on the right side. Look for the large pond and drive up past the pond to parking on right side.

Fairfield County
Sunday, September 9

★ There are additional gardens open on this date in nearby Westchester County, NY. See page 268.

Fairfield County
WILTON
THE HARRIS GARDEN
9 Shagbark Place, Wilton
Hours: 10 a.m. to 4 p.m.
📷 | ♿PARTIAL | **2017**

It began as a flower garden in 1994. Initially every plant was chosen because it made a good cut flower or had great foliage or a beguiling scent—preferably all three! From the onset, the intention has been to convey a wild, exuberant abundance; annuals are inter-planted with perennials. Structural elements have been added to provide balance and suggest premeditation. Boxwoods and unusual trees play an important role. As the two-acre site was naturalized, the original concept was adapted to shaded and woodland areas. Designer's notes: My name is Laura Tuttle Stabell. This garden has been twenty-two years in the making—since I first met Tom and Doreen Harris—so I'm excited to share the garden. The Harris home is modern and the garden follows to a degree. (I was working with Helene Verglas on designing Horsefeathers, a traditional Colonial garden, at the time, and some of her structural ideas filtered through.) It was designed to provide cut flowers as well—and also has a prairie vibe, with lots of grasses, and gets a little wild in places. A neighbor's field has been "borrowed" by planting grasses and keeping it open along that border. This garden is also about color, with much thought going into the ever-changing color schemes throughout the year...[Read full description online]

DIRECTIONS—From Wilton Center, take Route 7 North. Turn left on Route 33 north. Go approximately 2.5 miles north. Turn right on Nod Hill Road (you will see Signal Hill Road on the left just before turn). Proceed to stop sign. Turn left, continuing on Nod Hill Road for approximately 2.5 miles. You will see Charter Oak Drive on the left. Just past it turn on Hillbrook Road. The very next turn is Shagbark Place. Park on the cul-de-sac. The house is #9.
—From Danbury, take Route 7 south to Branchville. Turn right on Route 102 and head toward Ridgefield center. Turn left on the second road on the left, Old Branchville Road. At the top of the hill there is a 3-way stop. Turn left onto Nod Hill Road and proceed down it through next 3 stop signs and past the Weir Farm Historic Site. The last stop is Whipstick Road. Stay on Nod Hill for 1 mile more. You will see Millstone Road on the right. Continue around

the corner on Nod Hill. The turn is the next right: Hillbrook Road. The very next turn is Shagbark Place. Park on the cul-de-sac. The house is #9.

The Harris Garden
DIGGING DEEPER
3 PM
Art and Science in the Garden
Free with garden admission

Underlying the painterly palette of flowering plants and the grading and sculpting of the earth, lies the mechanics of horticulture and the secrets of garden science. Explore the Harris Garden with landscape gardener Laura Tuttle Stabell. This garden, built on a ledge with sloping terrain, presented many challenges that were solved by focusing on both the art and the science of gardening. Aspects of the garden—fragrance, color, style—all have a science to them which can be used to create sensual experiences. Other sciences can be used to create a sense of place, lead you, stop you, or help create rooms. See your garden as you never have before and learn how to use science to make a better garden.

ANNOUNCING HOLLISTER HOUSE
GARDEN STUDY WEEKEND VIII
A Passion for Plants

Presented by Hollister House Garden and the Garden Conservancy

September 8–9, 2018
Symposium, Great Vendors, & Open Day Garden Tours

Saturday, September 8

Symposium at the Heritage Hotel
in Southbury, CT, featuring talks by:

Sarah Price – one of Britain's most prominent and distinctive garden designers who achieved worldwide recognition for her work on London's Olympic Park

Kelly Norris – director of horticulture at Greater Des Moines Botanical Garden, plantsman, and author

Lynden Miller – award-winning author and garden designer renowned for her work beautifying New York's public spaces

Ed Bowen and Taylor Johnston – collaborators in Issima, a nursery, garden design, and cut flower studio

Barbara Paul Robinson – passionate gardener and author, introducing her new book, *Heroes of Horticulture: Americans Who Transformed the Landscape*

At the conclusion of the symposium, enjoy cocktails and early buying at the Sale of Rare and Unusual Plants at Hollister House Garden.

Sunday, September 9

Garden Conservancy Open Day
will feature private gardens in Litchfield County.

The Sale of Rare and Unusual Plants will open to the public at Hollister House Garden.

For a full schedule of participating gardens, see the Open Days schedule at www.gardenconservancy.org.

For more information and to register for the Saturday program, visit www.hollisterhousegarden.org or call 860.868.2200.

Litchfield County
Sunday, September 9

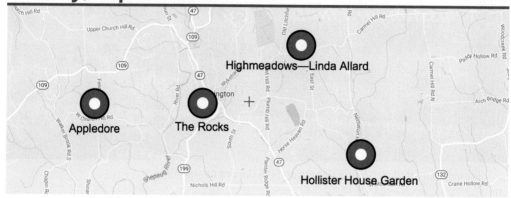

★ Start your day at Hollister House Garden, 300 Nettleton Hollow Road, Washington, 9 a.m. to 4 p.m. Admission: $10, including access to plant sale.

Litchfield County
WASHINGTON
HIGHMEADOWS—LINDA ALLARD
156 Wykeham Road, Washington
Hours: 10 a.m. to 4 p.m.
2017

Highmeadows sits on a hillside overlooking meadows, an apple orchard, rolling hills of woods, and fields with beautiful panoramic views of the Litchfield Hills. In the walled garden, the walls are covered with espaliered fruit trees, climbing roses, and hydrangeas. A lush rose arbor filled with pale pink and white roses interwoven with *Clematis* separates the formal garden and the *potager*. Boxwood hedges define the white formal garden. The geometric beds of the *potager* overflow with vegetables, herbs, and flowers. A woodland garden has evolved from a section of woodland trail winding through the property. Original trees and shrubs have been enriched with additional plantings of dogwoods, azaleas, *Helleborus*, ferns, spring-flowering bulbs, and woodland flowers. The courtyard garden, covered in pink and red roses mingled with *Clematis* and edged with lavender, leads to a hidden pine grove and artist's studio. The studio looks out to an old granite rock formation converted into a waterfall. A small pond is surrounded with moss, ferns, and woodland plants.

DIRECTIONS—From Washington Green at Gunn Memorial Library, turn onto Wykeham Road. Follow for about 1.5 miles until Old Litchfield Road forks left. Stay right on Wykeham for about 0.25 mile. Go up a small hill to a red barn on right. The entrance to garden is opposite barn. A sign for #156 is on a stone wall. Proceed through gate to garden.

THE ROCKS
21 Kirby Road, Washington
Hours: 10 a.m. to 4 p.m.
NEW

The Rocks is the pre-eminent example of the many summer cottages built by notable New York architect Ehrick Rossiter in and around Washington's green a century ago. Nearly twenty years in the making, the large rambling Shingle- style house offers views over the Shepaug River Valley. In the garden, he framed formal gardens with colonnaded pergolas and sculpted the land to highlight the rocky ledges. Equally impressive as the house and landscape is the extraordinary collection of trees that have now grown to enormous proportions. The house has recently been restored and the gardens reimagined; this is the first opportunity to explore this magnificent landscape and garden.

DIRECTIONS—From the center of Washington Depot, head southeast on Route 47S for 0.8 mile. Turn right on Kirby Road. In 0.2 mile the destination will be on your right.

WASHINGTON DEPOT
APPLEDORE
47 Fenn Hill Road, Washington Depot
Hours: 10 a.m. to 4 p.m.
NEW

Appledore is a two-acre garden of shrubs, trees, and perennials that grew without a plan on the site of an old farm. Each year I would add another bed, avoiding straight lines and seeking to create vistas from every room of the house that would be pleasing in every season. Some of the beds have names: pool garden, birch grove, wood garden, crabapple meadow. Others are nameless, their character evolving according to the light and their neighbors. Much of what I have planted is unusual, but there are plenty of old favorites, too. After two decades some of the little trees have grown, older beds have required reimagining, and the more than three dozen kinds of daffodils have spread all over!

DIRECTIONS—From the center of Washington Depot, head northeast toward CT-109 East. Turn left onto CT-109 West and head toward New Milford for 1.5 miles. Turn left onto Fenn Hill Road. Third driveway on right, 47 Fenn Hill Road.

PUBLIC GARDEN PARTNER

Litchfield County
WASHINGTON
HOLLISTER HOUSE GARDEN
300 Nettleton Hollow Road, Washington
🏷 PLANT SALES—RARE AND UNUSUAL
(860) 868-2200
hollisterhousegarden.org
Hours 2018: Special Garden Conservancy Open Days June 2, June 16, July 14, 10 a.m. to 4 p.m.; September 9, 9 a.m. to 4 p.m. Otherwise open every Friday, 1 p.m. to 4

p.m., and every Saturday 10 a.m. to 4 p.m., April 27 to October 6.
Admission: $5 suggested donation. *Please note: Open Days admission tickets will not be accepted on Sunday, September 9, during garden study weekend. Admission on September 9 is $10 and includes plant sale.*

Situated around an eighteenth-century farmhouse in the Litchfield Hills of northwest Connecticut, this romantic country garden features exuberant plantings set in rambling formal structure and is noted for its subtle and sometimes surprising color combinations. Reminiscent of such classic English gardens as Great Dixter and Sissinghurst, the garden is divided into a series of rooms, which open to vistas over the garden and out onto the natural landscape beyond. The garden has been a preservation project of the Garden Conservancy since 2005.

DIRECTIONS—From I-84, take Exit 15/Southbury. Take Route 6 north through Southbury and Woodbury. Turn left onto Route 47 North. Go 4 miles, past Woodbury Ski Area on left, and turn right onto Nettleton Hollow Road. Go 1.7 miles. Garden is on right. Please park along the road or follow parking signs through the gate.

Fairfield County
Sunday, September 16

Fairfield County
GREENWICH
SLEEPY CAT FARM
146 Clapboard Ridge Road, Greenwich
Hours: 10 a.m. to 4 p.m.
📷 | 2017

The thirteen acres of Sleepy Cat Farm have evolved over the last twenty five years through a close collaboration between the present owner and Virginia based landscape architect Charles J. Stick. The landscape bordering Lake Avenue includes an extensive greenhouse and potager. The "Barn," distinguished by its half-timbered French Normandy vocabulary is surrounded by thyme-covered terraces providing an elegant stage set for a fine collection of garden ornament, sculpture and boxwood topiary. The visitor's experience of the garden unfolds as pathways lead from garden room to garden room in a carefully orchestrated series of discoveries. The central portion of the garden is distinguished by two parallel garden spaces; the first is dominated by a long reflecting pool, terminated on the north end by a wisteria-covered arbor, and on the south end by a pebble mosaic terrace and fountain basin. One of the great surprises of the tour is the adjacent garden space. Bordered by a precisely clipped hornbeam hedge, the green architecture of this room is meant to frame the view to the Chinese pavilion (Ting dynasty), positioned on a small island in the middle of a pond teeming with koi... [Read full description online]

Sleepy Cat Farm
DIGGING DEEPER
4 – 5:30 PM
Garden Bounty
with Chef Seen Lippert
A shuttle will be provided
to the garden.
REGISTRATION: $70 Garden
Conservancy Members / $80 general

Seen Lippert is a chef at Chez Panisse restaurant in Berkeley, California and co-owner of Sleepy Cat Farm. Her demonstration class will focus on using the early fall harvest to the fullest, with little or no waste. Seen will share some delicious nibbles and easy basics to use all of your garden bounty with ease.

Registration required — space limited
Go to opendaysprogram.org
or call 1 (888) 842-2442

DIRECTIONS—For safety reasons, there is no parking this year along Clapboard Ridge Road. Instead, attendees will meet at Camp Simmons, 744 Lake Avenue, Greenwich. There will be signage indicating both Camp Simmons as well as Garden Conservancy signage. Once there, guests will be directed to parking, and board a shuttle van which will take you to the gardens, as well as pickup. The shuttle will operate from 10 a.m. to 4 p.m.

WILTON
PIXIE PERENNIALS
200 Nod Hill Road, Wilton
Hours: 10 a.m. to 4 p.m.
📷 | 2017| 🏷 PLANT SALES

Terraced perennial gardens with a wide variety of unusual plants surround a 1740 homestead set on four acres, overlooking a reservoir and home to mature and specimen trees. A small rock garden tucked into the exposed ledge leads to a fishpond. A frog pond is nestled in between rows of flowers. The property features peach trees, an old leaning apple tree, fig trees, kiwi, blueberry bushes, strawberries, raspberries, and a vegetable garden. The kitchen courtyard garden hosts shade-loving plants: *Hellebores, Brunnera, Heuchera, Ligularia*, shaped boxwoods, and other varieties of perennials that live nestled under a giant maple tree. Peonies border one length of the paddock fence, leading you to the lilac bushes. A back garden built around exposed stones showcases tall plants that can be seen from the house. In late summer a stand of *Perovskia* creates a blue backdrop for fall-flowering perennials. The garden is a work in progress, ever-changing from year to year. The "party barn" boasts quarter-sawn oak floors, and hosted town dances during Prohibition. Homegrown perennials and shrubs will be for sale on the back patio and adjacent areas. There will be a pop-up boutique in the barn featuring wonderful items for sale by local artisans.

DIRECTIONS—It is 0.9 mile up on the right from the intersection of Route 33/Ridge-field Road and Nod Hill Road.

Fairfield County
Saturday, October 13

Highmeadows—Linda Allard
156 Wykeham Road, Washington

DIGGING DEEPER
1 – 3 PM
An Autumn Afternoon
with Linda Allard
REGISTRATION: $60 Garden
Conservancy Members / $70 general

Join owner Linda Allard as she leads an intimate group through Highmeadows during one of her favorite moments in her extraordinary garden, a peak fall afternoon. She will talk about the design ideas and choice plants that make the autumn here so spectacular, as well as some of the sustainable techniques used to keep her garden so healthy and lush. Fruit trees framing a golden meadow will be laden with their colorful bounty, the layered plantings in the woodland garden will be decked in jewel tones, the enclosed potager will be filled with winter crops, and sweeping vistas of the Litchfield Hills will form a blazing backdrop to the entire property. Wine and light hors d'oeuvres will be served. (To read a description of Highmeadows, please go to page 99.)

Registration required — space limited
Go to opendaysprogram.org
or call 1 (888) 842-2442

PUBLIC GARDEN

Fairfield County
NEW CANAAN
WAVENY WALLED GARDEN AT WAVENY
HOUSE IN WAVENY PARK
677 South Avenue & Route 124
New Canaan
(203) 594-3600
Hours: April through October, daily, dawn
to dusk
Admission: Free

The Waveny Walled Garden was originally
designed by Frederick Law Olmsted's firm
as a formal rose garden. In 1995, the garden was redesigned as a Wedding Garden
by a committee of the New Canaan Garden
Club horticulture devotees. The design today incorporates roses in a long rose border along one side. The remaining three
sides, bordered by brick walks, showcase
deep herbaceous borders which include
perennials, small trees, flowering shrubs,
bulbs, and annuals. Three seasons of the
year this very special space is used weekly
for weddings and special events. In this
civic endeavor, the New Canaan Garden
Club collaborates with the Town Parks and
Recreation department. The Garden Club
is responsible for the weekly maintenance.

DIRECTIONS—From the Merritt Parkway/
Route 15, take Exit 37 and follow South
Avenue into town. Driveway entrance to
Waveny Park is on left. The garden is adjacent to Waveny House on the left. Ample
parking is available. Dogs must be on leads
at all times.

Our new book is now for sale online & via our website
www.smilandscapearchitecture.com

THE
MAKING
OF
THREE
GARDENS

Jorge Sánchez
SMI Landscape Architecture

Foreword by
The Duke of Devonshire

MERRELL

J.P. FRANZEN ASSOCIATES ARCHITECTS, P.C.

AWARD-WINNING ARCHITECTURE
LANDSCAPE ARCHITECTURE
PRESERVATION AND PLANNING

PROJECTS FROM MAINE TO HAWAII WITH
OFFICES IN SOUTHPORT AND FAIRFIELD, CONNECTICUT

Photo by Stacy Bass

203.259.0529
www.franzenarchitects.com
• MEMBERS OF THE AMERICAN INSTITUTE OF ARCHITECTS •

Washington D.C.
Sunday, June 10

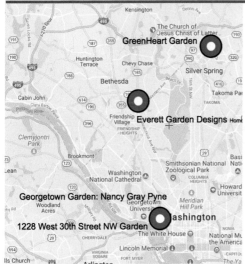

★There are additional gardens open on this date in nearby Montgomery County, MD. See page 146.

GEORGETOWN

1228 30TH STREET NW GARDEN
1228 30th Street NW, Georgetown
Hours: 10 a.m. to 4 p.m.
NEW

This tiny gem of a garden was designed originally by Perry Wheeler around 1960. In 2015, F2 Environmental Design redesigned this garden. The goal was to create a serene environment in this very narrow space. The renovation process started with excavating and amending the soil to create a natural nutrient cycling system that would not require the use of fertilizers and chemical amendments. Andrea Filippone and Eric T. Fleisher of F2ED limited their palette to fastigate hornbeam and boxwood. The hornbeams give great verticality while the boxwood is used as

a string of pearls underneath the trees. A gravel terrace was added and the small lawn surrounds the fountain. The garden now is maintained completely organically. Three boxwood cultivars are featured: *Buxus sempervirens* 'Fastigiata,' an upright cultivar which create a low privacy hedge on the gravel terrace; *Buxus microphylla* 'Grace Hendrick Phillips,' a beautiful dwarf boxwood located above the ivy covered stone wall; and *Buxus insularis sinica* 'Justin Brouwers,' lays like a string of pearls under the *Carpinus fastigiata* (fastigate hornbeam).

DIRECTIONS—The garden is located between M and N Streets in the historic neighborhood of Georgetown.

GEORGETOWN GARDEN: NANCY GRAY PYNE
1224 30th Street NW, Georgetown
Hours: 10 a.m. to 4 p.m.
📷 | 2016

A journey through this secret garden in the heart of Georgetown takes the visitor up a series of formal terraced gardens and past a number of outbuildings that include a library, two greenhouses, and a freestanding theater. It culminates in a decorative walled vegetable garden designed and planted by *Washington Post* garden writer, Adrian Higgins. The garden had been assembled over the course of a century or more, but it was given its character in the 1930s as one of the major Washington projects of a pioneering landscape architect named Rose Greely. The main terrace is a walled garden perched above the house. Its most animated feature, a geometric fountain, is aligned with both the rear entrance of the house and, at right angles to it, a rectangular lawn framed by a path and boxwood plantings. The upper garden functions as its own formal garden of shrubs and small trees, as well as an entrance for the theater, known as the playhouse, and the larger greenhouse (and potting shed). The upper garden is also a place of paths. One leads to a parking lot at the end of an alley...[Read full description online]

DIRECTIONS—The garden is located between M and N Streets in the historic neighborhood of Georgetown.

Georgetown Garden: Nancy Gray Pyne

DIGGING DEEPER
12 PM
Boxwood for the Future
REGISTRATION: $30 Garden Conservancy Members / $35 general

Andrea Filippone is a boxwood expert who is on a crusade to get people to move beyond the sickly standard English and American box varieties to embrace lesser-known hybrids that are elegant and agreeably pungent, but better garden plants. The latest influx of the boxwood blight, *Cylindrocladium buxicola*, emphasizes the need for a shift to new hybrids and new, organic

cultural practices. With proper soil management, the use of cultivars specifically chosen for the site, and the absence of chemical fertilizers and pesticides, the plants will thrive in their new location for years to come. Andrea and Eric T. Fleischer operate a boxwood nursery at their home as well as F2 Environmental Design.

Registration required — space limited
Go to opendaysprogram.org
or call 1 (888) 842-2442

Georgetown Garden: Nancy Gray Pyne

DIGGING DEEPER
1 PM
Compost Tea for Healthy Soil and Healthy Gardens
REGISTRATION: $30 Garden Conservancy Members / $35 general

In 2011, Nancy Gray Pyne hired the New Jersey-based firm, F2 Environmental Design. Andrea Filippone is a boxwood expert who is on a crusade to get people to move beyond the sickly standard English and American box varieties to embrace lesser-known hybrids that are elegant and agreeably pungent, but better garden plants. Eric T. Fleischer is the organic guru in the firm, who believes that the basis of all successful gardening is an understanding and nurturing of the soil biosphere. Healthy soil is rich in beneficial bacteria and fungi, some of which work directly with plant roots to nourish and protect their symbionts. Fleisher explained that some of these microbes are eaten by tiny creatures which release nitrogen as they feed. This is a system that relies on good soil structure, lots of choice compost incorporated into the earth, and the absence of chemical fertilizers and pesticides.

Registration required — space limited
Go to opendaysprogram.org
or call 1 (888) 842-2442

FLORIDA
Jacksonville
Saturday, April 14

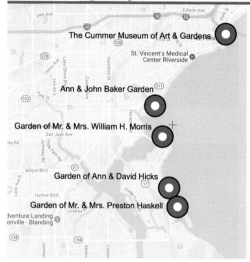

★ Start your day at Cummer Museum of Art & Gardens, 829 Riverside Avenue, Jacksonville, 10 a.m. to 4 p.m. Admission: free for Open Days visitors when purchasing a day pass.

OUR PARTNER IN FLORIDA

Cummer Museum of Art & Gardens

This Open Day is part of the Cummer Museum of Art & Gardens year-round garden programming. The Museum celebrates its historic gardens through a variety of garden-related programs throughout the year for visitors of all ages. This year's activities include tours, lectures, concerts, workshops, and more.

www.opendaysprogram.org

Duval County
JACKSONVILLE
ANN & JOHN BAKER GARDEN
3710 Richmond Street, Jacksonville
Hours: 12 p.m. to 4 p.m.
NEW

Anne and John Baker spent their early years of marriage living in the Avondale neighborhood of Jacksonville. When an opportunity came their way to buy an empty property on the river in Avondale, they purchased it. The Bakers began to create a home and garden that would look as if they had always been there. David Case of Richard Skinner & Associates designed their home while Sunscapes Landscape Design's Gerry Crouch and Judy Drake created the gardens. John Baker requested that live oak trees be planted on the nearly treeless property. A signature oak has replaced the large live oak at the property's entry, damaged by Hurricane Irma in September 2017. Anne Baker always wanted a white garden in the style of the old gardens of the southeast. At the garden entry are an inviting courtyard and fountain, a seating area, and pots filled with seasonal flowers. *Ligustrum* hedges provide privacy for the entire garden site...[Read full description online]

DIRECTIONS—From the Cummer Museum, go south (left) on Riverside Avenue. Turn left onto King Street, at hospital. Turn right (south) on St. Johns Avenue. Turn left on Shadowlawn Avenue. Turn left on Richmond Street.

IN THE GARDEN

FEBRUARY 2 THROUGH APRIL 22

From famous public spaces to the simplest home vegetable garden, and from worlds imagined by artists to food production recorded by journalists, this exhibition broadens our understanding of how photography has been used to record gardens and document humans' relationship to nature.

Organized by the George Eastman Museum

For more information, visit **cummermuseum.org**.

CUMMER MUSEUM

ART | GARDENS | EDUCATION

GARDEN OF ANN & DAVID HICKS
4705 Ortega Boulevard, Jacksonville
Hours: 12 p.m. to 4 p.m.
2016

In 1991, two riverfront properties and houses were joined, creating one family house and garden. Mary Palmer Dargan of Dargan Landscape Architects (Atlanta, Georgia) was engaged to integrate the grounds. In keeping with the formal Colonial Revival style of the "new" house, Dargan created terraces and private garden rooms on the front, shaded side of the property. A walk through an arched pergola along the side of the property opens to a sunny, expansive view of the St. Johns River. A classical arbor with limestone columns overlooks an oval lawn and a lovely terraced parterre rose garden, reached by a set of English steps. Judy Drake and Gerry Crouch of Sunscapes Landscape Design installed the garden in 1995 and have maintained and augmented it for twenty years.

DIRECTIONS—Driving south on Route 17/ Roosevelt Boulevard, turn left onto Verona and then right onto Ortega Boulevard.

GARDEN OF MR. & MRS. PRESTON HASKELL
4971 Morven Road, Jacksonville
Hours: 12 p.m. to 4 p.m.
2016

The Haskell gardens comprise three acres of lush plantings, a contemporary house, and fourteen large abstract outdoor sculptures that are integrated into the landscape. The initial design for the riverfront property was created by landscape architect Wayne O. Manning, Jr., *circa* 1978. The landscape scheme for the property includes medium-density woods of live oaks and magnolias, with screening shrub-bery including *Viburnum*, holly, *Ligustrum*, anise, and oleaster. The road to the west is screened by a tall multi-layered hedge with azaleas, Sago palms, and holly ferns planted in the foreground. Curving hedges of varying heights define spaces within the property and set off the outdoor sculpture. A lawn opens to St. Johns River on the east side of the estate. Other plantings include *Aspidistra, Pittosporum, Podocarpus*, and *Ilex*, while Jasmine covers an arbor and the fences around the tennis court. Ground-covers include *Liriope, Juniper*, and mondograss. Flowering annuals are added for color.

DIRECTIONS—Driving south on Route 17/ Roosevelt Boulevard, turn left onto Verona. Then turn right onto Ortega Boulevard. Continue and turn left onto Morven Road.

GARDEN OF MR. & MRS. WILLIAM H. MORRIS
3700 Oak Point Avenue, Jacksonville
Hours: 12 p.m. to 4 p.m.
2016

This property was purchased as a vacant lot in 1996. Over the next few years, plans for the gardens and house were developed. Construction was completed in 2003. Formal gardens surround the English Baroque-style house, with more natural gardens away from the house. It is one of the few riverfront properties without a bulkhead, which allows for a natural transition to the river. A number of water features complement the riverside setting of the gardens, which were designed and laid out by the owners. The gardens provide a setting for a collection of outdoor sculptures that the owners have collected over the years. The gardens continue to evolve as the owners visit other gardens on their travels.

DIRECTIONS—Driving south on Route 17/ Roosevelt Boulevard, turn left onto Verona. Then turn left onto Ortega Boulevard. The garden is on the right on Oak Point Avenue.

PUBLIC GARDEN PARTNER

Duval County
JACKSONVILLE
THE CUMMER MUSEUM OF ART & GARDENS

829 Riverside Avenue, Jacksonville
(904) 356-6857
cummermuseum.org/visit

★ Start your tour here on Saturday, April 14, 10 a.m. to 4 p.m. Tickets and maps will be available here.

Hours: Special Garden Conservancy Open Day Saturday, April 14, 10 a.m. to 4 p.m. (regular Saturday hours). Otherwise, Tuesday 10 a.m. to 9 p.m.; Wednesday through Saturday 10 a.m. to 4 p.m.; Sunday, 12 p.m. to 4 p.m. Closed Mondays and July 4th, Thanksgiving, Christmas Eve & Christmas Day, New Years Eve & New Years Day.
Admission: $30 which includes access to the museum's historic gardens as well as the five private gardens. The Museum is free on Tuesdays from 4 p.m. to 9 p.m. and the first Saturday of every month. Otherwise $10 adults, $6 seniors (62+), military, and students (with ID). Children 5 and under free. College students with ID free Tuesday through Friday.

The Cummer Gardens, acknowledged by the National Register of Historic Places, have a fascinating history and bear the imprint of some of the foremost names in landscape design and horticulture, including Ossian Cole Simonds, Ellen Biddle Shipman, Thomas Meehan and Sons, and the fabled Olmsted firm. The Museum's two-and-one-half acres of historic gardens are unique examples of early twentieth-century garden design, featuring reflecting pools, fountains, arbors, antique ornaments, and sculptures. The majestic Cummer Oak has a canopy of more than 150 feet and is one of the oldest trees in Jacksonville.

DIRECTIONS—Travelling north on I-95 South, take Exit 352A. Take ramp right for Forest Street toward Riverside Avenue. Turn left onto Forest Street. Turn right onto Route 211S/Riverside Avenue. Bear right onto Route 211/Riverside Avenue. Museum is on left.
—Travelling south on I-95 North, take Exit 351A. Take ramp right and follow signs for Park Street. Turn left onto Park Street. Turn left onto Riverside Park Place. Turn right onto Riverside Avenue. Museum is on left. Museum parking is available on Riverside Avenue (directly across from the Museum), with an additional lot on the corner of Riverside Avenue and Post Street.

ILLINOIS
Chicago's North Shore
Sunday, May 20

Gardens of Nicole Williams and Larry Becker, 11 Rockgate Lane, Glencoe

DIGGING DEEPER
3 – 5 PM
Visions of Nature
REGISTRATION: $60 Garden Conservancy Members / $70 general

Nicole Williams and Larry Becker garden on a dramatic, largely wooded site bounded by a sharp drop in grade, and a ravine running to Lake Michigan filled with rare native plants. Their overarching goals are to celebrate these natural features, and create a harmonious setting where interior and exterior spaces flow together. To accomplish this, they turned for inspiration to Japanese gardens and architecture, as well as to Jens Jensen's respect for the lines and native plants of the Midwest. While different, these aesthetics celebrate the experience of being in nature. The result is a house and series of gardens that sit comfortably and naturally on the site, and draw visitors through an appreciation of each aspect of its distinctive character. The house, which abuts the ravine, was remodeled in a Japanese mode, and is surrounded by Japanese-style gardens. Gardens further from the house are more naturalistic. There remains a small bridge from the historic Hermann Paepcke estate, which was designed by Jens Jensen. Surrounding the remnants of a stone porch now serving as the upper terrace, meadow and boulder gardens, as well as native woodlands, flow down the slope to a birch grove adjacent to a traditional Japanese bridge and teahouse. Spend a very special afternoon with Nicole and Larry as they narrate their garden visions during a walking exploration of the site, and share wine and hors d'oeuvres with an intimate group of guests.

Registration required — space limited
Go to opendaysprogram.org
or call 1 (888) 842-2442

Chicago's North Shore
Saturday, June 23

Cook County
WINNETKA
GOTHIC VICTORIAN GARDEN
Winnetka
NEW
Hours: 10 a.m. to 4 p.m.

My house was built in 1860, with an addition constructed around 2003, and I have been working on the gardens since then. I have beautiful oaks in the front yard that complement the house—they are both more than 100 years old! I have a courtyard garden with a conservatory, and a weeping beech. In the backyard I have an herb/lavender-themed garden, and a perennial garden (both designed by Craig Bergmann Landscape Design). I have a beautiful shade garden, and a twenty-yard-long pool and a poolhouse.

DIRECTIONS—At the request of the garden host, directions will be provided by calling the Garden Conservancy office toll-free weekdays, 9 a.m. to 5 p.m. EST, 1 (888) 842-2442.

Chicago's North Shore
Sunday, June 24

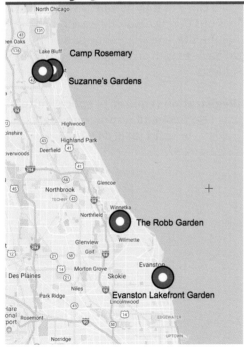

Cook County
EVANSTON
EVANSTON LAKEFRONT GARDEN
707 Sheridan Road, Evanston
Hours: 10 a.m. to 4 p.m.
📷 | ♿PARTIAL | **2017**

With a stone fountain at its center, the front garden of this lovingly restored Queen Anne house is an exuberant flowering tapestry that is only a foretaste of what is to come, upon passing through the garden gates. As visitors follow the brick drive around the side of the house beneath a hedge of hybrid dogwoods, their first view of this expansive lakefront garden is framed by a magnificent poplar tree of monumental proportions. Four hundred feet in the distance, an open garden pavilion beckons from atop a lakefront dune at the end of a carpet of manicured lawn. The journey to the lake passes a formal koi pond, fabulous pieces of Southeast Asian garden art, a naturalistic white birch grove, a bubbling fountain, and a collection of linked gardens featuring Japanese maples, hydrangeas, roses, and rhododendrons tied together by an ever-changing combination of perennials, grasses, and groundcovers. A water garden that is home to an extensive collection of marginal plants and generations of goldfish terminates the view and fronts the lakefront pavilion and adjoining beach house. At the lake, quartzite revetments and a breakwater protect a private beach planted with dune grasses, colorful sedums, roses, and sculptural Japanese white pines. Relax, have a seat, and take in the aquamarine view.

DIRECTIONS—From the Edens Expressway, exit at Dempster Street. Travel east on Dempster Street 4.1 miles toward Ridge Avenue. Turn right onto Ridge Avenue and head south 1 mile to Main Street. Turn left onto Main Street toward Sheridan Road. Main Street will turn into Sheridan Road. Follow Sheridan Road to #707 (on lakeside of Sheridan Road)
—From Lake Shore Drive, take the Hollywood Exit and turn onto Sheridan Road, heading north. Take Sheridan Road 4.2 miles to #707.

WINNETKA
THE ROBB GARDEN
23 Indian Hill Road, Winnetka
Hours: 10 a.m. to 4 p.m.
📷 | 2015

The Robb Garden, featuring native Midwest shrubs and perennials and large bluestone/fieldstone/paving brick hardscapes, is designed to create complementary views surrounding a re-designed contemporary house by architect Paul Konstant. Oehme and van Sweden originally designed the garden to highlight native grasses and flowers. The garden was installed and has been maintained by Rocco Fiore and Sons, Inc. The garden's mosaic "quilt" pattern of colors and textures changes throughout the year. A dramatic granite sculpture by Jesus Bautista Moroles, "Ellipse," bridges the transition from the large bluestone terrace to the contemporary interior spaces of the house. Located in an old shagbark hickory and swamp white oak grove, the garden is bordered by white pine, hemlock, and Norway spruce, providing both privacy from Indian Hill Road and informal framing of the garden features. Introduced trees and shrubs include Norway maple, sugar maple, saucer and star magnolia, Japanese lilac, hawthorn, hemlock, Kousa dogwood, flowering crabapple, *Viburnum*, hydrangea, forsythia, boxwood, and witch hazel... [Read full description online]

DIRECTIONS—From the Edens Expressway/I-94 North, exit at Willow Road East and follow to Hibbard Road. Turn right and go south on Hibbard Road to Hill Road. Turn left and go east on Hill Road to stop sign at Locust Street. Continue across Locust east to a small bend in Hill Road. Just past the bend, turn right onto Indian Hill Road. Number 23 is the third house on right, just past the first stop sign on Indian Hill Road.
—From the Edens Expressway/I-94 South, exit at Lake Avenue East. Take Lake Avenue to Hibbard Road. Turn left and go north on Hibbard to Hill Road. Turn right and go east on Hill Road to stop sign at Locust Street. Proceed as directed above. Please park only along the east side (golf course side) of Indian Hill Road, as marked.

Lake County
LAKE FOREST
SUZANNE'S GARDENS
283 West Laurel Avenue, Lake Forest
Hours: 10 a.m. to 4 p.m.
📷 | ♿ | **2016**

Situated adjacent to the Lake Forest Open Lands, Suzanne's Gardens transition seamlessly from native vegetation to more formal perennial beds. Here, you'll find indigenous plants that flow from the neighboring prairie and woodlands to mix with non-natives that are typical of more traditional European gardens. Plant selection has concentrated on ensuring that non-natives remain in aesthetic and ecological harmony with the conservation lands. Healthy land stewardship has been a priority throughout.

DIRECTIONS—From the intersection of Green Bay Road and Deerpath Road, go north about 0.25 mile on Green Bay Road to Laurel Avenue. Turn left and go west on Laurel Avenue. Please park on Laurel near the "T" with Private Lane. Go south on Private Lane to #283.

Camp Rosemary
DIGGING DEEPER
3 – 5 PM
Garden Enchantment—An Afternoon at Camp Rosemary
REGISTRATION: $90 Garden Conservancy Members / $100 general
Address will only be sent to registered guests

Spend an extraordinary Sunday afternoon in one of the nation's most spectacular private gardens, Posy Krehbiel's Camp Rosemary. This ex-

pansive Lake Forest estate, designed by Rose Standish Nichols in the 1920s and later enhanced by other prominent landscape designers, includes an array of captivating garden rooms, a lush wooded ravine garden, and an exquisite pool house.

Marion Brenner

Head gardener, Marya Padour, will lead visitors through this intensely and imaginatively cultivated oasis, discussing historic garden elements, features Posy Krehbiel has added over the years, and the expert horticultural techniques used to make this garden shine. In addition to visual riches, guests will be lavished with attention, from valet parking to wine and hors d'oeuvres while exploring the garden. This very special experience is not to be missed.

Registration required — space limited
Go to opendaysprogram.org
or call 1 (888) 842-2442

Chicago's North Shore
Sunday, July 22

Lake County
HIGHLAND PARK
HIGHLAND PARK RESIDENCE

1057 Lincoln Avenue South,
Highland Park
Hours: 10 a.m. to 4 p.m.
📷 | ♿PARTIAL | **2015**

A sweeping driveway and naturalistic planting of bold masses of *Spirea* and hydrangea create a subtle plinth for this refined white Georgian house set on a raised knoll in a quiet sun-dappled neighborhood. A hint of classic English formality is established around the architectural details and access points of the house. Boxwood hedges, juneberry, espaliered crabapple, pachysandra, and dimensioned bluestone paths lead you through each garden room. Sweeping and undulating lawn panels layered with purpleleaf wintercreeper create a solid composition along with sequence of spaces unified by a clear sense of movement and vistas terminating into modern and antique focal points that include garden benches, a fountain, staddle stones, and classically inspired raised urns

dripping with seasonal annuals. Taking advantage of the existing change in elevation, a raised bluestone terrace frames a screened pavilion for entertaining. Stone walls and wide graceful steps lead down to a formal allée of Armstrong maples accented and framed by white lattice panels and perennial gardens, creating a playful contrast to the surrounding landscape borders. Long and short sight lines and axial line movement clearly articulate and frame a garden that displays "art in harmony with Nature."

DIRECTIONS—From Chicago, take North Lasalle Street toward West Randolph Street. Turn left onto West Randolph Street. Take ramp right and follow signs for I-94 West/I-90 West. Keep right onto I-94 W/Edens Expressway. Keep left onto Route 41 North/Edens Expressway. Take ramp right and follow signs for Clavey Road. Turn right onto Clavey Road. Turn left onto Green Bay Road. Turn right onto Roger Williams Avenue. Bear left onto Dean Avenue. Turn left onto Cedar Avenue. Continue to #1057 Lincoln Avenue South.
—From Milwaukee, take ramp left for Route 41 South/I-43 South/I-94 East toward Chicago. Keep left onto I-94 East/Route 41 South. Take ramp right and follow signs for Route 60. Turn left onto Route 60. Bear right onto Route 60 E/West Kennedy Road. Bear right onto Route 60/West Kennedy Road. Turn right onto Route 41 South/South Skokie Highway. Take ramp right and follow signs for East Central Avenue. Keep straight onto Central Avenue. Turn right onto St Johns Avenue. Bear left onto Sheridan Road. Turn right onto Cedar Avenue. Continue to 1057 Lincoln Avenue South.

LAKE FOREST
THE GARDENS AT 900
1065 Acorn Trail, Lake Forest
Hours: 10 a.m. to 4 p.m.
♿PARTIAL | **2017**

The Gardens at 900 are a sensitive renovation and interpretation of the original entry building complex and gardens of Elawa Farm. Originally designed by architect David Adler in 1917 for A. Watson and Elsa Armour, the buildings had been abandoned for nearly a decade before being acquired by Craig Bergmann and Paul Klug. Used as both private residence and the design offices for Bergmann and Klug, the buildings and garden areas regard the history of the site, while also fostering creativity. Formal borders, a shade garden, an orchard laden with old roses, a swimming pool garden, and a motor court constitute the garden today. A relatively young garden (2010), The Gardens at 900 is an excellent example of how quickly a landscape can be transformed with a focused, collaborative vision.

DIRECTIONS—From Waukegan Road/Route 43, the garden is 2.7 miles north of Route 60, 1.4 miles north of Deerpath Road. At the traffic light for Middlefork Drive/Westmoreland Road, turn west onto Middlefork Drive and take the first left onto Acorn Trail. Please park on the street and walk down the designated path at #1065.

METTAWA
METTAWA MANOR
25779 St. Mary's Road, Mettawa
Hours: 10 a.m. to 4 p.m.
📷 | **2017**

The house and grounds were built in 1927 as a family compound. Donna LaPietra and Bill Kurtis are only the second owners in the manor's rich history and have been working for the past twenty-three years to refurbish some garden areas and create new ones. The centerpiece is a walled English-style garden with forty-foot perennial borders on either side of a sunken lawn that leads to a spring walk and rose room centered on an old fountain. Outside the east gate is a golden garden and an orchard/meadow bordered by a fenced *potager*, cutting garden, and circular herb garden. The sixty-five-acre property has two ponds, a fifteen-acre prairie, and a parkland of specimen trees; it is surrounded by a newly reclaimed oak-hickory forest. The most recent additions include a silver garden, a bronze garden, an ornamental lily pool, aqua-theatre, a three-tiered mound, a grass labyrinth with central fire pit with a tree house overlook, and a shrubbery with island beds. This year's Open Day will be celebrated with activities and festivities throughout the grounds, such as a club-car guided tour of the restored native prairie and beehives, and a honey tasting as well as all-day refreshments on the terrace, which will include a sampling of local and sustainable foods. There will also be separately ticketed house tours (tickets are limited and all proceeds go to the Garden Conservancy).

DIRECTIONS—Take I-94 / Edens Expressway to Route 41. Exit at Route 60 West, go 3 miles to St. Mary's Road, and turn left just past horse stables to Open Days signs on left of St. Mary's Road, marking driveway entrance.

Mettawa Manor

DIGGING DEEPER

10 AM – 4 PM
(Bee activities 1 PM – 2:30 PM)
A Day-Long Garden Celebration
Free with garden admission

Longtime Open Days hosts, Bill Kurtis and Donna LaPietra, invite guests of all ages to spend the day touring their extraordinary garden and enjoying many special activities.

Prairie Tours: Walk or join Bill on a club car ride to explore twenty acres of Midwest tall grass prairie in full bloom. Terrace Tastings: Enjoy local, artisanal treats and learn more about green markets and environmentally conscious food choices. Garden Selfies: A photographic and video exhibit of this garden through the seasons, plus pointers on better smart phone photos. The Buzz: To bring back pollinators, Mettawa Manor has three beehives which produce more than 100 pounds of honey each year. A beekeeper will show how the hives work, and visitors can sample "Bill's Bees Mettawa Prairie Honey."

Camp Rosemary

DIGGING DEEPER

3 – 5 PM
Garden Enchantment—An
Afternoon at Camp Rosemary
REGISTRATION: $90 Garden
Conservancy Members / $100 general
Address will only be sent to
registered guests

Marion Brenner

Spend an extraordinary Sunday afternoon in one of the nation's most spectacular private gardens, Posy Krehbiel's Camp Rosemary. This expansive Lake Forest estate, designed by Rose Standish Nichols in the 1920s and later enhanced by other prominent landscape designers, includes an array of captivating garden rooms, a lush wooded ravine garden, and an exquisite pool house. Head gardener, Marya Padour, will lead visitors through this intensely and imaginatively cultivated oasis, discussing historic garden elements, features Posy Krehbiel has added over the years, and the expert horticultural techniques used to make this garden shine. In addition to visual riches, guests will be lavished with attention, from valet parking to wine and hors d'oeuvres while exploring the garden. This very special experience is not to be missed.

West Chicago
Sunday, August 5

Du Page County
WEST CHICAGO
THE GARDENS AT BALL

622 Town Road, West Chicago
Hours: 10 a.m. to 4 p.m.
📷 | ♿ | **2017**

Guests will enjoy the opportunity to visit The Gardens at Ball, usually reserved for the wholesale customers of the 112-year-old Ball Horticultural Company, a world leader in the breeding, production, distribution, and marketing of horticultural products. There will be more than ten acres of gardens to view, including *Calibrachoa* container trials with more than 200 varieties, and coleus trials featuring the top new introductions from recent years. Thousands of annual, perennial, and vegetable varieties will be showcased in beds, containers, and baskets along with flowers and vegetables in the All-America Selections evaluation trials. Guides will be available throughout the day to give garden tours and answer questions. Allow two or more hours to visit these exceptional gardens. Portable toilets will be available for guests.

DIRECTIONS—Turn north onto Town Road off Roosevelt Road/Route 38 in West Chicago. Watch for signs to turn left into the parking and main garden entrance just north of the main building complex.

PUBLIC GARDENS

Cook County
EVANSTON
THE SHAKESPEARE GARDEN
Northwestern University, Garrett Place/2133 Sheridan Road, Evanston
(847) 332-1159
www.thegardenclubofevanston.org/html/gardens.php
Hours: Year round, daily, dawn to 11 p.m.
Admission: Free. The Shakespeare Garden is open to the public, but special tours and events may be scheduled.

Shakespeare Garden is nestled in a quiet central section of Northwestern University, on Garrett Place, behind Howes Memorial Chapel, hidden from view by a double wall of hawthorn hedges. The 70-by-100-foot garden was established a century ago, during WWI in 1915, as a project of The Garden Club of Evanston. Members wished to express wartime sympathy for our British allies and to commemorate the 300th anniversary of Shakespeare's death. It was a way to celebrate the ties between England and America, as promoted by the Drama League of America. The Shakespeare Garden was designed by renowned Danish-American landscape architect and conservationist Jens Jensen (1860-1951). The flowers, shrubs, trees and herbs in the garden are mentioned in Shakespeare's plays and are varieties best suited to the garden's location and Midwestern climate. The Shakespeare Garden still contains many of the original hawthorns that were started from seed in France and which form the formal garden's base. The hawthorns of Jensen's plan and the fact that it represents the type of project that flourished in 1916 are the reasons the Shakespeare Garden was listed on the National Register of Historic Places in 1988. At the entrance to the garden, is a stone fountain and bench, with a bronze plaque and relief sculpture, designed and donated in 1930 by architect Hubert Burnham, son of internationally known Chicago architect Daniel H. Burnham, in memory of his mother, Margaret Sherman Burnham, an early Shakespeare Garden chairman. Following a visit in 1990, John Brookes, a distinguished English garden designer and writer, suggested a few changes that are now reflected in the garden. In 2016, in honor of its Centennial, the garden underwent a major renovation/restoration, a collaborative effort funded by a gift from Northwestern University, which received the Historic Preservation award from the Illinois chapter of the American Society of Landscape Architects. The garden continues to be maintained by The Garden Club of Evanston members, and is integral to campus life at Northwestern University. It is the site of numerous marriage proposals and weddings each year.

DIRECTIONS—The lakeshore suburb of Evanston is north of Chicago, the first town beyond the city limit. Take Sheridan Road to Garrett Place, Northwestern University campus, directly east of the Ford Motor Company Engineering Design Center at 2133 Sheridan Road, hidden from view by a double wall of hawthorn hedges, north of Garrett Seminary's Howes Memorial Chapel.

Cook County
GLENCOE
CHICAGO BOTANIC GARDEN
1000 Lake Cook Road, Glencoe
(847) 835-5440
www.chicagobotanic.org
Hours: Year round, daily, 8 a.m. to dusk, with extended summer and winter holiday season hours
Admission: Free; parking fees apply
Located 0.5 mile east of Edens Expressway/Route 41 on Lake Cook Road.

The Chicago Botanic Garden, one of the treasures of the Forest Preserve District of Cook County, is a 385-acre living plant museum featuring twenty-seven distinct display gardens surrounded by lakes, as well as four natural areas. The Garden's programs educate visitors of all ages about plants and the natural world, from day campers to high school students, to certificate, Masters and PhD students, to lifelong learners. The Regenstein Center houses the Plant Information Service, exhibition halls, and the Lenhardt Library and Greenhouses. The Plant Conservation Science Center houses the Green Roof Garden and Visitor Gallery with interactive interpretation of the plant research being done behind the scenes.

MARYLAND
Frederick County
Saturday, June 2

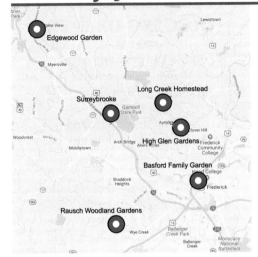

Frederick County
FREDERICK
BASFORD FAMILY GARDEN
144 Kline Boulevard, Frederick
Hours: 10 a.m. to 4 p.m.
📷 | ♿ | **NEW**

As you enter our retreat over a curved river-stone pathway, you will notice the many shade-loving plants that surround the entire garden. Included are dogwoods, hollies, hydrangeas, azaleas, and *Aucuba* and many others. At the gardens center is a brick patio accented by a cascading water feature. Between the street and the Cape Cod-style home, there stands a majestic black oak, said to be at least 130 years of age, transplanted in 1951 from Maryland's Eastern Shore.

DIRECTIONS—From US I-5 North or South, take Rosemont Avenue to Patrick Street,

East. At the first traffic light, take a left onto Kline Boulevard and go approximately 1 mile to residence on right. Parking on both sides of street.

HIGH GLEN GARDENS
6450 Christophers Crossing, Frederick
Hours: 10 a.m. to 4 p.m.
📷 | **2017**

High Glen Gardens is a young, sixty-four-acre estate at the base of the Catoctin Mountains with approximately ten acres of impressive formal gardens, including a large perennial border, a rose garden, koi pond, Japanese garden, Mediterranean garden, and an English cottage-style garden. There are also extensive perimeter plantings and open fields, as well as newly restored natural areas that include a wet meadow. As part of a master plan created in 2013, High Glen Gardens is developing many new gardens, including a grand allée of bur oaks, an earth sculpture of warm-season grasses, and a woodland reforestation.

High Glen Gardens
DIGGING DEEPER
10 AM – 4 PM
Guided garden tours
Free with garden admission

Peter Couchman, Executive Director, and the staff of High Glen Gardens will offer free, hourly guided tours of the formal gardens as well as the natural

areas under development, such as the wetland, woodland, and earth sculptures.

DIRECTIONS—From Route 15, which runs through Frederick, take the Rosemont Avenue exit, heading about 2 miles west on Rosemont (away from downtown Frederick), passing Fort Detrick on the right. Rosemont becomes Yellow Springs Road immediately after Fort Detrick. At the intersection of Christophers Crossing, turn left. We are the first driveway on the right (mailbox #6450) about 0.125 mile down. Once you turn into the driveway, proceed past the house toward the adjacent barn. Someone will be there to direct you to the parking area.

LONG CREEK HOMESTEAD
8955 Indian Springs Road, Frederick
Hours: 10 a.m. to 4 p.m.
📷 | ♿PARTIAL | **NEW** | 🏷PLANT SALES

Long Creek Homestead sits on twenty-five acres of mixed woodland, food forests, and gardens. It celebrates more than 100 varieties of fruits and useful perennials. Landscapes are ecologically designed to harvest rainwater, build soil, and balance insect populations. Living willow dome

and circular straw-bale home is open to explore. A small on-site nursery will be open and selling paw paws, elderberries, chokeberries, juneberries, ornamental willows, inoculated mushroom logs, etc.

Long Creek Homestead
DIGGING DEEPER
3 PM
Edible Landscaping with a Permaculture Twist
Free with garden admission

Join Michael Judd, permaculture teacher, ecological garden designer, and author of *Edible Landscaping with a Permaculture Twist*, for a tour of his homestead. Often used as his outdoor classroom, this private landscape includes several food forests, raised bed swales, and hugelkultur raised beds, that passively harvest water and create microclimates to boost food production. A range of fruits, nuts, vegetables and medicinals are grown across the site.

DIRECTIONS—Parking at Brook Hill Church, 8946 Indian Springs Road, Frederick. Volunteer will direct visitors down a lane to the gardens and house. Visitors with handicap needs can drive directly to the gardens.

RAUSCH WOODLAND GARDENS
5527 Woodlyn Road, Frederick
Hours: 10 a.m. to 4 p.m.
📷 | ♿PARTIAL | **NEW**

The Rauschs purchased their home on one acre of land in 1979. The home is located west of Frederick in a second-growth mixed woodland with red, white, and black oaks, tulip poplars, and beech. Over the ensuing thirty-nine years, the Rauschs have transformed their yard into a woodland wonderland with wandering paths leading to azaleas, rhododendrons, hydrangeas, and tree peonies anchoring mixed borders of ferns, hellebores, hostas, wild ginger, wildflowers, and ephemerals, and chainsaw-carved stumps. The gardens provide year-round interest and beauty. They actively compost leaves and garden trimmings to improve the soil and promote organic practices.

DIRECTIONS—Take Alt US 40 west from Frederick, and turn right on Maryland Avenue in Braddock Heights. Turn right on Jefferson Boulevard, then drive 3 miles and take a left on Woodlyn Road. Curve left and go down hill to #5527 on your right.

MIDDLETOWN
SURREYBROOKE
8610 Baltimore National Pike
Middletown
Hours: 10 a.m. to 4 p.m.
📷 | ♿PARTIAL | **2017** | 🏷PLANT SALES

Surreybrooke is nestled in beautiful Middletown Valley. Over the past four decades the property has been transformed from a dairy farm to the lovingly tended gardens that flourish today. Herbaceous borders, dwarf conifers, and a scented garden surround the historically restored outbuildings. Native plantings encircle three earthen ponds that empty into the creek as it meanders through the center of the twenty-acre garden. Specimen trees and deciduous shrubs dot the rolling landscapes. Terraces, artful pergolas, and garden rooms are accessed by brick pathways. Guest are invited to enter the 1860s farmhouse and private gardens that surround the home. Visitors may bring lunch to eat in our back pavilion.

Surreybrooke
DIGGING DEEPER
10 AM – 4 PM
Guided tours
Free with garden admission

Staff members will lead informative discussions on the plantings as well as the history of the gardens, outbuildings, and the Civil War-era house. Special attention will be given to the unique collection of plants.

DIRECTIONS—From Baltimore, take I-70 to Exit 53B/Route 15 North. Take Exit 13B/Route 40 West. Proceed 6.5 miles, past Gambrill State Park. Surreybrooke is on left.
—From Washington, DC, take I-270 to Exit 13B/Route 40 West. Proceed 6.5 miles. Surreybrooke is on left.
—From Hagerstown, take Route 40 East towards Frederick for 7 miles past Greenbriar Sate Park. Surreybrooke is on right. Park in special events parking lot. There will be someone to direct you.

MYERSVILLE
EDGEWOOD GARDEN

10813 Baltimore National Pike
Myersville
Hours: 10 a.m. to 4 p.m.
📷 | **NEW**

Edgewood private gardens of Jeff, Tina, Emilee, and Ida Mae, is comprised of fifteen-and-one-half acres and fifteen gardens, a field, and a woodland with natures trails. The house was built in 1986, and the gardens were started shortly after. There is a cottage garden with a winding stone path ending at a small log cabin, with hydrangea trees, perennials, shrubs, and more. There are annuals interspersed throughout the gardens. Included in the design are three water features, a shade garden, and a rock garden. Sheds on the property were all built from reclaimed lumber. All the gardens were designed, planted, and maintained by owners of the property. Edgewood has been featured in *Country Gardens, Cottage Garden, Frederick and Hagerstown Magazine*, and Maryland's House and Garden Tour.

DIRECTIONS—From Baltimore/Washington, D.C., go west on I-70 to Exit 42 Myersville/Route 17 North and bear right to Myersville. Bear right on Route 17 North and go 0.5 mile to stoplight. Turn left onto Route 40 West/Baltimore National Pike and go 2 miles. The garden will be on your right.
—From the west: Take Route 40 East/Baltimore National Pike towards Myersville. Go 1 mile into Frederick County, passing the Appalachian Trailhead. Garden is on left past Pleasant Walk Road; second driveway.

District of Columbia Area
Sunday, June 10

★There are additional gardens open on this date in nearby District of Columbia. See page 126.

Montgomery County
CHEVY CHASE
EVERETT GARDEN DESIGNS
HOME GARDEN

3 Newlands Street, Chevy Chase
Hours: 10 a.m. to 4 p.m.
📷 | ♿PARTIAL | **NEW**

This garden is the home and studio of Everett Garden Designs and beautifully demonstrates how space can be divided. A brick wall lined with hollies forms the backdrop of the garden, with a koi pond providing a strong focal point from the central axis of the house. The stand-alone garage was recently converted to a studio/office, with part of the driveway reclaimed to enlarge the garden. Strong geometric lines and mixed materials provide structure and an architectural framework, which contrast with abundant plantings. The garden features unique sculptures, artful screening devices, and decorative accents.

DIRECTIONS—From I-495, take Exit 33 onto MD-185 south. Turn left onto Connecticut Avenue toward Chevy Chase. Head 2.3 miles south before making a left turn onto Newlands Street. Number 3 Newlands is on the left at the top of the street. Parking is available on the street.

SILVER SPRING
GREENHEART GARDEN
805 Dale Drive, Silver Spring
Hours: 10 a.m. to 4 p.m.
📷 | ♿PARTIAL | **NEW**

We live in a small 1934 house on a busy road and wanted multiple sensual outdoor living spaces in the rear. The wisteria-clad Zuri deck is used daily for meals; the yellowwood tree provides privacy and a delightful overhead canopy. The auto court and trellis garden are our sunny spaces: peonies, irises, roses, *Amsonia*, lilies, catmint, and hardy geraniums grow here. An invisible two-foot-tall retaining wall on the right and cut-and-fill grading made space for the screened pavilion and back patio at the end of a woodland path.

DIRECTIONS—The GreenHeart garden is located 1 mile inside the Beltway near downtown Silver Spring, Chevy Chase, and northwest Washington D.C. From I-495, go south on Route 29, Colesville Road, toward downtown Silver Spring. Turn left on Dale Drive (Mrs. K's Toll House restaurant is on the corner), cross Kingsbury Drive, and #805 is a brick Cape Cod-style house, the fourth on the left. Park on Kingsbury Drive or Ellsworth Drive, as Dale Drive is a busy street. GreenHeart's red gravel driveway is to the right of the house. Enter the back garden through the driveway gate.

MASSACHUSETTS
Bristol County
Sunday, June 3

McIlwain Garden

Landscape Designer Andrew Grossman's
Display Gardens

Seekonk

Bristol County
REHOBOTH
MCILWAIN GARDEN
37 Medalist Drive, Rehoboth
Hours: 10 a.m. to 4 p.m.
2016

This young garden abuts a golf course, providing expansive views in the English landscape tradition. Optimal plantings have been chosen for the range of challenging ecosystems, from rocky, dry soil to windy sites with wet soil. A cluster of trees with filtered sunlight hosts rhododendrons, azaleas, *Pieris, Enkiantus, Hellebores*, and more. Most of the garden enjoys full sun. This is a garden for all seasons with the blossoms of Okame cherries and saucer and star magnolias ushering in early spring, followed soon thereafter by daffodils, grape hyacinth, Spanish bluebells, ground phlox, and PJM azaleas. Early May sees the arrival of tulips, azaleas, the

sweetly fragrant *Viburnum carlessi*, and lilies of the valley. By mid-May, the bearded irises have opened, along with the chives, allium, bleeding heart, and rhododendrons. By June, this is followed in swift succession by dogwoods, Virginia magnolias with lemon-scented blossoms, peonies, Dutch irises and 'Gumpo' azaleas, coral bells, catmint, *Campanula, Clematis*, and *Geranium bikova*. By late June, summer has arrived with hydrangeas, roses, foxgloves, garden phlox, daisies, veronica, lavender, *Astilbe*, blue salvia, anise hyssop, and Russian sage...[Read full description online]

DIRECTIONS—From I-195 take Exit 1 in Massachusetts for Route 114A. (Do NOT take Exit 7 in Rhode Island to Barrington via Route 114.). Proceed north on Route 114A through several traffic lights to Route 44/Taunton Avenue. Turn right and go east through Seekonk and into Rehoboth, where you will see a flashing yellow light. Proceed east about 0.9 mile to Mills Plaza on left. Drive another 0.3 mile to Bairos Construction followed by the cluster of stores of Winthrop Commons on left. Immediately after Winthrop Commons, turn left onto River Street (it is hard to see). On River Street, cross the 4-way stop, continue about 0.4 mile (passing Tranquil Lake Nursery on right) and turn left onto Hillside Avenue. Drive 0.8 mile, passing the Hillside Country Club on right, and turn right at the next road, marked by a sign for Hillside Estates. This is Medalist Drive; proceed to the first house on the right, which is #37 (red brick with white columns).

SEEKONK
LANDSCAPE DESIGNER ANDREW GROSSMAN'S DISPLAY GARDENS
393 Fall River Avenue, Seekonk
Hours: 10 a.m. to 4 p.m.
📷 | ♿PARTIAL | **2016**

My gardens, which border the Martin Wildlife Refuge and the Runnins River, showcase a wide variety of perennials, shrubs, and grasses. The property includes a blue-and-white garden, a hot-colored garden with a checkerboard thyme patio, a cottage garden planted with roses and other old-fashioned favorites, and a rustic pond surrounded by bog plantings. There is also a cutting garden currently planted with tea roses and dinner plate dahlias. The property is featured in *Design New England's* 2016 March/April issue and was a finalist in HGTV's Gorgeous Gardens competition.

DIRECTIONS—From Providence, take 195 East to Exit 1/Seekonk/Barrington/Route 114A. You are now about 5 minutes from the house. At exit traffic light, bear left for Seekonk. Go through two more lights. At flashing light, bear left and stay on Route 114A/Fall River Avenue (do not go straight). Gristmill Restaurant and parking lot are on right, then a large yellow house on left. Take gravel driveway, marked by two white wooden columns, immediately past the yellow house on left, opposite parking lot for Vinny's Antiques. The gardens are at end of driveway. Please park in driveway or in lot across street.
From I-95 West, proceed as directed above, but turn right off the exit and only go through one light before flashing light.

What our Garden Hosts recommend in Bristol County

Tranquil Lake Nursery
45 River Street Rehoboth, MA
(508) 252-4002
www.tranquil-lake.com

Greater Boston Area
Saturday, June 9

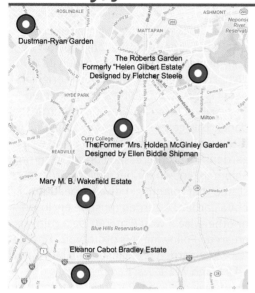

★ Start your day at the Mary M.B. Wakefield Estate, 1465 Brush Hill Road, Milton, 10 a.m. to 4 p.m. Admission: $7 on Open Day.

OUR PARTNER IN THE MILTON AREA

Mary M.B. Wakefield Estate

Each June, the Wakefield Estate welcomes visitors to celebrate the annual blooming of hundreds of Polly Wakefield's Kousa dogwood trees during "Dogwood Days". As host garden, the Wakefield Estate has helped us line up several remarkable gardens, some with important historical horticultural pedigrees and others reflecting remarkable accomplishments of local

gardeners and landscape designers. Begin your day at the Wakefield Estate, pick up a map and head out to see some or all of these great and inspiring gardens. A guided tour of the Wakefield Estate will be offered at 1p.m., rain or shine.

Norfolk County
CANTON
ELEANOR CABOT BRADLEY ESTATE
2468B Washington Street, Canton
Hours: 10 a.m. to 4 p.m.
NEW

Once a colonial farmstead known as Cherry Hill Farm, the Bradley Estate was transformed in 1902 into a classic country estate. Dr. Arthur Tracey Cabot hired noted architect Charles Platt to design a great house, landscaped grounds, and a complex of farm and estate buildings. Platt adorned the lovely natural setting with manicured lawns, a walled garden, and a brick-edged parterre garden. In 1945, Cabot's niece Eleanor Cabot Bradley acquired Cherry Hill Farm and lived there with her husband until its bequest to The Trustees of Reservations in 1991. Mrs. Bradley made some notable additions to the property, including a greenhouse and a studio. Today, the Trustees' Bradley Estate is open to the public and offers a variety of workshops, concerts, and other special events throughout the year. A guided tour of the Bradley Estate will be offered at 12:00 p.m., rain or shine. Mrs. Bradley's Formal Garden has recently been planted with a stunning display of spring and summer bulbs, including varieties that Eleanor Cabot Bradley had in her garden when she lived here. This spring, stroll through over 5,000 tulips and other spring bulbs, and come back in the summer to take a break among the 500 lilies (ten varieties) that were particular favorites of Eleanor, and will stand tall among the fragrant roses and perennials in the Formal Garden.

DIRECTIONS—From Route 128 (I-93), take Exit 2A and follow Route 138 South toward Stoughton. Immediately after crossing bridge (if exiting from Route 128 North) or coming off exit ramp (if exiting from Route 128 South), turn right into first driveway on the right (it comes up fast!). Follow signs to parking area. The drives on the property utilize a one-way system, so please take notice of signs.
—From the Wakefield Estate, turn right onto Brush Hill Road, then turn right onto Route 138/Blue Hill Avenue. Travel approximately 1.5 miles south over 128 and turn right into first driveway on the right (it comes up fast!). Follow signs to parking area. The drives on the property utilize a one-way system, so please take notice of signs.

MILTON
THE FORMER "MRS. HOLDEN MCGINLEY GARDEN" DESIGNED BY ELLEN BIDDLE SHIPMAN
582 Blue Hill Avenue, Milton
Hours: 10 a.m. to 4 p.m.
📷 | ♿ PARTIAL | **2017**

Coinciding with publication of Judith Tankard's new book, *Ellen Shipman and the American Garden*, a highlight of this year's Open Day is The Former "Mrs. Holden McGinley Garden." An intact garden designed for Mrs. Holden McGinley by Ellen Biddle Shipman in 1925, at the peak of her illustrious career as one of America's premier landscape architects, it is a stunning example of Shipman's garden design philosophy of closely integrating house and garden. Its key axis lures the visitor out from the house across the lawn into the walled garden. There, another axis transitions through a series of three long, narrow descending garden rooms, each with its own distinctive character. Most of the original detail is intact, including an original bluestone rill, which traverses the uppermost panel. This garden shows how Shipman often skillfully combined formal and wild gardens in a compressed suburban setting. Shipman, known for her walled gardens stated that "planting, however beautiful, is not a garden. A garden must be enclosed... or otherwise it would merely be a cultivated area." Following this prototypical layout here, the garden is enclosed and surrounded by high white-washed brick walls that match the mansion. Recently acquired by Ellen Shapiro and her husband, Michael Bloomberg, this important garden now receives the protection and care it so richly deserves. Open Day visitors are fortunate to have this rare opportunity to glimpse an intact masterwork by the "Dean of American Women Landscape Architects."

DIRECTIONS—From Rt. I-93, take Exit 2B in Canton for Route 138 North. Travel 3.2 miles, continuing on Route 138/Blue Hill Avenue (bearing left when Canton Avenue forks to the right). #582 is on the right.
—From the Wakefield Estate, turn right onto Brush Hill Road, then turn left onto Route 138/Blue Hill Avenue. Travel approximately 2 miles north to #582 on the right.

THE ROBERTS GARDEN—FORMERLY THE "HELEN GILBERT ESTATE" DESIGNED BY FLETCHER STEELE

173 School Street, Milton
Hours: 10 a.m. to 4 p.m.
📷 | ♿PARTIAL | **2017**

This lovingly restored Fletcher Steele garden is not to be missed! The Roberts Garden was formerly the Helen Gilbert Estate, designed by Fletcher Steele between 1953 and 1960. When Darrol and Amy Roberts acquired their property in 2004, it was like many of the great Milton properties whose full-time gardener had long gone: with upkeep long neglected, the garden designer's original vision had become obscured. Crumbling walls leaned on diseased Himalayan birch. Flowering trees, deciduous shrubs, roses, irises, and various groundcovers grew wild and unchecked. Nature reclaimed and reforested the sightlines, walkways, garden art, and vistas that renowned garden designer Fletcher Steele had crafted sixty years prior.

It was not until the Roberts' moved into the house that they uncovered Steele's hand in every aspect of the property's landscape design—from the front garden's brick walkway and distinctive Chippendale fence, to the placement of the Persephone statue at the back of the one-acre property as a focal point to capture the eye. Their four-year restoration recovered Steele's original vision while modifying it to work for a modern gardener-less, family. "The garden...must be—in proportion and detail—private, comfortable in all seasons and well fitted to the use of its owner," said Steele...[Read full description online]

DIRECTIONS—From Route 128, take ramp right for Route 1 North/I-93 North toward Braintree/Boston 2.9 miles. At Exit 5B, take ramp right for Route 28 North toward Milton 0.3 mile. Keep straight onto Route 28/North Main Street, 3.1 miles. Keep straight onto Randolph Avenue 1.0 mile. Turn left onto School Street 0.1 mile. The last intersection is at Randolph Avenue. If you reach Canton Avenue, you've gone too far. From the Wakefield Estate, depart Brush Hill Road toward Route 138/Blue Hill Avenue 128 feet. Turn right onto Route 138/Blue Hill Avenue 0.7 mile. Turn right onto Dollar Lane 456 feet. Turn left onto Canton Avenue. Pass Gulf station in 1.3 miles. Keep left to stay on Canton Avenue 0.8 mile. Turn right onto School Street 384 feet. The last intersection is Canton Avenue. If you reach Randolph Avenue, you've gone too far.

Suffolk County
WEST ROXBURY
DUSTMAN-RYAN GARDEN

353 Park Street, West Roxbury
Hours: 10 a.m. to 4 p.m.
📷 | ♿ | **2017**

This garden reflects the creative efforts of a mighty team: Christie Dustman, professional garden designer, and Patti Ryan, a professional furniture maker. In their own personal garden, these two artists have let nothing hinder their zeal for plants, stone, and whimsy. The garden is in its eleventh season, and its transformation was done in phases, keeping only a privet hedge and one andromeda. The garden uses plants and objects as sculptures in an array of vignettes and intentional views. By showcasing some plants and objects against a background of other plants and elements, this garden has many levels of complexity and interest. The owners are members of the Conifer Society, and you will find more than fifty different conifers, as well as rare and unusual plants. It is the reclaimed and castoff items used as art and decoration, like basketball hoops and organ pipes, that often command the most "ooohs and ahhhs."

DIRECTIONS—From Route 128/I-95 North, take Route 1/Providence Highway inbound from Exit 15a or 15b. At Washington Street, bear slightly right and proceed inbound about 2 miles. Turn left onto Lagrange Street about 0.2 mile past Maplewood Street. Go 0.3 mile and turn right onto Robin Street, just past Searle Road. Take the third left onto Park Street. The garden is at #353. Please park along street.

From the Wakefield Estate, turn left onto Brush Hill Road and travel approximately 0.8 mile. Keep left onto Neponset Valley Parkway. Follow until Milton Street, turning left. At "T" intersection, turn right to continue on Neponset Valley Parkway again. Go 0.5 mile and turn right onto River Street. Quickly bear left onto Turtle Pond Parkway. Turtle Pond Parkway turns into Enneking Parkway and then West Roxbury Parkway (after crossing Washington Street). Turn left onto Woodard Road, then left again onto Park Street. Number 353 is on the right.

PUBLIC GARDEN PARTNER

Norfolk County
MILTON
**MARY M. B. WAKEFIELD ESTATE— LISTED ON THE NATIONAL REGISTER OF HISTORIC PLACES
LEVEL II CERTIFIED ARBORETUM**

1465 Brush Hill Road, Milton
(617) 333-0924
wakefieldtrust.org
Hours: Special Garden Conservancy Open Day Saturday, June 9 from 10 a.m. to 4 p.m.; otherwise the estate is open some Sunday afternoons, 1 p.m. to 4 p.m. during the growing season, and Monday through Friday during business hours by appointment only. A guided tour of the Wakefield Estate will be offered at 1:00 pm, rain or shine.
Admission: $7 during Open Day

★ Start your tour here on Saturday, June 9, 10 a.m. to 4 p.m.

Open Days coincides with the Wakefield Estate's own Dogwood Days, timed to give the public a rare opportunity to enjoy our collection of hundreds of Chinese dogwoods (*Cornus kousa*) at their spectacular peak bloom. Polly Wakefield grew most of these trees from seed or cuttings collected from the Arnold Arboretum. The dogwoods are planted throughout Polly's Formal Garden and Terrace Rooms along with other rare trees and shrubs, as well as lining either side of the Fountain Path Allée, that spans the entire length of the property—it is truly a magnificent sight to behold. This year, in addition to celebrating the kousa dogwood collection's annual bloom, the Wakefield Estate is excited to be celebrating its recent approved listing on the National Register of Historic Places, and formal certification as a Level II Arboretum by Arbnet, granted to certified arboreta that have at least 100 species of woody plants, employ paid staff, and have enhanced public education programs and a documented collections policy. Gardens and nurseries surround a farmhouse circa 1730 and a Georgian mansion circa 1794. The Wakefield-Davenport Estate takes its name and purpose from Mary "Polly" Wakefield, who lived most of her life at the estate. The estate is managed by the Mary M. B. Wakefield Charitable Trust, which is committed to promoting life-long participatory learning using the land and resources of the Wakefield estate. Through collaborative partnerships with schools and community organizations, the Wakefield Trust carries out this mission through providing educational opportunities, tours, presentations, workshops, hands-on training, internships, and other programs covering a variety of subjects, including local history, ecology, horticulture, agriculture, archival work, and historic preservation.

DIRECTIONS—From Route I-95/128, take Exit 2B in Canton for Route 138 North. Bear right on Canton Avenue, immediately stay in the left lane in order to effectively turn left onto Brush Hill Road. Wakefield Estate entrance is the first left, 200 feet from the intersection and across from Fuller Village.

Berkshire County
Sunday, June 24

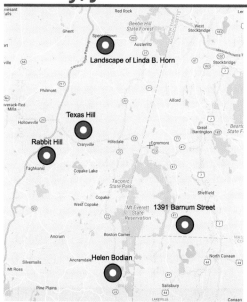

★ There are additional gardens open on this date in nearby Columbia County, NY. See page 237.

Berkshire County
SHEFFIELD
1391 BARNUM STREET
1391 Barnum Street, Sheffield
Hours: 10 a.m. to 4 p.m.

📷 | ♿PARTIAL | 2017
The first garden you see while walking up the driveway is the "Rabbit Garden," so named for the wooden rabbit in its midst. This chainsaw-carved animal is one of many on the property. Under the crabapple tree is a primrose garden. Walking up the stairs toward the house gives you your first view of the pond and waterfall area. From the deck, a series of stone steps and landings leads down past a rock garden to the patio and pond, home to goldfish and frogs. The patio fronts a mixed border of perennials, shrubs, and trees. From the screened-in porch the pond and waterfall can be seen and heard. The woodland garden behind the house, with its winding paths and many shade plantings, is a cool retreat. The garden on the pool side of the house has a variety of butterfly- and hummingbird-friendly plantings.

DIRECTIONS—From the south, travel north on Route 41 from Salisbury CT. From the White Hart Inn in Salisbury drive north on Route 41 about 6 miles. Turn right (after passing into MA) on Kelsey Road (a dirt road). Proceed about 1.5 miles to a "T" and bear left. Number 1391 is the first house on the right.

—From the north, travel south on Route 41. From the Great Barrington police station proceed about 6 miles through the town of Sheffield and turn right onto Berkshire School Road. Take the first left onto Salisbury Road. Proceed through the turns in the road and take the first left onto Barnum Street. Proceed past the Transfer Station where the road turns to dirt and after 1 mile bear right onto Lower Barnum. After another mile bearing right, the house and gardens are on the left.

—From the northwest, go east on Route 23 from Hillsdale, NY, to South Egremont, MA. Turn right onto Route 41 and go south about 7.5 miles. Turn left onto Kelsey Road (dirt), proceed about 1.5 miles to a "T," and bear left. The house and gardens are on the right.

10th Annual Nantucket Garden Festival

July 17-19, 2018
www.nantucketgardenfestival.org

Nantucket
Thursday, July 12

Nantucket County
NANTUCKET
BLUEBERRY HILL—DOUGLASS AND CAROLINE ELLIS
8 Quaise Pastures Road, Nantucket
Hours: 10 a.m. to 4 p.m.
 | 2014

An oak forest and tupelo grove protect the house and garden from ocean winds. The naturalistic landscape, designed by Lucinda Young, contrasts with rolling serene meadow views of West Polpis Harbor. An enclosed garden, set in a small building envelope on a conservation restriction, consists of heaths, heathers, and a crabapple espalier. A hidden garden contains a flower and shade garden. Chickens roam the property.

DIRECTIONS—Located 3.3 miles on Poplis Road from Milestone Road turnoff. Turn left after mailbox #209 onto Quaise Pastures Road. Hardtop road turns to gravel. Please park at circle before gate (except wheelchairs). We are #8. Walk through gate and bear left up hill.

THE GARDEN AT 7 POCOMO
7 Pocomo Road, Nantucket
Hours: 10 a.m. to 4 p.m.
 | NEW

A cottage resting atop a knoll surrounded by Nantucket's natural beauty, the land itself is a tapestry of undisturbed native plants. Interwoven grass paths connect a series of protected rooms. The garden was created to bring joy to many generations of family. There are cutting and vegetable gardens to supply the house and friends all summer, as well as a flock of chickens! The cutting garden focuses on the color palette of summer, and the vegetable garden is chockfull of reliable food all summer long. This property is sure to be a treat for novice and experienced gardeners.

DIRECTIONS—Take Polpis Road to Wauwinet Road, then turn left onto Pocomo Road. Garden is at the first driveway on the right.

GARDEN OF GALE H. ARNOLD
110 Wauwinet Road, Nantucket
Hours: 10 a.m. to 4 p.m.
 | NEW

The gardens at 110 Wauwinet Road are reflective of its place in time, architecture, and utility. Tree, shrub, and perennial plantings are integrated into the natural landscape. Walkways and lawn space allow for free movement throughout and provide a clear view of the inner harbor and sunset. A collection of scented plants and fruit grow inside the 18th-century-style glass house. An enormous native oak, typical of Wauwinet, dominates the back of the

Queen Anne-style residence.

DIRECTIONS—From town, get on Mile-stone Road and turn left at Island Lumber (Polpis Road). At end of Polpis Road, turn left onto Wauwinet Road. As you pass gatehouse to Great Point area, make an immediate left at #110 (see huge num-bered rock) or park in gatehouse lot.

HOUSE IN THE WOODS
251-249 Polpis Road, Nantucket
Hours: 10 a.m. to 4 p.m.
♿ | **NEW**

House in the Woods is a naturalistic land-scape design. The property wraps around a large wetland, which has determined the aesthetic of the landscape, embracing native meadows, pollinator gardens, pool gardens, and native groundcovers. The connecting property emphasizes edibles in extensive vegetable gardens with won-derful woodwork and stonework details throughout.

DIRECTIONS—From the Hyannis ferry dock, head southwest on Steamboat Wharf, which turns into Broad Street. Turn left onto South Water Street. Go through the downtown historic district, and continue straight, the road changes into Washington Street. Turn right onto Francis Street. Francis Street turns left and be-comes Union Street. Turn left onto Orange Street. Continue onto Lower Orange Street. At James Coffin Memorial Rotary, take the third exit onto Milestone Road. Turn left onto Polpis Road. Go 3.8 miles, destination will be on the right. Parking on street & marked areas on shell driveway.

MORASH VICTORY GARDEN
41 Shawkemo Road, Nantucket
Hours: 10 a.m. to 4 p.m.
📷 | ♿PARTIAL | **2012**

The Morash Victory Garden has expanded several times during the past thirty years. Today, polypropylene deer fencing pro-tects twenty earthen raised beds that were built on native sandy soils amended gen-erously with local and site-made compost. Benefitting from such strategies as winter cover cropping, grass mulching, plastic sheeting, and clean cultivation, the garden grows the usual suspects found in most backyard vegetable gardens. Potatoes and pumpkins, tomatoes, and cut flowers are important crops. Sufficient water, abun-dant sunshine, and a hardworking home-made greenhouse, together with countless happy hours from an old gardener, are some of the secret weapons to be found in this vegetable and flower display.

DIRECTIONS—From town, take Polpis Road past Moor's End Farm to Rabbit Run Road on left. Go 0.7 mile on Rabbit Run, which eventually turns left. Stay right at this fork (you're now on Shawkemo Road) and go straight for a few hundred yards to a driveway on the right and a sign welcom-ing you to the Morash property. Please park as suggested by the signs.

Berkshire County
Saturday, July 21

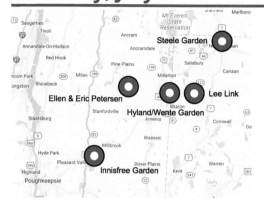

★ There are additional gardens open on this date in nearby Litchfield County, CT (see page 107), and Dutchess County, NY (see page 254).

Berkshire County
ASHLEY FALLS
STEELE GARDEN
159 Ashley Falls Road, Ashley Falls
Hours: 10 a.m. to 4 p.m.
📷 | **2017** | 🏷 PLANT SALES

The garden has been created over the last twenty years, with many changes along the way, to complement a small Greek Revival house. No master plan was ever drawn, the garden (all self-maintained) evolving according to whim, available time, and, of course, funds. The intent was to make an attractive and interesting garden to be in and wander through, with views and focal points throughout and from the house. The result is a series of seven connected circles, with both formal and informal side gardens of favorite plants, particularly hostas and daffodils.

DIRECTIONS—From Sheffield, go south on

Route 7 for 2 miles. Bear right onto Route 7A. Left at first street, Pike Road. Garden on the right corner. Park along Pike Road.

What our Garden Hosts recommend in Berkshire County

Whalen Nursery
1820 North Main Street,
Sheffield, MA 01257
(413) 528-4077
www.whalennursery.com

NO. 6 Depot Café
6 Depot Street (the old train station)
West Stockbridge, MA 01266
(413) 232-0205
www.sixdepot.com

PUBLIC GARDEN

Berkshire County
STOCKBRIDGE
BERKSHIRE BOTANICAL GARDEN
Routes 102 & 183, Stockbridge
(413) 298-3926
www.berkshirebotanical.org
Hours: Berkshire Botanical Garden is open year round for classes, lectures, workshops and exhibits. The gardens can be toured from May 1 through Columbus Day, 9 a.m. to 5 p.m. Group tours available by appointment.
Admission: $15 adults, $14 seniors and students; members and children 12 and under, free.

Established in 1934 and revered as one of the older public display gardens in the Northeast, Berkshire Botanical Garden encompasses fifteen acres of land in the heart of the Berkshire Hills of Western Massachusetts. Visitors to the Garden enjoy over 3,000 species and varieties of herbaceous and woody plants that thrive in Zone 5b. Twenty-five display gardens blend intimate landscapes with seasonal palettes and tapestries of fragrant and colorful perennials and over 2,000 annuals. Two mixed border gardens, perennial borders for sun and shade, The Children's Garden, The Foster Rock Garden, the historical Daylily Walk, and native plant gardens are among the many favorite display areas. Former guest gardeners include Martha Stewart (Heirloom Flower Garden), Page Dickey (Terraced Herb Garden), Jack Staub (Vegetable and Fruit Gardens), and Anthony Archer-Wills (The Pond Garden) and Michael Marriott (David Austin Rose Garden). The 2018 theme, ART/GARDEN features paintings by Ellsworth Kelly and a sculpture exhibition throughout the Garden.

DIRECTIONS—GPS address: 5 West Stockbridge Road, (corner of Routes 102 and 183), Stockbridge, MA.
—From the east, take I-90/Massachusetts Turnpike to Exit 2. Follow Route 102 west through Stockbridge. Entrance on left 0.1 mile past intersection with Route 183.
—From the west, take the New York State Thruway to Exit B-3. Follow Route 22 South 0.8 miles to Route 102, then 5.9 miles east through west Stockbridge to entrance on right.

MISSOURI
St. Louis
Saturday, June 16

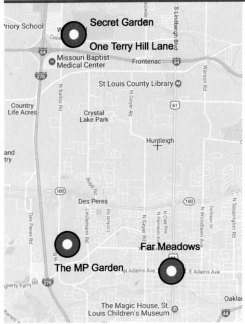

St. Louis County
LADUE
FAR MEADOWS
Ladue
Hours: 10 a.m. to 4 p.m.
NEW

In 1922 the present owner's grandparents purchased 150 acres next to the Log Cabin Club on Log Cabin Lane. In 1923 the architects Jamieson and Spearl, who had designed many houses on Westmoreland and Portland Place, began to build the house. The owners called the property Far Meadows, as it extended across what is now Highway 64/40 to where the Racquet Club West has its parking lot. The property presently comprises twenty-nine-and-a-

half acres, which extend west to Magnolia Drive over the creek and is very wooded, and south on Log Cabin Drive. The gardens were designed in 1924 by Warren Manning, of Boston, who received his training from Frederick Law Olmstead. Much of the garden is now a meadow, and, in the early spring, a large field of daffodils fills the view from the back of the house. The English perennial border, the pool placement, and the white peony English boxwood garden are Manning's work. The log cabin, which visitors will see as they stroll through the grounds, was used as a bathing house and a children's playhouse. An addition to the house in the late 1990s was designed by Paul Fendler...[Read full description online]

DIRECTIONS—At the request of the garden host, directions to this garden will be provided at additional gardens open on this date.

KIRKWOOD
THE MP GARDEN
1819 Cheswick Place, Kirkwood
Hours: 10 a.m. to 4 p.m.
📷 | ♿PARTIAL | **NEW**

Anchored by a double koi pond with a peninsula waterfall and a meandering stream from the crest of the hill, this garden has year-round interest. Oaks, catalpa, elm, black gum, buckeye, hickory, hackberry, dogwood, bald cypress, and sugar maple, some more than a century old, are focal points of the property. Towering Norway spruce provide defining elements and privacy in various areas of the property, including a small stone patio alongside the pond. A variety of flowerbeds display both sun- and shade-loving perennials interspersed with conifers, roses, and deciduous shrubs. Steppingstones and pavers wind through the beds, while benches and large "sitting" boulders beckon you to rest. The spring brings blooms of dogwood, hellebore, clematis, daffodil, and peony. Summer blooms include phlox, *Ligularia, Coreopsis,* and hydrangeas. Sweet autumn clematis, *Callicarpa* (beautyberry), *Tricyrtis* (toad lily), mums, and Russian sage bring us into fall. This garden has a way of making you think you are "in the country" far from the hubbub of civilization. Come, and enjoy!

DIRECTIONS—From I-270, take the Manchester Road exit and go east on Manchester Road. Next go south (right) on Ballas Road. Turn left onto Brookcreek Lane; right onto Bridlebrook Lane; right on Lynkirk Lane, and then right on Cheswick Place. Park on street, either on Cheswick Place or Lynkirk Lane.

ST. LOUIS
ONE TERRY HILL LANE
1 Terry Hill Lane, St. Louis
Hours: 10 a.m. to 4 p.m.
📷 | &PARTIAL | **NEW**

Situated on a beautiful one-and-four-fifths-acre lot with a natural, hilly terrain and mature trees, the landscape of 1 Terry Hill Lane was originally designed by Edith Mason in the late 1930s for one of the founding families of nearby Westwood Country Club. Her signature brick and stone walls and paths create a hardscape framework for many diverse garden views and private settings. Subsequent design improve-

ments were done by horticulturalist Robert Dingwall from 2010 to the present. Most recent landscape renovations, container designs, and maintenance projects are the work of Bellinger Botanicals. It is a varied, interesting garden, and there is always something to see. The entry driveway and perennial beds feature boxwoods, *Abelia*; nandinas; and 'Limelight,' 'Strawberry Vanilla,' and 'Little Quick Fire' hydrangeas, Michael Dirr's 'Razzle Dazzle' dwarf crape myrtle and *Chamaecyparis* are set against background yews, hollies, magnolia, *Viburnum*, and rose of Sharon. The circular center of the driveway features an antique French limestone statue surrounded by 'Otto Luyken' cherry laurel and annuals for color...[Read full description online]

DIRECTIONS—Exit I-64 at New Ballas Road. Head north to Conway Road, then east on Conway Road for 0.2 mile. Turn left onto Terry Hill Lane. The garden is #1 Terry Hill Lane.

SECRET GARDEN
3 Terry Hill Lane, St. Louis
Hours: 10 a.m. to 4 p.m.
NEW

The owners purchased this 1930s home with a dream to create a backyard garden sanctuary. Beautiful brickwork and iron fences provided structure and pathways. The garden has evolved over the past 15 years despite numerous rabbits who feast on the plants. Potted plants have become a strategy to overcome the challenges of wildlife. There are many containers that add color and texture. This is a garden that offers solitude and pleasure in all seasons. The fountains, chimes, and music bring peace and tranquility, and garden rooms encourage strolling, sitting, and reflection. This private and tranquil sanctuary spills with azaleas, hydrangeas, viburnums, butterfly bushes, magnolia trees, Japanese maples, gigantic boxwoods, green giants, dogwoods, cedars, hollies, redbuds, *Styrax japonicus*, nandinas, and hostas. The owners start and end each day in the garden to enjoy nature and to appreciate the seasons of life. "Enjoy the moment. The butterfly counts not months but moments, and has time enough." ~Rabindranath Tagore

DIRECTIONS—Exit I-64 at New Ballas Road. Head north to Conway Road, then east on Conway Road for 0.2 mile. Turn left onto Terry Hill Lane. The garden is at #3.

What our Garden Hosts recommend in St. Louis

Tomasovic Greenhouse & Nursery
1251 Meier Ln, St. Louis, MO 63131
(314) 821-4963
www.tomasovics.com

Bowood Farms: Nursery and Café
4605 Olive St, St. Louis, MO 63108
(314) 454-6868
www.bowoodfarms.com

NEW HAMPSHIRE
Monadnock Area
Saturday, June 16

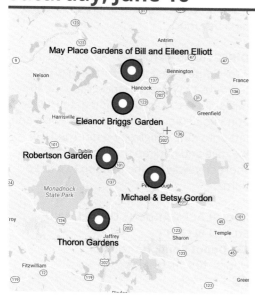

Map labels: May Place Gardens of Bill and Eileen Elliott · Eleanor Briggs' Garden · Robertson Garden · Michael & Betsy Gordon · Thoron Gardens · Antrim · Bennington · Hancock · Greenfield · Harrisville · Nelson · Dublin · Monadnock State Park · Peterborough · Jaffrey · Sharon · Temple · Fitzwilliam

Cheshire County
DUBLIN
ROBERTSON GARDEN
162 Gerry Road, Dublin
Hours: 10 a.m. to 4 p.m.
 | ♿ | 2002

The inspiration to create our garden came during a visit to southeastern England in 1986. The geometric design of the perennial bed was drawn on an American Airline's napkin during the return flight. Upon entering our property, visitors are met with some 12,000 daffodils during the month of May. The garden itself is bounded by fruit trees, a vegetable garden, a pergola, and a large barn. A fairly productive bluebird trail ambles through peripheral meadows. Among the specimen trees on our proper-

ty are horse chestnuts, seven sons (*Heptacodium miconioides*), a variegated Japanese red pine ('Dragon's Eye'), and a Tennessee yellowwood tree. Recent additions are several Japanese maple species and Slovenian beehives. Although a difficult struggle, inducing some color from the granite is very rewarding.

DIRECTIONS—Gerry Road leaves Route 101 about 0.8 mile west of the junction of Routes 101 and 137. Carr's store and Citgo gas station are located at this junction. Gerry Road, primarily a dirt road through a wooded area, is 0.7 mile long and dead ends at our property.

JAFFERY
THORON GARDENS
139 Harkness Road, Jaffery
Hours: 10 a.m. to 4 p.m.
📷 | NEW

The property includes a 230-year-old cottage/farmhouse, renovated and surrounded by gardens, a view of Mount Monadnock, an eleven-acre wetland with beavers, an old/new orchard, mowed fields, and stone walls. Help was given from garden designers Gordon Hayward and Kristian Fenderson, who put up with owner's strong ideas and vision, 2006 to present, intermittently. Additional features include sixteen different gardens covering two acres: wetland, woodland, a formal/informal vegetable/cutting garden above a forty-foot perennial bed, roadside and driveway perennial borders, two formal boxwood gardens, a grove of river birch, eighty-five garden pots, climbing roses on the fence and trellis of the house, perennial curved lawn gardens, tall perennials adjacent to barn, a brick walkway, plus four small gardens and a kitchen garden adjacent to house.

DIRECTIONS—Take Route 101 east/west highway to Route 137 south toward Jaffrey. Go 5 miles. Turn right onto the second Procter Road, which runs into Harkness Road. Continue for 0.8 mile to Route 139. Do not turn onto the first Procter Road. Parking will be in the roadside field.

Hillsborough County
HANCOCK
ELEANOR BRIGGS' GARDEN
86 King's Highway, Hancock
Hours: 10 a.m. to 4 p.m.
📷 | ♿ | **2016**

The gardens surround Hancock's first house, built in 1776 by the town clerk, Jonathan Bennett. Since it is a farmhouse, the plantings are informal and blend into surrounding fields and woods. On each side of the "front" door are raised beds reminiscent of Colonial gardens. The real front door (never used) is flanked by plantings of old roses and *Nepeta*. Behind the 1970 kitchen wing is a forty-eight-foot-long koi pond designed by landscape architect Diane McGuire and planted with lotuses, irises, and water lilies. McGuire also laid out the perennial bed and woodland border. The AIA-award-winning screened porch was designed by Dan Scully. Sculptures in the terraced vegetable garden are by Noel Grenier, and a pair of 200-year-old granite Korean rams graze on the back lawn. I followed McGuire's brilliant layout of the parallel borders but deepened the perennial bed to make a bit more room to

"paint" with annuals and perennials. The woodland border is planted with witch hazel, azaleas, snakeroot, and *Rodgersia*. Walking beyond the borders, one comes to a new bog garden surrounded by marsh marigolds, skunk cabbage, and sedges. A trail of cardinal flowers brightens the wetland beyond.

DIRECTIONS—From I-91 North, take Exit 3 for Route 9 East into Brattleboro. Go to Route 123 toward Hancock (about 40 miles). Take the second right onto Hunt's Pond Road (about 5 miles). Go 0.5 mile and left onto King's Highway, a dirt road. Go 0.5 mile and park on the road next to the short driveway on the right up to a large barn.

MAY PLACE GARDENS OF BILL AND EILEEN ELLIOTT
191 Depot Road, Hancock
Hours: 10 a.m. to 4 p.m.
📷 | **2011**

Two compulsive plant collectors have been making gardens on a wooded hillside clearing for thirty-seven years. We continue to do all of the planning, landscaping, planting, and maintenance ourselves. Gardening offers us ample challenges and satisfaction as the garden continues to expand, change, die back, thrive, disappoint, and exhilarate. Within the green wall of mature woodland is a two-acre clearing, which contains a mix of trees, shrubs, perennials, biennials, annuals, herbs, and vegetables. The garden features mixed borders, an ornamental vegetable garden, and a formal peony/clematis garden. A path leads to the shade gardens by the house.

DIRECTIONS—From Route 123/Main Street in Hancock, with the Hancock Inn and church on right, go north on Route

123 and turn right on Depot Road, the first right past Norway Pond. The garden is 2 miles up road. At the "T" junction, with a green mailbox "220," go left up hill. The garden is on right. Please drive past garden to a wide junction for an easy place to turn around. Park on right side of road, facing downhill.

PETERBOROUGH
MICHAEL & BETSY GORDON
14 High Street, Peterborough
Hours: 10 a.m. to 4 p.m.
📷 | ♿PARTIAL | **2016**

This small garden in the village was designed by a plantsman to be an extension of the house. The house and garden are situated on a hill, and the garden is terraced on three levels. The upper level was intended to be enjoyed from the street. The middle level is laid out formally, using yew hedges and a century-old granite wall foundation to create a garden room. The lowest level, an informal woodland garden, has shade-loving plants from North America and Asia. The garden was planted with a mixture of unusual trees, shrubs, perennials, grasses, annuals, and bulbs. Plants were selected primarily for interesting form, foliage, and texture. The garden is chronicled on instagram.com/thegardenerseye.

Michael & Betsy Gordon's Garden
DIGGING DEEPER
4 PM
Succession Planting for Mere Mortals
REGISTRATION: $30 Garden Conservancy Members / $35 general
Join Michael B. Gordon for a walking tour of his garden where he will reveal how he has incorporated a simplified version of the succession planting

concepts used by the late Christopher Lloyd and Fergus Garrett at Great Dixter, England, in his small private garden.

Michael will explain how he uses combinations of woody and herbaceous plants to extend the season as long as he possibly can in New Hampshire. The talk will be of interest to the plantsman as well as the designer. Refreshments will be served. Michael B. Gordon is an optometrist by profession but a gardener by obsession. He has designed public gardens in Peterborough for nearly two decades. He has a passion for visiting gardens in the United States and abroad. Each year, he leads a tour of English Gardens and brings back ideas for his own garden.

Registration required — space limited
Go to opendaysprogram.org
or call 1 (888) 842-2442

DIRECTIONS—From the traffic lights at the intersection of Route 101 and Route 202 in Peterborough, take Route 101 west up the hill to Elm Street. Turn right onto Elm Street. At the stop sign, cross the intersection and take gentle left turn up the hill onto High Street. The garden is the third house on the left: a white clapboard house with a picket fence across the street from the Elementary School.

Merrimack Valley
Saturday & Sunday, July 14 &15

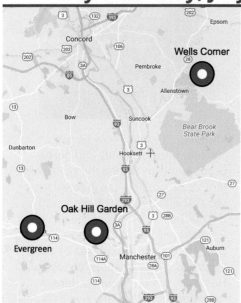

"I have never seen this plant before" is the spontaneous reaction of visitors to this garden, bright with seasonal perennials and more than 200 varieties of shrubs and trees. Gardens include a slope garden, Japanese maple garden, birch grove, cottage garden, shade gardens, tree and shrub beds, daylily bed, blueberry patch, stonework including a large stone staircase, and beautiful lawns that set off the garden beds. A farmer's porch and two patios provide retreats for relaxing.

DIRECTIONS—From Route 293: Exit 6 (Amoskeag Street/Goffstown Road). Follow rotary and exit onto Goffstown Road. Continue on Goffstown Road about 3 miles and turn right onto Langan Drive. Last house on the left, blue with black shutters and white trim.
—From downtown Goffstown's Main Street, turn onto Elm Street (turns into Goffstown Road). Travel about 5 miles and turn Left onto Langan Drive. Last house on the left, blue with black shutters and white trim.

OUR PARTNER IN MERRIMACK VALLEY

EVERGREEN FOUNDATION

Evergreen Foundation owns and operates Evergreen, its woodland garden in Goffstown, New Hampshire, and opens it to the public without charge. It also promotes excellent landscape design through garden tours, lectures, and its forthcoming website.

Hillsborough County
GOFFSTOWN
OAK HILL GARDEN
51 Langan Drive, Goffstown
Hours: 10 a.m. to 4 p.m.
📷 | ♿PARTIAL | **NEW**

Merrimack County
EPSOM
WELLS CORNER
5 Wing Road, Epsom
Hours: 10 a.m. to 5 p.m.
📷 | ♿ | **2017**

Mine is a garden in the dooryard of an eighteenth-century farmhouse. It is both country and casual. When I moved here twenty-nine years ago, there was a narrow border of *Vinca minor* (dwarf periwinkle, now covered by a widened porch), large clumps of orange daylilies (*Hemerocallis*), and an old grape arbor. None of these remain. I garden on glacial sandy moraine. Soil preparation is intensive. What I meant to be two or three borders is now an acre of gardens set around an eighteenth-century post-and-beam barn (thirty-five-feet by fifty-six-feet) and other period buildings. There are deep mixed borders, low dry-laid stone walls, a koi pond, a small woodland, and a small ornamental *potager*. I have tried not to lose sight of the fact that this is an informal country garden. The garden rooms are defined by sight lines rather than formal hedging.

DIRECTIONS—From I-93, take Exit 11. After you pass through the toll, turn left onto Hackett Hill Road. In 0.25 mile turn left again onto West River Road. In a little over 0.5 mile you will come to a traffic light. Turn right and go over the river. In 0.5 mile you will come to a crossroad. Go straight up the hill to the traffic light. Turn left onto Route 3/Route 28. In about 2.5 miles, at Sully's Market, stay on Route 28 to the right. Turn right onto Route 28/Pinewood Road. Proceed an additional 3 miles on Route 28. On right you will see a large brown wooden sign for Bear Brook State Park. Turn right into the park. Cross over Catamount Pond and pass the Old Allentown Meetinghouse on the left. In 1.5 miles you will come to New Rye Road. The sign is on the right, the road is on the left. Turn left up the hill for 1 mile. On the right you will see a dark red center chimney Colonial. —From the Seacoast, take Route 4 to the Epsom Traffic Circle. Take the third exit, and turn left onto Route 28. Drive approximately 5.5 miles. Turn left into Bear Brook State Park and proceed as directed above.

PUBLIC GARDEN PARTNER

Hillsborough County
GOFFSTOWN
EVERGREEN
42 Summer Street, Goffstown
(603) 497 8020
Hours: Open every year on the first weekend in June, when the Catawba rhododendrons are at or near peak bloom: this year Friday to Sunday, June 1–3, 10 a.m. to 5 p.m. Also open during the Monadnock Area Open Days, Saturday, June 16 , 10 a.m. to 5 p.m., when the mountain laurel (*Kalmia latifolia*) are in bloom; and during the Merrimack Valley Open Days, Saturday & Sunday, July 14 & 15, 10 a.m. to 5 p.m., when the rosebay rhododendrons are blossoming.
Admission: $7 on Open Days, July 14 & 15; otherwise free.

Created by landscape designer Robert Gillmore, Evergreen is an idealized woodland comprised of mature white pines, broadleaf evergreen shrubs—including sweeps of 220 Catawba rhododendrons (*Rhododendron catawbiense*) and 175 rosebay rhododendrons (*Rhododendron maximum*)— plus colorful evergreen ground covers and other low-maintenance, shade-tolerant plants. The one-acre garden is ringed with berms, some of them twelve feet high and all of them planted with rhododendrons, which screen the garden from neighboring houses. The sloping site also has a seasonal cascading brook with pools, a quarter-mile of paths, and rooms defined by granite boulders, berms, and plants.

www.opendaysprogram.org

The White Room is named for its sweeps of variegated 'Emerald Gaiety' euonymus and white-variegated hosta, the Gold Room for its carpets of 'Emerald 'n Gold' euonymus and *Vinca minor* 'Illumination.' Gillmore is the author of *The Woodland Garden* and *Beauty All Around You: How to Create Large Private Low-Maintenance Gardens, Even on Small Lots and Small Budgets.* Open to the public every year since 1994 and an Open Days garden from 2012 to 2017, Evergreen is now owned and operated by the non-profit Evergreen Foundation.

DIRECTIONS—From east, take Route 114 to Goffstown village. Just after Sully's Superette (near where Route 13 goes north from Route 114), turn right onto Summer Street. Go to eighth house on right.
—From west, take Route 136 to New Boston, then Route 13 to Goffstown, then left onto Routes 13 & 114. Just beyond Sully's Superette (near where Route 13 goes north from Route 114), turn right onto Summer Street. Go to eighth house on right.

PUBLIC GARDEN

Merrimack County
NEWBURY
THE FELLS

456 Route 103A, Newbury
(603) 763-4789
www.thefells.org
Hours: Gardens and trails are open daily year round. Members may visit dawn to dusk, nonmembers, 9 a.m. to 4 p.m.
Admission: Main House open: adults, $10; seniors and students, $8; children ages 6 to 17, $4; 5 and under, free; families of two adults and two or more children ages 6 or above, $25. Main House closed: adults $8; seniors and students, $6; children, $3; families of two adults and two or more children ages 6 or above, $15. Winter admission: December through March is $5 per household, payable at our self-serve Welcome Kiosk. The Fells is proud to participate in Blue Star Museums 2018, providing free site admission for active-duty military personnel and their immediate families.

The historic gardens at The Fells—created and nurtured by three generations of Hay family until 1969—surround the twenty-two-room Colonial Revival-style summer home first established by statesman John Milton Hay (1838-1905) in 1891. By then, Hay had served as President Lincoln's private secretary; he later served two other U.S. Presidents as Secretary of State. Over the years, the property changed hands and the gardens fell into disrepair. In 1995, volunteers began to manage the property. In 1997, they formed a nonprofit known today as The Fells. In 2008, The Fells became the owners of eighty-four acres of the original 1,000-acre site. Aided by the Garden Conservancy in 1995, The Fells began the meticulous process of renovating the beautiful gardens. Visitors may now see five formal garden areas, wide sweeping terraced lawns, and lichen-covered stonewalls that result in a varied landscape that includes both natural and cultivated elements. Lake and mountain views prevail. The Pebble Court entrance is home to boxwood, lilacs, a yew hedge, a magnificent *Enkianthus*, and the beautiful "Hebe." A hundred-foot-long stone wall provides structure for a dazzling perennial border, and high walls and a cascading fountain frame a rose garden of hybrid tea roses. A large rock garden, bordered by an impressive heather bed, was created with onsite granite and contains 650 alpine and rock garden plants. The Old Garden, the first to be created on the property, consists of rhododendron-lined "secret" paths, fountain, and stone tea table, and was restored in 2011.

DIRECTIONS—From I-89 south take Exit 12/Route 11. Turn right and take an immediate left. Continue 5.6 miles. The Fells is on right. Park in lot and walk the quarter-mile driveway to the house and gardens.

NEW JERSEY
Essex County
Sunday, April 15

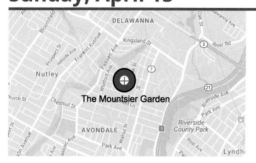

Essex County
NUTLEY
THE MOUNTSIER GARDEN
205 Rutgers Place, Nutley
Hours: 10 a.m. to 4 p.m.
📷 | ♿PARTIAL | **2017**

I love my garden! Do come in spring to see it bursting forth and enjoy it with me! It is the best time to see the strong bones of the garden and the bright colors of thousands of spring bulbs illuminating it! Then from my garden it is one-and-one-half miles to the largest display of flowering cherries in the United States—so you can really feast on the glory of spring from here. Return again on September 8, (Garden Description found on page 188) and see the garden in full flush. Over the last twenty-two years, Richard Hartlage, the talented garden designer, has designed my garden. Garden clubs and other groups are welcome for a guided tour by appointment, making contributions to the Open Days program. Contact: graemehard@aol.com.

DIRECTIONS—From the Lincoln Tunnel or Exit 16 from I-95/New Jersey Turnpike, go west on Route 3. From Garden State Parkway, go east on Route 3. From both directions, go to Main Avenue/Nutley/Passaic exit. At end of exit ramp, turn left and go through two traffic lights (three lights if coming from west). Then go straight ahead. Rutgers Place is fourth street on left. Come up Rutgers Place to top of hill; when road flattens, #205 is on right.

Northern New Jersey
Saturday, May 5

Essex County
EAST ORANGE
THE SECRET GARDEN @ 377—
THE GOTELLI GARDEN AT
HARRISON PARK TOWERS

Harrison Park Towers
377 South Harrison, East Orange
Hours: 10 a.m. to 4 p.m.
📷 | 2017

This one-acre, formal Italianate garden designed by William T. Gotelli celebrated its sixtieth birthday in 2016! This unique garden sits atop our parking garage at Harrison Park Towers and is entered through our lobby. We have a number of dwarf conifers and other shrubs that came from Gotelli's personal gardens in South Orange prior to his donation of plants and trees to The National Arboretum (Google: Gotelli Dwarf Conifer Collection for a walking tour of the collection.) At the end of his life, he moved into this building so that he could enjoy his lifetime's rooftop design achievement. The garden has just completed a number of major restoration steps to recover from a large construction project in 2009 involving the drainage system and garage. This garden has extensive collections of azalea, hydrangea, lilac, hosta, peony, tree peony and spring-blooming trees.

The Secret Garden @ 377 is a very special feature of this almost 300-unit cooperative apartment community. Other than on our Open Days dates, the garden is available for tours by appointment only by calling Ron Carter at (973) 202-4728 or emailing him at rcarter31@aol.com.

DIRECTIONS—From I-280 East, take exit for Harrison Street/Clinton Street/East Orange. Turn right onto Harrison Street and cross Central Avenue. Proceed along Harrison past a large open lot on right. Pass East Highland Avenue and turn right into 377 South Harrison. Note the large sign "377" and turn immediately prior to it. Park in The Visitors Parking Lot and walk to the front entrance under the overhang nearest South Harrison Street. Alternate parking is available along Elmwood Avenue, which is a left turn off Harrison immediately in front of the building. Ignore the signs about permits and be careful crossing South Harrison at the crosswalk.
—From I-280 West, take Exit 12A toward Clinton Street/East Orange. Follow along onto Freeway Drive westbound. Turn left onto South Harrison Street. Cross Central Avenue. Proceed as directed above.

Morris County
CHATHAM
JACK LAGOS
23 Pine Street, Chatham
Hours: 10 a.m. to 4 p.m.
📷 | ♿ | **2003**

I have been developing this one-acre property, which backs onto a lovely wood, for twenty-five years. The first garden, with island perennial border, is now one among many. A 100-year-old barn is backdrop for shade-loving plants, and on its sunny sides lie an herb garden and another perennial border. Ten graceful clematis vines climb beautifully designed lattice fencing, which defines the dwarf conifer collection. A woodland garden, my latest project, lies beneath a very large white oak and features a natural rock fountain.

DIRECTIONS—From Garden State Parkway or New Jersey Turnpike/I-95, take I-78 west to Route 24 west. Take Chatham exit (immediately after Short Hills Mall). Follow signs to Route 124 West/Main Street and, at fifth traffic light, turn left onto Lafayette Avenue. Go all the way to top of hill and, when Lafayette bends to right, turn right onto Pine Street. Number 23 is the fourth house on left. From I-287, exit onto Route 24 East. Continue to The Mall at Short Hills exit. At end of exit ramp, turn right onto River Road. At first traffic light, bear right and continue straight (River Road becomes Watching Avenue) to fifth light. Turn left onto Lafayette Avenue. Proceed as directed above. Please park on street.

Somerset County
FAR HILLS
THE HAY HONEY FARM
130 Stevens Lane, Far Hills
Hours: 10 a.m. to 5 p.m.
2017

The extensive gardens of The Hay Honey Farm lie nestled between rolling hills along the North Branch of the Raritan River. The transition from cattle farm to garden began in 1989, and while Black Angus cattle still graze the nearby hayfields, honeybees have become the only "livestock" allowed within the gates. Over the years, a wide variety of plant material, including hundreds of trees and shrubs, has been carefully added to the landscape in a naturalistic manner, with a respect for the history and topography of the site, and consistent with the broader surrounding atmosphere of Pleasant Valley. The plant collections reflect the diverse interests of the owners and the resident horticulturists, and show the results of a long-term vision and dedicated horticultural attention to plant care. Garden areas created near the homes include a dwarf conifer/spring bulb garden, a large walled perennial border, hosta gardens, a native meadow, and a large kitchen garden. Year-round springs feed a small stream, which originates in the wild garden and flows through a collection of rhododendron and companion wild flowers and woodland plants...[Read full description online]

There is something to prune every day of the year at The Hay Honey Farm. In addition to the "right plant, right place" philosophy, we also embrace "use the right tool for the job," and we make sure that tool is in proper working order. By far our hardest working

tools are the bypass pruners— we like Felco #2s. After touring the gardens, we invite you to bring your pruners or loppers to the tune-up table and spend some time with gardener Michael Clayton. Michael will provide hands-on instruction to help you get your tools in tiptop shape, in time to prune the tender new growth of spring in your garden.

DIRECTIONS—From I-95/New Jersey Turnpike, take I-78 West. Then take I-287 North to Exit 22B (or Exit 22 if coming from north). Stay on Route 206 North. At fourth traffic light, turn right onto Holland Avenue. At end, turn left onto Peapack. Turn right onto Willow Avenue. Go 1 mile and turn left onto Branch Road. At 0.7 mile, cross the green steel bridge onto a private gravel road. Please follow signs to the parking area, as weather conditions don't always allow us to use the hayfields. Park here for the Stone House Garden also and volunteers will direct you.

STONE HOUSE GARDEN
121 Stevens Lane, Far Hills
Hours: 10 a.m. to 4 p.m.
2017

All the buildings and walls are of old Pennsylvania stone; the paths and terrace are of Vermont schist. One goes through the beech hedge into the courtyard, planted with low-growing *Rhus aromatica* and Spanish bluebells. The path, which encircles the house, leads through the medallion garden to the crescent border, planted for spring bloom and fall color; past the kitchen garden, terrace, and Mimi's garden; and down stone steps to the bog, which, in the spring, hosts an explosion of primula candelabra, fern, and skunk cabbage.

DIRECTIONS—Follow directions to park at The Hay Honey Farm, and walk next door to the Stone House Garden; volunteers will be on hand to direct you.

PUBLIC GARDEN

Essex County
SHORT HILLS
GREENWOOD GARDENS
274 Old Short Hills Road, Short Hills
(973) 258-4026
greenwoodgardens.org
★ See full listing on page 192.

Essex County
Saturday, June 16

Essex County
MONTCLAIR
CLAIRE CILIOTTA

279 Park Street, Montclair
Hours: 10 a.m. to 4 p.m.
📷 | ♿PARTIAL | **2017**

Welcome to my garden! There are lots of lovely changes that I've made in the last two years! The front garden now has a nice curving path and new broad steps to the house. You will get to see what I've done with the plantings! Then, follow the brick path around the side of the house and look for the climbing roses, *Baptisia*, smoke bushes, and a Japanese maple. Open the new gate to a meditation garden—watch the birds at the feeder, notice the Mayan rock wall with its spirit windows surrounding a moon-shaped pond. Enjoy the mounds of *Hakonechloa*, and the clump bamboo, but don't miss the tree bench with the tree's newly made clay animal totems surrounded by hydrangeas, roses, and hellebores. Follow the path to the Balinese platform floating in a sea of ferns and daylilies. Take a moment to enjoy the privacy, then walk back to the new deck with its wonderful steel-wire railing. Come up and see the garden from this vantage point! Welcome to my garden! Iced tea will be served!

DIRECTIONS—From the Garden State Parkway, take Exit 151/Watchung Avenue. Turn right if you are coming from the north, left if from the south. Continue for 5 traffic lights or so on Watchung Avenue. The last traffic light will be at North Fullerton. Go through traffic light and make the next right (Valero gas station on corner) onto Park Street. Number 279 Park is about 10 houses later on right.
—From Route 3, take Grove Street Exit and turn left onto Grove Street. Continue past the cemetery. Turn right (only way possible) at the traffic light at end of cemetery. Go halfway up hill, turn left onto Park Street, continue about 1.5 miles to #279 (right past Gordonhurst intersection). The garden is on the left.

Bergen County
Saturday, June 23

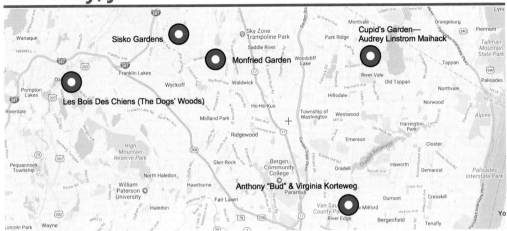

Bergen County
ALLENDALE
MONFRIED GARDEN
15 Stone Fence Road, Allendale
Hours: 10 a.m. to 4 p.m.
📷 | 2017

My garden is always evolving. The front beds, exposed to the street, are a magnet for deer, so I have planted many alliums and mint family plants, so far with some success. The back garden is fenced and features beds filled with many lush perennials, a large variety of interesting shrubs, small trees, vines, and potted tropicals. The woodland garden includes spring ephemerals, ferns, *Epimedium*, and other shade lovers. Hedgerows on both sides of the yard provide more protection from deer and showcase evergreen and deciduous shrubs under-planted with bulbs and perennials. A small raised bed provides vegetables in season.

DIRECTIONS—From the south, take Route 17 North to second Sheridan Avenue exit,

go under Route 17 and up ramp. Turn left on Prospect Avenue. At traffic light, turn left onto Franklin Turnpike. At next light, turn right onto Wyckoff Avenue. Go to third traffic light, then turn right onto Crescent Avenue. Go 1 mile to Allendale. Turn left onto Beresford Road, then right onto Schuyler Road, and then right again onto Stone Fence Road to #15.
—From the north, take Route 17 South to Lake Street exit. Bear left through the traffic light onto Crescent Avenue. Go through 4 more lights, then turn right onto Beresford Road, right onto Schuyler Road, and then right again onto Stone Fence Road to #15.

MAHWAH
SISKO GARDENS
113 Fardale Avenue, Mahwah
Hours: 10 a.m. to 4 p.m.
📷 | 2017

Paul has been working on this three-and-one-half acre property for over thirty years. The property was completely wooded within 100 feet of all sides of the original house. Major tree removal has opened the property to sunlight and sunset views. The fishpond and pool area are surrounded by terraced gardens from relocated stone farm walls that were on the property, along with larger stones unearthed from additional construction to the home. The terraces and upper gardens have been planted with mostly perennials and numerous annuals for spring through fall color. A new raised-bed vegetable garden has been added to an adjoining plot of land, which now receives sun due to the loss of several mature spruces. All of these gardens, as well as additions to the original home and his art studio/barn building have been developed by Paul. With more than 1,000 feet of recently installed deer fencing and electric driveway gates, Paul hopes his gardens will now be much safer from the resident deer population which live within the surrounding forest. We still have the groundhogs, raccoons, and chipmunks to deal with, but have taken a big step in protecting the major part of our gardens from wildlife...[Read full description online]

DIRECTIONS—From Route 208, take Russell Avenue Exit toward Wyckoff business district (left). Follow Wyckoff Avenue through 4 stoplights and turn left onto Fardale Avenue.
—From Route 17, exit at Lake Street to Ramsey business district (Main Street). Go through town where Main Street becomes Wyckoff Avenue. Turn right onto Fardale Avenue. If you come to a stoplight, you've gone 2 blocks past Fardale Avenue. Please park on either side of Fardale Avenue and check in with the garden docents upon entering the property through the stonewall entry.

OAKLAND
LES BOIS DES CHIENS (THE DOGS' WOODS)

90 Martha Place, Oakland
Hours: 10 a.m. to 4 p.m.
NEW

We are delighted to welcome guests to our gardens and woods, which are a source of great sustenance and joy to us. We urge you to enjoy our three acres of formal gardens, which include a wonderful balance of flowering perennials, varied annuals, a multitude of herbaceous and woody plants, and other garden amenities. One word of advice: GOOD WALKING SHOES WITH TRACTION are a must! Make sure to check out The Shakespeare Herb Garden before you enter the gardens themselves, and then glimpse the unusual showcase vegetable garden with its nice mixture of edible fruits and vegetables and annual flowers, before you leave for the woods. Once you exit the formal gardens and enter *Les Bois Des Chiens* (The Dogs' Woods) through one of the two gates we suggest (either the gate behind the bar or the main gate, located slightly to the left of the vegetable garden), a garden guide will help you find your way to some of the gems hidden among the various trees, shrubs, and ferns. As you pass through the main gate, take a peek at the carved collie heads on the gateposts. Our woods were named after the collies we have owned for over fifty years...[Read full description online]

DIRECTIONS—From New York City and other points east, take New Jersey State Route 4 west. Merge onto NJ-208 N / State Route 208 toward Oakland/Pompton Lakes/Greenwood Lake/Erskin Lake. Merge onto I-287 South via the exit on the left, toward Oakland / Morristown. Take the US-202 exit/Exit 58, toward Oakland. Turn left

onto Ramapo Valley Road/US-202 South. Continue to follow Ramapo Valley Road. Turn left onto Long Hill Road/US-202 North. Continue to follow Long Hill Road. Turn right onto Martha Place.
—From the south or west, take I-287 North toward Mahwah. Take Exit 58 toward US-202/Oakland. Turn left onto County Highway 4/W Oakland Avenue. Turn right onto Ramapo Valley Road/US-202 South. Continue to follow Ramapo Valley Road. Turn left onto Long Hill North. Continue to follow Long Hill. Turn right onto Martha Place.

RIVER EDGE
ANTHONY "BUD" & VIRGINIA KORTEWEG
800 Summit Avenue, River Edge
Hours: 8:30 a.m. to 4 p.m.
📷 | ♿ | **2017**

Edgecroft is a unique terraced property laid out in 1910 by Italian artisans. One hundred Carrara marble steps lead to a swimming pool surrounded by a stone-columned pergola draped in roses, wisteria, and honeysuckle. A gated brick courtyard entrance with a slowly maturing allée of hydrangeas greets guests. Hydrangeas provide a warm welcome with hues of pink and lavender interspersed with a variety of mixed perennials. There are also rare *Cryptomeria 'Lobbii,'* rhododendrons, azaleas, a *Magnolia virginiana*, a tiered bronze angel fountain, a Victorian-style perennial garden with David Austin antique roses and favorite perennials, a formal garden with crape myrtles, azaleas, and a fountain with a copy of Verricchio's fifteenth-century bronze "Cupid with Dolphin." A series of three koi ponds are interspersed with nine waterfalls that cascade down terraces edged with aged pines, golden larches, flowering cherry trees, dogwoods, *Styrax japonicus*, hydrangeas, wild strawberries,

and creeping roses. Bronze water statuary, stone benches, and stone statuary can be enjoyed throughout the grounds. A crushing 2010 winter storm transformed the white Bridal Room, but American Heritage river birch trees remain to frame this garden room with their tall leafy canopy... [Read full description online

DIRECTIONS—From George Washington Bridge, take Route 4 West to Route 17 North. Take Midland Avenue/River Edge exit. Go east about 2 miles to "T" and turn right onto Kinderkamack Road. Go south to first traffic light. Turn right onto Lincoln Avenue up a cobblestone hill. Walled property on right is Edgecroft. Turn right onto Summit Avenue. Number 800 is immediately on right. Please park along street and enter through open gates.
—From I-80/Garden State Parkway, take Route 17 North and proceed as directed above.

RIVER VALE
CUPID'S GARDEN—
AUDREY LINSTROM MAIHACK
690 Edward Street, River Vale
Hours: 10 a.m. to 4 p.m.
📷 | ♿ | **2017**

Due to a severe storm in 2011, the center of my garden changed from a patio shaded by tall trees to a sun garden full of color. A surrounding border of conifers, pines, and shrubs form a private semi-shaded garden. Short paths lead from decks to ponds, patio, and greenhouse. Varied gardens are adorned with rocks, shells, ground covers, rose trellises, early perennials, potted tropicals, and bonsai plants. Spring has many azaleas, bulbs, wisteria, dogwoods, weeping cherry, and Scotch broom. Later, flowering shrubs, iris, peonies, dianthus, and roses make way for foxgloves and assorted perennials, as well as water plants, daylilies, hostas, ferns, and herbs. Fall color starts the retreat to the potting shed and cedar greenhouse, my winter garden. Outside, under the watchful eye of Cupid, hawks and doves, as well as many other birds, frogs, rabbits, chipmunks, "Woody" the woodchuck, raccoons, and Mr. Skunk all visit the fish in the ponds.

DIRECTIONS—From the Garden State Parkway North, take Exit 172, last exit in New Jersey. Turn right onto Grand Avenue east. Pass Kinderkamack Road (railroad tracks) and go over hill to "T" (about 3 miles). Turn right onto South Middletown Road, which becomes River Vale Road, for 0.5 mile to right on Thurnau Drive (first right after Forcellati Nursery). First right is Edward Street. Ours is first house on right. Please park on street.
—From Palisades Parkway, take Exit 6W. Travel west on Orangeburg Road to fourth traffic light and turn left onto Blue Hill Road at end of reservoir. Go 1.4 miles to a stop sign. Turn left onto River Vale Road and proceed as directed above.
—Locals: Take Kinderkamack Road north from River Edge or Route 4. Pass Oradell, Emerson, Westwood business intersec-tions. Continue several miles to right turn onto Prospect Avenue. Continue to the end at River Vale Road. Turn left, two streets to Thurnau Drive. First right on Edward Street, to first house on right.

What our Garden Hosts recommend in Bergen County

Allendale Eats
101 West Allendale Avenue, Allendale, NJ
(201) 825-0110
www.allendaleeats.com

Rohsler's Allendale Nursery
100 Franklin Tpke, Allendale, NJ
(201) 327-3156
www.rohslers.com

Daveys Irish Pub
5 Park St, Montvale, NJ
(201) 391-9356
www.daveyspub.com

DePiero's Farm Stand and Greenhouses
156 Summit Ave, Montvale, NJ 07645
(201) 391-4576

Hunterdon County
Saturday, July 14

★ There are additional gardens open on this date in nearby Bucks County, PA. See page 296.

STOCKTON
BELLSFLOWER GARDEN
33 Rittenhouse Road, Stockton
Hours: 10 a.m. to 4 p.m.
📷 | ♿ | **NEW**

Bellsflower is a garden of flowers from spring through fall. In 1995, the year following our purchase of the farm, I started garden beds with little knowledge and lots of enthusiasm. Plants were chosen for color and size and often just because they caught an eye at the garden center. Knowledge came with time. Plants that survived and thrived began to shape the garden. *Phlox subulata* covers large swaths and hangs over stone walls. The pink and yellow of early *Nepeta* and *Allysum* signal spring. Irises, roses, and a succession of *arborescens, paniculata*, and *macrophylla* hydrangeas follow. July and August find crape myrtle and summer phlox in pink, blue, white, and coral. Come September the asters begin, and the final chapter is all about blue with tall roses adding their exclamation points and grasses flowing in the breeze. Flowering shrubs and spec-

imen trees bloom from March through September. As the leaves color and fall, the bright holly berries herald winter, when they feed robins as the snow flies.

DIRECTIONS—From Stockton, go north on Route 523 to the blinking light in the Village of Sergeantsville, and turn right onto Route 604 / Rosemont-Ringoes Road. Take first right onto Rittenhouse Road to #33, on left.

THE GARDEN AT FEDERAL TWIST
208 Federal Twist Road, Stockton
Hours: 10 a.m. to 6 p.m.
📷 | **2017**

When we moved into a mid-century house overlooking the woods, I immediately knew only a naturalistic garden would be appropriate to the place. The garden is hidden. You enter through the house, where you first glimpse the landscape, a sunny glade, through a wall of windows. Huge perennials and grasses evoke an "Alice in Wonderland" feeling (many plants are taller than you). The garden is in the New Perennial tradition: plants are massed in interwoven communities and emphasize structure, shape, and form—which are long-lasting—rather than flower. Begun as an experiment to explore garden making in the challenging conditions of unimproved, heavy, wet clay, the garden is ecologically similar to a wet prairie and is maintained by cutting and burning. Flowering begins in mid-June and peaks in mid-July, when the perennials and grasses reach maturity; then a second peak occurs in October, when low sunlight makes the grasses glow in yellows, russets, and golds.

Two small ponds attract hundreds of frogs, insects, and wildlife. Many gravel paths make garden exploration an immersive experience...[Read full description online]

DIRECTIONS—From the New York City area, take I-78. Take Exit 29 for I-287 toward Route 206/Route 202/Morristown / Somerville. Keep left at the fork and continue onto I-287 South for about 4 miles. Take Exit 17 onto Route 202 and continue to Flemington (about 19 miles). At the traffic circle, continue to the opposite side, and continue on Route 202 (about 10.8 miles) to the last exit in New Jersey, to Lambertville and Route 29. At the foot of the exit, turn left, then at the bottom of the exit, turn right onto Route 29/River Road/Daniel Bray Highway. Continue north, passing through the village of Stockton, for a total of 5.1 miles from Lambertville. On the right is a large sign for Hidden Valley Nursery. Federal Twist Road is immediately past the sign. Turn right and drive up Federal Twist Road 2.9 miles to #208. Park on the right side of the road (the house side), taking care to leave the left lane open.
—From western Philadelphia suburbs, take the I-276 East/Pennsylvania Turnpike east to Exit 343. Exit on Route 611 North toward Doylestown. In about 10 miles, exit onto Route 202 North/New Hope. In about 10 miles, continue on Route 202 past New Hope, and cross toll bridge over Delaware River, exiting immediately on the New Jersey side toward Lambertville. At the foot of the exit, turn left onto Route 29 North/ River Road/Daniel Bray Highway. Proceed as directed above.
—From northern New Jersey or the Hudson River Valley, take I-287 south, then take Exit 17 onto Route 202 and continue to Flemington (about 19 miles). At the traffic circle continue to the opposite side, and continue on Route 202 (about 10.8 miles)

to the last exit in New Jersey, to Lambertville and Route 29. At the foot of the exit, turn left, then at the bottom of the exit, turn right onto Route 29 / River Road/ Daniel Bray Highway. Proceed as directed above.

THE GORRELL-SHUCKER GARDEN
36 Brookville Hollow Road, Stockton
Hours: 10 a.m. to 4 p.m.
NEW

Paul Gorrell and John Schucker's late eighteenth-century home is surrounded by three-and-one-half acres of recently deer fenced land with the garden comprising roughly half of this while the rest is natural woodland. It is a traditional landscape garden made up of several terraced areas, each supported by dry-laid stone walls, several quite old. The surrounding woodland seems to have demanded that the garden be created with an emphasis on woody plants and ground covers and so it includes many rhododendrons, viburnums, witch hazels, hydrangeas, and various small ornamental trees.

DIRECTIONS—The nearest large highway is Route 202. Exit for Stockton/Lambertville and head north on Route 29 for a couple of miles. As one approaches Stockton, there is a sharp "S" curve in the road. Turn RIGHT onto Brookville Hollow Road. Number 36 is 0.5 mile up the road on the right side. If approaching from the north on Route 29, Brookville Hollow Road will be found as a left turn only at the southern end of the town. The old stone house and stone garage and carriage house are situated very close to the road and so there is no driveway leading to the house. Instead, there is plenty of room to pull off the road to park in front of the house along a stone retaining wall.

Morris County
Saturday, July 14

Morris County
CHATHAM
JACK LAGOS
23 Pine Street, Chatham
Hours: 10 a.m. to 4 p.m.
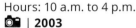 | 2003

I have been developing this one-acre property, which backs onto a lovely wood, for twenty-five years. The first garden, with island perennial border, is now one among many. A 100-year-old barn is backdrop for shade-loving plants, and on its sunny sides lie an herb garden and another perennial border. Ten graceful clematis vines climb beautifully designed lattice fencing, which defines the dwarf conifer collection. A woodland garden, my latest project, lies beneath a very large white oak and fea-

tures a natural rock fountain.

DIRECTIONS—From Garden State Parkway or New Jersey Turnpike/I-95, take I-78 west to Route 24 west. Take Chatham exit (immediately after Short Hills Mall). Follow signs to Route 124 West/Main Street and, at fifth traffic light, turn left onto Lafayette Avenue. Go all the way to top of hill and, when Lafayette bends to right, turn right onto Pine Street. Number 23 is the fourth house on left. From I-287, exit onto Route 24 East. Continue to The Mall at Short Hills exit. At end of exit ramp, turn right onto River Road. At first traffic light, bear right and continue straight (River Road becomes Watching Avenue) to fifth light. Turn left onto Lafayette Avenue. Proceed as directed above. Please park on street.

Monmouth County
Saturday, July 21

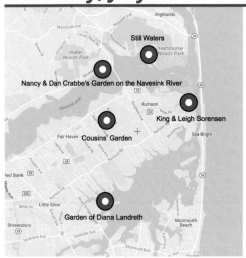

LITTLE SILVER
GARDEN OF DIANA LANDRETH
585 Little Silver Point Road, Little Silver
Hours: 10 a.m. to 4 p.m.
📷 | ♿PARTIAL | **NEW**

In 2001, I bought an old house with a wonderful view of the Shrewsbury River. Although the house needed some tender loving care, I couldn't wait to get my hands on the garden. I have always been a great fan of the traditional English perennial border, but this Victorian house seemed to call for something else entirely. In my mind's eye, I saw a perfectly symmetrical formal parterre lined up with the central axis of the house. To the surprise and consternation of the neighbors, I carefully staked out a pattern and began to dig up the front lawn. For lovers of vast lawns and bigger driveways, this was a really radical plan. But, for me, this step outside my comfort zone was the best design decision I ever made. The parterre has become a canvas on which I can experiment with color and

form in the eight sections delineated by low boxwood hedges. In spring, 1,500 tulip bulbs, different combinations of pastels each year, announce the beginning of the season, and complement the surrounding cherry blossoms and redbuds. June brings roses, pale pink 'New Dawn' on four anchoring *tuteurs*, with red Drift® roses in two of the sections, and 'Phenomenal' lavender close by...[Read full description online]

DIRECTIONS—Take the Garden State Parkway South to Exit 109 Red Bank/Tinton Falls. Turn left onto Newman Springs Road after leaving exit. Proceed 0.7 mile to Hance Avenue. Keep right and take the right exit onto Hance. Proceed 1.1 miles to Sycamore Avenue. Turn left onto Sycamore Avenue and proceed 2.3 miles, passing Shrewsbury Avenue and Route 35. Continuing across the tracks at Little Silver train station, go through the intersection (station and large gas station on your right). Sycamore Avenue turns slightly to left and becomes Willow Drive for 1 mile. Turn right onto Little Silver Point Road and proceed 1.2 miles, continuing through intersection at Seven Bridges Road. (Point Road Elementary School is at intersection.) You are now on the Point, and #585 is on the left, clearly marked on mailbox post. White Victorian house with dark green shutters, red brick driveway—lots of flowers! Route from the Parkway should take 15 to 20 minutes.

LOCUST

NANCY & DAN CRABBE'S GARDEN ON THE NAVESINK RIVER

904 Navesink River Road, Locust
Hours: 10 a.m. to 4 p.m.
 | 2016

The property, at an elevation of 150′ over-looking the Navesink River, was originally developed to showcase a Japanese bonsai collection created by the owner's aunt. The bonsai have moved on to a county park, and the garden has been extended and currently reflects its original bones coupled with naturalistic English garden flowers and shrubs. It is a peaceful and rustic space.

DIRECTIONS—Take Exit 109 on the Garden State Parkway. Continue east onto Half Mile Road until it dead-ends. Turn right onto West Front Street and continue to the first traffic light. Turn left onto Hubbard Road and at the first light turn right onto Navesink River Road. Continue 4.5 miles to Deep Hollow Drive on the left, where you can park. Walk east (left as you leave Deep Hollow Drive) to the Crabbe garden at #904 Navesink River Road (black mailbox with a red crab), which is on the right side of the road.

STILL WATERS

19 Wigwam Road, Locust
Hours: 10 a.m. to 4 p.m.
 | & | NEW

My garden looks directly up the Navesink River. We have a large terrace overlooking the garden, and a curvy path runs through it with a gate in the center toward the river. Our three-bowl fountain attracts all the birds in the neighborhood. The garden is encircled by mature boxwoods. There always seems to be something blooming,

from peonies to irises to old hydrangeas, asters, daisies, lilies, roses, azaleas. The location is exquisite between the river and the 750-acre Hartshorne Woods Park. There are gardens around the whole house as well.

DIRECTIONS—Take Hartshorne Road, across From All Saints Episcopal Church, and go 2 miles. Drive along causeway, pass pond on left, and go around a curve to first street on your right, marked Wigwam Road. We are the third house on the right, #19. Park on street.

RUMSON

COUSINS' GARDEN

2 Orchard Lane, Rumson
Hours: 10 a.m. to 4 p.m.
 | & | NEW

At the suggestion of their daughter Michele, Michael and Jill Sullivan created Cousins' Garden on their one-acre proper-ty in Rumson as a way for their ten grand-children to garden together and give back to the local community. The cousins weed and harvest fruits and vegetables in 120 raised beds. Their first year, the cousins contributed 6,500 pounds of produce to Lunch Break, a soup kitchen in nearby Red Bank. "It's given much more back to us than we put in," Michael says of the project. Renee Mongiovi of Oasis Backyard Gar-dens in Colts Neck, New Jersey, designed the attractive layout.

DIRECTIONS—From Garden State Park-way, take Exit 109. Turn east onto Newman Springs Road (Route 520), and after 1.5 miles turn left onto Broad Street. After 0.75 mile, turn right onto Harding Place and go east 3 miles (road name changes to Ridge Road). Turn left onto Buena Vista Avenue and take first right onto Orchard

Lane. House is at the end of the lane.

KING & LEIGH SORENSEN
7 North Ward Avenue, Rumson
Hours: 10 a.m. to 4 p.m.
📷 | ♿PARTIAL | **2016**

The house, a former windmill and barn, looks out at five miles of salt marsh, a river, and the distant Manhattan skyline. The design of the landscape reflects this view to the north—islands of perennials, shrubs, and trees that are saltwater-tolerant and grouped naturalistically. Numerous publications have featured the gardens starting with the January 1983 issue of *House Beautiful*. Leigh, who is a landscape designer, has a collection of bonsai and a flock of chickens. After a trip to Japan last year, Leigh added a small stone garden. King raises honeybees and five varieties of lettuce. The property floods in storm tides.

DIRECTIONS—From Garden State Parkway, take Exit 109. Turn east onto Newman Springs Road, and after 1.5 miles turn left onto Broad Street. After 0.75 mile turn right onto Harding Place and go east 5 miles (road name changes to Ridge, then Hartshorne). At end, turn left onto North Ward Avenue. Our driveway is a continuation of North Ward Avenue.

What our Garden Hosts recommend in Monmouth County

Sickles Market
1 Harrison Ave, Little Silver, NJ 07739
(732) 741-9563
www.sicklesmarket.com

Guaranteed Plants & Florist
504 Locust Point Rd, Rumson, NJ 07760
(732) 291-3241
www.guaranteedplants.com

Fresh Bistro
144 Bay Ave, Highlands, NJ 07732
(732) 708-0328
www.freshhighlands.com

Anjelica's
1070 Ocean Ave, Sea Bright, NJ 07760
(732) 842-2800
www.anjelicas.com

Hunterdon County
Saturday, August 4

DIRECTIONS—From Route 202 South, proceed to Route 29. Follow directions from Route 29.
—From Route 29, take 519 N through Rosemont. House is on left, 0.5 mile north of Rosemont.
—From Route 78, continue to Route 202. Follow directions from 202.

★ There is an additional garden open on this date in nearby Bucks County, PA. See page 297.

Hunterdon County
STOCKTON
PRETTY BIRD FARM
137 Kingwood Stockton Road, Stockton
Hours: 10 a.m. to 4 p.m.
📷 | ♿PARTIAL | **NEW**

Pretty Bird Farm is a vegetable and flower garden nestled in scenic Hunterdon County. We grow primarily heirloom tomatoes and a wide variety of cut flowers to sell to our neighbors and local small businesses. 2018 will be our fifth summer here, growing everything as organically as possible. We have a low- water-use site and plant and care for our garden to support the bees, butterflies, and birds. Our goal is to treat our farm as one balanced and harmonious ecosystem.

Northern New Jersey
Saturday, September 8

Essex County
NUTLEY
THE MOUNTSIER GARDEN
205 Rutgers Place, Nutley
Hours: 10 a.m. to 4 p.m.
📷 | ♿PARTIAL | **2017**

For the last twenty-three years Richard Hartlage has worked with Silas Mountsier and Graeme Hardie on their garden in Nutley. Says Hartlage, "Our collaboration and friendship grew through a chance meeting with Graeme in Raleigh, North Carolina. The outcome is the most favorite in my portfolio. The original property has expanded from a half-acre to over two acres during the last two decades, as Silas and Graeme purchased adjacent parcels. The garden evolved through collaboration, with not an ill-considered decision; sometimes with disagreement, sometimes embraced immediately, but always with consensus. The garden has deep personal meaning for the three of us and represents the history of a friendship built in physical space. For visitors, the emotional content is palpable with every detail and vista. Though a strolling garden at its heart, the garden offers many places to sit and rest the eye and contemplate the crucible of a visitor's life and the vast collection of figurative and modern art. The garden is bold in its layout and unfolds through a progression of spaces, each more beautiful than the last...[Read full description online]

DIRECTIONS—From the Lincoln Tunnel or Exit 16 of the I-95/New Jersey Turnpike, go west on Route 3. From Garden State Parkway, go east on Route 3. From both directions, go to the Main Avenue/Nutley/Passaic exit. At end of exit ramp, turn left and go through two traffic lights (three lights if coming from west). After this light, go straight ahead. Rutgers Place is fourth street on left. Come up Rutgers Place to top of hill; when road flattens, #205 is on right.

Morris County
FLANDERS
STERLING GARDEN
110 Bartley-Flanders Road, Flanders
Hours: 10 a.m. to 4 p.m.
📷 | ♿PARTIAL | **NEW**

Susan Olinger is a landscape designer, certified with the APLD and employed by Sterling Horticultural Services. She designed Sterling garden in 2004 and has been adding to and maintaining it ever since. The property is four acres, but the gardens encompass about one-and-one-half acres. This includes a patio, a small pond with waterfall, a woodland garden, and diverse mixed borders. Most of the trees were planted, although a 100-year-old (or more) Kentucky coffee tree (*Gymnocladus dioicus*) adorns the front yard. There is also a meadow of naturally occurring wildflowers and grasses.

DIRECTIONS—Bartley-Flanders Road is just off Route 206, approximately 5 miles south of Route 80 and 4 miles north of Chester Borough. There is ample parking if you pull into driveway.

Somerset County
FAR HILLS
THE HAY HONEY FARM
130 Stevens Lane, Far Hills
Hours: 10 a.m. to 5 p.m.
2017

The extensive gardens of The Hay Honey Farm lie nestled between rolling hills along the North Branch of the Raritan River. The transition from cattle farm to garden began in 1989, and while Black Angus cattle still graze the nearby hayfields, honeybees have become the only "livestock" allowed within the gates. Over the years, a wide variety of plant material, including hundreds of trees and shrubs, has been carefully added to the landscape in a naturalistic manner, with a respect for the history and topography of the site, and consistent with the broader surrounding atmosphere of Pleasant Valley. The plant collections reflect the diverse interests of the owners and the resident horticulturists, and show the results of a long-term vision and dedicated horticultural attention to plant care. Garden areas created near the homes include a dwarf conifer/spring bulb garden, a large walled perennial border, hosta gardens, a native meadow, and a large kitchen garden. Year-round springs feed a small stream, which originates in the wild garden and flows through a collection of rhododendron and companion wild flowers and woodland plants...[Read full description online]

DIRECTIONS—From I-95/New Jersey Turnpike, take I-78 West. Then take I-287 North to Exit 22B (or Exit 22 if coming from north). Stay on Route 206 North. At fourth traffic light, turn right onto Holland Avenue. At end, turn left onto Peapack. Turn right onto Willow Avenue. Go 1 mile and turn left onto Branch Road. At 0.7 mile, cross the green steel bridge onto a private gravel road. Please follow signs to the parking area, as weather conditions don't always allow us to use the hayfields. Park here for the Stone House Garden also and volunteers will direct you.

STONE HOUSE GARDEN
121 Stevens Lane, Far Hills
Hours: 10 a.m. to 4 p.m.
📷 | **2017**

All the buildings and walls are of old Pennsylvania stone; the paths and terrace are of Vermont schist. One goes through the beech hedge into the courtyard, planted with low-growing *Rhus aromatica* and Spanish bluebells. The path, which encircles the house, leads through the medallion garden to the crescent border, planted for spring bloom and fall color; past the kitchen garden, terrace, and Mimi's garden; and down stone steps to the bog, which, in the spring, hosts an explosion of primula candelabra, fern, and skunk cabbage.

DIRECTIONS—Follow directions to park at The Hay Honey Farm, and walk next door to the Stone House Garden; volunteers will be on hand to direct you.

PUBLIC GARDEN

Essex County
SHORT HILLS
GREENWOOD GARDENS
274 Old Short Hills Road, Short Hills
(973) 258-4026
greenwoodgardens.org

★ See full listing on page 192.

Hunterdon County
Sunday, September 9

Hunterdon County
POTTERSVILLE
JARDIN DE BUIS
129 Pickle Road, Pottersville
Hours: 10 a.m. to 4 pm.
📷 | 2017

The gardens and landscape are part of an ongoing project begun in 1992 as a complete renovation and expansion of an eighteenth-century dairy farm on thirty-five acres. The original four barns and a single wooded hedge-row was all that was left of the abandoned farm in the heart of deer country. The gardens closest to the barn/house complex were structured around three courtyards formed by the barns, stone walls, and boxwood. The stone parking court leads to the entry/west courtyard which is adjacent to the formal sycamore and boxwood garden off the kitchen. Continuing around the house is a thyme garden that leads to the eastern court with the pond and white garden. Moving westward away from the house you encounter the formal French *potager* surrounded by privet and fence. This vegetable garden was laid out on axis to the north side of an old cowshed and the orangery. The greenhouse was salvaged from Rutgers University and designed around an English-style orangery. It is solar powered and heated... [Read full description online]

DIRECTIONS—From New York City, take

www.opendaysprogram.org

Holland Tunnel to I-78 West to Exit 29/I-287 North. Do not follow sign towards I-287. Stay on I-78 West to Exit 29.
—From I-287 North take Exit 22B/Routes 202/206 North Bedminster/Netcong (second exit). Keep left on Route 206 North. Go to sixth traffic light at Route 512/Pottersville Road. Turn left and go to the end. Turn right onto Black River Road. Then stay left, cross bridge, pass Black River Market and take Route 512/Fairmont Road East. Go 1.6 miles, (pass Pickle Road on right). Turn right onto Van Pelt Road and go to end. Turn left onto Pickle Road. Entrance is 0.2 mile on left or the fourth drive with four barns and a silo.

Jardin de Buis
DIGGING DEEPER
12 PM
Boxwood for the Future
REGISTRATION: $30 Garden Conservancy Members / $35 general

Andrea Filippone is a boxwood expert who is on a crusade to get people to move beyond the sickly standard English and American box varieties to embrace lesser-known hybrids that are elegant and agreeably pungent, but better garden plants. The latest influx of the boxwood blight, *Cylindrocladium buxicola*, emphasizes the need for a shift to new hybrids and new, organic cultural practices. With proper soil management, the use of cultivars specifically chosen for the site, and the absence of chemical fertilizers and pesticides, the plants will thrive in their new location for years to come.

Andrea and Eric T. Fleischer operate a boxwood nursery at their home as well as F2 Environmental Design.

Registration required — space limited
Go to opendaysprogram.org
or call 1 (888) 842-2442

Jardin de Buis
DIGGING DEEPER
1 PM
Compost Tea for Healthy Soil and Healthy Gardens
REGISTRATION: $30 Garden Conservancy Members / $35 general

Andrea Filippone and Eric T. Fleischer run F2 Environmental Design, where their clients include Harvard University, Storm King Art Center, and the Museum of Modern Art. "T" is the organic guru in the firm, who believes that the basis of all successful gardening is an understanding and nurturing of the soil biosphere. Healthy soil is rich in beneficial bacteria and fungi, some of which work directly with plant roots to nourish and protect their symbionts. Fleisher explained that some of these microbes are eaten by tiny creatures which release nitrogen as they feed. This is a system that relies on good soil structure, lots of choice compost incorporated into the earth, and the absence of chemical fertilizers and pesticides.

Registration required — space limited
Go to opendaysprogram.org
or call 1 (888) 842-2442

PUBLIC GARDENS

Essex County
SHORT HILLS
GREENWOOD GARDENS
274 Old Short Hills Road, Short Hills
(973) 258-4026
greenwoodgardens.org

Hours: Special Garden Conservancy Open Days 2018: May 5 and September 8, 10 a.m. to 5 p.m., otherwise May through mid November, Thursday through Sunday from 10 a.m. to 5 p.m.
Admission: $7 on Garden Conservancy

days. All other days $10 for adults, $5 for senior citizens and students, Children under 12 free.

Since the early twentieth-century, Greenwood Gardens was a private retreat with formal Italianate gardens graced by colorful tiles, rustic stone tea houses, mossy-pebbled walks, and vistas stretching for miles into the surrounding wooded hillsides. Careful preservation work and imaginative horticulture have returned much of the garden to its original Arts and

Crafts design. Greenwood Gardens is a Garden Conservancy preservation garden.

DIRECTIONS—From Garden State Parkway, take Exit 142. Take I-78 west to Millburn and take Exit 50B. At top of exit ramp, turn right onto Vauxhall Road and proceed to its end, about 0.8 mile. At end of Vauxhall Road, turn left onto Millburn Avenue. In about 1 mile, road jogs slightly to right and changes to Essex). At third traffic light turn right onto Old Short Hills Road and go up hill about 0.5 mile to stone gateposts marking entrance of Greenwood Gardens, #274, on right. Turn here and follow signs to parking lot.
—From New Jersey Turnpike/I-95 South, take Exit 14/Newark Airport. Stay right through tollbooth, and take I-78 local west to Millburn, and get off at Exit 50B. Proceed as directed above.
—From Route 24 West, take Hobart Gap Road exit. Turn right at light onto Hobart Gap Road. At blinking light, road name changes to White Oak Ridge Road. At next light (1 mile), turn right onto Parsonage Hill Road. Continue to "T" junction. Turn left onto Old Short Hills Road and go about 0.6 mile where road widens at stone gate marked with signs for Greenwood Gardens.

Essex County
MONTCLAIR
VAN VLECK HOUSE & GARDENS
21 Van Vleck Street, Montclair
(973) 744-4752
www.vanvleck.org
Hours: Year round, daily, dawn until dusk
Admission: Free

Begun at the turn of the century, these gardens have been developed by several generations of committed horticulturists. The plan is largely formal, responding to the Mediterranean style of the house. The extensive collection of rhododendrons and azaleas, including several named for family members, is renowned. Also of note are the many mature plant specimens.

DIRECTIONS—From Garden State Parkway North, take Exit 148/Bloomfield Avenue. Stay in left lane of exit ramp through first traffic light and take jug-handle under the Garden State Parkway back to Bloomfield Avenue; turn right (west) at light. Proceed for 2.5 miles through Bloomfield, Glen Ridge, and Montclair town centers. Turn right onto North Mountain Avenue (Montclair Art Museum is on left). Proceed through one light (Claremont Avenue) and take next left onto Van Vleck Street; Van Vleck House & Gardens is on left.
From Garden State Parkway South, take Exit 148/Bloomfield Avenue. Follow service road (paralleling the Garden State Parkway) through one stop sign and two lights. Turn right (west) at the third light onto Bloomfield Avenue. Proceed as directed above.
—From New York City, take Lincoln Tunnel to Route 3 West. Exit at Grove Street/Montclair. Turn left at top of exit ramp onto Grove Street, proceed 3.9 miles to Claremont Avenue, turn right. Proceed 0.9 mile to fifth light. Turn right onto North

Mountain Avenue and proceed as directed above.

—From I-280, take Exit 8B/Prospect Avenue. Proceed north 2 miles to Bloomfield Avenue, turn right, and proceed 0.5 mile to third light. Turn left onto North Mountain Avenue. Proceed through one light (Claremont Avenue) and take next left onto Van Vleck Street. Van Vleck House and Gardens is on left.

M. Doren

STONECROP GARDENS

81 Stonecrop Lane, Cold Spring, New York 845.265.2000
www.stonecrop.org

Stonecrop Gardens consists of 15 acres of gardens at a windswept elevation of
1,100 feet in the Hudson Highlands in Cold Spring, New York.

Come see our diverse collection of gardens and plants
• Conservatory • Enclosed Flower Garden • Woodland Garden
• Mediterranean Garden • Alpine Rock Ledge • Systemic Order Beds

❋ Plants for sale / Membership available ❋
....

*Our mission is to uphold and demonstrate the highest standards of horticultural practice
and to promote the use of such standards among amateur and professional gardeners
through aesthetic displays and educational programs.*
....

Stonecrop is open Monday – Saturday
April – October, 10 a.m. – 5 p.m.
Admission *$10*
Seniors 65 and older, students with an ID - *$5*
Children ages 3 through 18 - *$5*
Children under 3 - ***Free***
Guided group tours (10 or more people) available by appointment

❋ **2018 Garden Conservancy Open Days** ❋

April 22, May 13, June 10, July 8, August 12, September 2, October 7

Join us for Tea in the Garden (noon – 4 p.m.)

NEW YORK
Ithaca Area
Saturday, March 24

Tompkins County
TRUMANSBURG
HITCH LYMAN'S GARDEN
3441 Krums Corners Road, Trumansburg
Hours: 11 a.m. to 3 p.m.
 | **2017**

This garden features a collection of more than 500 snowdrop varieties (*Galanthus*) planted in a woodland setting, in addition to early spring flowers. By the end of March, there may still be some late snowdrops in bloom, as well as cyclamen and early daffodils. The 1848 Greek Revival-style farmhouse was moved to this site in 1990. Plants will be offered for sale from the Temple Nursery. Please note: due to rough terrain this garden is not handicapped accessible nor appropriate for small children. In case of inclement weather, please check the website for schedule changes.

DIRECTIONS—From Ithaca, go north on Route 96 about 6 miles. Turn right onto Krums Corners Road. Go to sixth driveway on left. Please park on road.

Dutchess County
Saturday, March 24

Cary Institute of Ecosystem Studies
2801 Sharon Turnpike, Millbrook
DIGGING DEEPER
2 PM
I Plant, Therefore, I Am—Stories from
a Connecticut Kitchen Garden
—
Lecture co-sponsored by
Cary Institute and Innisfree Garden
REGISTRATION: $30 Garden
Conservancy Members / $35 general

At her private "Ho Hum Hollow Farm," Pamela Page maintains a 10,000 square foot kitchen garden where she grows almost 200 different kinds of fruits and vegetables, everything from the usual farmer's market produce to rare or heirloom varieties such as Chinese watermelon radish, purple carrots, multi-colored cucumbers, white beets, and black tomatoes. In more than 300 images, Pamela takes us through the evolution of her kitchen garden, from early inspirations to the challenges and rewards of growing your own. Her garden has been open through the Garden Conservancy Open Days and featured in *Country Living* magazine as well as *Connecticut Cottages & Gardens*. Pamela also helps clients around the globe, from New England to Tuscany, Panama, and the Bahamas, achieve the same dream of creating and maintaining a flower and vegetable garden. As part of her educational outreach activities, Pamela designed and built a kitchen garden at Glynwood Center, a historic 225-acre demonstration farm dedicated to rural conservation located in Cold Spring, New York, where she also oversaw their kitchen gardening apprentice program. Pamela frequently lectures on how to create a kitchen garden, whether on a rooftop, in a window box, or a suburban back yard.

Registration required — space limited
Go to opendaysprogram.org
or call 1 (888) 842-2442

Dutchess County
Saturday, April 14

Cary Institute of Ecosystem Studies
2801 Sharon Turnpike, Millbrook
DIGGING DEEPER
11 AM
The Budget-Wise Gardener
—
Lecture co-sponsored by
Cary Institute and Innisfree Garden
REGISTRATION: $30 Garden
Conservancy Members / $35 general

Plant the best for less! Money-saving tips for purchasing plants plus cost-saving garden designs. Discover a wealth of ideas for getting the best price and value for exceptional plants. The plant sources and strategies will surprise you! Also covered are striking design concepts for eye-popping, pollinator-friendly landscapes requiring less maintenance and water. And, container gardening takes on a whole new spin with these cost-effective, creative ideas!

This lecture is based on Kerry Ann Mendez's newest book, *The Budget-Wise Gardener*—an essential guide to creating the garden of your dreams without breaking the bank. An award-winning speaker, author, and designer, Kerry Ann has more than twenty-five years of professional and personal garden experience with a special interest in low-maintenance gardening.

Registration required — space limited
Go to opendaysprogram.org
or call 1 (888) 842-2442

What our Garden Hosts recommend in Dutchess County

Babette's Kitchen
3293 Franklin Avenue, Millbrook NY 12545
(845) 677-8602
www.babetteskitchen.com

The Farmer's Wife
3809 ROUTE 44, Millbrook, NY 12545
(845) 605-1595
www.thefarmerswife.biz

Twin Brook Gardens
3424 Franklin Avenue, Millbrook, NY 12545
(845) 677-5050
www.twinbrooksgardens.com

Adams Fairacre Farms
765 Dutchess Turnpike
Poughkeepsie, NY 12603
(845) 454-4330
www.adamsfarms.com

Putnam County
Sunday, April 22

Putnam County
COLD SPRING
STONECROP GARDENS
81 Stonecrop Lane, Cold Spring
(845) 265-2000
stonecrop.org

★ For full listing please see page 279.

Dutchess County
Saturday, April 28

Cary Institute of Ecosystem Studies
2801 Sharon Turnpike, Millbrook

DIGGING DEEPER
11 AM
The Garden in Every Sense and
Season—A Bootcamp for the Senses
—
Lecture co-sponsored by
Cary Institute and Innisfree Garden
REGISTRATION: $30 Garden
Conservancy Members / $35 general

Your garden could be so fulfilling—if you plug in. Created to coincide with the publication of Tovah Martin's new book, *The Garden in Every Sense*

and Season, this lecture explores the garden on all levels by attuning your nose to the scents and training your ears to listen. Learn to garden with eyes wide open, ears to the ground, and hands outstretched. Tailored to the current season to make each presentation dynamic, this lecture will lead your group through an odyssey of exploration to awaken the senses and arouse your abilities of perception on all levels. Sharing advice and ideas to deeply enhance the gardening experience while also incorporating a "Smellathon" to help get nostrils in gear, this lecture is beautiful and fun as well as highly practical. Want to broaden your horizons? After this presentation, your garden will be more savory, you will know its touch, smell its aromas, hear its voice, and see it anew.

Registration required—space limited
Go to opendaysprogram.org
or call 1 (888) 842-2442

Westchester County
Sunday, April 29

Westchester County
LEWISBORO
THE WHITE GARDEN
199 Elmwood Road, Lewisboro
Hours: 10 a.m. to 3 p.m.
📷 | **2017**

The native oak-hickory forest provides a "sacred grove" setting for the modern Greek Revival-style house. The gardens were designed by Patrick Chassé, ASLA, and completed in 1999. Nearest the house the gardens are classically inspired, including a nymphaeum, pergola garden, labyrinth, and theater court, and additional hidden gardens include a perennial ellipse and "annual" garden, a conservatory "jungle" garden, and an Asian-inspired moss garden.

Several water features accent the landscape, and native plantings dominate in areas outside the central gardens. Many sculptures enrich this landscape, and one can visit a Temple of Apollo on an island in the main pond. In spring, over 300,000 daffodils bloom in the woodland, where walking paths weave over a meandering brook and through a shady dell. Several glasshouses can be seen, including a new state-of-the-art greenhouse that supports the gardens. Head gardener Eric Schmidt, who ably orchestrates the rich garden plantings throughout the property, is on hand for questions.

DIRECTIONS—From Route 15/Merritt Parkway, take Exit 38 and follow Route 123 North through New Canaan into New York state. Town of Lewisboro and village of Vista are first signs encountered. Go past Vista Fire Department about 0.25 mile. Just after shingled Episcopal church on right, Route 123 bears left and Elmwood Road bears right. Go about another 0.25 mile, just over a hill. At beginning of a gray stockade fence on right is driveway at #199.

The White Garden
DIGGING DEEPER
Family Time — 10 AM & 2 PM
The Magic of Making More Plants—A Workshop for Kids
Free with garden admission

Celebrate spring at the fabulously imaginative White Garden with Eric Schmidt, estate manager, as he leads a hands-on workshop for gardeners of all ages. In the large greenhouse, kids will get their hands in the soil, investigating and planting different seeds and discussing what they need to germinate. The group will also explore how some plants grow from cuttings (pieces of existing plants). Each child will take home a free seedling to observe and enjoy. This program is appropriate for children ages seven and up. Adults must stay with the children in their care at all times.

What our Garden Hosts recommend in Westchester County

Purdy's Farmer & the Fish
100 Titicus Rd, North Salem, NY 10560
(914) 617-8380
www.farmerandthefish.com

Rosedale Nurseries Inc
51 Saw Mill River Rd, Hawthorne, NY 10532
(914) 769-1300
www.rosedalenurseries.com

Susan Lawrence Gourmet Food
26 N Greeley Ave, Chappaqua, NY 10514
(914) 238-8833
www.susanlawrence.com

Crabtree's Kittle House
11 Kittle Rd, Chappaqua, NY 10514
(914) 666-8044
www.kittlehouse.com

Columbia County
Saturday, May 5

Columbia County
COPAKE FALLS
MARGARET ROACH
99 Valley View Road, Copake Falls
Hours: 10 a.m. to 4 p.m.
📷 | **2017** | 🏷 BROKEN ARROW NURSERY

The garden, about thirty years of age, reflects my obsession with plants, particularly those with good foliage or of interest to wildlife, and also my belief that even in Zone 5B the view out the window can be compelling and satisfying all 365 days of the year. Sixty-five kinds of birds have been my longtime companions, along with every local frog and toad species, and we are all happy together. Informal mixed borders, shrubberies, frog-filled water gardens, and container groupings cover the steep two-and-one-third-acre hillside.

It's a former orchard with a simple Victorian-era farmhouse and little outbuildings set in Taconic State Park lands on a rural farm road.

DIRECTIONS—From Route 22 (5 miles south of Hillsdale, 13 miles north of Millerton) take Route 344 toward Taconic State Park signs. Bear right onto Valley View Road after park entrance and brown store, over metal bridge, and past camp. After High Valley Road on left, stay right another 100' to green barn and house on left. Parking on High Valley or opposite house.

www.opendaysprogram.org

What our Garden Hosts recommend in Columbia County

Hawthorne Valley Farm Store &
327 County Route 21c, Ghent, NY 12075
(518) 672-7500
www.store.hawthornevalley.org

Crossroads Food Shop
2642 NY-23, Hillsdale, NY 12529
(518) 325-1461
www.crossroadsfoodshop.com

Ca'Mea
333 Warren St, Hudson, NY 12534
(518) 822-0005
www.camearestaurant.com

Pondside Nursery
5918 RT9G, Hudson, NY 12534
(518) 828-1179
www.pondsidenursery.com

Suffolk County
Sunday, May 6

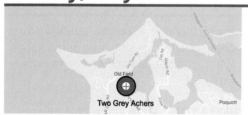

Suffolk County
OLD FIELD
TWO GREY ACHERS
88 Old Field Road, Old Field
Hours: 10 p.m. to 4 p.m.
📷 | ♿PARTIAL | **2016**

Designed, executed, and largely maintained by its owners to provide seasonal interest every day of the year, this garden, adjacent to Conscience Bay on Long Island's North Shore, has conifers large and small, rhododendrons, azaleas, Japanese maples, and companions to create a tapestry of color, texture, and form. Its favorable maritime microclimate is reflected in the broad range of taxa thriving on this extensively planted site. Those visitors returning to the garden since it was last included in the Garden Conservancy Open Days program will see a somewhat expanded and much matured landscape. In addition, the favorable 2017 summer season has resulted in exuberant growth and a phenomenal rhododendron flower bud set promising an exceptional show in May.

DIRECTIONS—Take Route 495/Long Island Expressway to Exit 62. Take Route 97/ Nicolls Road North to end at Route 25A. Turn right onto Route 25A and then left at the first traffic light. Go through 4 stop signs to end at the stone bridge. Turn left over stone bridge onto Old Field Road. Go about 2 miles to #88 on the left. There is no name on the mailbox, but the number 88 shows clearly. There is no roadside parking in the Village of Old Field. Cars should pull off the roadside onto the front lawn.

Dutchess County
Saturday, May 12

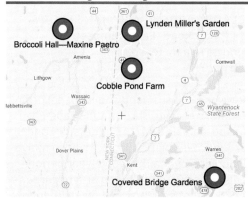

★ There are additional gardens open on this date in nearby Litchfield County, CT. See page 83.

Dutchess County
AMENIA
BROCCOLI HALL—MAXINE PAETRO
23 Flint Hill Road, Amenia
Hours: 10 a.m. to 4 p.m.
📷 | ♿PARTIAL | **2017**

Visitors to Broccoli Hall describe this English-style cottage garden as "incredible," "inspirational," "magical"—and they come back again and again. Starting in 1985 with one-and-one-half acres of bare earth, Maxine Paetro collaborated with horticulturist Tim Steinhoff to create a series of enchanting garden "rooms." Broccoli Hall offers an apple tunnel, a brick courtyard, a lavish display of spring bulbs blooming with crabapples in May; an extensive border of irises, peonies, and old shrub roses flowering in June; a tree house with long views; and a secret woodland garden with a teddy bears' picnic. We have some whimsical rustic carvings by woodsman/artisan Hoppy Quick; new bears, new stairs, new

chairs, and some exceptionally charming bird feeders. Photos and magazine stories about Broccoli Hall can be viewed at www. broccolihall.com. In 2010, Broccoli Hall was expanded to five acres and two new mud ponds were installed. This is where we began a breeding program—but we don't sell our fish. To see the "elusive ki shusui" project in progress, go to www.kishusui. com. We look forward to seeing you in the garden in 2018!

DIRECTIONS—From Route 22 North or South, go toward Amenia. Go west on Route 44 to Route 83 North/Smithfield Road. Go 2.5 miles to dirt road on right, Flint Hill Road. Turn right. Garden is first on left. Please park on Flint Hill Road. Be careful of ditches.

Suffolk County
Saturday, May 12

Suffolk County
EAST HAMPTON
BIERCUK & LUCKEY GARDEN
18 Sayres Path, East Hampton
Hours: 10 a.m. to 4 p.m.
📷 | **2017**

Our four-season woodland garden under a high oak canopy shelters a collection of rhododendrons, azaleas, *Kalmia*, *Pieris*, understory trees, perennials, bulbs, and tropicals in season. A mostly sunny, rear corner contains a pool designed as a pond with a waterfall and is surrounded with plantings that peak mid-July through October. Winding paths and stone walls enhance a sense of depth and elevation change on a mostly flat acre. There is something in bloom every season.

DIRECTIONS—From Montauk Highway/Route 27, turn right onto Sayre's Path. House is first driveway on right. Please park along road.

GLADE GARDEN—ABBY JANE BRODY
44 Glade Road, East Hampton
Hours: 10 a.m. to 4 p.m.
📷 | **2017**

Rare and unusual (and some not so) ornamental trees and shrubs and shade-loving perennials form the understory and groundcover in this niche carved in native woodland over a thirty-five-year period. This is a playground for an ardent gardener and plant collector, and plants that do not meet high standards of performance quickly give way to others waiting in the wings. Planted for year-round interest, in mid-spring camellias that rise above carpets of hellebores, woodland phlox, wood anemones, and minor bulbs capture the most attention, and are succeeded by *Epimedium, Daphne*, fragrant rhododendrons, species peonies, and more. During the summer, color and fragrance are provided by a progression of hydrangeas, Asiatic and American *Clethra*, crape myrtles, and a range of *Stewartia*, together with the newest treasure, a purple-leaved *Styrax japonica*.

DIRECTIONS—From Route 27/Montauk Highway, turn left at traffic light in East Hampton. Pass town pond, go through village, and turn left at windmill. Pass under railroad bridge and turn right at fork to Springs Fireplace Road. In about 3 miles, turn left onto Woodbine and take an immediate right onto Glade Road. Please park along road, not on grass.

LEVY-BARNETT GARDEN
31 Woodbine Drive, East Hampton
Hours: 10 a.m. to 2 p.m.
📷 | ♿ | **2017**

My vision was a country garden that wouldn't feel suburban. There were two caveats: no lawn, no irrigation. Landscape designer Julie Strong embraced my vision, and worked within these demanding parameters. The garden is very natural, as Julie planted ornamental grasses, drought tolerant shrubs, perennials and trees. I supplement her design by planting hundreds of bulbs each autumn, along with maintaining a container garden of tender foliage perennials and *Colocasia*. Self-seeders are welcomed and embraced, and the abundant butterflies, bees, moths, and birds are a bonus. The profusion of blooms begin in early spring and continue through late autumn. Both hardscape and mulched pathways encircle the garden, cohesively bringing it together. The result is a Zen-like environment which has become a contemplative retreat that relaxes and stimulates at the same time.

DIRECTIONS—Take Route 27 East, passing East Hampton village to a left at the windmill (opposite Citarella Gourmet Market) onto North Main Street. Then, bear left onto Three Mile Harbor Road. Proceed about 3+ miles to a right on Woodbine Drive. (If you pass East Hampton Point, you went a block too far). We are 7th house on the left.

Hertenhof
17 Terry's Trail, East Hampton
DIGGING DEEPER
10 AM
An Evocative Vision—The Designers' Country Place with Peter van Hattum
REGISTRATION: $30 Garden Conservancy Members / $35 general

Surrounded by the preserved open spaces of the historic Grace Estate in Northwest Harbor, Peter van Hattum and his late partner, Harold Simmons, had the unique opportunity to create a new home on a site rich with history. Deeply evocative of a traditional country place, the house and garden at Hertenhof (Deer Court in Dutch), were designed as a single composition, each integral to the other. Completed in 2000, the Georgian-style residence is filled with beloved and carefully collected modern pieces as well as English, French, and Dutch antiques. Interior spaces flow seamlessly out into an exquisitely landscaped six-acre park, choreographing a way of living in the country that is comfortable and understated. While Peter started his career with major roles on Broadway, he opened his own interior design firm in the 1970s. For twenty years, Harold ran the architecture department at

Parish-Hadley, one of America's iconic design firms. In 1987, they opened their own office, working on important residential commissions throughout the Americas. Hertenhof is featured in *Parish-Hadley Tree of Life: An Intimate History of the Legendary Design Firm*, by Brian J. McCarthy and Bunny Williams.

Registration required—space limited
Go to opendaysprogram.org
or call 1 (888) 842-2442

Putnam County
Sunday, May 13 — Mother's Day

Putnam County
COLD SPRING
STONECROP GARDENS

81 Stonecrop Lane, Cold Spring
(845) 265-2000
stonecrop.org

★ For full listing please see page 279.

Westchester County
Saturday, May 19

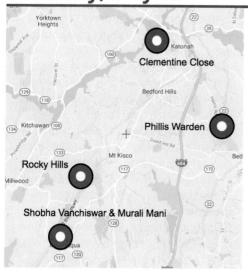

Westchester County
BEDFORD HILLS
PHILLIS WARDEN

531 Bedford Center Road, Bedford Hills
Hours: 10 a.m. to 4 p.m.
📷 | 2017

This garden of many facets includes perennial borders, three water gardens, a formal vegetable garden, wildflower garden, fern garden, marsh garden, a tree platform overlooking the marshlands, a woodland walk, a hidden garden, and a formal croquet court. The garden extends over seven acres, the back four acres of which are a study in what deer do not eat.

DIRECTIONS—From Bedford Village, take Route 22 toward Katonah to intersection at Bedford Cross. Garden is on left. Please park at Rippowam School and walk to #531.

CHAPPAQUA
SHOBHA VANCHISWAR & MURALI MANI
76 Castle Road, Chappaqua
Hours: 10 a.m. to 4 p.m.
📷 | ♿PARTIAL | **2017**

This modest-sized organically maintained garden won the 2007 Golden Trowel award from *Garden Design* magazine. It features a cottage garden of bulbs and perennials, a Belgian espalier of fruit trees, a grape arbor, an herb garden, a checkerboard garden, and a "meadow" with naturalized bulbs, native plants, a Domenico Belli sculpture, and a greenhouse. There are many European touches, like rose arbors, window boxes, a fountain, and Anduze pots. There is also a terrace with a wisteria-covered pergola for outdoor dining. A vertical garden of mostly ferns and *Heuchera* and inspired by Patrick Blanc was installed four springs ago. It has been a steep learning curve and we look forward to when it is mature. Presently, we are enjoying sharing it during its growing pains. Modest in size, our garden is rich in detail and has a great deal of visual appeal. This garden was featured in the 2010 "Best of" issue of *Westchester Home* magazine.

DIRECTIONS—From lower Westchester County and New York City, take Saw Mill Parkway north to Exit 32. Follow signs for Route 120 South through hamlet of Chappaqua. Cross the parkway. Turn left at "Y," and then left onto South Greeley, then right onto King Street. Halfway up King Street, turn left onto Castle Road. Look for Samalin Investment Counsel at crossing. House is #76 with post-and-rope railing.

Please park on street, staying clear of front of garden, driveway, and walkways.
From upper Westchester County, take Saw Mill Parkway south to Exit 32. Make two right turns and proceed as directed above from Route 120 South.

KATONAH
CLEMENTINE CLOSE
107 Cherry Street, Katonah
Hours: 10 a.m. to 4 p.m.
📷 | ♿PARTIAL | **NEW**

From the moment you enter this sun-splashed horticultural oasis, you will be awestruck by the amazing diversity of the plantings. Over the years, a wide variety of plants, including hundreds of trees and shrubs, have been introduced to the landscape in a deliberate, mostly naturalistic manner. Particularly, they reflect a genuine interest in plants by the owners, a characteristic rarely seen, even in stateside botanical gardens. The gardens, embellished with two natural ponds fed by a small, intermittently flowing stream, are designed as a series of natural rooms dictated by the topography, soil, and water conditions: woodland, wetland, manicured, rhododendron, formal, English, Japanese. Unusual trees have been placed throughout. Encompassing nearly three heavily planted acres, the star of the show is the sixty-foot-long golden chain (*Laburnum anagyroides*) tunnel. Historically this blooms in the middle of May. But the gardens also have been designed to promote interest from spring through September, and in late July a stunning collection of crape myrtle trees/shrubs takes center stage. Located within a nine-acre compound, the gardens have been constructed piecemeal over a period of fifteen years...[Read full description online]

DIRECTIONS—Turn onto Cherry Street from the Route 35 traffic light. Proceed 0.5 mile south and #107 is on the right. We are the yellow house at the very bottom of the common driveway. Be aware that GPS often will bring you to Quicks Lane, which means that you have gone too far south on Cherry Street. Parking is limited, and the driveway is narrow for two-way traffic. Enter and proceed with caution.

MOUNT KISCO
ROCKY HILLS

95 Old Roaring Brook Road, Mount Kisco
Hours: 10 a.m. to 4 p.m.
📷 | ♿PARTIAL | **2017**

At Rocky Hills, William and Henriette Suhr began planting among the stone walls some fifty years ago. You will find mature specimens of black walnut and ash, complemented by recent additions of weeping beech, dawn redwood, *Stewartia*, dogwood, and an impressive collection of magnolias and conifers. Tree peonies and an extensive planting of rhododendrons and azaleas compete for attention with the carpet of bulbs throughout the thirteen acres. Most impressive in May and June are the forget-me-nots, which are allowed full freedom throughout the garden. Starting on the hillside meadow, clouds of perfect blue flowers appear among an ever-expanding rock garden, through the hills and terraces, walls and paths, through fern woodlands, finding good company with self-sown *Primula* along the natural brook that serves as the heart of the garden.

DIRECTIONS—From Saw Mill River Parkway, go north to Exit 33/Reader's Digest Road. At traffic light, turn left, then make a sharp right onto Old Roaring Brook Road. Rocky Hills, #95, is 1 mile farther on right. Please park at Lawrence Farms Crossways

as directed.
—From Merritt Parkway/Route 15, go to I-287 West and exit at Saw Mill River Parkway North. Proceed as directed above. From Taconic Parkway South, take Route 100/Route 133 exit toward Briarcliff Manor/Millwood. Turn right onto Route 100/Route 133/Saw Mill River Road/Somerstown Turnpike. Turn right onto Station Road, continue for 0.5 mile, and then turn right onto Millwood Road. Take a slight right onto Quaker Road, proceed for about 0.5 mile, and then make a sharp left turn onto Seven Bridges Road. Turn right onto Lawrence Farms Crossway, left onto Old Roaring Brook Road, and go to #95. Proceed as directed above.

Rocky Hills
DIGGING DEEPER
2 PM
Tovah Martin's
Bootcamp for the Senses
Free with garden admission

Your garden could be so meaningful, if you plug in. To coincide with the publication of Tovah's new book, *The*

Garden in Every Sense and Season, this event explores the garden on all levels by attuning your nose to the scents and training your ears to listen. Keying into the bounty of stimuli at Rocky Hills, we'll learn to garden with eyes wide open, ears to the ground, and hands outstretched. As we engage, we'll talk about making your own garden more fulfilling on all levels. And a special bonus—expand your nose and its vistas with a Smellathon! Together, we'll come to our senses. Tovah Martin is an award-winning author,

garden writer, freelancer, and fanatical gardener. Her books include her most recent title: *The Garden in Every Sense and Season* (Timber Press, April 2018) as well as *The Indestructible Houseplant, The New Terrarium*, and *Tasha Tudor's Garden*. Her writing appears in the publications *Gardens Illustrated, Garden Design, Country Gardens, Cottage Journal, Milieu, Traditional Home*, and many other magazines. An organic gardener, she digs into the land as well as growing indoors at Furthermore, her Litchfield County home.

Nassau County
Sunday, May 20

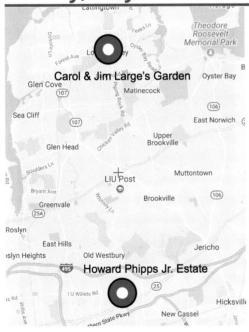

Nassau County
LOCUST VALLEY
CAROL & JIM LARGE'S GARDEN
14 Underhill Road, Locust Valley
Hours: 10 a.m. to 4 p.m.
♿PARTIAL | **2014**

This garden truly reflects the personality of its owners, having been redesigned and altered over their nineteen years of ownership. The bones of the original garden were designed through Innocenti and Webel in the late 1930s around a much older frame farmhouse that was moved to the site and altered in 1936 by architect Bradley Delahanty. The property encompasses ten acres of mature woodlands, streams, ponds, and fields placed in a framework of Long Island's signature rhododendron, mountain laurel, and azalea. There are several more formal garden areas planted with specimen woody plants, herb and perennial gardens, lawns, and terraces.

DIRECTIONS—Take Long Island Express-way to Glen Cove Road. Go north 1.8 miles to Route 25A, turn, and go 3.3 miles to Wolver Hollow Road. Turn left at the Old Brookville Police Station and go a short distance to stop sign at Piping Rock Road. Turn left and drive through two traffic lights (past Friends' Academy). Underhill Road is 0.3 mile past Duck Pond Road. Turn left onto Underhill Road and follow the road to the left to #14, a yellow frame house. Parking is in the drive or on the road.

OLD WESTBURY
HOWARD PHIPPS JR. ESTATE
75 Post Road, Old Westbury
Hours: 10 a.m. to 4 p.m.
2017

Built in 1935, the house was designed by Adams and Prentice with a landscape by Umberto Innocenti. Rhododendrons have been bred and raised here since the be-ginning, and their hybridization continues today. Entering through a formal flower garden, one crosses a grass terrace, set be-tween two diagonal avenues of American beech, that overlooks the swimming pool and meadow. To the east, a wide grass path climbs a hill planted with hybrid rho-dodendrons and uncommon shrubs. An easy walk of about three-quarters of a mile takes visitors through a Japanese garden and down the meadow to the trial grounds of new rhododendron seedlings. The walk returns to the house through mature plantings of flowering shrubs, trees, and a hydrangea garden.

DIRECTIONS—Take the Long Island Ex-pressway to Exit 39. Proceed straight along the service road for 2 miles. Turn right at traffic light intersection of Post Road, and bear right at far end of pond. Take first driveway on the left, 75 Post Road, "Erch-less." Go up winding driveway to house. —From the Grand Central Parkway/North-ern State Parkway, take Exit 32 to Post Road in Westbury. Turn left at end of ramp. Cross traffic-light intersection of Jericho Turnpike. Continue past Westbury High School on right. Take second driveway on the right after the high school, 75 Post Road, "Erchless." Continue up drive to the house.

Howard Phipps Jr. Estate
DIGGING DEEPER
10:30 AM
Looking for Little Epiphanies
with George Woodard
REGISTRATION: $30 Garden
Conservancy Members / $35 general

Nearly 100 years old, the Phipps Estate is a classic American country place with a rich horticultural history. When the 10,000 rhododendrons grown on site from seed are in peak bloom, join Superintendent George Woodard for an intimate tour of this remarkable landmark. Drawing on his thirty-five years working for the Phipps, George will give visitors a rare behind-the-scenes look at the estate. This will include the design, its extensive, historic rhododendron breeding program, contributions to horticulture and world wildlife preservation made (mostly anonymously) by Mr. & Mrs. Phipps, key organic maintenance practices including the composting and compost tea programs, and some of the more spectacular plant collections. Trained at Cornell University, George is a noted horticulturist and garden designer. He is a member of the Hortus Club, an exclusive group of professional horticulturists, and the American Rhododendron Society, where he ran their seed exchange for many years. He is also a longtime student of Tibetan Buddhism.

Registration required — space limited
Go to opendaysprogram.org
or call 1 (888) 842-2442

What our Garden Hosts recommend in Nassau County

American Café
5 School St, Glen Cove, NY 11542
(516) 656-0003
www.americancafe.org

Pauls Nursery
200 Glen Cove Rd, Glen Head, NY 11545
(516) 676-0630
www.paulsnursery.com

Toku Modern Asian
2014 Northern Blvd, Manhasset, NY 11030
(516) 627-8658
www.pollrestaurants.com/restaurants/tok

Suffolk County
Saturday, May 26

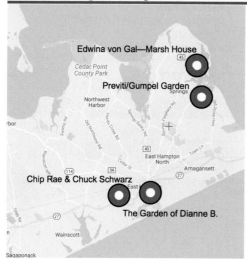

Suffolk County
EAST HAMPTON
CHIP RAE & CHUCK SCHWARZ
16 Greenway Drive, East Hampton
Hours: 10 a.m. to 4 p.m.
NEW

Hidden away on a short private lane at the edge of East Hampton Village, our house and gardens have been the object of our affection for thirty years. The 1976 saltbox house sits on two-thirds of an acre, yet the property feels much larger due to the clever siting of the house and the undulating change in elevation from the front to the rear. The house began its life as a plain barn-inspired structure, but has evolved into a Colonial Revival residence inside and out. A row of eight gingko trees flank the street and driveway, bursting in to a chartreuse extravaganza for a brief moment every fall. Dozens of oak trees were removed from the property to open up the lawns and provide a large swath of sky

and sun. The mature hemlock hedge along the north side of the front lawn survived a bout with the woolly adelgid blight only after annual spray treatments stopped. Moving up the driveway and through the white gates, a peony bed frames the deck. The plants were lovingly moved from a family farm in New Jersey twenty-five years ago, and should be at their peak in late May... [Read full description online]

DIRECTIONS—Approaching East Hampton Village from Bridgehampton on Route 27 east, turn left at the Exxon station onto Toilsome Lane. Go 1 block, and take the first left onto Wireless Road. Go 1 block and Greenway Drive is on your right. Please park along Wireless Road, or at the very end of Greenway Drive in our nice neighbor's gravel parking area. We are the yellow house with green shutters.

EDWINA VON GAL—MARSH HOUSE
962-964 Springs Fireplace Road, East Hampton
Hours: 10 a.m. to 4 p.m.
📷 | ♿ | **2017**

I am a landscape designer and environmentalist, and my goal is to create beautiful gardens without synthetic chemicals. My garden is my laboratory as well as an ecological refuge of sorts. It is on a protected salt marsh, so much of the land is not available for me to intercede, which makes the fabulous view stress free.

The rest of the four-plus acres contains a variety of natural restoration and garden areas, in various stages of progress: a meadow, woodland, and moss garden—all magnets for voracious deer. I explore different ways to create interest with plants they don't eat, and selectively plant and protect those they do. My one deer-proof area, a fenced garden that contains vegetables, shrubs, and flowers, is where I get to do most of my gardening. It is surrounded by beds full of attempts at growing reliably deer-proof flowering plants, for the bees and butterflies. I do not remove any biomass from the property, so I explore various uses of the materials generated, such as log walls from invasive trees, and hay stacks of the meadow cuttings.

DIRECTIONS—Follow North Main Street out of East Hampton and bear right onto Springs Fireplace Road. Property is 4.5 miles on the left. Please park on the street.

Edwina von Gal's Marsh House

DIGGING DEEPER
2 PM
Perfect Earth Seed Bomb Workshop
with Edwina von Gal
Free with garden admission, but
advance registration is required

Adults are invited to come and make Fukuoka-style seed bombs (don't worry, we'll explain!). We will use clover and pollinator attracting wildflower mixes and learn about the importance of native pollinators, how to promote and protect their populations, and the best ways to ensure your seed bombs grow and become healthy habitat for wildlife. Children are welcome! Materials and refreshments will be provided.

Registration required — space limited
Go to opendaysprogram.org
or call 1 (888) 842-2442

Edwina von Gal's Marsh House

DIGGING DEEPER
10:30 AM – 4 PM
Tea for Two, the Soil and You!
with Edwina von Gal
Free with garden admission

Sip delicious tea in the garden while we demonstrate how to create aerated compost tea for soil health and productivity! Learn about the equipment, the process, and the benefits of adding compost tea into your organic gardening routine.

DIGGING DEEPER
11 AM & 3 PM
Guided garden tours
Free with garden admission

Walk with Edwina von Gal to explore the garden she calls her "play pen, laboratory and retreat...an unruly, willful version of what I do for my clients."

THE GARDEN OF DIANNE B.
86 Davids Lane, East Hampton
Hours: 10 p.m. to 2 p.m.
 | ♿ | 2017

To the usual array of several kinds of *Fritillaria*, hyacinths, *Arum, Allium*, and tons of tulips, this year you will find new species of *Ornithogalum* and *Camassia*. Beautiful small wonders like cyclamen, trillium, and hepatica nestle among the cultivated-moss valley under a huge seventy-five-year-old pink *Magnolia grandiflora*. Variegation thrives in this garden along with the gloriously poignant leafing out of many Japanese maples and elegant small specimen treasures. Her collection of Jack in the Pulpits grows as she can source new ones (difficult to do), but *Arisaema ringens* 'Black Mambo' should be at its most seductive.

Look under trees and around corners—you never know what you might find in this ever-evolving, layer-upon-layer garden. Unexpected sculptures pop up among twisted trees, weepers, and odd woodland plants. Dianne labels herself a "garden stylist" to suit her modus operandi—weaving together texture, accessories, color, patterns, and layered shapes that echo her twentieth-century career in fashion. Her garden provides the pizzazz for her blog, Dirtier, which is the progeny of her '90s gardening book, *Dirt* (still available at amazon.com).

DIRECTIONS—On Route 27/Main Street going east, pass East Hampton Town Pond and Guild, then turn right onto Davids Lane (just after the big white-columned church). The garden is three-quarters of the way down the street on left—just before the East Hampton Duck Pond. Enter through the garden gate. Please park in the direction of traffic.

PREVITI/GUMPEL GARDEN
230 Old Stone Highway, East Hampton
Hours: 10 a.m. to 4 p.m.
 | 2016

This garden is a series of rooms. Numerous outdoor sculptures by the owners are scattered throughout. Paths wind through cedar groves past casual lawns and plantings. There is a sun garden with stone terraces and fountain, a cool and restful shade garden, and a fire pit area. Go through Pop's Garden to the tented "dining room," then the arbor at the base of the artist's studio, which will be open for viewing accessed by a stair tower. Move past the games lawn to the pool, where you may rest in the shaded pergola at the end of the patio.

DIRECTIONS—From East Hampton, take Route 27 to first traffic light past windmill. Turn left on Accabonac Highway and drive 4 miles to stop sign. Turn right onto Old Stone Highway. Drive 0.25 mile to #230. Please park on main road and walk to first house on right.

What our Garden Hosts recommend in Eastern Long Island

Trimbles Nursery
20985 Main Rd, Cutchogue, NY 11935
(631) 734-6494
www.trimblesnursery.com

La Fondita
74 Montauk Hwy, Amagansett, NY 11930
(631) 267-8800
www.lafondita.net

Fowlers Garden Center
175 North Sea Road
Southhampton, NY 11968
(631) 283-5515
www.fowlersgardencenter.com

Love Lane Kitchen
240 Love Ln, Mattituck, NY 11952
(631) 298-8989
www.lovelanekitchen.com

Suffolk County
Saturday, June 2

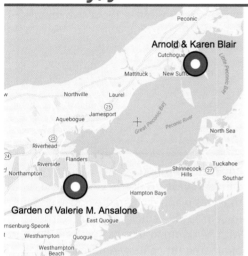

Arnold & Karen Blair (map label)

Garden of Valerie M. Ansalone (map label)

Suffolk County
CUTCHOGUE
ARNOLD & KAREN BLAIR
4560 Vanston Road, Cutchogue
Hours: May: 10 a.m. to 4 p.m.
📷 | 2017

Our three-acre Peconic Bay-front property overlooks a seventeen-acre beach-and-wetland protected preserve deeded to The Nature Conservancy; it's a haven for migratory and nesting sea birds. The gardens flow from an eighty-foot elevation down to sea level via numerous winding paths with various landings and overlooks. A park-like one-and-one-half-acre woodland garden features numerous spring flowering shrubs and trees under towering oaks. A wandering rustic path leads to a massive log gazebo fronting a wetland we lovingly rescued from invasive vines and replanted with indigenous bayberry, high tide bush, and native grasses, which put on a delightful burst of color in late fall. Extensive

stone walls surround a pool tucked into the hillside. Rolling lawns, numerous specimen evergreens, antique and salvaged garden ornaments, and 180-degree bay views with magnificent sunsets enhance a magical spot on the North Fork. Our garden is self-designed and boasts plenty of natives. It has evolved over twenty-seven years of experimenting, transplanting, learning, and re-transplanting. Our garden is a living, breathing, perpetual work that will never finish.

DIRECTIONS—Take Route 25 East from Riverhead. At the second traffic light in Cutchogue, turn right onto Eugenes Road. Turn right onto Skunk Lane. Bear right and continue all the way to the bay, where the road curves right over the causeway. At end of causeway, road forks. Take right fork, which is Vanston Road. House is 0.9 mile on right on Vanston Road.

FLANDERS
GARDEN OF VALERIE M. ANSALONE
86 Risa Court, Flanders
Hours: 10 a.m. to 4 p.m.
2017

Welcome to my garden. It has been evolving for many years. My original goal has not changed: create a park-like setting that will welcome me home. The one-acre property was originally filled with oaks, pitch pines, and berryless blueberry bushes. Today there is a native oak canopy as you stroll through winding garden paths to find rhododendrons, azaleas, conifers, magnolias, perennials, hydrangeas, landscape trees, and bulbs. The woodland walk, with sitting areas to enjoy the environment, leads to my 4,000-gallon koi pond, where you will meet Chester, Parker, and Bella—a few of my Japanese koi. My garden was featured on the East End, on News 12, and in the Home and Garden supplement to the *News Review* and other North Fork local newspapers. My garden is designed to provide color and foliage every season.

DIRECTIONS—From Route 27/Sunrise Highway, take Exit 64 North/Route 104. Take first right onto Pleasure Drive, then first left onto Risa Court. Number 86 has white gate. Garden is about two minutes from Route 27 exit.

Nassau County
Sunday, June 3

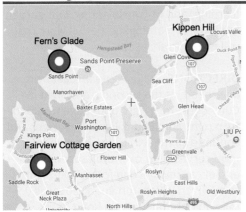

Nassau County
GLEN COVE
KIPPEN HILL

89 Walnut Road, Glen Cove

Hours: 10 a.m. to 4 p.m.

📷 | ♿PARTIAL | **2017**

Kippen Hill is an eight-year-old garden that encompasses five smaller gardens situated on one-and-one-half acres. The variegated garden grows 'Dragon's Eye' pine and Japanese forest grass, variegated *Hosta* and *Acuba*. A formal garden of English-style borders with a central-axis bubbler fountain is the anchor to the site. An Asian garden, with an aviary pagoda, is home for our Asian-native egg-laying hens. Coltsfoot from the Humes Japanese Stroll Garden

and black bamboo are featured here along with a majestic centenary boulevard cedar that was planted when the house was first built in 1910. A small vegetable garden with heirloom tomatoes hosts a collection of nineteenth-century American garden equipment. The roomy front lawn is our croquet gaming garden, with English-style borders making a perfect backdrop for this quintessential British pastime. A Lord and Burnham greenhouse dating to 1925 was rescued and restored from a famed Gold Coast estate about three years ago by Dean and Jonathan. This outbuilding doubles as a site for our collection of tropicals, including bananas and orchids, as well as a dining room for guests during all four seasons...[Read full description online]

DIRECTIONS—Take Exit 39 North on Glen Cove Road from the Long Island Expressway/I-495. Follow Glen Cove Road several miles to the town of Glen Cove. Turn right at the light onto Bridge Street in front of the Glen Cove Police Station. Proceed to Highland Road and turn right on Highland Road. Drive up the hill to the first stoplight. Cross Walnut Road and park on the lawn marked with parking signs, on left. Walk to our garden by following the signs to #89 Walnut Road, around the corner.

GREAT NECK
FAIRVIEW COTTAGE GARDEN
5 Fairview Avenue, Great Neck
Hours: 10 a.m. to 4 p.m.
 | NEW

Curb appeal is off-the-charts: a stolid 1899 clapboard farmhouse and barn, at short remove from the storefronts of Middle Neck Road in the Old Village of Great Neck, with dignified simplicity, presents an ideal foil to exuberant plantings in the English cottage garden style that spill onto Fairview Avenue. A large brick patio at front and a gravel driveway leads to an antique barn, bamboo screening, and, of course, more roses and dahlias, lavender, hydrangeas, *Viburnum*, *Echinacea*, clematis—a fine example of a delightful flowery oasis, heedless of the surrounding bustle.

DIRECTIONS—On the north side of Fairview Avenue, about 100-feet east of Middle Neck Road. Free street parking on south side of Fairview Avenue; on West Park Place; and in the municipal lot behind the garden.

SANDS POINT
FERN'S GLADE
221 Sands Point Road, Sands Point
Hours: 10 a.m. to 4 p.m.
 | 2000
Naturalized Japanese maples, antique garden ornaments, sophisticated planting design, and open lawns harmonize an expansive two-acre garden featuring rose, woodland, and kitchen gardens; an English glasshouse; and low boxwood hedges enclosing perennial gardens. There are numerous benches to sit on and contemplate the ivy-clad brick house surrounded by understated horticultural aplomb: a tree-form wisteria, *Sorbaria aitchisonii*, azaleas, roses, hydrangeas, *Viburnum*, magnolias, clematis, and perennials of all kinds. An antique stone frog spouts water into a koi pond, a lichened-stone dog presides over a charming old swimming pool, and a pair of cranes perches on a sod bench.

DIRECTIONS—Take the Long Island Expressway to Exit 36. Travel north on Searingtown Road, which, at the intersection with Northern Boulevard/Route 25 A, becomes Port Washington Boulevard/Route 101, and then Middle Neck Road at Sands Point Country Club. Continue farther north along Middle Neck Road to Sands Point Road and turn left. The garden is at the second driveway on the right. Park on Cedar Knoll Road just past #590 Sands Point Road.

Columbia County
Saturday, June 9

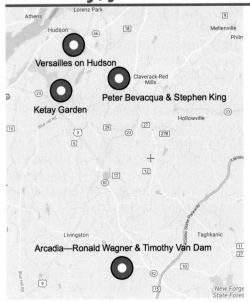

is a great place to sit in spring when the irises and redbuds are in bloom. Looking over the garden behind the house and meadow beyond is a large pergola covered with yellow trumpet vine. From this garden, a curving mown path leads down the hill, through the meadow and then along the side of the property bordered by our homage to Tuscany: a line of tall, narrow Irish juniper, which ca...[Read full description online]

DIRECTIONS—From Hudson, take Route 23 B toward Great Barrington, MA. Turn right onto Route 9 H/Route 23. The garden is about 0.8 mile on the right. The driveway is bordered by a black rail fence. It is right before you get to the big Victorian house also on the right.

Columbia County
CLAVERACK
KETAY GARDEN
6121 Route 9H & Route 23, Claverack
Hours: 10 a.m. to 4 p.m.
📷 | ♿PARTIAL | **2017**

An allée of large maples and ash trees, bordered by meadows on either side, forms the entrance to the garden. Our ten-acre property can be viewed as three large sections—even though these sections contain divisions within them. There is a large garden in front of the house and a smaller, intimately planted one behind, which leads to the third section—an expansive meadow framed in the distance by views of the Catskill Mountains. The front garden, which consists of rooms created with shrubs, perennials, and trees, is shielded from the road by a semicircle of forsythia. An iron bench that encircles an oak tree

PETER BEVACQUA & STEPHEN KING
443 New York State 23 B / Willmon Road & Route 23 B, Claverack
Hours: 10 a.m. to 4 p.m.
📷 | ♿PARTIAL | **2017**
🏷PONDSIDE NURSERY

Enter this magical garden and discover an intimate and beloved world that has been evolving with devotion and care for the last twenty-eight years. New this past year is the addition of a half-acre expanse, the Nearly Native Garden featuring a bold sculpture by prominent local artist Mark Wasserbach. Garden designer Peter Bevacqua has taken his governing design principles of color, form, texture, and layering and focuses here primarily on native plants supported by non-natives to create a special environment. In this space, he collaborates with native plant expert Heather

Grimes. This new addition complements the other garden spaces in this almost three-acre haven where one area unfolds upon the next, each with its own sense of individuality and charm. Among the features are the Sun Garden (surrounded by walls of yew hedge), the Hydrangea Walk, the greenhouse borders, many unusual trees and shrubs, as well as architectural fragments. What was once a small orchard has become a conifer garden. A boxwood cloud hedge, inspired by Jacques Wirtz, replaces an old rose border......[Read full description online]

DIRECTIONS—From Taconic State Parkway, take Exit 82 and go northwest toward Hudson and Rip Van Winkle Bridge. At first traffic light, turn right onto Route 9 H/Route 23. At next light (Claverack Market and post office will be on right), turn left onto Route 23 B. After about 0.8 mile turn right onto Willmon Road. Please park on left.

HUDSON
VERSAILLES ON HUDSON
5 Rossman Avenue, Hudson
Hours: 10 a.m. to 4 p.m.
📷 | 2017

We wanted to create a garden that looked as if it had been planted when the house was built, in 1903. The entire land formation presented a real challenge—from the house to the bottom of the garden was a steep thirty-foot drop. We needed to create an elegant way to move through the garden—so we carefully designed multi-level stone patios and easy access stairways to guide you down to the fountain. We chose a most unexpected plan that would take advantage of the dramatic views of the river, hills, and sunsets. By turning the garden on its axis, we created

the illusion of a massive property—with grand, sweeping lawns; long, flowing hydrangea and hornbeam hedges; and architectural boxwood balls. Our fountain and the hornbeam curve are the highlights of this quiet garden—complete with fish, frogs, and water plants. In the spring and early summer, the garden is predominately green and white, and it turns ever more pink as the summer progresses. In the winter, this garden makes an equally strong statement due to its framing by many evergreens. Versailles on Hudson offers ever-changing vistas as you walk around the property. From the upper and lower patios, the grand porch, the four staircases, the long lawns and the bubbling fountain, this special garden always delights and soothes the soul.

DIRECTIONS—Warren Street is the main street of Hudson. It runs gently uphill from the river for about 1.5 miles. Cross streets start at 1st Street near the river and go up in numbers from there. For our garden (5 Rossman Avenue), go to the top of Warren Street, turn left onto Prospect Avenue, and then right onto Rossman Avenue. (Columbia Memorial Hospital is on Prospect Avenue opposite Rossman Avenue.) Our house is a big pink Victorian on the right, the third house from the corner.
—From the south, take the Sawmill Parkway North to the Taconic State Parkway North. Take the Hudson exit onto Route 82 west. It becomes Routes 9 and 23. Continue straight until Route 9 turns right toward Hudson at a traffic light (Route 23 goes straight on to the Rip Van Winkle Bridge). WARNING: Do not turn right onto Route 9H at an earlier traffic light. Route 9 runs straight into Prospect Avenue with the top of Warren Street on left. Proceed as directed above.
—From the New York State Thruway/I-87

North to Exit 21/Catskill. Exit toll plaza and turn left onto Route 23 B, then left again onto Route 23 East. Soon after crossing the Rip Van Winkle Bridge, turn left onto Route 9 G and go north toward Hudson. You will enter Hudson on 3rd Street. The second traffic light is Warren Street. Turn right and proceed as directed above. From Massachusetts and New England, take the Massachusetts Turnpike West to Exit B-2/Taconic Parkway South. Stay on the parkway to the exit for Route 23 West, Hudson. This will turn into Route 23 B and take you directly into Hudson. Turn left onto Prospect Avenue. You will be at the non-Warren Street end of Prospect and so Rossman Avenue is the first on the left. Proceed as directed above. Please park anywhere on the right side of Rossman Avenue going uphill. Do not park in the driveway.

WEST TAGHKANIC
ARCADIA—RONALD WAGNER & TIMOTHY VAN DAM
733 Taghkanic Road, West Taghkanic
Hours: 10 a.m. to 4 p.m.
📷 | ♿ | 2016

Our early Greek Revival-style farmhouse is set in a pastoral landscape. An avenue of sweet gum trees lining the formal drive is planted in forced perspective to visually extend the approach to the house. The gently rolling hillside is punctuated by a magnificent grove of black locust trees and a developing grove of deciduous conifer trees including bald cypress, dawn redwood, and larch. A wildflower meadow rises to the north. The informal plantings include the lilac walk and rhododendron and hydrangea beds. A large pond is the focus of surrounding naturalistic plantings giving onto views of the wetland beyond. Symmetrical twin terraces at the house feature an arbor-covered stone dining table on the south and a perennial border on the north.

DIRECTIONS—From center of village of Livingston /Route 9, go east on Church/ Livingston Road, passing red brick Dutch Reformed Church, and continue about 2 miles, to Taghkanic Road. Turn right and go to third house on right, #733.
—From the Taconic State Parkway, take Hudson/Ancram, Route 82 exit. Drive northwest on Route 82, past Taconic Diner with neon Indian. About 1 mile from Taconic Parkway, turn left onto Livingston Road. Go 0.5 mile up a winding hill to Taghkanic Road on left. Turn left and go to third house on right, #733.

Greater Rochester Area
Sunday, June 10

Livingston County
PAVILION
LINWOOD GARDENS
1912 York Road West, Pavilion
Hours: 10 a.m. to 4 p.m.
📷 | ♿PARTIAL | **NEW**

Linwood Gardens is located in the farm-lands of the Genesee Valley. The original garden landscape was designed in the early 1900s, with an Arts and Crafts-style summer house and walled gardens with pools, fountains, ornamental trees, and a view of the valley beyond. The gardens include a distinguished collection of Japa-nese and American tree peonies featured each spring at the Tree Peony Festival of Flowers. During the summer months, Lin-wood Gardens offers a peaceful sanctuary for workshops, Open Garden Days, and wedding ceremonies. Our mission is to preserve the gardens and the tree peony collection for future generations to enjoy. Take the New York State Thruway/I-90 to Route 390 south/Exit 10 for Avon.

DIRECTIONS—Follow Routes 5 and 20 west, through Avon. Go left on Route 20 West for 6 miles. Go left on Route 36 south for 3 miles to town of York. Turn right onto York Road West, and go 2.9 miles. At the top of the hill, turn left at Linwood Gadens.

Putnam County
Sunday, June 10

This garden is a series of vignettes that flow into each other on five acres overlooking the Hudson River. The gardens are designed and maintained by the owner, Arthur Ross, and include a water garden, a moon (white) garden, meditation garden, rock garden, interesting daylilies, a fern garden, shrub garden (azaleas, rhododendrons, mountain laurels), cutting gardens, and garden sculptures, along with a waterfall and a new koi pond. Garden paths give easy access to many unusual flowers.

Putnam County

GARRISON

ROSS GARDENS

43 Snake Hill Road (Travis Corners)
Garrison
Hours: 10 a.m. to 4 p.m.
📷 | **2017**

DIRECTIONS—Take Route 9 to Garrison Golf Course. Turn west onto Snake Hill Road. Garden is 0.25 mile on left. Parking is available for 30 cars at any one time.

PUBLIC GARDEN PARTNER

Putnam County

COLD SPRING

STONECROP GARDENS

81 Stonecrop Lane, Cold Spring
(845) 265-2000
stonecrop.org
Hours: Special Garden Conservancy 2018 Open Days featuring Tea in the Garden, April 22, May 13 (Mother's Day), June 10, July 8, August 12, September 2, October 7, 10 a.m. to 5 p.m. Visitors will have the chance to purchase tea and cake from 12 p.m. to 4 p.m. Also open, April through October, Monday through Saturday, 10 a.m. to 5 p.m.
Admission: Adults, $10. Seniors 65 and older, students with an ID, $5. Children

ages 3 through 18, $5. Children under 2 free.

Stonecrop Gardens, originally the home of Frank and Anne Cabot, became a public garden in 1992 under the direction of Caroline Burgess. Frank Cabot is also the founder of the Garden Conservancy. At its windswept elevation of 1,100 feet in the Hudson Highlands, Stonecrop enjoys a Zone 6a climate. The display gardens cover an area of about twelve acres and incorporate a diverse collection of gardens and plants including woodland and water gardens, a grass garden, raised alpine stone beds, a cliff rock garden, perennial beds, and an enclosed English-style flower garden. Additional features include a conservatory, display alpine house, a pit house with an extensive collection of choice dwarf bulbs, and systematic order beds representing more than fifty plant families.

DIRECTIONS—From Taconic State Parkway, take Route 301/Cold Spring exit. Travel 3.5 miles to Stonecrop's entrance on right. A sign reading "Stonecrop Gardens" marks the driveway.

—From Route 9, take Route 301 east 2.7 miles and turn left at the entrance.

What our Garden Hosts recommend in Putnam County

Maple Lawn Farm Market
2461 U.S. 9, Garrison, NY 10524
(845) 424-4093

Vera's Marketplace and Garden Center
3091 Route 9 Suite 102
Cold Spring, NY 10516
(845) 265-2151
www.verasmarketplaceandgardencenter.com

B&L Deli (Cash Only)
3182 U.S. 9 #108, Cold Spring, NY 10516
(845) 265-3007
www.bldeli.com

Hudson Hil's Café
129-131 Main St, Cold Spring, NY 10516
(845) 265-9471
www.hudsonhils.com

SPENCERTOWN ACADEMY ARTS CENTER
PRESENTS

Hidden Gardens 2018

SATURDAY JUNE 17
COCKTAIL PARTY
GARDEN TOUR
MARKET ON THE GREEN
GALLERY EXHIBITION
LECTURE

Information and Reservations visit
www.spencertownacademy.org

SPENCERTOWN
NEW YORK

Dutchess County
Saturday, June 16

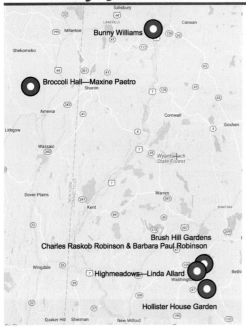

★ There are additional gardens open on this date in nearby Litchfield County, CT. See page 99.

Dutchess County
AMENIA
BROCCOLI HALL—MAXINE PAETRO
23 Flint Hill Road, Amenia
Hours: 10 a.m. to 4 p.m.
📷 | ♿PARTIAL | **2017**

Visitors to Broccoli Hall describe this English-style cottage garden as "incredible," "inspirational," "magical"—and they come back again and again. Starting in 1985 with one-and-one-half acres of bare earth, Maxine Paetro collaborated with horticulturist Tim Steinhoff to create a series of enchanting garden "rooms." Broccoli Hall offers an apple tunnel, a brick courtyard, a lavish display of spring bulbs blooming with crabapples in May; an extensive border of irises, peonies, and old shrub roses flowering in June; a tree house with long views; and a secret woodland garden with a teddy bears' picnic. We have some whimsical rustic carvings by woodsman / artisan Hoppy Quick; new bears, new stairs, new chairs, and some exceptionally charming bird feeders. Photos and magazine stories about Broccoli Hall can be viewed at www.broccolihall.com. In 2010, Broccoli Hall was expanded to five acres and two new mud ponds were installed. This is where we began a breeding program—but we don't sell our fish. To see the "elusive ki shusui" project in progress, go to www.kishusui.com. We look forward to seeing you in the garden in 2018!

DIRECTIONS—From Route 22 North or South, go toward Amenia. Go west on Route 44 to Route 83 North/Smithfield Road. Go 2.5 miles to dirt road on right, Flint Hill Road. Turn right. Garden is first on left. Please park on Flint Hill Road. Be careful of ditches.

Westchester County
Sunday, June 17

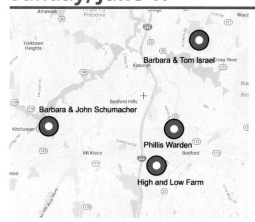

Westchester County
BEDFORD
HIGH AND LOW FARM
649 South Bedford Road, Bedford
Hours: 10 a.m. to 4 p.m.
📷 | 2007

A French-inspired garden that *House & Garden* said "combines echoes of antiquity with a startling modernism that is rare in a private landscape." Integrating the physical changes in the land into garden features, High and Low Farm is a balance of geometry and nature.

DIRECTIONS—From the north, take I-684 south to Exit 4. Turn left off the exit ramp. After about 0.5 mile, Foxlane High School will be on right and Succabone Road on left. The house is at first driveway on left after Succabone Road.
—From Connecticut, take I-95, exit at Stamford and get onto Route 104. Follow Route 104 into New York. The road turns into Long Ridge Road, which ends at a "T" intersection with Route 172/Pound Ridge Road. Turn left. At a blinking traffic light at

Shell station, turn right onto South Bedford Road (which is a continuation of Route 172). The next blinking light is at Foxlane High School. Proceed as directed above.

BEDFORD HILLS
PHILLIS WARDEN
531 Bedford Center Road, Bedford Hills
Hours: 10 a.m. to 4 p.m.
📷 | 2017

This garden of many facets includes perennial borders, three water gardens, a formal vegetable garden, wildflower garden, fern garden, marsh garden, a tree platform overlooking the marshlands, a woodland walk, a hidden garden, and a formal croquet court. The garden extends over seven acres, the back four acres of which are a study in what deer do not eat.

DIRECTIONS—From Bedford Village, take Route 22 toward Katonah to intersection at Bedford Cross. Garden is on left. Please park at Rippowam School and walk to #531.

KATONAH
BARBARA & TOM ISRAEL
296 Mount Holly Road, Katonah
Hours: 10 a.m. to 4 p.m.
📷 | ♿ | 2015

This historic property includes formal box-hedged perennial borders, a meditation garden, an orchard within a meadow, a rose garden, many specimen trees, and examples of antique garden statuary.

DIRECTIONS—From I-684, take Exit 6/Katonah/Cross River. Coming off the exit, turn toward Cross River, heading east on Route 35. Go about 3 miles and turn left onto Holly Branch Road. Follow this windy, hilly road to end. Turn right at "T" onto Mount Holly Road and make immediate left into driveway, #296 on mailbox. Gate will open automatically.

Barbara Israel's Garden
DIGGING DEEPER
11 AM
Skillful or Showy—Placing Ornament in the Garden
REGISTRATION: $30 Garden Conservancy Members / $35 general

Barbara Frelinghuysen Israel founded Barbara Israel Garden Antiques in 1985, after a serendipitous purchase of a large collection of estate statuary led her down the garden antiques path. Now in her thirty-second year in business, Barbara is recognized as an authority on the subject. Barbara's exhaustively researched book, *Antique Garden Ornament: Two Centuries of American Taste* (1999), is the definitive work in the field. She is also the author of *A Guide to Buying Antique Garden Ornament* (2012), a user-friendly handbook packed with tips on conservation, identification, and more.

Barbara has served as a consultant to both the Metropolitan Museum of Art and the Smithsonian Institution for their collections of nineteenth-century cast iron, and sold pieces to the Winterthur Museum, the Smithsonian Institution, and the Baltimore Museum of Art, as well as to many important private collectors. As an active board member of Historic Hudson Valley and the Untermyer Gardens Conservancy, she is devoted to preserving historic gardens and, of course, their antique garden ornament.

Registration required — space limited
Go to opendaysprogram.org
or call 1 (888) 842-2442

YORKTOWN
BARBARA & JOHN SCHUMACHER
315-317 Crow Hill Road, Yorktown
Hours: 10 a.m. to 4 p.m.
📷 | **2010**

At least four acres of this fifty-acre property have been developed into gardens by Barbara and John Schumacher, owners of the garden antiques shop Fleur. The large rose garden below the house colors the landscape with 400 roses. A perennial garden features *Hosta*, tree peonies, and sweeps of Asiatic lilies. Other attractions are a fern garden and a generous and varied collection of hydrangeas.

DIRECTIONS—From I-684 south take Exit 6 for Route 35/Cross River/Katonah. Turn right onto Route 35. Go 1.6 miles and turn left onto Route 100. Go 4.6 miles and turn left onto Crow Hill Road. Parking is not allowed on Crow Hill Road. Park on side streets and take care walking to garden. —From Saw Mill River Parkway, take exit for Route 133/Millwood Road in Mount Kisco. Go west on Route 133 (an extension of Main Street) toward Millbrook and turn right onto Crow Hill Road. The Schumacher's driveway will be on left. Parking is not allowed on Crow Hill Road. Please park on side streets and take care walking.

Dutchess County
Saturday, June 23

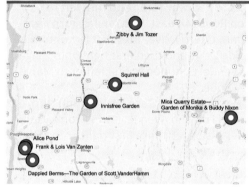

★ There is an additional garden open on this date in nearby Litchfield County, CT. See page 102.

★ Start your day at Innisfree Garden, 362 Tyrrel Road, Millbrook. Extended Open Day hours: 9:30 - 5. Admission: $8

OUR PARTNER IN DUTCHESS COUNTY

INNISFREE GARDEN

INNISFREE GARDEN

We are proud to partner with Innisfree Garden to bring you the June 23, July 21, and September 22 Dutchess County Open Days. Innisfree Foundation preserves and shares Innisfree Garden and the legacy of landscape architect Lester Collins. His iconic mid-twentieth century design exalts the beauty of nature enhanced by subtle and sustainable human intervention.

A small nonprofit, Innisfree has opened this sublime 185-acre landscape to the public since 1960, and is now expanding its educational offerings and working to preserve and protect this living landmark.

Dutchess County
MILLBROOK
SQUIRREL HALL
83 Maple Avenue, Millbrook
Hours: 10 a.m. to 4 p.m.
2017

Squirrel Hall is a surprisingly witty garden, formally designed on a tiny village lot of less than one acre. The central axis is defined by an allée of sixteen hornbeams with two secret niches. The garden is organized into a series of rooms with features usually reserved for large estates. The front lawn is enclosed by shrubs and an asparagus bed. A boxwood walkway leads to the front door as well as through an antique gate to the sunken garden, across the gravel and up the steps to a pavilion terrace and dining courtyard. Walk a few more steps up to the allée. The apiary is to the east, the petite orchard to the west, and a border of peonies is enclosed by a

collection of hydrangea and other shrubs to the north. Two English terra-cotta chimneys mark the entrance to a secret woodland stroll garden featuring hemlocks, shade-loving perennials and shrubs, and a bungalow.

DIRECTIONS—From Taconic State Parkway, take Route 44 exit and go east toward Millbrook.
—From west, follow directions on Route 44 from here. Go 1.8 miles from the Taconic State Parkway ramp and turn left to stay on Route 44 east. In 2.7 miles, turn right onto Ciferri Drive. Take first left onto Hillside Drive and then first right onto Haight Avenue. Continue to first left onto Maple Avenue.
—From the east, Take 44 west and turn left onto Franklin Avenue. (Twin Brooks Gardens is on left) Take first right onto Maple Avenue.

POUGHKEEPSIE
ALICE POND
94 Wilbur Boulevard, Poughkeepsie
Hours: 10 a.m. to 4 p.m.
📷 | **2017**

A "hidden treasure," this small Japanese-influenced, small suburban garden follows the Oriental philosophy of a series of rooms, with successive areas opening up and becoming visible as you meander down the stone paths and walkways. Each one treats visitors to a different sense of place and vantage point. They experience contemplative feelings of tranquility, from the soothing sound of the small waterfall emptying into the goldfish pond, to a rustic cedar wood gazebo overlooking it all. Slip off your shoes and come inside the teahouse, or do a "walking meditation" around the circular stone patio. This small garden won't take much time, and

TWIN BROOKS GARDENS
FROM OUR FIELDS TO YOUR GARDEN

; squirrel
; hall
; gifts
...because life should be amusing.
3424 Franklin Avenue | Millbrook NY 12545 | telephone 845.677.5050

utilizes a monochromatic natural growth selection—but the peaceful feeling might remain with you forever.

DIRECTIONS—From Route 9 North or South to Route 113/Spackenkill Road, and then 0.8 mile through a traffic light near Oakwood School's entrance. At second traffic light, turn left; dedicated lane into Wilbur Boulevard. Garden is 1.5 miles on left, past Christo's Restaurant/McCann Golf Course on right, baseball fields on right. Slow down and look for small sign on right for Spratt Park swimming pool; go up driveway to recommended parking. (You've gone too far if you see Miller Road on right).
—From Taconic State Parkway North or South, go to exits for either Route 44 or Route 55, continue west to merge with Maple Street/East-West Arterial, and continue west until Route 9 south. Follow directions above. No parking available at garden itself. Suggested parking at Spratt Park ball field lots, opposite 138 Wilbur Boulevard (also an Open Garden) or else diagonally across at the Spratt Park swimming pool driveway. No pets, please. Entrance to garden is via 13 wide stone slabs, then 3 stone steps; once inside the cedar archway gate, then 5 more steps down. There are other steps throughout the garden.

DAPPLED BERMS—THE GARDEN OF SCOTT VANDERHAMM
74 Colburn Drive, Poughkeepsie
Hours: 10 a.m. to 4 p.m.
📷 | ♿PARTIAL | **2017**
🏷ADAMS FAIRACRE FARMS

The garden is situated on a one-acre property within a 1950s (IBM-era) suburban community. As a result of the mature trees, which dominate the grounds, a shade perennial garden was created and cultivated over twenty seasons of weekend gardening. The assembled collection of plants, spread throughout numerous beds and man-made berms, relies heavily on the juxtapositions of color, texture, and form to bring interest and natural beauty to the garden. One of the highlights of the garden is the collection of more than 250 different *Hosta* cultivars numbering more than 470 specimens, all labeled for ease of identification. The garden will host a pop-up plant sale with Adams Fairacre Farms.

DIRECTIONS—From Route 9, take Spackenkill Road/Route 113 East 2 miles to Colburn Drive. (Please note: Colburn Drive is a U-Shaped street with two entrances onto Spackenkill Road. Number 74 Colburn is closer to the more western entrance.) Turn right off Spackenkill Road onto Colburn Drive to #74 on the left; please park on the street.
—From the Taconic State Parkway heading south, exit at Route 44 West and go approximately 12 miles to Main Street, Poughkeepsie. Continue on Main Street to Raymond Avenue/Route 376. Turn left on Raymond Avenue. Travel south on Raymond Avenue (past Vassar College) to Hooker Avenue. Turn left and continue on Route 376 to Zack's Way. Turn right at Zack's Way (which becomes Boardman Road) and follow to Spackenkill Road/

Route 113. Turn right on Spackenkill Road and then left onto Colburn Drive. Please park on the street.

—From the Taconic State Parkway heading north, exit at Route 55 West. Take Route 55 West approximately 14 miles to Raymond Avenue and follow the directions above.

FRANK & LOIS VAN ZANTEN
138 Wilbur Boulevard, Poughkeepsie
Hours: 10 a.m. to 4 p.m.
◎ | ♿ | **2017**

Our one-third-acre city lot, seventy-feet-wide by 200-feet deep is half shady. The objective is to have maximum color throughout the season, therefore a balanced mix of perennials, annuals, and some vegetables. We use hardscape (glass, metal sculpture, stone, etc.) and moveable pots, hanging and ground level, to maintain an attractive appearance throughout season. Potential value to the Garden Conservancy program is to show/inspire owners of small properties how to have an attractive garden without hired help.

DIRECTIONS—From Route 9, turn east on Spackenkill Road/County Road 113. Go approximately 0.7 mile to Wilbur Boulevard, at second traffic light. Turn left on Wilbur Boulevard and go north 1.1 mile to parking lot on right.
—From Taconic State Parkway, go west on either Route 55 or Route 44, direction Poughkeepsie, until it merges with Route 9 (approximately 20-25 minutes). From right lane turn onto Route 9 South, direction Wappingers Falls. Go 3.3 miles to Spackenkill Road; follow directions from above. Our garden is located 0.3 mile from the Van Aken/Roper garden and 2.8 miles from Scott Vanderhamm's Dappled Berms garden.

STANFORDVILLE
ZIBBY & JIM TOZER
840 Hunns Lake Road, Stanfordville
Hours: 10 a.m. to 2 p.m.
◎ | ♿ | **2017**

Uplands Farm includes a range of gardens in an Arcadian setting. The circular Romantic Garden, with its forget-me-nots, bleeding hearts, blue trapezoidal loveseats, and blue Moorish gate, all by Madison Cox, is of special interest. The white gate, with its Chippendale-style latticework and its ball and chain, was designed by Charles Stick of Virginia. The Pool Folly, which was inspired by the teahouse at Kykuit, has latticed walls, pagoda lanterns, and an eternity gate. Between two large paddocks, there are arches covered with 'William Baffin' roses, under which *Nepeta* and lavender create a path to a meadow. The Playhouse and the Tennis Cottage have their own charming gardens. The main garden is a seventy-foot herbaceous border filled with flowering perennials, grasses, Alberta spruces, topiaries, and shrubs. Other gardens dot the larger property of rolling hills, grand old trees, a lush meadow of rye, and paddocks with miniature horses, Babydoll miniature sheep, miniature donkeys, and Belted Galloway cows.

DIRECTIONS—From Taconic State Parkway, take Millbrook/Poughkeepsie exit. Turn right, direction Millbrook, at end of exit ramp onto Route 44. Go about 0.2 mile. Turn left onto Route 82 and go about 8 miles. At "Y" intersection at Stissing National Bank, bear right onto Route 65. Go 2 miles, passing Hunns Lake on left. Main house is third house past lake on right. Please park where indicated.

PUBLIC GARDEN PARTNER

Dutchess County
MILLBROOK
INNISFREE GARDEN

362 Tyrrel Road, Millbrook
(845) 677-5268
innisfreegarden.org
Hours: Daffodil viewing: April 21 & 28,
11 a.m. to 5 p.m. Regular hours May 5
through October 21, Wednesday through
Friday, 10 a.m. to 4 p.m.; weekends and
bank holidays, 11 a.m. to 5 p.m.; closed
Mondays and Tuesdays except bank holidays. Guided curator's tours and wildflower walks offered monthly. Garden opens
before sunrise three times each year.
Please see website for calendar details.
Admission: $6 weekdays; $8 weekends
and holidays; children 3 and under free.

Recognized as one of the world's ten
best gardens, Innisfree is a powerful icon
of mid-twentieth century design. Over
fifty years in the making, it is the work of
landscape architect Lester Collins, FASLA
(1914–1993), with important contributions
by his clients, artist and teacher Walter
Beck and gardener and heiress Marion
Burt Beck. Innisfree merges the essence of
Modernist and Romantic ideas with traditional Chinese and Japanese garden design
principles in a form that evolved through
subtle handling of the landscape and slow
manipulation of its ecology. The result is
a distinctly American stroll garden — a
sublime composition of rock, water, wood,
and sky achieved with remarkable economy and grace.

DIRECTIONS—Tyrrel Road is on the south
side of Route 44, 1.6 miles east of the
Taconic State Parkway overpass and 1.9
miles west of the traffic light at the intersection of Routes 82, 343, and Franklin Avenue. Blue and white signs for Innisfree on
Route 44 mark the turn. Innisfree is about
1.1 miles off Route 44, on the left side of
Tyrrel. The street number is out of order
so watch for the white Innisfree sign and a
dirt driveway through stone pillars to the
right of a stone gatehouse. The parking
area is about 0.5 miles in along the drive.
—If coming from the Taconic State Parkway,
please do NOT take the Tyrrel Road exit (it
is impassible in the middle). Instead, take
the Route 44 exit east toward Millbrook. If
using GPS, the Innisfree driveway is now
called Innisfree Lane. You can key in Tyrrel
Road & Innisfree Lane, Millbrook, New
York 12545.

Saratoga Springs Area
Saturday, June 23

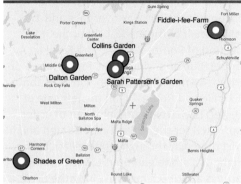

DIGGING DEEPER
2:30 PM
Shades of Green—The Lush Beauty of a Shady Garden
Free with garden admission

Wynn Trowbridge

Join passionate shade garden expert Wynne Trowbridge to explore her garden and the extensive plant collection that inspired her to start a small nursery specializing in shade plants.

Saratoga County
CHARLTON
SHADES OF GREEN
2036 Cook Road, Charlton
Hours: 10 a.m. to 4 p.m.
📷 | ♿PARTIAL | **NEW**

Come take a quiet stroll through the woods, relax for a spell on a shady bench and listen to the birds, while taking in the beautiful woodland gardens of Shades of Green. Discover hidden treasures among the hundreds of different varieties of shade-loving perennials including *Hosta*, ferns, *Heuchera, Polygonatum,* and *Primula* in this peaceful country setting. Picnic tables are available, so bring your lunch. Purchase one of the many perennials available, or just come for inspiration.

DIRECTIONS—Shades of Green is located approximately 13 miles east of Amsterdam, New York. From Highway 67 to Cook Road, then 5.1 miles.
—From west of Ballston Spa, New York, take Highway 67 for 9 miles to Cook Road, then 5.1 miles. Parking is available in driveway or along Cook Road. For Saratoga

MIDDLE GROVE
DALTON GARDEN
284 Middle Grove Road, Middle Grove
Hours: 10 a.m. to 4 p.m.
📷 | ♿PARTIAL | **NEW**

The garden surrounds the house and covers two-and-one-half acres. It is woodland in nature with large collections of native plants (trillium, *Clintonia*, ferns, *Arisaema*), shade perennials (*Astilbe, Heuchera*, primrose, *Cimicifuga, Hosta*), shrubs (peonies, hydrangea, *Viburnum*, rhododendron), and trees (Japanese maple, dogwood, minia-ture gingko). Adding interest throughout the garden you will find statues, urns, and other ornaments reflecting the theme of the area in which they are located.

DIRECTIONS—Take Exit 24 of the NYS Thruway. Follow sign to I-87 North/ I-90 East/ Albany/Montreal. Merge onto I-87 for 25 miles. Take Exit 13N, US-9 North/Sara-toga Springs. Follow US-9 for 4 miles into Saratoga (to just past Congress Park on the right). Turn left onto Route 29 (Washing-ton Street). (Starbucks on the corner). Go 4 miles and turn right onto North Milton Road (cemetery and driving range on corner). At the first stop sign, turn left onto Middle Grove Road.

SARATOGA SPRINGS
COLLINS GARDEN
339 Clinton Street, Saratoga Springs
Hours: 10 a.m. to 4 p.m.
📷 | ♿PARTIAL | **NEW**

We've enjoyed creating and maintain-ing our garden, which is surrounded by wetland and forest on the border of Saratoga Springs, "The City in the Country." For twenty-five years we've let the path of the sun and the flow of seasons guide our decisions. From dogwoods flowering to tamaracks turning gold, plants peak at different times. You'll find shady fern gardens and Hosta-lined paths along with daylilies, hydrangeas, irises, and sunflow-ers. Ornamental grasses and evergreens soften stone walls. Flowers surround the greenhouse, waterfall, and gazebo. Birds and animals seem to like the blurring of garden and wildlife habitat. We hope you do too.

DIRECTIONS—From Saratoga Springs, take Clinton Street north past Skidmore College, go down the hill, then two houses past the Alpine Sport Shop on left. The garden is 1 mile from downtown Saratoga Springs.

SARAH PATTERSON'S GARDEN
65 Central Avenue, Saratoga Springs
Hours: 10 a.m to 4 p.m.
 | **NEW**

My garden has evolved over the past ten years from all lawn to none. I have tried to create a peaceful garden that can be enjoyed while wandering along paths. To create some shade, I have incorporated small-scale trees and shrubs. These in-clude *Cornus, Betula, Acer griseum, Chamae-cyparis, Viburnum, Ilex* and *Syringa*. Added to those are dwarf *Betula, Fagus, Abies, Picea, Taxus*, and *Thuja*. Vines and ferns mixed with *Papaver atlanticum, Lathyrus vernus, Digitalis, Helleborus, Hemerocallis, Geranium*, and many other perennials add the final layer. As always I am proud to say all work I have done by myself.

DIRECTIONS—From downtown Sarato-ga, turn at the Adirondack Trust building, Church St. From the traffic light at the hospital, take your fourth left (there is a doctors office sign on the left just before you turn). Number 65 Central Avenue is the first building on the right.

SCHUYLERVILLE
FIDDLE-I-FEE-FARM
167 West River Road, Schuylerville
Hours: 10 a.m. to 4 p.m.
📷 | ♿ | **NEW**

Our farm, a melange of fields, woodlands, and wetlands, rolls to a bluff above the Hudson, with vistas east to Vermont and north to the Adirondacks. My husband, Neil, is the woodsman. I am the cultivator. We have enriched the hedgerows and swales with missing species including arborvitae, cedar, larch, bald cypress, sycamore, tulip, oak, willow, and copses of pawpaw and persimmon. A prairie reconstruction shares a field with an orchard and vegetable garden. An expansive informal garden billows around an Arts and Crafts-style house, borrowing views from surrounding nature.

DIRECTIONS—In Schuylerville, take Routes 32/4 north. When routes diverge, bear left on Route 32. At top of hill, take first right onto West River Road/County 29. At 0.25 mile on the left is our mailbox, #167, next to gravel drive. Enter drive, park in field on right.

What our Garden Hosts recommend in Saratoga Springs

Brookside Nursery
824 Route 67, Ballston Spa, NY
(518) 885-6500
www.brooksidenursery.com

Columbia County
Sunday, June 24

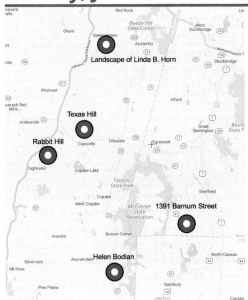

★ There is an additional garden open on this date in nearby Berkshire County, MA. See page 155.

Columbia County
CRARYVILLE
RABBIT HILL
158 Maiers Road, Craryville
📷🖼 | ♿ | **2017**
Hours: 10 a.m. to 5 p.m.

Forty years ago, my husband Richard and I bought a tiny "get-away". A nineteenth-century farmhouse set in fifty-seven acres of a second-growth woodland. Today, the tiny house, wrapped in additions, is unrecognizable. The gardens, then non-existent became our joy and creating a landscape was Richard's passion for years. Unfortunately he passed away in May 2015 and all of the plants and trees miss him. I am continuing to work on the garden without him. We cleared a woodland for a large lawn and opened land to reveal a view of the Berkshires. Richard raised the canopy of a large wooded area and planted many species and varieties of decorative understory trees, shrubs, shade perennials, and ground-covers that are now seen by strolling on a network of stone paths that interlace the woodland grove. A moss garden is contained within the grove and it is bordered by an allée planted with specimen trees and shrubs and, to the east, by "Moby Dick", a rock outcropping, several hundred feet long, uncovered by hand digging over several years. Whale-shaped and white when uncovered, the name was inevitable. [Read the full description online]

DIRECTIONS—From the Taconic State Parkway, exit east at Manor Rock Road. Go 1 mile to fork and turn right onto Maiers Road. Ten feet on left are five mailboxes and our driveway with a sign, "158 Maiers Road." Park on the road and walk into the property. If you are handicapped have a friend drive you in.
—From intersection of Route 22 and 23 at Hillsdale, go west on Route 23 exactly 4 miles to County Route 11/Beauty Award Highway. Go south 2.2 miles to Craryville Road. Turn right and go 0.8 miles to fork in road. Bear right onto Manor Rock Road and go 1.5 miles to Maiers Road fork. Keep left about ten feet. Our driveway is just past five mailboxes. Please park on Maiers Road and walk in.

HILLSDALE
TEXAS HILL
411 Texas Hill Road, Hillsdale
Hours: 10 a.m. to 4 p.m.
2017

Our garden atop Texas Hill in Hillsdale began ten years ago, after we completed the
restoration of our newly purchased house,
having left behind our Germantown house
and garden after twenty-five years. We
acquired this 1967 "modern ranch" from
the family of the original owners. There
was no garden to speak of—just a few
peonies, rhododendron, lots of *Vinca*
and *Epimedium*, and a few sad tulips. But
the rocky ridge-line property had much
to offer: excellent big views, interesting
terrains, old and newer stone walls and patios, established trails through the woods,
and a beautifully sighted spring-fed pond.
Accentuating these assets has been our
over-riding goal from the outset. However,
the elevation (Zone 4), brutal exposure,
deer herds, and the terribly rocky soil
presented unusually difficult challenges.
Initially we created two protected courtyards, using existing structures and new
fencing, and planting beds with perennials
and small scrubs and dwarf trees. Beyond
these early beds and courtyards, we planted large groups of evergreen trees (hemlock, pine, spruce) for visual variety and
wind protection. Around them we made
island beds of so-called deer-resistant
plants. Within three years, after a particularly devastating deer attack one harsh
winter, we were forced to enclose......[Read
full description online]

DIRECTIONS—From the Taconic State
Parkway, exit onto Route 23 East. Go 0.2
mile and turn left onto County Road 11.
Go another 0.2 mile and turn right onto
Carlson Road. Road becomes Texas Hill
Road after intersection of Lockwood Road.
Number 411 is on the right, about 3 miles
from the Taconic.

MILLERTON
HELEN BODIAN
359 Carson Road, Millerton
Hours: 10 a.m. to 4 p.m.
📷 | ♿PARTIAL | **2017**

The setting is a broad landscape of hayfield and meadows crested by a forested
ridge. Within it are four self-contained
gardens established sequentially over
twenty-five years, sited at the base of the
surrounding slopes. The gardens, made
at different times and in different styles,
are not entirely adjacent, so a network
of paths connects them with one another and then out to a pond and the larger
landscape. The first garden, a rock garden,
was spurred by construction of a modern
addition to the house. This garden presented several design challenges at the start:
first, scaling the rocks and plantings both
to a shale hill suspended above and to the
elongated house addition, and then, breaking up the linear view from the house. The
solution was to use massed shrubs and
small trees at the rim and to allow some
to wander down into the garden area. Not
a conventional rock garden, it is instead a
place for small perennials to flourish and
show their colors. Next, across a dirt road,
was a quasi-classic, rather romantic garden in the form of an open square framed
on two parallel sides by hornbeam hedges
and planted with crabapples, ornamental
shrubs, and perennials. A greenhouse and
modernist walled garden followed, with
a small square pool and rectilinear gravel
areas for summer staging of potted tender
plants from the greenhouse. The vegetable
garden came last and with it an opportunity to make a striking and colorful composi-

tion every year, using kale, amaranth, and cardoon as structure and annual flowers for color.

DIRECTIONS—From Millerton, take Route 22 to intersection of Routes 44 and 22 and go north on Route 22 for 4 miles. On right, you will see a sign for Columbia County and on left, Carson Road. Turn onto Carson Road and go up hill for 1 mile. On left are a tennis court and a metal barn; on right, a white farmhouse with a modern addition. Please park in field next to barn.
—From Hillsdale, take Route 22 South about 14 miles from traffic light in Hillsdale. Look for a sign on left for Dutchess County and Carson Road on right.

SPENCERTOWN
LANDSCAPE OF LINDA B. HORN
5015 County Route 7, Spencertown
Hours: 10 a.m. to 2 p.m.
📷 | ♿PARTIAL | **2017**

The restoration of my landscape has been the goal for the fifteen years of living here after a move from Chicago. There are four restored ecosystems: wetlands, waterfall, domestic area of native grasses, and woodland. The last section of restoration was started last fall with eliminating dead trees and then new seeding. This year goldenrod was weed-wacked and new trees planted. The landscape was featured in the September issue of *New York Cottages & Gardens* with a five-page spread (images are available). Native restoration workshops have been held here through the Columbia Land Conservancy, Spencertown Academy, and Berkshire Botanical Garden.

DIRECTIONS—From Chatham, go south on Route 203, stay right onto County Route 7/Crow Hill Road in Spencertown. The

garden is exactly 1 mile south of the post office. The driveway is on the right after Pratt Hill Road. Look for pillar with #5015.
—From Hillsdale/Route 22 North, turn left onto Route 21 and then right onto County Route 7/Crow Hill Road. Look for #5015 pillar on left. If you reach Punsit Hill Road on the right or Pratt Hill Road on the left, you have gone a block too far. (For Garmins, use Austerlitz Township as our town; for Google Maps, use Chatham.) Please park on Punsit Road or on side of driveway if not used.

The Garden of Linda Horn
DIGGING DEEPER
10 AM – 4 PM
A Meadow Restoration Through the Seasons—Late Spring
Free with garden admission

Mick Hales

Owner and artist Linda Horn, land stewardship designer Barbara Hughey, and landscape designer Heather Grimes will be on hand to introduce guests to Linda's dynamic landscape, discuss the concepts and practices of landscape restoration, and provide practical ideas for creating healthy, beautiful, and low maintenance native ecosystems. In addition to landscape restoration basics, they will focus on the special tasks and stand-out plants of the season.

Ulster County
Sunday, June 24

Nestled in an old apple orchard with a view of the Shawangunk Ridge, this intricate garden is comprised of intimate spaces and surprises in unexpected places. Garden designer Teri Condon and sculptor Richard Gottlieb have combined their talents to create a feast for your eyes. An *Akebia*-draped pergola, recessed patio, and stone fire circle are woven together with serpentine stepping stone paths that seduce you from one delicacy to the next. Striking foliage combinations paired with architectural forms create a serene yet whimsical garden experience.

DIRECTIONS—From the New York State Thruway, take Exit 18. Turn right at first light after toll onto Route 299. Go 0.2 mile to next light and turn left onto North Ohioville. Turn right onto Old Route 299 (there is an antiques store on corner). Go about 0.7 mile to Plutarch Road and turn left. Go another 0.5 mile to Hillside Avenue and turn left. Bear left where drive splits. Garden is on top of hill.

Ulster County
HIGHLAND
TERI CONDON—GARDENSMITH DESIGN
50 Hillside Avenue, Highland
Hours: 12 p.m. to 4 p.m.
📷 | 2016

KINGSTON
GARDEN OF PEGGY & FRANK ALMQUIST
107 Beth Drive, Kingston
Hours: 10 a.m. to 4 p.m.
 | NEW

An American *Hemerocallis* Society "display garden" of approximately 200 daylilies enhanced with a jubilant mix of perennial favorites (*Astilbe, Helleborum*, Asian lilies) and prized specimens (dawn redwood, Japanese umbrella pine, 'Green Panda' bamboo). The garden is laid out in a series of rooms and raised beds, with sun, shade, a waterfall, many surprises, and two very avid and knowledgeable gardeners.

DIRECTIONS—Take the New York State Thruway to Kingston/Exit 19, after toll bear slight left to traffic circle. Stay in right lane and take second exit, Washington Avenue. Stay in right lane through first traffic light. For next two traffic lights use center lane. Road narrows to one lane. After two more traffic lights, turn right on Pear Street at next light. Proceed 0.75 mile to top of hill and "T." Turn right onto Lynette Boulevard. At next stop sign turn right onto Hillside Terrace, and at next intersection turn right onto Beth Drive. House is almost at end on right, #107. Park on roadside opposite the home.

NEW PALTZ
SPRINGTOWN FARMDEN
387 Springtown Road, New Paltz
Hours: 1 p.m. to 4:30 p.m.
 | PARTIAL | **2016**

A writer once proclaimed my garden to be very much a "man's garden"; perhaps it is. The emphasis is on fruits and vegetables, but the whole works, as they are woven into plantings of flowers and ornamental shrubs. I try to grow a year-round supply of pretty much every kind of vegetable except rhubarb, parsnips, and Jerusalem artichokes. Fruits include many varieties of dwarf apples and pears, grapes, and numerous uncommon fruits such as pawpaws, persimmons, gooseberries (twenty or so varieties), currants, and medlars. Out in the adjoining hayfield is a 100-foot trellis of hardy kiwis and a swale bordered by chestnut and hazelnut trees.

DIRECTIONS—From I-87/New York State Thruway, take New Paltz/Route 299 West exit through New Paltz. Cross bridge and take first right onto Springtown Road. Bear right at fork; house is #387, about 3 miles on left.
—From Kingston, take Route 32 South. Go about 2 miles, after passing Rosendale, to Tillson Road. (Postage Inn is on left.) Turn right and then left at stop sign onto Springtown Road. House is #387 and is about 1.5 miles on right. Please park along street or driveway.

What our Garden Hosts recommend in Ulster County

Hash
3928 Main St, Stone Ridge, NY 12484
(845) 687-9794
www.hashfoodny.com

Dutchess County
Saturday, June 30

DIRECTIONS—Take I-684 to Route 22/ Pawling exit. Go about 9 miles to Route 311 and turn right onto South Quaker Hill Road. At stop sign (about 3 miles along), turn right onto Birch Hill Road. We are #10 on right. Please park on road.
—From Connecticut, take Route 37 through Sherman and turn onto Wakeman Road. Akin Hall Library is on right, Hill Farm on left. Turn left and continue south; this becomes Birch Hill Road. Please park on road.

★There is an additional garden open on this date in nearby Fairfield County, CT. See page 103.

Dutchess County
PAWLING
SCHERER GARDEN
10 Birch Hill Road, Pawling
Hours: 11 a.m. to 4 p.m.
📷 | 2016

Over thirty years ago, we moved a 200-year-old house and barn to our scrubby, rocky site on Quaker Hill. In collaboration with Robin Zitter, we have created the garden we dreamed of, a naturalistic, traditional cottage garden. Woodland paths are filled with rhododendrons, ferns, and spring-blooming bulbs. In the garden close to the house the beds are now deeper and filled with shrubs, sedges, grasses, and perennials. The pool area is a hidden, rocky gem filled with color. A knot/herb garden in the back is a focal point and enhances the western views. Our garden is featured in Jane Garmey and John M. Hall's book *Private Gardens of the Hudson Valley*.

Suffolk County
Saturday, June 30

Suffolk County
MT. SINAI
TRANQUILITY
42 Jesse Way, Mt. Sinai
Hours: 10 a.m. to 4 p.m.
📷 | ♿PARTIAL | **2017**

The Becker garden can be described as an explosion of color, fragrance, sound, and texture. Hundreds of perennials, shrubs, trees, and annuals are combined with water features, lawn art, and recently relocated garden trails that allow the visitor to enter the owner's vision of an Impressionistic garden painting. Footpaths wind through the extensive garden, allowing visitors to immerse themselves in the sights and sounds of nature and escape the general stress of modern lifestyles.

DIRECTIONS—Take the Long Island Expressway to Exit 63/Route 83. Go north to Canal Road. Turn left and then take the first right onto Autumn Road. Go to end. Turn right onto Wheat Path and then take the first left onto Jesse Way. Number 42 is on left.

Dutchess County
Saturday, July 7

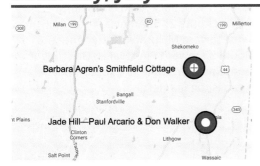

Dutchess County
AMENIA
JADE HILL—PAUL ARCARIO & DON WALKER
13 Lake Amenia Road, Amenia
Hours: 10 a.m. to 4 p.m.
📷 | **2017**

Starting as a rocky hillside that was mostly lawn, Jade Hill has grown into a stroll garden designed to be a tapestry of texture and color. Favorite plants went in first: Japanese maples, conifers, and a bamboo grove. Innumerable wheelbarrows of compost and mulch (wheeled uphill!) helped create beds of shrubs and perennials; hand-dug pools were put in for goldfish and lotus. The main bed along the driveway is anchored by golden barberries and purple smoke trees (coppiced each year)— with roses, peonies, Siberian irises, phlox, and other perennials filling in—and backed by a 'Purple Fountain' weeping beech. Jade Hill borders the wetlands that were once Lake Amenia, and our property is on the site of what was intended to become a lakeside community consisting of dozens of small lots. Over the years, we were able to acquire some of the adjacent parcels, which quickly became new garden rooms. One addition was the rose garden; another was a gold-themed garden, viewed from a cantilevered "Oriental" pavilion meant to show off carved wooden window panels purchased at a flea market years ago. The garden was featured in the September 2006 issue of *Better Homes & Gardens* and the July 2007 issue of *Hudson Valley* magazine.

DIRECTIONS—From the traffic light in Amenia at the intersection of Routes 22, 44, and 343, take Route 44 west. Make first left after 55 mph sign onto Lake Amenia Road. A gated driveway is after fifth house on right. Please park on road.

MILLERTON
BARBARA AGREN'S
SMITHFIELD COTTAGE
56 Moadock Road, Millerton
Hours: 10 a.m. to 4 p.m.
 | 🖒 | **2015**

Barbara's garden atop, the beautiful Smithfield Valley in the heart of the Millbrook Hunt Country, is exhibited in vibrant colors in her perennial landscape around her cottage. Her fashion background shows in the mix of color from an array of roses, *Crocosmia*, Russian sage, 'Globemaster' *Allium*, lilies, phlox, and many more amongst stone and cast-iron sculptures and stone walls on different levels. A peach and apple espalier is featured against the charming cottage. The views show the magnificent landscape of the Smithfield Valley—not a house in sight.

DIRECTIONS—From the Taconic Parkway North, take Millbrook exit and turn right onto Route 44 East. Continue on Route 44 toward Amenia, make left turn onto Route 83 toward Pine Plains, and go straight onto Route 5. Moadock Road is first left.
—From Route 22 in Amenia, take Route 44 West toward Millbrook. Turn right onto Route 83 toward Pine Plains. Go straight onto Route 5/Smithfield Road. Moadock-Road is the first left.

Suffolk County
Saturday, July 7

Suffolk County
JAMESPORT
WINDS WAY FARM
73 Winds Way, Jamesport
Hours: 10 a.m. to 4 p.m.
📷 | ♿PARTIAL | **2017**

Welcome to Winds Way! Located on the shore of Great Peconic Bay, our North Fork gardens occupy land that was once potato field and pasture. The gardens are designed to complement the historic buildings we've moved to our property —an 1836 Greek Revival-style whaling captain's house, an 1872 one-room schoolhouse, an early-nineteenth-century barn—and to create a compelling sense of place. Included are a small orchard featuring heirloom apples and espaliered fruit trees, a large-scale vegetable garden, a soft-fruit area, and herbaceous and shrub borders teaming with plants that appeal to butterflies and other pollinators. As avid birders, we've planted many natives to provide food, shelter, and nesting sites for feathered friends. Plantings vary in style from more formal gardens with historically appropriate plant material to naturalistic

settings. They feature shaded and woodland gardens in addition to full-sun areas and a small meadow. All the gardens are connected with meandering paths, and garden spaces are defined by picket fences, rail fences, and hedges. We started as weekend gardeners in the mid-1980s and, since retiring in 2001, continue to add new gardens to parts of our property that are not protected by conservation easements... [Read full description online]

DIRECTIONS—From I-495/Long Island Expressway, take Exit 73/Route 58 and follow to Route 25 and traffic light in Jamesport (about 8 miles). Turn right onto South Jamesport Avenue, pass under railroad tracks, and at 4-way stop sign turn right onto Peconic Bay Boulevard. Cross Washington Avenue. About a quarter mile farther, Winds Way is a dirt road on the left passing through the middle of a large field. Please parallel park along the edge of Winds Way.

MATTITUCK
DENNIS SCHRADER & BILL SMITH
1200 East Mill Road, Mattituck
Hours: 10 a.m. to 4 p.m.
📷 | ♿ | **2017** | 🏷PLANT SALES

Set in the heart of the North Fork's wine region, this three-plus-acre garden surrounds a restored 1840s farmhouse. In 2008, the house went through a major renovation, and the gardens and terraces around it have since been redesigned. The deck, porches, and stone terraces are filled with hundreds of container plantings. There are many perennial and mixed-shrub borders throughout the garden that can be accessed by numerous winding paths. Garden rooms hedged in by hornbeam and boxwood reflect various themed gardens within. Additionally, there is a vegetable/herb garden, a formal knot garden, several bog plantings, meadow gardens, and a woodland shade area. The garden also features rustic arbors, trellises, stone walls, and a Tiki hut that contains a collection of exotic plants. The newest meadow garden surrounds the "Ruin"—a subterranean stone grotto partially covered with a sedum-planted green roof. The three roundels located in the eastern part of the garden are made from locust wood harvested from the property. The roundels support climbing roses and seasonal exotic vines and are under-planted with a collection of shade-loving plants...[Read full description online]

DIRECTIONS—From I-495/Long Island Expressway, take Exit 73/Route 58 and follow to Route 25. Go through town of Mattituck, past Love Lane to Wickham Avenue. Turn left and go past railroad tracks and traffic light. Stay straight on Wickham and it will turn into Grand Avenue. Take Grand about 1 mile to East Mill Road. Turn left and look for #1200. Please park along street.

SHELTER ISLAND HEIGHTS
BIRDHOUSE GARDEN

3A Wesley Avenue, Shelter Island Heights
Hours: 10 a.m. to 4 p.m.
2017

Tim Purtell's garden in Shelter Island Heights mixes trees, shrubs, grasses, and flowering perennials with the goal of attracting and supporting wildlife such as bees, butterflies, birds, and small mammals. There's no lawn. Instead, the fifteen-year old landscape is planted predominantly with natives that provide color, texture, and fragrance from June to October. Aside from the pleasure of its natural form, which mimics wilder places but on a small scale, the garden also functions as a lab to test plants for deer resistance, drought tolerance, and other qualities.

DIRECTIONS—From the North Fork, take Grand Avenue to Waverly Place. Make a right onto Waverly Place and then a left onto Wesley Avenue. The house is near the end of Wesley.
—From the South Fork, take 114 across the island to Chase Avenue. Go up the hill on Chase Avenue and at the top take a right onto Grand Avenue. Make a left onto Grand Avenue, go to Waverly Avenue, and then take a left onto Wesley Avenue. The house is near the end of Wesley.

Ithaca Area
Saturday, July 7

Tompkins County Towns and Villages for beautification projects. The Community Beautification Program is funded by the Tompkins County Tourism Program and administered by Cornell Cooperative Extension.

Tioga County
SPENCER
MYERS GARDENS
1071 Michigan Hollow Road, Spencer
Hours: 10 a.m. to 4 p.m.
📷 | 2015

Wayne's gardens are a wonderland of gorgeous plantings, unique hardscaping, and interesting historical features. Six acres of rolling lawn and perennial beds contain more than 550 different varieties nestled between fieldstone walls and outbuildings. Features include a covered bridge, a working water wheel on a post-and-beam-constructed feed mill, a blacksmith shop, and a glass sponge fossil rock enclosed in a unique display case. Other unusual features include a thirty-foot-diameter stone sundial and a potting-shed garden. Wayne also constructs sculptures, found throughout the gardens, from discarded farm machinery parts.

DIRECTIONS—From downtown Ithaca, take Route 13/34/96 south. About 3 miles south of Ithaca, take left exit onto Route 34 / 96 and go about 9 miles, then turn left onto Hillview Road. Stay on Hillview Road for 3 miles, until the stop sign and intersection with Michigan Hollow Road. The garden is directly in front of you. Please park on road.

OUR PARTNER IN THE ITHACA AREA

THE TOMPKINS COUNTY COMMUNITY BEAUTIFICATION PROGRAM

The Tompkins County Community Beautification Program was established in 2002 to improve the landscaping and appearance of public spaces in Ithaca and Tompkins County. In the City of Ithaca, this is accomplished through the efforts of a group of volunteers called the Beautification Brigade. This program also hosts a Rural Beautification Grant program through which matching funds are made available to rural

Tompkins County
FREEVILLE
MANZANO GARDEN
418 Caswell Road, Freeville
Hours: 10 a.m. to 4 p.m.
📷 | **2016**

Spacious gardens at Ann and Carlton Manzano's 1800s farmhouse are well integrated with the sloping topography. Near the house, the pool area is surrounded by lush, tropical plantings, while the steep slopes behind the house are planted with a dense mix of perennials, shrubs, and ground covers. Carlton is a plein-air artist, and dozens of his paintings are on display in the barn, which he built himself in the architectural style of 1800s barns. His whimsical sculptures made of natural wood pieces can also be found along the woodland paths at the rear of the property.

DIRECTIONS—From Route 13 in Ithaca, turn north onto Hanshaw Road. Go 2.7 miles and turn right onto West Dryden Road. Go 2.9 miles and turn left onto Caswell Road. Go 0.5 mile to #418.

ITHACA
SHELIA AND LOUIS OUT'S GARDEN
247 Valley Road, Ithaca
Hours: 10 a.m. to 4 p.m.
📷 | **NEW**

Louis and Sheila's garden is a hidden gem in the city. Plantings in front of their home are low-maintenance, with shrubs and stone retaining walls on the steep slope. The backyard features exuberant borders of bright summer perennials at the base of a high wall, to which Louis added a black locust grid to create a geometric focal point behind the gardens. Shade-loving perennials surround a weeping cherry tree, and a small pond with a wooden bridge and stone terrace provides a restful place to observe wildlife that visit the pond.

DIRECTIONS—From downtown Ithaca, take Route 79 East. After 1 mile turn left onto Valley Road. Stay on Valley Road for 0.3 mile and the Out residence will be on your right, just before the intersection with Elmwood Avenue. Park on Valley Road.

LANSING
LION GARDEN
219 Lansing Station Road, Lansing
Hours: 10 a.m. to 4 p.m.
📷 | ♿PARTIAL | **2013**

Flowers welcome you from the moment you arrive. Entrance plantings embrace the street, and hundreds of blooming perennials line the brick driveway. The sound of flowing water emanates from three connected ponds containing lotuses, water lilies, and koi. Large flowerbeds around the house are filled with perennials, and dozens of planted pots grace the deck on the shady hillside. The gardens continue down a steep, wooded hill, where borders of shade-loving perennials, ground covers, and shrubs surround a gazebo and folly. Woodland trails lead to a small ravine below the garden.

DIRECTIONS—From Ithaca, take Route 34 north along Cayuga Lake. Turn left onto Route 34 B and go 5.5 miles. Turn left onto Lansing Station Road and go 1 mile. The house is on left, and wooden mailbox reads #219. Please park on left past driveway.

Putnam County
Sunday, July 8

Putnam County
COLD SPRING
STONECROP GARDENS

81 Stonecrop Lane, Cold Spring
(845) 265-2000
stonecrop.org

★ For full listing please see page 279.

Suffolk County
Saturday, July 14

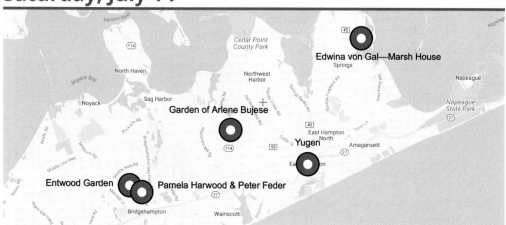

Suffolk County
BRIDGEHAMPTON
ENTWOOD GARDEN
100 Chase Court, Bridgehampton
Hours: 10 a.m. to 4 p.m.
📷 | ♿ | 2017

This is an informal but structured seven-acre, contoured landscape intended to combine intimate gardens, intriguing plants, tree and rock specimens, welcoming habitats, expansive views, and recre-

ational spaces. Originally a flat potato field, it centers around two large naturalistic koi ponds nurtured by wetland filter systems. The ponds are surrounded by open lawn and arboretum areas, which in turn give way to border plantings of mature evergreen and deciduous trees, hidden paths, and shade gardens. Entering through the front gate, you are greeted by a colorful cottage garden partially shaded by a mature crabapple, a Japanese pagoda tree, and yellow deodar cedar. Continuing west under a weeping Atlas cedar archway, you pass a small Asian-style pond and garden on the left and, on the right, a kitchen, lily, and rose garden. A partially hidden path under a stand of cedars of Lebanon leads to a hidden koi pond overhung by Himalayan pines. Crossing north through the pond on stones set in the water, the path opens onto a lawn bordered on the left by Alaska cedars, *Cryptomeria*, Skyrocket English oaks, sweetgums, Callery pears, and tulip trees. ...[Read full description online]

DIRECTIONS—Take Route 27 to Bridgehampton. Go north onto Sag Main Turnpike, then take immediate left fork onto Lumber Lane. Go north 1 mile. Turn left onto Chase Court. Number 100 is last house on right.
—If coming from Sag Harbor, go south onto Sag Main Turnpike. Turn right onto Scuttle Hole Road. Then turn left onto Lumber Lane. Take the first right onto Chase Court and continue to #100 (last house on right). Please park on the street.

Entwood Gardens
DIGGING DEEPER
2 PM
**Rocks, Ponds, Waterfalls, and Exotic Trees—A Strolling Garden
to Soothe and Stimulate
REGISTRATION: $30 Garden Conservancy Members / $35 general**

Spend an afternoon strolling through a park-like landscape of intimate, naturalistic gardens, contoured vistas, and whimsical surprises created over the past twenty years. Garden owners, Marlene Marko and Loren Skeist, will describe their efforts to create a beguiling, all-season refuge. Along with gardeners Dan and Laura Reilly, and

water expert Ed Drohan, Marlene and Loren will share how their fascination with individual garden elements—especially trees and rocks—expanded to include shrubs and flowers, ponds, woodland, shade and water gardens, and ultimately, the relationships and flow between gardens. They hope to share their joy in discovering beauty in so many unexpected places and of starting gardens which then continue to surprise and challenge as they mature. Practicing medicine and raising three children in Manhattan, Marlene and Loren bought a small weekend cottage on two-thirds of an acre in Bridgehampton in 1996. Two years later they acquired an adjacent six-acre potato field and began to recruit a team of creative and passionate garden specialists to help them imagine and realize outdoor spaces that were interesting and fun. Each year, one or two gardens or other features were added, not as part of a predetermined cohesive vision, but as a new element, often to create just the right place for an extraordinary rock or a newly discovered rare plant or tree. The result is a garden that is best experienced not by just looking, but by taking the time—strolling, sitting, touching, listening—to feel a part of it.

**Registration required — space limited
Go to opendaysprogram.org
or call 1 (888) 842-2442**

PAMELA HARWOOD & PETER FEDER
371 Woodland Drive, Bridgehampton
Hours: 10 a.m. to 4 p.m.
♿PARTIAL | **2017**

This all-organic garden has evolved over the last twenty-six years, created and entirely tended by its' two self-taught owners, one of whom is a board member of the Horticultural Alliance of the Hamptons. When deer began decimating the plantings, the owners rethought the design, fenced in the rear of the property, and dedicated the accessible front portion entirely to proven, deer-resistant varieties, like the lengthy hedge of *Lavendula* 'Hidcote' (Hidcote lavender) that runs along the semi-circular pebble driveway. At the same time, they "took back" the fenced-in rear garden, enjoyed blooms that had been easy prey for years, but also redesigned the space, continually adding new varieties. In early June, visitors will see not only the evergreen and deciduous tree and shrub "bones" of the garden, but also blooms on trees, shrubs, and perennials, among them *Helleborus orientalis* (Lenten rose), *Myosotis* (forget-me-not), azalea, *Viburnum*, *Geranium macrorrhizum* (scented geranium), *Amsonia* (blue star), *Allium*, perennial *Salvia sylvestris*, columbine, chives, *Euphorbia*, *Spirea*, rhododendrons, daisies, *Papavar* (poppy), *Thalictrum* (meadow rue), *Digitalis* (foxtail), *Baptisia* (false indigo), *Philadelphus* (mock orange), *Cornus kousa* (Korean dogwood), roses, *Gaillardia* (blanket flower), peonies, *Nepeta* (catmint), *Gillenia trifoliata* (bowman's root), *Anemone Canadensis* (windflower), *Kalmia* (mountain laurel), and *Iris siberica* (Siberian iris) ...[Read full description online]

DIRECTIONS—From Montauk Highway/ Route 27 or Scuttle Hole Road, turn onto Lumber Lane, then onto Elliston Way to the end, then turn right onto Woodland Drive. Park along the road.

EAST HAMPTON
EDWINA VON GAL—MARSH HOUSE
962-964 Springs Fireplace Road,
East Hampton
Hours: 10 a.m. to 4 p.m.
📷 | ♿ | **2017**

I am a landscape designer and environmentalist, and my goal is to create beautiful gardens without synthetic chemicals. My garden is my laboratory as well as an ecological refuge of sorts. It is on a protected salt marsh, so much of the land is not available for me to intercede, which makes the fabulous view stress free. The rest of the four-plus acres contains a variety of natural restoration and garden areas, in various stages of progress: a meadow, woodland, and moss garden—all magnets for voracious deer. I explore different ways to create interest with plants they don't eat, and selectively plant and protect those they do. My one deer-proof area, a fenced garden that contains vegetables, shrubs, and flowers, is where I get to do most of my gardening. It is surrounded by beds full of attempts at growing reliably deer-proof flowering plants, for the bees and butterflies. I do not remove any biomass from the property, so I explore various uses of the materials generated, such as log walls from invasive trees, and hay stacks of the meadow cuttings.

DIRECTIONS—Follow North Main Street out of East Hampton and bear right onto Springs Fireplace Road. Property is 4.5 miles on the left. Please park on the street.

Edwina von Gal's Marsh House
DIGGING DEEPER
1 – 3 PM
The Dirt on Soil Health
Free with garden admission, but advance registration is required

Join toxin-free land care crusader Edwina von Gal to get all of the good dirt on soil health! It is the new frontier. Healthy soil means healthy, strong and resilient plants, no need for chemicals. Learn the importance of soil tests: how to send soil samples for testing and more importantly how interpret the results! Take a look into the guts of your garden as we explore the soil biome under the microscope. Learn all about the world of compost tea: how to make, how to know when it is good. Get familiar with the equipment, the process and the benefits of adding compost tea into your organic gardening routine by making your own or becoming an educated consumer.

**Registration required — space limited
Go to opendaysprogram.org
or call 1 (888) 842-2442**

DIGGING DEEPER
10:30 AM – 4 PM
Tea for Two, the Soil and You!
with Edwina von Gal
Free with garden admission

Sip delicious tea in the garden while we demonstrate how to create aerated compost tea for soil health and productivity! Learn about the equipment, the process, and the benefits of adding compost tea into your organic gardening routine.

DIGGING DEEPER
11 AM
Guided garden tour
Free with garden admission

Walk with Edwina von Gal to explore the garden she calls her "play pen, laboratory and retreat...an unruly, willful version of what I do for my clients."

GARDEN OF ARLENE BUJESE
**40 Whooping Hollow Road,
East Hampton**
Hours: 10 a.m. to 2 p.m.
📷 | 2017

Situated on a sloping half-acre, the landscape comprises four rooms. A flower garden bordered by evergreens surrounds a goldfish pond at the rear of the house. Brick walkways weave throughout. The front property is terraced into three levels, each with evergreen backdrops to create a "green" environment in winter. More than twenty sculptures are strategically placed around the property, including large works by William King, Han van de Bovenkamp, Alfonso Ossorio, Dennis Leri, Arline Wingate, and Calvin Albert. Favored trees are flowering fruit specimens, conifers, and deciduous trees and shrubs, including a variety of hydrangeas. The garden has been personally created and maintained by the curator/art dealer over a period of twenty-five years, with the aim of offering a meditative "walk-around—sit here and there" environment for all seasons.

DIRECTIONS—Take Route 114 from Sag Harbor to East Hampton, about 4 miles. Turn right onto Whooping Hollow Road. Please park along street.

EAST HAMPTON
YUGEN
East Hampton
Hours: 10 a.m. to 4 p.m.

How do you create a unique Asian-influenced garden in the Hamptons? Start with acres and acres of deep emerald green moss. Add a special assortment of plants, including some that grew in Asia over 100 million years ago. Carve into the woods a Japanese stroll garden, a Japanese stone garden, a Japanese bridge garden, a Chinese pond garden, a Himalayan birch grove, sand dunes, and a waterfall hidden among the pines. Highlight the gardens with antique ornaments collected from Asia and other parts of the world. The result: a misty window into the Asian aesthetic. As an aside, Yugen is a Japanese aesthetic term relating to the subtle mystery and transience of beauty, like clouds passing across the moon. The garden has been featured in several newspapers and magazines.

DIRECTIONS—At the request of the garden host, directions to this garden will be provided at additional gardens open on this date, or by calling the Garden Conservancy office toll-free weekdays, 9 a.m. to 5 p.m. EST, 1 (888) 842-2442.

www.opendaysprogram.org

Yugen
DIGGING DEEPER
9:30 – 11:30 AM
Subtle and Mysterious Beauty—Exotic Plants and Asian Ideas in a Hamptons Garden
REGISTRATION: $30 Garden Conservancy Members / $35 general
Address will only be sent to registered guests

Spend the morning in an extraordinary twenty-acre garden in East Hampton that has evolved over more than twenty-five years. The owner, who now works to manage global public health crises, began as an expert collector of Japanese suiseki, small, naturally-formed stones that suggest larger landscapes or objects. This led to more stones in the garden, many on a massive scale, and finally to a passion for horticulture. Yugen is comprised of thirty-one individual gardens, including the 1491 Meadow—native plants that predate the arrival of Columbus in the New World—and Jurassic Park—plants that would have existed here in pre-history.

Registration required — space limited
Go to opendaysprogram.org
or call 1 (888) 842-2442

Dutchess County
Saturday, July 21

★There are additional gardens open on this date in nearby Litchfield County, CT (see page 107), and Berkshire County, MA (see page 159).

★Start your day at Innisfree Garden, 362 Tyrrel Road, Millbrook. Extended Open Day hours: 9:30 - 5. Admission: $8

Dutchess County
MILLERTON
HYLAND/WENTE GARDEN
95 Taylor Road, Millerton
Hours: 10 a.m. to 4 p.m.
 | 2017

The property consists of a modern barn-like structure located on rolling farmland overlooking Indian Mountain and Indian Lake. The house has eight doors leading to a series of distinct gardens, intentionally blurring house and gardens. Emphasizing grasses, textures, colors, and plant combinations, the gardens blend with surrounding wildflower meadows and are designed for interest in all seasons. There is a rill with bamboo, a secret garden, a

pool garden, a garden of solar panels, and a wooded walk down to Indian Lake.

DIRECTIONS—From Route 22 in Amenia, drive north 4.1 miles to Coleman Station Road/Route 58, and turn right. Go 1.1 miles, crossing Harlem Valley Rail Trail. Turn left immediately onto Regan Road, which, after 0.8 mile, dead-ends into Taylor Road. Turn right and go 0.1 mile up hill, and driveway for #95 is on left.
—From clock tower in Sharon, Connecticut, drive north on Route 41 along Sharon Green. Turn left onto Route 361 West at stop sign 0.1 mile in middle of Sharon Green, then make an immediate right, just after fire station, remaining on Route 361/Millerton Road. Follow for 2.1 miles and turn left onto Dakin Road (at a sign for Mole's Hill Farm Stables). Go up hill on Dakin Road, which becomes Taylor Road 0.4 mile from Route 361; #95 is on right.

STANFORDVILLE
ELLEN & ERIC PETERSEN
378 Conklin Hill Road, Stanfordville
Hours: 10 a.m. to 4 p.m.
 | 2017

Our garden keeps getting bigger! We keep making small changes, refining, renovating older plantings, and beginning new areas. We try to have interest every month of the year. In September, both annual and perennial sunflowers come into their own, along with many other tall daisy-type plants. The pokeweeds trained into standards by my helper will be looking spectacular. The *Heptacodium* should be showing its decorative red sepals and possibly the *Franklinia* will be in bloom. Probably the most spectacular part of the garden at this time is the meadow of *Sporobolus heterolepsis* (prairie dropseed), which frames a sculpture by Vivian Beer. On a sunny day, its scent is delicious. While I would definitely not call this a low-maintenance garden, we rarely water anything after the second year and fertilize only container plants. Compost suppresses weeds and feeds the soil without making it too rich. Consequently, in spite of all the very tall perennials, we need very little staking. My collection of plants includes more natives every year. I love finding interesting native cultivars like *Liquidambar* 'Slender Silhou-

ette' but still enjoy the thrill of searching out exotic rarities. The garden was included in Jane Garmey's book *Private Gardens of the Hudson Valley*.

DIRECTIONS—From Route 82 north, pass firehouse in Stanfordville. Go 5 miles to Old Conklin Hill Road and turn right. You will come to a "T" very soon. Turn right again there. Now you are on Conklin Hill Road. Continue about 2 miles up hill. The garden is on right after a sharp uphill turn. Please pull into the field on left. The house and garden are on right.

PUBLIC GARDEN PARTNER

Dutchess County
MILLBROOK
INNISFREE GARDEN

362 Tyrrel Road, Millbrook
(845) 677-5268
innisfreegarden.org
Hours: Daffodil viewing: April 21 & 28, 11 a.m. to 5 p.m. Regular hours May 5 through October 21, Wednesday through Friday, 10 a.m. to 4 p.m.; weekends and bank holidays, 11 a.m. to 5 p.m.; closed Mondays and Tuesdays except bank holidays. Guided curator's tours and wildflower walks offered monthly. Garden opens before sunrise three times each year. Please see website for calendar details.
Admission: $6 weekdays; $8 weekends and holidays; children 3 and under free.

Recognized as one of the world's ten best gardens, Innisfree is a powerful icon of mid-twentieth century design. Over fifty years in the making, it is the work of landscape architect Lester Collins, FASLA (1914–1993), with important contributions by his clients, artist and teacher Walter

Beck and gardener and heiress Marion Burt Beck. Innisfree merges the essence of Modernist and Romantic ideas with traditional Chinese and Japanese garden design principles in a form that evolved through subtle handling of the landscape and slow manipulation of its ecology. The result is a distinctly American stroll garden — a sublime composition of rock, water, wood, and sky achieved with remarkable economy and grace.

DIRECTIONS—Tyrrel Road is on the south side of Route 44, 1.6 miles east of the Taconic State Parkway overpass and 1.9 miles west of the traffic light at the intersection of Routes 82, 343, and Franklin Avenue. Blue and white signs for Innisfree on Route 44 mark the turn. Innisfree is about 1.1 miles off Route 44, on the left side of Tyrrel. The street number is out of order so watch for the white Innisfree sign and a dirt driveway through stone pillars to the right of a stone gatehouse. The parking area is about 0.5 miles in along the drive. —If coming from the Taconic State Parkway, please do NOT take the Tyrrel Road exit (it is impassible in the middle). Instead, take the Route 44 exit east toward Millbrook. If using GPS, the Innisfree driveway is now called Innisfree Lane. You can key in Tyrrel Road & Innisfree Lane, Millbrook, New York 12545.

North Country
Saturday, July 21

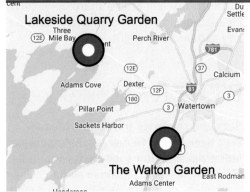

Jefferson County
CHAUMONT
LAKESIDE QUARRY GARDEN
11563 County Route 125, Chaumont
Hours: 10 a.m. to 4 p.m.
📷 | ♿PARTIAL | **NEW**

This garden is built around a summer home on the eastern shore of Lake Ontario. In some places the homeowner has cleaned the shallow surface soil off the limestone bedrock and created flowerbeds where the rock cracks are deep. There are five ponds, interesting fossils, and waves of glacially cut bedrock. In mid-July the day-lilies and Asiatic lilies will be in full bloom. The one-and-one-half-acre property allows for a lakeside stroll past the homeowner's current project: an enormous (100-feet by thirty-feet) flat rock surface that will eventually have elements of a Japanese garden.

DIRECTIONS—In downtown Chaumont, watch for signs for Point Salubrious. As soon as you turn, the road forks. Take the right fork. The garden is 1 mile down on the right. Parking is on the lawn.

WATERTOWN
THE WALTON GARDEN
17428 Old Rome Road, Watertown
Hours: 10 a.m. to 4 p.m.
📷 | ♿ | **NEW**

Extensive country is the setting for annuals, perennials, shrubbery, and man-made focal points. Large pond with fountain surrounded by dry-stacked limestone wall. There is a large stone structure simulating the gable end of an old stone house, including a large fireplace and a waterfall into a small pool. A sunken stone-walled patio with an elaborate pergola. The gardens include many large antique urns, antique statues, and treillage, or trellis, obelisks.

DIRECTIONS—From the north, proceed south on I-81 and get off at Exit 44. At the stop sign, turn right. At the next stop sign go straight for a short distance and cross over a small bridge. First place on the right. From the south, proceed north on I-81 and get off at Exit 44. Turn left at the stop sign, and left again at the next stop sign. After

passing under
—I-81, turn right onto Old Rome State Road.
In a short distance, cross over a bridge and
take the first driveway on right.

Westchester County
Saturday, July 21

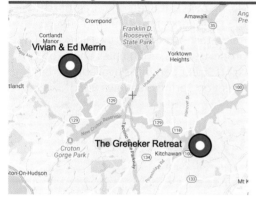

Westchester County
CORTLANDT MANOR
VIVIAN & ED MERRIN
2547 Maple Avenue, Cortlandt Manor
Hours: 10 a.m. to 2 p.m.
 | **2017**

The "Stumpery" garden is now complete
and is open (what a wonder to come out of
Hurricane Sandy). The Merrin garden has
been featured in several books and magazines; the most spectacular is *The New Garden Paradise: Great Private Gardens of the
World*. On a pond with a "pond house" is a
paradise of lotus, 500 of them. More than
300 mountain laurels surround the garden,
in a planting that makes them part of the
total landscape. Mixed borders flow in and
out of the six- or seven-acre garden, containing indigenous plants as well as species
and rare cultivars. Rare tropical plants, all
of which are on display during the summer
months, are kept in four greenhouse struc-

tures. A lotus pond will be in bloom. It is a
sight to behold. A dramatic lookout made
of glass and wood allows the visitor to look
out over the property and its lake. The garden has been done with the expertise of
Patrick Chassé. There are many rare trees,
hundreds of *Helleborus*, twenty-five magnolias, a garden of giant bamboo, a large
and beautifully designed succulent and
cactus garden, and several rare orchids
and other tropicals. A large vegetable garden is seen at the end of the tour. In July,
visitors will see fifty to seventy-five lotuses
in bloom and as many tropical plants and
orchids; three gardenia trees of various
sizes; many hibiscuses, some unique; a
cactus garden; the Stumpery; and the giant
bamboo garden.

DIRECTIONS—From the Taconic State
Parkway, take Route 202 exit. Turn left
toward Peekskill. Go 2.5 miles, then turn
left at traffic light onto Croton Avenue, just
past Cortland Farm Market. Go 1.2 miles
to blinking light / stop sign and turn right
onto Furnace Dock Road. Go 0.8 mile to
blinking light / stop sign and turn left onto
Maple Avenue. Go 0.9 mile to private road
on right. Go 0.2 mile to #2547 on left.

MT. KISCO
THE GRENEKER RETREAT
375 Crow Hill Road, Mt. Kisco
Hours: 10 a.m. to 4 p.m.
📷 | NEW

This 1925 home in Mount Kisco is one of five designed and built by Lillian Greneker, whose works are now curated in Harvard's Arthur and Elizabeth Schlesinger Library on the History of Women in America. Her husband, C. P. Greneker, was then director of publicity for the Shubert Theater. This two-acre property has meandering wood-chip trails, two streams, seven small bridg-es, and two "secret" gardens. It includes a natural fern garden and other beautiful perennial gardens, created by the owners, that contain *Astilbe*, roses, statuary, a kitchen stone garden, and other whimsical features. The home, on this undulating property, is enchanting.

DIRECTIONS—From the Taconic Parkway Norht, take Exit 8 left onto Campfire Road, then right onto Route 100 N. After 3.5 miles, turn right onto Crow Hill Road. The property, #375, is 0.4 miles ahead on the right. Street parking is available across the street on Spring Meadows Road.

Columbia County
Sunday, July 29

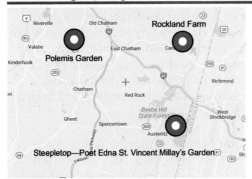

Columbia County
CANAAN
ROCKLAND FARM
180 Stony Kill Road, Canaan
Hours: 10 a.m. to 4 p.m.
📷 | ♿ | 2017

The garden occupies about ten acres of our property. There's a 450-foot-long rock ledge, topped by a dry garden, a raised terrace featuring exotic and tropical plants, a lavender garden, a perennial garden, a water garden, a sundial garden, a rock gar-den, and a fenced vegetable and cutting garden. A hydrangea allée leads to steps up to a wooded knoll, with paths connecting a folly, a water feature, and a stumpery. We have been featured in the books *Great Gardens of The Berkshires*, *Private Edens*, and *Private Gardens of The Hudson Valley*.

DIRECTIONS—From west, take Route 295 (last exit before toll going north on Taconic State Parkway) through East Chatham to flashing traffic light at intersection of Route 5 in Canaan. Immediately after intersection, turn left onto Upper Queechy Road and then left again at end. Look for a parking sign.
—From east, take Route 295 from Route 41 in Massachusetts or from Route 22 in New York past Queechy Lake on right, and Stony Kill Road is the first dirt road on right. Go about 0.5 mile and look for a parking sign.

CHATHAM CENTER
POLEMIS GARDEN
31 County Route 13, Chatham Center
Hours: 10 a.m. to 4 p.m.
📷 | ♿PARTIAL | **NEW**

The garden is at its best in late May through June and again in the autumn. The garden primarily consists of a number of borders framing open lawns or drives. The borders are tiered shrubs, with trees or large shrubs in the rear, ending in perennials in the front. The trees and shrubs are mostly evergreens (*Thuja*, hemlock, holly, rhododendron) as well as deciduous plants such as *Stewartia*, fothergilla, *Aesculus*, and oak leaf hydrangea, which are chosen for their autumn color. The borders have been planted so that they provide interest during late autumn, winter and early spring. The front of the borders contain hostas, *Epimedium*, daylilies, *Leucothoe*, hellebore and *Mertensia* as well as spring bulbs. There are also extensive plantings of peonies and lilacs. The lawn expanses are increasingly being planted with specimen trees such as weeping *Cornus mas*, weeping beech, *Acer griseum, Acer triflorum* and a selection of magnolias.

DIRECTIONS—From New York City and points south via the Taconic State Parkway northbound: take exit marked Austerlitz / Chatham. At stop sign at end of exit ramp turn right onto Route 203 West. Cross over Taconic and turn right after 0.1 mile on to County Route 61. Proceed on Route 61 for 1 mile to stop sign at bottom of hill. Speed limit in village is 30 MPH and is STRICTLY enforced. Continue straight across road and railroad tracks to traffic circle. Take first right off traffic circle for NY 66 North. Continue on NY 66 North for 3.8 miles. You will see a sign for Chatham Center then a sign for Fire House - SLOW DOWN. Turn right on Lover's Lane. At end of road turn right and immediately turn left into driveway.

PUBLIC GARDEN

AUSTERLITZ
STEEPLETOP—POET EDNA ST. VINCENT MILLAY'S GARDEN
440 East Hill Road, Austerlitz
(518) 392-3362
millay.org

★ For full listing please see page 281.

Westchester County
Sunday, July 29

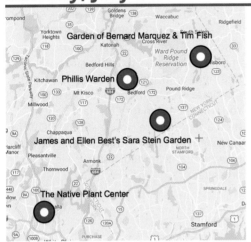

Westchester County
BEDFORD HILLS
PHILLIS WARDEN
531 Bedford Center Road, Bedford Hills
Hours: 10 a.m. to 4 p.m.
📷 | **2017**

This garden of many facets includes perennial borders, three water gardens, a formal vegetable garden, wildflower garden, fern garden, marsh garden, a tree platform overlooking the marshlands, a woodland walk, a hidden garden, and a formal croquet court. The garden extends over seven acres, the back four acres of which are a study in what deer do not eat.

DIRECTIONS—From Bedford Village, take Route 22 toward Katonah to intersection at Bedford Cross. Garden is on left. Please park at Rippowam School and walk to #531.

POUND RIDGE
JAMES AND ELLEN BEST'S
SARA STEIN GARDEN
8 Fox Hill Road, Pound Ridge
Hours: 10 a.m. to 4 p.m.
📷 | ♿PARTIAL | **2017**

This ecological restoration by Sara Stein, the native plant pioneer, spans five-and-one-half acres and includes upland and wetland meadows, woodlands, and thickets. Documenting her planting experiences in her books (*Noah's Garden, Planting Noah's Garden, My Weeds*), she included many native species important to wildlife but not often used in landscaping. Other features include a stone terrace planted with grasses and sedges, an herb garden within openings in a brick patio, and a planted moss garden and path around the pond. There are numerous paths through the various habitats, all showing a viable, sustainable alternative to the conventional suburban landscape design. The meadows will be in full bloom. Ellen and James Best acquired the property in 2007 and have been maintaining it since then.

DIRECTIONS—From I-684, take Exit 4/ Route 172 east to the blinking light at the gas station. Turn left, merging onto Routes 172 & 22 through Bedford. Go 1 mile, bearing right at the Bedford Village Green, staying on Route 172. At traffic light (Gulf gas station), turn right onto Long Ridge Road, south toward Stamford, Connecticut. Continue 2.4 miles to Fox Hill Road. Turn right. Number 8 is the first driveway on the left. Please park on Fox Hill Road.
—From the Merritt Parkway, take Exit 34/ Long Ridge Road/Route 104. Go 6.5 miles

north toward Bedford. Turn left onto Fox Hill Road. Number 8 is the first driveway on the left. Please park on Fox Hill Road.

SOUTH SALEM
GARDEN OF BERNARD MARQUEZ & TIM FISH
74 Hemlock Road, South Salem
Hours: 10 a.m. to 6 p.m.
📷 | ♿PARTIAL | **2017**

The garden, recently featured in *Garden Design* magazine, is a hybrid of discipline and fun! It consists of several garden rooms that flow harmoniously into each other on different levels. Existing natural stone outcrops accentuate many of the spaces. The various garden compositions utilize conifer cultivars and broad-leaf evergreens including a variety of box-woods, some uncommon in the Northeast, as the main structural elements. A koi and orf pond, considerable stonework, and views of the Pound Ridge Reservation and Lake Kitchawan are highlights. Annuals, perennials, artifacts, water features, and containers complete the experience. The gardens make creative use of what was difficult terrain.

DIRECTIONS—From the west, take I-684 to Exit 6/Route 35. Go east to Route 123, then south to Mill River Road to Lake Kitchawan Road to Hemlock Road. All are one-directional turns. Please park where indicated with signage. There are spots where you CANNOT park, also indicated.

PUBLIC GARDEN

VALHALLA
THE NATIVE PLANT CENTER
Westchester Community College
75 Grasslands Road, Valhalla
(914) 606-7870
nativeplantcenter.org

★ For full listing please see page 282.

Greene County
Saturday, August 4

Greene County
CATSKILL
ABEEL HOUSE PRAIRIE
739 Route 23 A, Catskill
Hours: 10 a.m. to 4 p.m.
NEW

The Abeel House Prairie is four acres of

wildflowers and native grasses. It blankets a small holler in a secluded valley next to an eighteenth-century Dutch stone house once owned by David Abeel, an early settler in the Hudson Valley. The owners planted the prairie eight years ago, a decision they regretted almost immediately. Apparently they thought the prairie would be a low-maintenance solution to a brush-covered hillside that was too steep to mow. In hindsight, they say it would've been easier to cut the brush weekly with a pair of hand sheers. They learned that establishing and maintaining a wildflower prairie is a non-stop battle against invasives. Today, however, the results are magnificent. The prairie is full of more than two dozen varieties of flowers and grasses. Bordered by a small brook and bisected by a short hiking trail, it is an easy walk. While strolling through the prairie you may hear a noticeable buzz—a collective celebration of bees that visit here for one of the finest dining experiences of their lives. In fact, there is a huge honeybee nest in the trunk of a large cedar tree next to the estate's cemetery.

DIRECTIONS—From points west of the Hudson River via the Rip Van Winkle bridge, turn left at the first traffic light onto Spring Street/NY-385. After 0.5 mile, turn right at the stop sign onto Bridge Street and continue for 1.5 miles. It will merge with Route 9W, but don't let that confuse you. Just keep plowing ahead. You can do this. When you get near the Price Chopper, the street name will change yet again. The road is now called 23 A. Don't get frustrated or intimidated. This is merely the highway department's way of trying to get people to stay home. You will drive another 3.5 miles past the Price Chopper. Number 739 will be on the left, 0.1 mile past Underhill Road. You'll see a large brown mailbox and a break in the guardrail.

—From points south of Catskill on the New York Thruway, take Exit 20 and follow Route 32 north for about 8 miles. There will be a few turns and a veer to the right; just make sure you stay on Route 32. At Story Farms, turn right onto Route 23 A. Go just about 2.5 miles. The road will turn sharply to the left, and you will see a break in the guardrail on the right. The driveway is at that break in the guardrail. If you get to Underhill Road you've gone too far. Should that happen, you can either give up and go home, or you can turn around and go 0.1 mile back in the other direction.

—From points north of Catskill on the New York State Thruway, take Exit 21/Catskill/Cairo and turn left onto Route 23 B. After about 1.5 miles take the ramp to the right onto Route 9W south. After about another 1.5 miles, Route 9W will turn to the left near the Price Chopper. Don't make that turn. Keep going straight. You're now on Route 23 A. Drive another 3.5 miles to # 739. It will be on the left, 0.1 mile past Underhill Road. You'll see a large brown mailbox and a break in the guardrail.

Join a passionate meadow gardener as he takes a small group through his spectacular four-and-one-half-acre Hudson Valley prairie. He will explain how he got hooked on weeds by his "dealer," Neil Diboll, owner of Wisconsin's Prairie Nursery, through gateway plants like purple coneflower, compass plant, and smooth aster, and how his addiction grew as he endeavored to turn a weed-infested hillside into the beautiful prairie you see today. He maintains that he still knows very little about the plants and the process, but the results tell quite a different story, perhaps what an enthusiastic novice really can achieve.

Registration required — space limited
Go to opendaysprogram.org
or call 1 (888) 842-2442

HIGH FALLS
1624 High Falls Road, Catskill
Hours: 1 p.m. to 7 p.m.
📷 | 2011

Central to this garden is the barberry hedge and stone-walled Oval Garden. Built, planted, and maintained by the owner himself, the Oval is crossed by seven paths, each garden slice with its own character influenced by sun exposure and species grouping. Enter the Oval through the clipped Triumph Arch and leave through the stone dry wall to see the ten-foot semi-circular hemlock hedge. Boxwood-edged paths, topiaries, and stone walls throughout the garden complement the Catskill bluestone terraces, steps, benches, and staircases throughout the property. A wrought-iron wisteria structure is flanked by an old wood shed painted with faux Greek columns on one side and grape arbors and fruit trees on the other. Three spring-fed interconnected ponds filled with bass and carp, named Alpha, Beta, and Gamma, serve as a summer swimming pond, a reservoir for the elaborate sprinkler system, and a playground for the water fountain jets. The shady areas of the property are home to six-foot-tall fern groupings. The old part of the High Falls house was built in 1780 and expanded in 1919 to house Camp Rip Van Winkle for Catholic Boys. The camp thrived until 1968.

DIRECTIONS—From the New York State Thruway, take Exit 20/Saugerties. After the toll booth, reset odometer. Turn left and cross the thruway. Turn right at 0.3 miles onto Route 32 North. At 2.1 miles, turn right onto Route 34/Old King's Highway. Pass a stop sign at 2.2 miles and pass the old stone Dutch Reformed Church and cemetery at 3.0 miles, the Katsbaan Golf Club and Fire Station at 3.8 miles. Slow down at 4.4 miles. Turn left onto School Road and then take first right, at 4.7 miles, onto C. Smith Road. Cross bridge at 5.1 miles. Go another 1.2 miles to a big white clapboard house on right.

Columbia County
Saturday, August 11

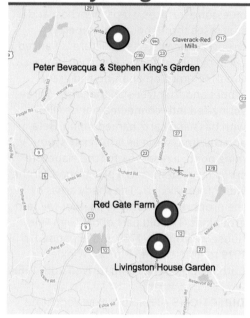

Peter Bevacqua & Stephen King's Garden

Red Gate Farm

Livingston House Garden

Columbia County
HUDSON
LIVINGSTON HOUSE GARDEN
20 Water Street Road, Hudson
Hours: 10 a.m. to 4 p.m.
 | NEW

Located on four acres overlooking the magnificent Churchtown Dairy, the garden at Livingston House has been a labor of love for owner Deborah D'Arcy for over a decade. After caring for the beautiful, natural garden left by the previous owner, she engaged Peter Bevacqua in 2012 to imagine and design a new vision for what the garden could become. Together, they embraced their shared love of classic English gardens such as Great Dixter and Hidcote Manor (albeit on a much smaller scale!). The garden was laid out as a pattern of

different rooms for the visitor to discover, each dedicated to a different concept and connected with pebbled paths lined with hydrangeas, navigated by a large wall of red tumbled brick. The generous raised-bed vegetable garden borders the small orchard of plums, apples, pears, and peaches and leads to an Italianate terrace planted with a wonderful weeping ginkgo, roses, lilacs, *Clethra* and *Buddleia*. Here you can enjoy a view of the tennis court, lined with magnolias and arborvitaes, and an extensive field of wildflowers. Take the path back along the lawns, and the space around the pool takes you to a different place entirely... [Read full description online]

DIRECTIONS—Take Water Street Road off Route 82, and drive for 2 miles. Or take Bells Pond Road off Route 82 for 1.5 miles to junction with Water Street Road. Take a hard right onto Water Street Road. Property is on your right.

RED GATE FARM
219 Millbrook Road, Hudson
Hours: 10 a.m. to 4 p.m.
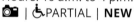 | ♿PARTIAL | NEW

I bought my eight-acre property in the summer of 2013 and spent that fall getting it ready for my horses and putting the plants I brought with me in holding beds. I'm a mad plant collector. The first two borders, the Backlit Border and the Yellow Garden, went in the following spring, and I've been adding to the garden every year since. I put up a poly tunnel for last year so I could get a head start on seedlings and my dahlia collection. There is always more to do.

DIRECTIONS—From the south, take Route 9 North to Route 9H toward Claverack, go 1 mile and turn right onto Orchard Road (dirt). At end of Orchard Road turn left onto Millbrook Road, and the driveway is first on the right.
—From the north, take Route 9H South, 2.5 miles, turn left onto Route 27, take first right onto Millbrook Road, go through intersection, and my drive is first left after bridge.

**Peter Bevacqua &
Stephen King's Garden
443 New York State 23B/Willmon Road
& Route 23B, Claverack**

DIGGING DEEPER
4 PM
**Creative Pragmatism—An Innovative Approach to Reclaiming Land and Developing a "Nearly Native Garden"
REGISTRATION: $30 Garden Conservancy Members / $35 general**

Garden designer Peter Bevacqua and artist Stephen King's garden is usually open to the public in early June, but in high summer the garden takes on a completely different vibe. During that moment which few others see, Peter and Stephen will lead a small group through their gardens, with an empha-
sis on a new area, the "nearly native garden." This recently acquired half-acre plot, once overrun with rampant growth, has become an experiment in turning an overgrown piece of property into a manageable and sustainable garden. Here, Peter and Stephen use mainly native plants but not to the exclusion of non-native options that may be better suited to the site or garden vision. Not wanting to spend the time and resources to kill off existing vegetation to start with a clean slate, they put their creative minds to work and developed an alternate method. Their aim is to create an overlay of plants that will hold their own and eventually dominate the space. As many people, gardeners and non-gardeners alike, find themselves with densely overgrown areas like this, finding a solution that does not involve pesticides or constant mowing holds great value.

**Registration required — space limited
Go to opendaysprogram.org
or call 1 (888) 842-2442**

Putnam County
Sunday, August 12

Putnam County
COLD SPRING
STONECROP GARDENS
81 Stonecrop Lane, Cold Spring
(845) 265-2000
stonecrop.org

★ For full listing please see page 279.

Columbia County
Saturday, August 18

Columbia County
COPAKE FALLS
MARGARET ROACH
99 Valley View Road, Copake Falls
Hours: 10 a.m. to 4 p.m.
📷 | 2017 | 🏷 BROKEN ARROW NURSERY

The garden, about thirty years of age, reflects my obsession with plants, particularly those with good foliage or of interest to wildlife, and also my belief that even in Zone 5B the view out the window can be compelling and satisfying all 365 days of the year. Sixty-five kinds of birds have been my longtime companions, along with every local frog and toad species, and we are all happy together. Informal mixed borders, shrubberies, frog-filled water gardens, and container groupings cover the steep two-and-one-third-acre hillside. It's a former orchard with a simple Victorian-era farmhouse and little outbuildings set in Taconic State Park lands on a rural farm road.

DIRECTIONS—From Route 22 (5 miles south of Hillsdale, 13 miles north of Millerton) take Route 344 toward Taconic State Park signs. Bear right onto Valley View Road after park entrance and brown store, over metal bridge, and past camp. After High Valley Road on left, stay right another 100' to green barn and house on left. Parking on High Valley or opposite house.

SPENCERTOWN

LANDSCAPE OF LINDA B. HORN

5015 County Route 7, Spencertown
Hours: 10 a.m. to 2 p.m.
📷 | ♿PARTIAL | **2017**

The restoration of my landscape has been the goal for the fifteen years of living here after a move from Chicago. There are four restored ecosystems: wetlands, waterfall, domestic area of native grasses, and woodland. The last section of restoration was started last fall with eliminating dead trees and then new seeding. This year goldenrod was weed-wacked and new trees planted. The landscape was featured in the September issue of *New York Cottages & Gardens* with a five-page spread (images are available). Native restoration workshops have been held here through the Columbia Land Conservancy, Spencertown Academy, and Berkshire Botanical Garden.

DIRECTIONS—From Chatham, go south on Route 203, stay right onto County Route 7/Crow Hill Road in Spencertown. The garden is exactly 1 mile south of the post office. The driveway is on the right after Pratt Hill Road. Look for pillar with #5015. From Hillsdale/Route 22 North, turn left onto Route 21 and then right onto County Route 7/Crow Hill Road. Look for #5015 pillar on left. If you reach Punsit Hill Road on the right or Pratt Hill Road on the left, you have gone a block too far. (For Garmins, use Austerlitz Township as our town; for Google Maps, use Chatham.) Please park on Punsit Road or on side of driveway if not used.

The Garden of Linda Horn

DIGGING DEEPER
10 AM – 4PM
A Meadow Restoration Through the Seasons—High Summer
Free with garden admission

Mick Hales

Owner and artist Linda Horn, land stewardship designer Barbara Hughey, and landscape designer Heather Grimes will be on hand to introduce guests to Linda's dynamic landscape, discuss the concepts and practices of landscape restoration, and provide practical ideas for creating healthy, beautiful, and low maintenance native ecosystems. In addition to landscape restoration basics, they will focus on the special tasks and stand-out plants of the season.

Putnam County
Sunday, September 2

Putnam County
COLD SPRING
STONECROP GARDENS
81 Stonecrop Lane, Cold Spring
(845) 265-2000
stonecrop.org

★ For full listing please see page 279.

Westchester County
Sunday, September 9

★ There is an additional garden open on this date in nearby Fairfield County, CT. See page 115.

Westchester County
SOUTH SALEM
GARDEN OF BERNARD MARQUEZ & TIM FISH
74 Hemlock Road, South Salem
Hours: 10 a.m. to 6 p.m.
📷 | ♿ PARTIAL | **2017**

The garden, recently featured in *Garden*

Design magazine, is a hybrid of discipline and fun! It consists of several garden rooms that flow harmoniously into each other on different levels. Existing natural stone outcrops accentuate many of the spaces. The various garden compositions utilize conifer cultivars and broad-leaf evergreens including a variety of box-woods, some uncommon in the Northeast, as the main structural elements. A koi and orf pond, considerable stonework, and views of the Pound Ridge Reservation and Lake Kitchawan are highlights. Annuals, perennials, artifacts, water features, and containers complete the experience. The gardens make creative use of what was difficult terrain.

DIRECTIONS—From the west, take I-684 to Exit 6/Route 35. Go east to Route 123, then south to Mill River Road to Lake Kitchawan Road to Hemlock Road. All are one-directional turns. Please park where indicated with signage. There are spots where you CANNOT park, also indicated.

WACCABUC
JAMES & SUSAN HENRY
36 Mead Street, Waccabuc
Hours: 10 a.m. to 4 p.m.
📷 | ♿ | 2012

A nineteenth-century farm is the setting for perennial gardens, specimen trees, a walled garden, cordoned apple trees, a vegetable garden, berries and fruits, a pond in a meadow, and a vineyard producing red and white wines.

DIRECTIONS—From I-684, take Exit 6/Route 35/Cross River/Katonah. Follow Route 35 east for 5 miles. After a long hill, look for Mead Street on left. Go 0.25 mile to #36 on left. Turn into driveway, then left into parking area.
From Connecticut, Mead Street is 4 miles from traffic light at intersection of Routes 35 and 123. Please park in field behind vineyard.

Dutchess County
Saturday, September 22

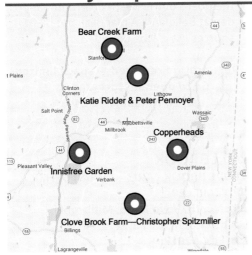

★ Start your day at Innisfree Garden, 362 Tyrrel Road, Millbrook. Extended Open Day hours: 9:30 - 5. Admission: $8

Dutchess County
DOVER PLAINS
COPPERHEADS
1249 Route 343, Dover Plains
Hours: 10 a.m. to 4 p.m.
📷 | 2016

Set on historic Plymouth Hill, the 1840s Greek Revival house has expansive views over the Berkshire foothills. The current property is forty acres, five of which are house and gardens. Influenced by English garden design, the present owners created a number of garden rooms, including a small orchard, a rhododendron teacup garden over which a statue of Pan presides, a perennial garden enclosed by tall hedges, and a boxwood parterre used as a vegetable and cutting garden. Most interesting is a large woodland shade garden, which is home to rare and unusual perennials, trees, and shrubs. Developing a garden on a significantly sloping site was a challenge. A perennial garden is enclosed by tall hedges. The upper half of this garden is guarded by bronze mastiffs, while the lower half has a frog pond. An extensive shade garden features unusual woodland plantings. Visitors walking along the woodland paths will come upon a *Laburnum* allée under-planted with *Hosta* and *Allium*. There is also a small apple orchard and a large pergola draped with *Aristolochia durior.* While there are no gnomes, there is a silly corner. The owners are presently developing a small teacup garden enclosed with rhododendrons in which a statue of Pan will nestle. A conifer garden atop the rubble of a long vanished building is also being developed.

DIRECTIONS—From the Taconic State Parkway, take Route 44 exit east toward Millbrook. After 1.8 miles, continue straight on Route 82 for 1.9 miles. At the traffic light continue straight on Route 343 for 6.3 miles to Bretti Lane parking. If Bretti Lane is not on your map/GPS, it is the north side of Route 343, 0.4 miles east of Route 24. From Route 22, take Route 343 west toward Millbrook for 1.6 miles to Bretti Lane parking. If Bretti Lane is not on your map/GPS, it is 1.6 miles west of Route 22. Access to site is from Bretti Lane. Please do not park on Route 343.

Copperheads
DIGGING DEEPER
10 AM
Amazing Annuals—Usual, Unusual, and Where to Find Them
REGISTRATION: $30 Garden Conservancy Members / $35 general

Annuals, long considered garden fillers, when properly used can become the standouts of both shady and sunny gardens. Rare and not-so-rare annuals contribute sparkle and variety to both the perennial garden and the woods garden. Copperheads, an historic Greek Revival house with views over the Berkshire foothills, has a variety of garden rooms and woodland walks that rely on annuals for continuous color and structure. Amy Pelletier Clark, landscape gardener and garden designer at Copperheads, will lead a walk through the gardens, talking about the annuals along the way. Guests will learn the best care and placement of standout annuals. Amy Pelletier Clark has curated many distinguished gardens of the Hudson Valley. She currently serves on the board of the Beatrix Farrand Garden at Bellefield. A plant list and plant sources list will be provided.

Registration required — space limited
Go to opendaysprogram.org
or call 1 (888) 842-2442

MILLBROOK
CLOVE BROOK FARM—CHRISTOPHER SPITZMILLER
857 North Clove Road, Millbrook
Hours: 10 a.m. to 4 p.m.
📷 | ♿ | 2017

The garden at Clove Brook Farm was designed by P. Allen Smith in collaboration with potter Christopher Spitzmiller in 2014. It was meant to complement the 1830s Greek Revival farmhouse, complete with a custom fence inspired by the balustrade on the Louisiana plantation "Felicity" in the movie *12 Years a Slave*. The garden, planted in 2014, sprang from the earth with great gusto and was influenced by the many visits to the garden of close friend Bunny

Williams. The horseshoe-shaped layout begins with two long, mixed perennial beds toward the front, filled with vibrant blooms, and the additional rectangular beds include a mix of mostly flowers and some vegetables planted to bloom seasonally, so there is always something to enjoy. In the spring and early summer, the wattle fence supports sweet peas and snap peas. Then dahlias grow up in their place, resembling colorful fireworks in late summer. Allen chose topiaries, Japanese willows, and white 'Phantom' hydrangeas to accent the front perennial beds and create a focal point...[Read full description online]

DIRECTIONS—From the south and east, take the Taconic State Parkway to the Beekman Road/Hopewell Junction/Sylvan Lake exit. Turn right onto Beekman Road. Go 10 miles to the farm off the Taconic. Go beyond two stop signs and then straight, through a roundabout. Beekman Road becomes Clove Road. Where Clove Road turns into Chestnut Ridge Road, turn left onto North Clove Road. Clove Brook is the first farm on your right.
—From the north, head east on Route 44. Continue straight on Route 82 south. Upon reaching Verbank, continue straight onto Route 9. Follow Route 9 to the left when it turns into North Clove Road and continue for about 4 miles. The house will be on the north side of the street. Parking is available at 851 North Clove Road or on street. Number 857 is a white building with a purple door.
—From the west, take Route 343 to Chestnut Ridge Road and bear right through the stop sign at Halls Corner Road. Chestnut Ridge Road ends, then turn right onto North Clove Road. The farm is the first house on the right.

Christopher Spitzmiller's Clove Brook Farm
DIGGING DEEPER
2 PM
Made By Hand—Ceramist Christopher Spitzmiller's Garden and Art
REGISTRATION: $30 Garden Conservancy Members / $35 general

Master potter Christopher Spitzmiller is best known for his iconic ceramic lamps, which have adorned the Oval Office and commissions of top interior designers around the world. His work, which also includes tableware and ceramic accessories, draws inspiration from classical forms and traditional gem-like glazes. The same could be said for his extraordinary garden, Clove Brook Farm, where, "There are no beds of single flowers, because for me, gardening is all about the mix, juxtaposition and seasonal change." This mixing of art forms dates to the earliest days of his career.

Christopher was discovered by designer Albert Hadley when working as a summer artist in residence at Mecox Gardens in Southampton, driving his kiln back and forth from his studio near Dumbarton Oaks. When his myriad dahlias are in peak bloom, spend the afternoon with Christopher exploring design ideas in both his garden and the adjacent nineteenth-century Grange Hall, which has been converted to a pottery studio where artisans make his tableware and accessories by hand.

**Registration required — space limited
Go to opendaysprogram.org
or call 1 (888) 842-2442**

KATIE RIDDER & PETER PENNOYER
366 Ludlow Woods Road, Millbrook
Hours: 10 a.m. to 4 p.m.
2017

Our hornbeam-enclosed flower garden with formal bluestone paths frames fourteen flowerbeds and was inspired by the flower garden at Wave Hill in The Bronx. Our house, designed by my husband, Peter Pennoyer, faces directly onto the garden. Our landscape architect, Edward Hollander, designed our property with simple hedgerows and trees, reserving the flower garden area for me to unleash a less disciplined approach. The property includes a cutting garden with vegetables, tomatoes, and dahlias. A new woodland garden encompasses a path from our house to the pond and to the cornfield beyond that defines the edge of the property.

DIRECTIONS—Ten minutes from the Taconic Parkway or 5 minutes from Route 22 in Millbrook. From US-44 east, turn north onto N. Mabbettsville Road and go 3.3 miles. Continue onto Ludlow Road and go 0.5 mile. Turn left onto Ludlow Woods Road. This address may not appear on certain maps. Please use Stanfordville as the town to get directions.

STANFORDVILLE
BEAR CREEK FARM
6187 Route 82, Stanfordville
Hours: 10 a.m. to 4 p.m.
📷 | ♿ | **2017**

This country garden invites you through an artful stone-pillared entrance along a long curving driveway framed by lilies, red maples, and river birches. The property includes acres of dahlias and peonies, part of an ever-evolving flower-growing operation. The 150-year old farmhouse is surrounded by impressive trees, including a 350-year old sycamore, one of the largest in Dutchess County, dressed with an apron of *Spirea*, as well as towering Norway spruces and unusual dawn redwoods. Each of the meadows and multiple garden areas carries its own aesthetic. White picket fences line some of the flower gardens, filled with hibiscus, iris, anemone, aster, and hydrangea. Wander among mature ninebark bushes framed by raspberry brambles with an old trumpet vine and even older tractor-trailer converted to an over-sized flower box. Meander along pathways among crabapple, pear, and katsura trees. There is a handmade stone grill along with various pottery pieces from around the world...[Read full description online]

DIRECTIONS—From the Taconic State Parkway traveling north, take Route 44 East/Millbrook exit (sign also says Poughkeepsie, though you will have passed prior exits for that) and turn right at end of ramp. Go 1.0 mile, and turn left onto Route 82 north, just after mini-mall on left and only gas station on the left. Go 7 miles to fork in the road (Stissing Bank in center), continue to bear left on Route

82 north, and slow down. On left, you will pass a house with a brown fence close to the road and our driveway is a bit hidden but marked by two small stone pillars just after the fenced house. Note: If you pass Carousel Antiques Center on right, you have gone too far.

PUBLIC GARDEN PARTNER

Dutchess County
MILLBROOK
INNISFREE GARDEN
362 Tyrrel Road, Millbrook
(845) 677-5268
innisfreegarden.org
Hours: Daffodil viewing: April 21 & 28, 11 a.m. to 5 p.m. Regular hours May 5 through October 21, Wednesday through Friday, 10 a.m. to 4 p.m.; weekends and bank holidays, 11 a.m. to 5 p.m.; closed Mondays and Tuesdays except bank holidays. Guided curator's tours and wildflower walks offered monthly. Garden opens before sunrise three times each year. Please see website for calendar details.
Admission: $6 weekdays; $8 weekends and holidays; children 3 and under free.

Recognized as one of the world's ten best gardens, Innisfree is a powerful icon of mid-twentieth century design. Over fifty years in the making, it is the work of landscape architect Lester Collins, FASLA (1914–1993), with important contributions by his clients, artist and teacher Walter Beck and gardener and heiress Marion Burt Beck. Innisfree merges the essence of Modernist and Romantic ideas with traditional Chinese and Japanese garden design principles in a form that evolved through subtle handling of the landscape and slow manipulation of its ecology. The result is a distinctly American stroll garden — a sublime composition of rock, water, wood, and sky achieved with remarkable economy and grace.

DIRECTIONS—Tyrrel Road is on the south side of Route 44, 1.6 miles east of the Taconic State Parkway overpass and 1.9 miles west of the traffic light at the intersection of Routes 82, 343, and Franklin Avenue. Blue and white signs for Innisfree on Route 44 mark the turn. Innisfree is about 1.1 miles off Route 44, on the left side of Tyrrel. The street number is out of order so watch for the white Innisfree sign and a dirt driveway through stone pillars to the right of a stone gatehouse. The parking area is about 0.5 miles in along the drive. If coming from the Taconic State Parkway, please do NOT take the Tyrrel Road exit (it is impassible in the middle). Instead, take the Route 44 exit east toward Millbrook. If using GPS, the Innisfree driveway is now called Innisfree Lane. You can key in Tyrrel Road & Innisfree Lane, Millbrook, New York 12545.

Putnam County
Sunday, October 7

Putnam County
COLD SPRING
STONECROP GARDENS

81 Stonecrop Lane, Cold Spring
(845) 265-2000
stonecrop.org

★ For full listing please see page 279.

Ulster County
Sunday, September 23

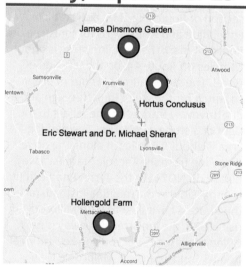

Ulster County
ACCORD
ERIC STEWART AND DR. MICHAEL SHERAN

3 Mary Davis Road, Accord
Hours: 10 a.m. to 4 p.m.
📷 | ♿PARTIAL | **NEW**

The garden is twenty-plus years old, with numerous raised beds filled with deer-resistant plantings of herbs, shrubs, flowering trees, native species, grasses, perennials, and flowering spring bulbs. It covers about one acre, and with lawns, meadows, and woodlands totals seven acres (three of them maintained). Gardens surround a restored farmhouse and carriage house *circa* 1840. There is a solar array. The property is in a rural, woodland setting with numerous mature trees and an abundance of wildlife.

DIRECTIONS—From New York State Route 209, turn onto County Route 2, passing through Town of Kripplebush. Go 2 miles and take a left onto Lower Bone Hollow Road. Go approximately 2 miles, then take a left fork onto Wynkoop Road. Go approximately 0.25 mile. House is on corner of Wynkoop Road and Mary Davis Road. Look for the red barn on the left. Parking areas can accommodate 5 to 7 cars, plus on-street parking.

HOLLENGOLD FARM
222 Lower Whitfield Road, Accord
Hours: 10 a.m. to 4 p.m.
📷 | ♿PARTIAL | **NEW**

Hollengold Farm is located in the Rond-out Valley, which is nestled between the Shawangunk and Catskill mountains in the hamlet of Accord. We use organic practices to grow fresh vegetables, herbs, flowers, fruits, and honey. We currently market through our farm store, which is self-serve and full of reasonably priced delicious food; we also sell to local restaurants. Hollengold Farm was started in the spring of 2009 by a family originally from New York City. Since then, we have continued to grow our gardens and watch as our perennials take root.

DIRECTIONS—From Route 209 turn onto Mettacahonts Road, go over a bridge, up a hill, and turn right onto Lower Whitfield Road. Look for signs and park in our lot outside of the solar pavilion.

OLIVEBRIDGE
JAMES DINSMORE GARDEN
11 Tongore Kill Road, Olivebridge
Hours: 10 a.m. to 4 p.m.
📷 | ♿PARTIAL | **2014**

The garden is best described as having a formal structure with hedges, paths, an arbor, and even trees laid out in a symmetrical and geometric design, which is softened by loose, exuberant plantings. There are four main perennial gardens, each with its own design and color scheme. There is also a long shrubbery, which ends with a stone Chinese pagoda, a latticework "temple," terraces, a Buddha garden with a teahouse, and a koi pond with a granite dragon in the center. Recent additions include a white marble gazebo, a wind garden, and a giant garden where everything is over-scaled so children feel Lilliputian walking through it. All and all the gardens extend over six acres.

DIRECTIONS—From New York State Thruway/I-87, take Exit 19/Kingston and take Route 28 west (toward Pine Hill) at traffic circle. Go about 5 miles, at which point you will see a turnoff for Route 375/Woodstock (coming from Woodstock, this is where you would turn right onto Route 28). Continue on Route 28 for 6.2 miles to sign pointing left for Olivebridge. Turn left. Go 2.2 miles (following detour signs after you cross reservoir) onto Route 28 A, bearing right. Go 1.8 miles to Route 213 and turn left. Go 1.1 miles to sign for Krumville and turn right. Go 1.4 miles to Weber Lane and turn right. Go 0.3 mile and turn left onto Tongore Kill Road. Property is first driveway on left with gate. Please park on street outside gate.

STONE RIDGE
HORTUS CONCLUSUS
76 Mill Road, Stone Ridge
Hours: 10 a.m. to 4 p.m.
📷 | NEW

Our goal is for Hortus Conclusus to be a "living textbook" of plant life that can be grown in the Hudson Valley. We began the process of creating a botanical garden/arboretum by planting native trees, shrubs, perennials, and unusual edible plants. In 2001 we began the process of recording what we planted with detailed plant tags. In 2017 we received Level II Accreditation by The ArbNet Arboretum Accreditation Program and The Morton Arboretum. As a young botanical garden/arboretum our goal is to grow the largest diversity of plant life in the Hudson Valley accessible to the general public.

DIRECTIONS—Take Route 209 South (coming from Kingston direction). At stoplight take right on Cooper Street. At stop sign go straight. Make a left on Scarawan Road, then another left on Mill Road. Please look for parking signs.

Hortus Conclusus
DIGGING DEEPER
1 PM
Unusual Edibles—Treasures for Garden and Table
REGISTRATION: $30 Garden Conservancy Members / $35 general

Allyson Levy and Scott Serrano are botanical artists who moved to the Catskill Mountains about twenty years ago. Their interests have expanded well beyond paper and canvas, and they now garden all year long at Hortus Conclusus, their accredited botanical garden and arboretum. Trialing plants from around the globe, their goal is to create a "living textbook" of plant life, particularly edibles, that can be grown in New York's Hudson Valley. These range from hardy citrus to ancient medlars, new types of quince that can be eaten raw, and a host of unusual berries and nuts. Prepare to get inspired (and hungry) during this walking tour, while Allyson and Scott share practical tips for surrounding your home and gracing your table with rare and beautiful fruits, nuts, and vegetables.

Steven Randazzo

Registration required — space limited
Go to opendaysprogram.org
or call 1 (888) 842-2442

Putnam County
Sunday, October 7

Putnam County
COLD SPRING
STONECROP GARDENS
81 Stonecrop Lane, Cold Spring
(845) 265-2000
stonecrop.org

★ For full listing please see page 279.

Dutchess County
Saturday, October 13

Dutchess County
PAWLING
THE BRINE GARDEN—DUNCAN & JULIA BRINE
21 Bluebird Inn Road, Pawling
Hours: 12 p.m. to 6 p.m.
📷 | 2017

This naturalistic, six-acre garden connects diverse ecological areas on a former dairy farm. Many, ironically unfamiliar, mature native shrubs and trees combine with select non-native plants to form a series of garden rooms with views joined by meandering paths. Duncan Brine, who works with his wife and partner, Julia, at GardenLarge, is a landscape designer and instructor at the New York Botanical Garden. Anne Raver of *The New York Times* writes that the Brine Garden is a dreamlike landscape. The garden has been published in books and magazines, and featured in Hudson Valley garden books. See garden-large.com for more.

DIRECTIONS—From the south (Westchester County, New York City), take Route I-684 north all the way to the end, where Route I-684 becomes Route 22. Continue north on Route 22 for about 25 minutes. From the intersection of Routes 55 and 22 in Pawling, continue north on Route 22 about 3 miles (passing Trinity Pawling High School and gazebos on right.) Turn right onto Route 68 / North Quaker Hill Road. Bear left at the first intersection onto Hurd's Corner Road. Go 0.5 mile. Park on right side of Hurd's Corner Road across from Bluebird Inn Road on left. Walk in on Bluebird Inn Road to the last house on left. —From the north (Northern Dutchess

County, Columbia County), take Route 22 south. At the intersection with Route 55 in Wingdale continue south on Route 22 about 4 miles. Turn left onto Route 68/ North Quaker Hill Road. Proceed as directed above.

—From northwestern Connecticut, take

Route 7 in Gaylordsville west on Route 55 into New York. At the "T" intersection turn left and continue to Route 22. Turn left (south) onto Route 22 and go 4 miles. Turn left onto Route 68/North Quaker Hill Road. Proceed as directed above.

PUBLIC GARDENS

Dutchess County
AMENIA
WETHERSFIELD
214 Pugsley Hill Road, Amenia
(845) 373-8037
www.wethersfieldgarden.org
Hours: June through September, Fridays, Saturdays and Sundays, noon to 5 p.m.
Admission: Special admission fee of $5 for Garden Conservancy dates. Otherwise, see website or call for more information and rates.

Wethersfield Garden is a three-acre formal garden created mainly in the Classical style. Inspired by gardens of the Italian Renaissance, it abounds with its use of water, sculpture, topiary, and terraces. The Garden was designed on an east/west and north/south axis and was claimed from sloping pastureland and fields. The Garden is located atop a hill, 1,200 feet in elevation, and provides commanding views in three directions which include the Catskills, Berkshires, and the Taconic Range. The entire Estate is 1,200 acres and visitors will enjoy our "two square miles of tranquility."

DIRECTIONS—From the Taconic State Parkway, north or south, take the Route 44/Poughkeepsie/Millbrook exit. Turn east on to Route 44 toward Millbrook. Continue 10.9 miles on Route 44 east to Bangall Amenia Road. Watch for the blue Wethersfield Garden sign. Turn left on Bangall

Amenia Road and continue for 2.4 miles. Turn right on Pugsley Hill Road and continue for 1.4 miles to the estate entrance on your left.

Dutchess County
ANNANDALE-ON-HUDSON
BLITHEWOOD GARDEN
Bard College, Blithewood Road Annandale-on-Hudson
(845) 758-7179
http://inside.bard.edu/horticulture
Hours: The Arboretum grounds are open sunrise to sunset daily and year round. The Arboretum office is open Monday through Friday, 7 a.m. to 3:30 p.m., located at Buildings and Grounds (Physical Plant) building on Campus Road. For more information, call the Arboretum office at 845-752-LEAF (5323).
Admission: Donations are gratefully accepted and appreciated. Memberships are encouraged.

Blithewood Garden is a formal Italianate walled garden located on the main campus of Bard College in Annandale-on-Hudson, New York. At 15,000 square feet, it is a garden on an intimate scale within a grand setting: the awe-inspiring backdrop of the Catskill Mountains and the Hudson River. The site has significant connections to the heritage of the Hudson Valley region and the evolution of American landscape design. Designed by Francis Hoppin in the early twentieth century, the garden's style is typically Beaux-Arts: highly architectural, with paths on geometric axes, symmetrical beds, a central water feature, statuary, and marble ornaments. The walls create a peaceful, green room that looks out over the Hudson River. The view is framed by a copper-roofed gazebo flanked by two wisteria-covered pergolas. The surrounding lawn areas of the Blithewood property contain many of the campuses most important and venerable tree specimens, including a former New York State Champion tree that is estimated to be more than 300 years old.

DIRECTIONS—Bard College is in Annandale-on-Hudson, New York, on the east bank of the Hudson River, about 90 miles north of New York City and 220 miles southwest of Boston.
From New York City, New Jersey, and points south, take the New York State Thruway to Exit 19/Kingston, then take Route 209 (changes to Route 199 at the Hudson River) over the Kingston-Rhinecliff Bridge to Route 9G at the second light, turn left onto Route 9G, and drive north 3.5 miles.
—From Albany and upstate New York, take the New York State Thruway to Exit 19 and proceed as from New York City.
From southern Connecticut, follow I-84 to the Taconic State Parkway, take the Taconic north to the Red Hook/Route 199 exit, drive west on Route 199 through the village of Red Hook to Route 9G, turn right onto Route 9G, and drive north 1.6 miles.
From Northern Connecticut, Take Route 44 to Route 199 at Millerton, drive west on Route 199, and proceed as from southern Connecticut.
—From Massachusetts and northern New England, take the Massachusetts

Turnpike to Exit B-2/Taconic Parkway, take the Taconic south to the Red Hook/Route 199 exit, and proceed as from southern Connecticut.

Putnam County
COLD SPRING
STONECROP GARDENS
81 Stonecrop Lane, Cold Spring
(845) 265-2000
stonecrop.org
Hours: Special Garden Conservancy 2018 Open Days featuring Tea in the Garden, April 22, May 13 (Mother's Day), June 10, July 8, August 12, September 2, October 7, 10 a.m. to 5 p.m. Visitors will have the chance to purchase tea and cake from 12 p.m. to 4 p.m. Also open, April through October, Monday through Saturday, 10 a.m. to 5 p.m.
Admission: Adults, $10. Seniors 65 and older, students with an ID, $5. Children ages 3 through 18, $5. Children under 2 free.

Stonecrop Gardens, originally the home of Frank and Anne Cabot, became a public garden in 1992 under the direction of Caroline Burgess. Frank Cabot is also the founder of the Garden Conservancy. At its windswept elevation of 1,100 feet in the Hudson Highlands, Stonecrop enjoys a Zone 6a climate. The display gardens cover an area of about twelve acres and incorporate a diverse collection of gardens and plants including woodland and water gardens, a grass garden, raised alpine stone beds, a cliff rock garden, perennial beds, and an enclosed English-style flower garden. Additional features include a conservatory, display alpine house, a pit house with an extensive collection of choice dwarf bulbs, and systematic order beds representing more than fifty plant families.

DIRECTIONS—From Taconic State Parkway, take Route 301/Cold Spring exit. Travel 3.5 miles to Stonecrop's entrance on right. A sign reading "Stonecrop Gardens" marks the driveway.
—From Route 9, take Route 301 east 2.7 miles and turn left at the entrance.

Putnam County
GARRISON
MANITOGA/THE RUSSEL WRIGHT DESIGN CENTER

584 Route 9D, Garrison
(845) 424-3812
www.visitmanitoga.org
Hours: Access to the house and studio are by guided tour only. For 2018 house, studio, and landscape tours of Manitoga will be offered May 18 to November 12, Fridays, Saturdays, Sundays, and Mondays,11a.m. and 1:30 p.m., unless otherwise posted. Reservations required. Hiking trails are open daily, dawn to dusk.
Admission: $20 general public; $15 for seniors, students with valid ID, members of docomomo, the National Trust, and Storm King Art Center; $10 for children under 12. Hiking trails only, $5 suggested donation.

A premier example of carefully designed naturalistic landscaping, industrial designer Russel Wright's woodland garden invites active participation with three miles of paths and links to the Appalachian Trail. This designed landscape abounds with native trees, ferns, mosses, and wildflowers and is meant not just to be seen, but to be experienced. The seventy-five-acre site, including Wright's Dragon Rock House and Studio, is a National Historic Landmark.

DIRECTIONS—Our public entrance is located at 584 Route 9D, 2.5 miles north of Bear Mountain Bridge. Manitoga's trails can be accessed via the Appalachian Trail and the Osborn Loop.

Suffolk County
EAST HAMPTON
LONGHOUSE RESERVE

133 Hands Creek Road, East Hampton
(631) 329-3568
www.longhouse.org
Hours: April through Columbus Day weekend, Wednesday and Saturday, 2 p.m. to 5 p.m.; July and August, Wednesday through Saturday, 2 p.m. to 5 p.m. Winter hours are by appointment.
Admission: $10 adults, $8 seniors, members free

By far, the sixteen acres of LongHouse Reserve are the most exciting gardens in the Hamptons. From the moment you enter through the impressive allée of statuesque *Cryptomeria*, you know you are in for a rarified experience. The varied and fascinating landscape includes a gigantic lotus pond, numerous walks, a dune garden, and a grass amphitheater. Collections of bamboo, conifers, broadleaf evergreens, and grasses are a compendium of each genus, and the springtime entices with more than 200 varieties of daffodils and 1,000 times as many blooms, at least. Aside from the fantastic gardens and arboretum, there is a museum-worthy collection of contemporary sculpture to intrigue you at every turn of every path. This is the one East End garden that is not to be missed. The large new house (not open to the public) was inspired by the seventh-century Shinto shrine at Ise, Japan.

DIRECTIONS—From East Hampton Village, turn onto Newtown Lane from intersection at Main Street. Go to Cooper Street, turn right, and go to end. Turn left onto Cedar Street and bear right at fork onto Hands

Creek Road. Go 0.7 mile to #133, on left.

Suffolk County
BRIDGEHAMPTON
PECONIC LAND TRUST BRIDGE GARDENS
36 Mitchell Lane, Bridgehampton
(631) 283-3195
www.peconiclandtrust.org/bridge_gardens
Hours: Bridge Gardens is open daily, 10 a.m. to 4 p.m.
Admission: Free, donations appreciated

A five-acre horticultural gem located in the heart of Bridgehampton, Bridge Gardens is a unique public garden with undulating hedgerows, expansive planting beds filled with perennials, annuals, native and non-native grasses, shrubs, and mature trees. Bridge Gardens also offers a large four-quadrant herb garden featuring culinary, medicinal, ornamental, and textile/dye plants. Donated in 2008 to the Peconic Land Trust by Jim Kilpatric and Harry Neyens, the Trust has maintained the characteristics of the gardens, while introducing new elements and programs that tie it to the organization's conservation mission, including an expansive vegetable garden and use of low impact, sustainable gardening practices as well as community garden plots for residents to lease for the season. Today, Bridge Gardens serves as a multi-purpose, multi-disciplinary outdoor classroom, demonstration garden, and community resource, under the direction of Garden Manager Rick Bogusch, and offers a wide variety of educational workshops for both the novice and expert gardener.

DIRECTIONS—From the West: take the Long Island Expressway to Exit 70, onto CR 111 to Route 27/CR 39 and head east through Southampton and into the hamlet of Bridgehampton. Turn north (left) onto Butter Lane, and immediately after the railroad trestle turn left onto Mitchell Lane. Bridge Gardens is the first entrance on the left.

Columbia County
AUSTERLITZ
STEEPLETOP—POET EDNA ST. VINCENT MILLAY'S GARDEN
440 East Hill Road, Austerlitz
(518) 392-3362
millay.org
Hours: Special Garden Conservancy Open Day on Sunday July 29; discounted house tours offered at 12:30 p.m. and 2 p.m. Space is limited so reservations are requested. Otherwise, open Friday through Monday, 10 a.m. to 4:30 p.m.
Admission: On July 29 Open Day, grounds $7; house tours $12. Otherwise, grounds & garden guided tour $16. Please note Open Days admission tickets are not accepted here.

Pulitzer-prize winning poet Edna St. Vincent Millay's home Steepletop, named for the wildflower found in its high fields, served the poet in very unique ways. This secluded sanctuary provided Millay with space to create gardens that satisfied her earth-ecstatic nature and gave her endless inspiration for some of her most beloved work. Over the twenty-five years that Millay lived at Steepletop she wrote volumes of poetry and created a series of garden rooms, a kitchen garden, and a spring-fed pool with an adjoining outdoor bar, dubbed "the ruins," where she could entertain her guests. Though some of these features are in various stages of restoration, they all can be toured and appreciated by today's visitors to Steepletop.

DIRECTIONS—East Hill Road is just off of Route 22 in Austerlitz, New York, just 4 miles south of Interstate 90 and the Massachusetts Turnpike.
—From the Taconic Parkway head east on Route 203 and follow the signs to Steepletop.

Westchester County
VALHALLA
THE NATIVE PLANT CENTER
Westchester Community College
75 Grasslands Road, Valhalla
(914) 606-7870
nativeplantcenter.org
Hours: Special Garden Conservancy Open Day guided tours, Sunday, July 29, 12 p.m. to 4 p.m.; otherwise year round, daily, dawn to dusk.
Admission: Free

The Native Plant Center at Westchester Community College in Valhalla, founded in 1998, is a program of the Westchester Community College Foundation and an affiliate of the Lady Bird Johnson Wildflower Center in Texas. The Native Plant Center maintains demonstration gardens and educates the public about the environmental necessity, economic value, and natural beauty of native plants. The Native Plant Center's demonstration gardens feature plants native to the northeastern United States:
• Lady Bird Johnson Demonstration Garden: Located near the College's East Grasslands entrance. Established in 1998 and dedicated in 1999 with a ceremony attended by Mrs. Johnson and her daughters, Lynda Johnson Robb and Luci Baines Johnson. Expanded and rededicated in 2012. Featured gardens: Native wildflower meadow planted in 1998 and now under restoration and berry-producing native shrubs and trees beneficial to birds, planted in 2012.
• Stone Cottage Garden: Behind the headquarters of The Native Plant Center. The space was renovated in 2017 and officially opens in 2018 as the New American Cottage Garden, featuring familiar aspects of a home garden such as a formal perennial bed, shrub border, seating area, and water feature using native plants exclusively. The garden showcases native plants in a less wild and more traditional setting.
• Rain Garden: Also located behind the headquarters of The Native Plant Center. Established 2008. The central element is a gravel/stone bed that carries stormwater runoff from the roof and downspouts of the cottage. The native plants in this garden can tolerate extreme fluctuations in moisture.

DIRECTIONS—Take Sprain Brook Parkway south to Eastview exit. Turn left onto Route 100. Enter Westchester Community College at East Grasslands Gate and bear right. Park in Lot #1. Greeting table at far edge of lot, near garden. From southern Westchester, take Sprain Brook Parkway to Eastview exit. Turn right onto Route 100. Proceed as directed above.
—From I-287, take Exit 4/Route 100A and go north 0.5 mile to entrance to Westchester Community College on right. At end of entrance road, turn right and follow to Parking Lot #1. Proceed as directed above.
—From I-287, take Exit 4/Route 100A and go north 0.5 mile to entrance to Westchester Community College on right. At end of entrance road, turn right and follow to Parking Lot #1. Proceed as directed above.

INNISFREE GARDEN

Innisfree is a post-war masterpiece — PERIOD.
Charles Birnbaum, President
The Cultural Landscape Foundation (2015)

Like the pyramids of Egypt or the Great Wall of China, Innisfree helps us to define what we mean by 'civilization.' It's one of the few places in this world that lived up to — nay, exceeded — my expectations.
David Wheeler, Editor, *Hortus* (2013)

www.innisfreegarden.org
Millbrook, New York

LongHouse Reserve
A Garden Conservancy Affiliate Garden

Founded by internationally known textile designer, author, and collector Jack Lenor Larsen, **LongHouse Reserve** is a 16-acre reserve and sculpture garden, which truly expresses landscape as an art form. The garden boasts a collection of more than 60 contemporary sculptures by Buckminster Fuller, Yoko Ono, William de Kooning, and many others.

LongHouse Reserve is a remarkable integration of nature, art, and design. It presents major art exhibitions, educational tours, family activities, festivals, and workshops each year.

Seasonal open hours run from April to November. Visit www.longhousereserve. org or call (631) 329-3568 for more information.

Special events for 2018 include:

Saturday, April 28, 2–5: Rites of Spring/ Season Opening. Rites of Spring kicks off the year with new art and spectacular garden displays ($10; members free).

Saturday, May 12, 11–2: Family Day: garden tours, refreshments and entertainment (free admission).

Saturday, June 23, 4:30–7: Planters ON+OFF the Ground IX ($20; $10 members)

133 Hands Creek Road
East Hampton, NY

OREGON
Eugene
Saturday, July 7

WILLAMETTE VALLEY
Hardy Plant Group

OUR PARTNER IN EUGENE

THE WILLAMETTE VALLEY HARDY PLANT GROUP

The Willamette Valley Hardy Plant Group is a nonprofit 501(c)(3) volunteer organization whose primary purpose is to educate the community about perennials, shrubs and other plants for use in the garden, share each others gardens and foster a love of gardening. The WVHPG has been active for more than 25 years and is governed by an elected volunteer Board of Directors. Directors set policy and manage the overall running of the organization.

Meetings and programs are held on the second Tuesday of the month, September through November, and January through May. WVHPG brings in speakers from throughout the west and occasionally from further reaches of the country. Additional member events may be held throughout the year and during summer months: open gardens for members and guests, field trips and garden bus tours, and summer and holiday gatherings. The WVHPG is the sponsor of a popular Hardy Plant Sale held at the Lane County Events Center and Fairgrounds on the Saturday of Mother's Day Weekend. Membership in the Willamette Valley Hardy Plant Group is open to all.

Lane County
EUGENE
BUELL STEELMAN & REBECCA SAMS
662 West 25th Place, Eugene
Hours: 12 p.m. to 4 p.m.
📷 | ♿PARTIAL | **2007**

In Buell and Rebecca's garden, a series of rooms is connected by pea gravel pathways and stonework. Galvanized metal fencing and stock tanks brighten the narrow space, especially in the Oregon winter. The garden originally doubled as a testing ground for plants that they could use for their company, Mosaic Gardens. As the plantings matured and light conditions changed, plantings were edited to masses of low-water favorites, with accents of unusual specimens. A third of the property is dedicated to food production, including a minimalist fruit orchard with one of Buell's stone sculptures. The garden has been featured in a variety of publications, including *Garden Design, Fine Gardening*, and *Sunset* magazines.

DIRECTIONS—From Jefferson Street, turn west/downhill onto 25th Place. Please note that 25th Place is one block south of 25th Avenue. The garden will be half a block down, on the left.

ENRIGHT GARDEN
2050 Monroe Street, Eugene
Hours: 12 p.m. to 4 p.m.
NEW

This garden, open for the first time, balances clean-lined, organized design with varied, full plantings. Chris enlisted the help of Mosaic Gardens to create her back garden, in which flagstone paving and a central lawn are surrounded by borders that mix uncommon plants with reliably attractive (but never boring) workhorses. Redwood decks and a stone terrace offer ample seating, but Chris's favorite spots are two benches—one tucked in a shady nook by a water feature and the other at the far side of the lawn, under a *Clematis*-covered steel arbor.

DIRECTIONS—From Jefferson Street, turn west onto 19th Avenue. Proceed two blocks on 19th and turn left on Monroe Street. The garden is on the west side of the street.

LAURELWOOD GARDEN
2475 Van Ness Street, Eugene
Hours: 12 p.m. to 4 p.m.
NEW

Featured on the cover of *Garden Design* in summer 2017, this garden blends contem-

porary and naturalistic elements. A stone terrace perched on raw steel retaining bench above the creek, and a floating ipe wood deck provide destinations and new views of the space. Masses of Oregon natives, pollinator-attracting flowering perennials, and tough, shade-loving plants weave together under mature elms. A rusty sphere sculpture anchors an ample, stone-bordered vegetable garden. The front garden is the homeowner's design, and the back garden's design is the result of a collaboration between the homeowner and Mosaic Gardens.

DIRECTIONS—From Hilyard Street and East 24th Avenue, proceed east on 24th, through the stop sign at Agate Street, to a "T" intersection with Columbia Street. Take a right on Columbia Street and an immediate left on East 25th Avenue. The garden is just northeast of the intersection of 25th and Van Ness Street.

NORTHWEST GARDEN NURSERY
86813 Central Road, Eugene
Hours: 12 p.m. to 6 p.m.
📷 | ♿PARTIAL | **2012**

Driven by a love of plants and gardening, we built our garden incrementally over thirty years. It is a real collector's garden of about one-and-one-half acres in the countryside, featuring choice plants from all over the world. The visitor will find extensive perennial borders in both sun and semi-shade and various woodland areas, a large sunny rock garden, a conifer/heather garden, and a chaparral garden, which is watered infrequently. A koi pond and many benches around the garden offer rest and repose.

DIRECTIONS—From Eugene, take West 11th Avenue toward Veneta. At exactly 6 miles past the Beltline intersection, at the end of the long guardrail, turn left onto Central Road. Go 2.8 miles to nursery, on left.

—From Cottage Grove, take Cottage Grove/ Lorane Highway to Lorane and turn right onto Territorial Road. Drive 14 miles to small town of Crow. Turn right onto Central Road at intersection just past the convenience market/gas station. Proceed 2.2 miles to nursery, on right. Entrance is 0.2 mile past Chapman Heights at end of bamboo hedge.

—Back way from Eugene, take Lorane Highway west. Go just over 6 miles and continue straight on Spencer Creek Road, which changes to Pine Grove Road 3.3 miles after a forced right turn. At bottom of hill (0.7 mile), turn left onto Erickson Road. After 1.7 miles, cross Crow Road onto Petzold Road. Drive 2.5 miles to Central Road, then turn right. The nursery is 0.4 mile on right after bamboo hedge.

Northwest Garden Nursery
DIGGING DEEPER
10 AM
A Tapestry Garden—The Art of Weaving Plants and Place
REGISTRATION: $30 Garden Conservancy Members / $35 general

Marietta and Ernie O'Byrne's garden—situated on one-and-one-half acres in Eugene, Oregon—is filled with an incredible array of plants from around the world. By consciously leveraging the garden's many microclimates, they have created a stunning patchwork of exuberant plants that is widely considered one of America's most outstanding private gardens.

Timber Press

In this very special Digging Deeper, they will share their deep knowledge of plants and essential garden advice. Marietta and Ernie will discuss design ideas for shade and drought-loving chaparral gardens, plant choices that have proven reliable for the local climate, many of them choice and underused, and maintenance practices including pruning, staking, and soil maintenance. Equal parts inspirational and practical, their goal is to help gardeners weave their own incredible gardens.

Registration required — space limited
Go to opendaysprogram.org
or call 1 (888) 842-2442

Portland
Saturday, July 14

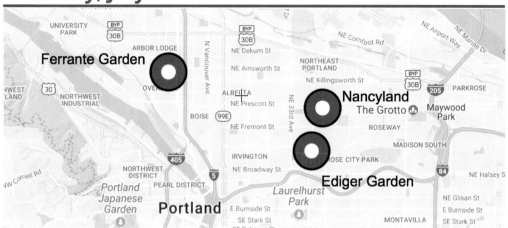

OUR PARTNER IN PORTLAND

HARDY PLANT SOCIETY OF OREGON

Our partner in the Northwest for many years, the Garden Conservancy has been a proud partner with the Hardy Plant Society of Oregon (HPSO) to share private gardens in the Portland Metro area. HPSO was founded in 1984 and dedicated to the promotion of hardy perennials, HPSO now has nearly 2,500 members in the Pacific Northwest and beyond. This year, the Open Days explores glorious garden in the neighborhoods of north and northeast Portland on Saturday, July 14.

Multnomah County
PORTLAND
EDIGER GARDEN

2506 NE 40th Avenue, Portland
Hours: 10 a.m. to 4 p.m.
📷 | ♿ | NEW

My garden is just six years old. It's on a sunny corner with nine-foot parking strips.

These hell strips are full of drought-resistant plants, native plants, and grasses integrated with vegetables. I particularly prize my peonies, daylilies, *Penstemon*, *Geum*, *Coreopsis*, and *Agastache*. The array of pollinators is astounding, and hummingbirds flit throughout the garden.

DIRECTIONS—The garden is at the corner of NE 40th and NE Brazee streets.

FERRANTE GARDEN
1825 North Jarrett Street, Portland
Hours: 10 a.m. to 4 p.m.
📷 | **2014**

I garden on a large corner lot, and my garden is all about foliage. Rusty garden art is nestled in amongst the many plants, and a rustic basalt pathway leads you around the house. There are quiet spaces to unwind in the shade and sunny spots to enjoy the uncommon daylilies. The deck, in the middle of lush plantings, is perfect for relaxing.

DIRECTIONS—From I-5 North or South, take the Rosa Parks exit and head west to Interstate Avenue (Max & New Seasons). Turn left at the traffic light and head south 0.3 mile to Ainsworth. Turn right and head west 0.2 mile to the second, at Campbell. Drive 0.1 mile to the house on the corner of Campbell and North Jarrett. Please park on street. Be certain you are at North Jarrett and not NE Jarrett; both streets have a house at #1825.

NANCYLAND
4527 NE Skidmore Street, Portland
Hours: 10 a.m. to 4 p.m.
📷 | ♿PARTIAL | **2002**

Nancyland garden was featured in the July 2016 issue of *Gardens Illustrated*. The front garden is a bit more staid, while the back garden, much cooler and green, is filled with interesting garden art, treasures, and a plethora of containers. The deep lot allows for surprises as you wander farther into the garden.

DIRECTIONS—Take I-84 east to the 33rd Avenue exit. Turn left (north) at the top of the exit ramp. Proceed north on 33rd Avenue for 1 mile to Fremont Street. Turn right onto Fremont to 42nd Avenue. Turn left onto 42nd Avenue (north) for 0.5 mile and turn right onto Skidmore Street. The home has a red brick front and red-and-white-striped awnings.

St. John Garden
5606 North Campbell Avenue
Portland

DIGGING DEEPER
10AM – 4PM
Book-Signing and Plant-Propagation Demonstrations
Free with garden tour pass

Timber Press authors Amy Campion and Paul Bonine will be signing their new book *Gardening in the Pacific Northwest*. Throughout the day, there will also be mini-classes on plant propagation and how to start plants from cuttings.

Eastman Griffin Garden
4120 North Michigan Avenue
Portland

DIGGING DEEPER
10 AM – 4 PM
Book-Signing
Free with garden tour pass

Timber Press author Donald Olson will be signing his award-winning book *The Pacific Northwest Garden Tour: The 60 Best Gardens to Visit in Oregon, Washington and British Columbia* as well as his new book *The California Garden Tour: The 50 Best Gardens to Visit in the Golden State*.

Garden Fever!
3433 NE 24th Avenue, Portland

DIGGING DEEPER

11AM, 1PM AND 3PM
Seminars: Succulents
Free with garden tour pass

Experts from the garden center will be giving brief classes on using water-wise plants throughout your garden and home, particularly focusing on succulents in containers for inside and out.

Thicket Garden Shop
4933 NE 23rd Avenue, Portland

DIGGING DEEPER

10AM, 12PM AND 2PM
Seminars: Pollinators
Free with garden tour pass

Come learn about the importance of pollinators. Experts will cover favorite pollinator plants, as well as tips for creating habitat for bees and other beneficial insects.

PUBLIC GARDEN

Marion County
SALEM
GAIETY HOLLOW

545 Mission Street, Salem
(503) 838-0527
www.lord-schryverconservancy.org
Hours: Open two days each month, March through September. Visitors are welcome to enjoy the gardens at their leisure the second Sunday and third Saturday, 1 p.m. to 4 p.m. Dates: March 17, April 8 & 21, May 13 & 19, June 10 & 16, July 8 & 21, August 12 & 18, September 9 & 15.
Admission: Children free; $5 for persons over age 16

The home garden of Elizabeth Lord and Edith Schryver, the tour de force of their life work. They designed more than 250 gardens in the Northwest from 1929–1969. A 0.4-acre urban garden, illustrating their design principles and plant palette, it is being restored to its period of significance.

DIRECTIONS—There is no public parking at Gaiety Hollow, 545 Mission Street. Free parking is available on nearby streets or at Bush's Pasture Park (600 Mission Street SE).

www.opendaysprogram.org

Hortulus Farm Garden and Nursery

A Garden Conservancy Affiliate Garden

Hortulus Farm is a one-hundred-acre, 18th-century farmstead and nursery in beautiful Bucks County, Pennsylvania. The gardens were created by renowned garden designer Renny Reynolds and noted garden author Jack Staub. In 2017, Hortulus Farm was the first garden featured in *Garden Design* magazine's "Great Gardens Across America" series.

The estate features twenty-four separate gardens, linked by paths, expansive lawns, and bridges. In spring, the lawns and woodlands are ablaze with daffodils, narcissus, bluebells, native dogwoods, and azaleas. Visitors can experience the perennial and summer borders, take a walk around the lake, or enjoy the charming kitchen garden. Hortulus Farm is also home to a variety of farm animals.

Owners Jack Staub and Renny Reynolds are working on a new book, *The Hortulus Farm Garden Book*. Many of the plants they grow and propagate for the Hortulus Farm Nursery can be viewed *in situ* in the Hortulus Farm gardens.

Hortulus Farm is open for both self-guided tours and tours led by one of the garden's creators, May–October, Tuesday–Saturday, 10–4. Visit www.hortulusfarm.com or call (215) 598-0550 for more information.

HORTULUS FARM

WHERE *history* AND *horticulture* MEET

60 Thompson Mill Road
Wrightstown, PA

Photo by Rob Cardillo

PENNSYLVANIA
Bucks County
Saturday, May 26

Bucks County
GARDENVILLE
TWIN SILO FARM
5727 Twin Silo Road, Gardenville
Hours: 10 a.m. to 4 p.m.
📷 | ♿PARTIAL | **2009**

Stands of specimen trees and gardens in abundance are scattered throughout the 100-acre farm. There are Italian, French, hoop, rose, and circular gardens; container and bog gardens are around the pool and on the terrace. A privet maze is found at the bottom of the farm. There are a pool and fountain filled with aquatic plants, and a wood-and-stone pavilion flanked by two limestone sphinxes. Antique sarcophagi, Roman marble tubs and well heads, enormous pre-war Italian clay pots, amphoras, urns, and bronze statuary are everywhere.

DIRECTIONS—From the intersection of Routes 202 & 413, take Route 413 north about 5 miles to Point Pleasant Pike. The Gardenville Hotel is on one corner, a convenience store on another, and a pet shop on the opposite corner. Turn right onto Point Pleasant Pike. In 0.2 mile turn right onto Twin Silo Road. You will pass a call box on left. The back entrance to the farm will be on left. There will be ample signs pointing the way.

NEW HOPE
GARDENS AT HALF MOON
2232 Holicong Road, New Hope
Hours: 10 a.m. to 4 p.m.
NEW

Garden owner is a nursery stock broker who also operates a small nursery specializing in grafted conifers. In calling on the trade I was exposed to a wide variety of unusual trees and shrubs and fell easily into the habit of collecting them. We purchased this property forty years ago which included the stone farm house, a tenant house, and the ruins of a large barn, but other than a lovely old 'Suffruticosa' boxwood hedge, now gone, was almost completely devoid of any landscaping. Our gardens grew and evolved over the years and are now populated with those plants collected in my travels in combination with selections of other compatible trees and shrubs. There is also a conifer garden which resulted from a long association with the Iseli Nursery in Oregon, which include quite a few forty-year-old specimens blended with newer additions. Throughout the property keep an eye out for rare and unusual plants that are everywhere and can pop up unexpectedly!

PAXSON HILL FARM
3265 Comfort Road, New Hope
Hours: 10 a.m. to 4 p.m.
📷 | **2017**| 🏷 PLANT SALES

Nestled in scenic New Hope, Paxson Hill Farm is twenty acres of stunning land-scapes. The property features a variety of disciplines, from a formal parterre garden to a 330-foot double-sided perennial bor-der and a naturalistic shade garden with ponds. The attention to detail is highlight-ed by a maze garden, a natural earthen structure, and a recently designed conifer garden. The gardens, known for numerous rare plants, have been designed to offer seasonal enjoyment. They are the perfect stop on a tour of Bucks County.

DIRECTIONS—From Lahaska/Peddler's Vil-lage, at the intersection of Routes 202 and 263, take Route 263 north for 3.2 miles, then turn left onto Comfort Road. Go 1 mile, and the farm is on left.
—From New Hope, take Route 32 north and turn left onto Route 263 south. At the top of hill, turn right onto Comfort Road. Go 1 mile, and farm is on left.

The Gardens at Mill Fleurs
27 Cafferty Road, Point Pleasant

DIGGING DEEPER
4 PM
Drama and Drainage—
The Gardens at Mill Fleurs
REGISTRATION: $30 Garden
Conservancy Members / $35 general

Join gardener, furniture designer, and owner of Tiffany Perennials, Barbara Tiffany, for a special tour through her extraordinary garden, which she has been cultivating for twenty-five years. The Gardens at Mill Fleurs, a 1742 grist mill on the often-raging Tohickon Creek, is set into massive rock out-croppings and steep woodland slopes. The site features drama and drainage—everything else is pure challenge.

Barbara is a hopeless collector of any plant family that thrives in shade, anything with a green or black flower, or any plant she hasn't seen before in Zone 6. Creating a landscape that will appeal to people who might be casual gardeners out of all these collections is a welcome challenge. Plants are or-ganized by color families: all the plants in a given area will have either foliage or flowers of the same color. For more information and pictures please vis-it www.millfleurs.garden.

Registration required — space limited
Go to opendaysprogram.org
or call 1 (888) 842-2442

Bucks County
Saturday, July 14

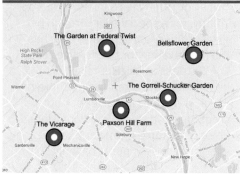

★ There are additional gardens open on this date in nearby Hunterdon County, NJ. See page 181.

Bucks County
CARVERSVILLE
THE VICARAGE
5925 Carversville Road, Carversville
Hours: 10 a.m. to 4 p.m.
 | NEW

The gardens at the Vicarage are varied include shade, water, vines, and traditional perennial gardens. The many gardens have been cared for and enlarged over twenty years. The property features pond, creek, poolside, patio gardens, and an 1763 stone farm house. The gardens have been included in other garden shows with admiring reviews. I hope you too will enjoy the property as much as I do.

DIRECTIONS—Take 413 West right onto Carversville Road. Proceed about 1.3 miles. Just after Street Road on your right, bear left on to Paunicussing Road (no outlet) and you have arrived.

NEW HOPE
PAXSON HILL FARM
3265 Comfort Road, New Hope
Hours: 10 a.m. to 4 p.m.
📷 | **2017**| 🏷 PLANT SALES

Nestled in scenic New Hope, Paxson Hill Farm is twenty acres of stunning landscapes. The property features a variety of disciplines, from a formal parterre garden to a 330-foot double-sided perennial border and a naturalistic shade garden with ponds. The attention to detail is highlighted by a maze garden, a natural earthen structure, and a recently designed conifer garden. The gardens, known for numerous rare plants, have been designed to offer seasonal enjoyment. They are the perfect stop on a tour of Bucks County.

DIRECTIONS—From Lahaska/Peddler's Village, at the intersection of Routes 202 and 263, take Route 263 north for 3.2 miles, then turn left onto Comfort Road. Go 1 mile, and the farm is on left.
—From New Hope, take Route 32 north and

turn left onto Route 263 south. At the top of hill, turn right onto Comfort Road. Go 1 mile, and farm is on left.

Bucks County
Saturday, August 4

ed by a maze garden, a natural earthen structure, and a recently designed conifer garden. The gardens, known for numerous rare plants, have been designed to offer seasonal enjoyment. They are the perfect stop on a tour of Bucks County.

DIRECTIONS—From Lahaska/Peddler's Village, at the intersection of Routes 202 and 263, take Route 263 north for 3.2 miles, then turn left onto Comfort Road. Go 1 mile, and the farm is on left.
—From New Hope, take Route 32 north and turn left onto Route 263 south. At the top of hill, turn right onto Comfort Road. Go 1 mile, and farm is on left.

★ There is an additional garden open on this date in nearby Hunterdon County, NJ. See page 187.

Bucks County
NEW HOPE
PAXSON HILL FARM
3265 Comfort Road, New Hope
Hours: 10 a.m. to 4 p.m.
📷🎫 | **2017**| 🏷 PLANT SALES

Nestled in scenic New Hope, Paxson Hill Farm is twenty acres of stunning landscapes. The property features a variety of disciplines, from a formal parterre garden to a 330-foot double-sided perennial border and a naturalistic shade garden with ponds. The attention to detail is highlight-

PUBLIC GARDEN

WRIGHTSTOWN
HORTULUS FARM GARDEN AND NURSERY

60 Thompson Mill Road, Wrightstown
(215) 598-0550
www.hortulusfarm.com
Hours: Open for both self-guided tours and tours led by one of the garden's creators, May to October, Tuesday through Saturday, 10 a.m. to 4 p.m. Visit www.hortulusfarm.com or call (215) 598-0550 for more information.

Hortulus Farm is a 100-acre, eighteenth-century farmstead and nursery in beautiful Bucks County, Pennsylvania. The gardens were created by renowned garden designer Renny Reynolds and noted garden author Jack Staub. In 2017, Hortulus Farm was the first garden featured in *Garden Design* magazine's "Great Gardens Across America" series. The estate features twenty-four separate gardens linked by paths, expansive lawns, and bridges. In spring, the lawns and woodlands are ablaze with daffodils, narcissus, bluebells, native dogwoods, and azaleas. Visitors can experience the perennial and summer borders, take a walk around the lake, or enjoy the charming kitchen garden. Hortulus Farm is also home to a variety of farm animals. Owners Jack Staub and Renny Reynolds are working on a new book, *The Hortulus Farm Garden Book*. Many of the plants they grow and propagate for the Hortulus Farm Nursery can be viewed in situ in the Hortulus Farm gardens.

DIRECTIONS—From New Hope, take Windy Bush Road/Route 232 South about 5 miles. At "Wrightstown Township" sign on right, turn immediately left onto Pineville Road. Go about 1 mile to right onto Thompson Mill Road. Go over bridge through series of steep, winding, uphill turns and up into a clearing and straightaway. Go to #60 for parking.
—From Philadelphia, take I-95 North towards Trenton about 40 miles to Exit 31/ New Hope. Turn left at end of exit ramp onto Taylorsville Road. Go north 3 miles to Wood Hill Road and turn left. Go about 2.7 miles to first stop sign. Turn right onto Eagle Road, go 0.3 mile, and make first left onto Pineville Road. Proceed as directed above.

RHODE ISLAND
Little Compton
Saturday & Sunday, May 26 & 27

Newport County
LITTLE COMPTON
SAKONNET

510 West Main Road, Little Compton
Hours: 9:30 a.m. to 6 p.m.
2016

Sakonnet Garden is an exotic cottage garden imbedded within a native coastal-fields landscape, a long-term project of John Gwynne and Mikel Folcarelli. It is a many decades, ongoing experiment in design, scale, and plantings. The acre-size main woodland garden is subdivided into a series of fourteen spaces separated by high windbreak hedges and stone walls. The whole is described as an outdoor folly. Each space has its own mood and horticultural objective. The yellow garden is planted with chartreuse or variegated foliage to catch sunlight on foggy coastal days. Elsewhere a silver zone has spires of weeping spruce emerging from pewter-colored foliage; another evokes the exuberant foliage of the subtropics, its centerpiece being a red Mughal pavilion imported from India. A Gothic woodpile is one of multiple tall wind-barriers installed to create microclimates for the experimental growing of plants rarely seen in Zone 7. A new one-acre pollinator-plus summer garden is adjacent, designed as a biodiversity maze for production of butterfly caterpillars and nectar for pollinating insects.

Sakonnet's spring Open Days for 2018 on Memorial Day weekend should occur at the garden's peak of spring bloom. Late tulips and hundreds of trilliums and other woodland wildflowers should be in flower. Blue poppies, blue *Camassias*, a gaudy azalea hedge and rhododendron punchbowl, a confection of pinks and whites, should be in full bloom. For more details, go to www.sakonnetgarden.com.

DIRECTIONS—From the north, Sakonnet is about 5.6 miles south of traffic light at Tiverton Four Corners (with Gray's Ice Cream stand). It is on left 0.07 mile after sign "to Commons" and just after Taylor's Lane. Small sign on tree reads "510". Park along street.

Washington County
Saturday, August 25

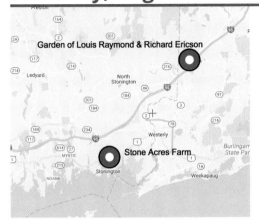

★ There is an additional garden open on this date in nearby New London County, CT. See page 111.

HOPKINTON
GARDEN OF LOUIS RAYMOND & RICHARD ERICSON

495 Main Street, Hopkinton
Hours: 10 a.m. to 3 p.m.
📷 | ♿ | 2017

This is landscape designer Raymond's own garden; it's all about explorations, whims, and manias. With "only" one-and-one-half acres, few trees or shrubs grow free-range. Instead, hedges, Belgian fences, and espaliers create the narrowest-possible separators. Woodies are also trained ornamentally as pollards, coppices, portals, standards, pillars, and topiary. All of this "hortitecture" rises from beds crowded with perennials, annuals, and tender woodies. A horde of container plants crowds the grass and the paths leading to the focal spots at the ends of the vistas.

DIRECTIONS—From Rhode Island Route 95, take Exit 1 onto Route 3/Main Street.

Go north just under one mile to the yellow blinking light. Number 495 Main Street is on far left just north of the light, immediately past the charming corner take-out. Unusual plants crowd the front of our center-chimney colonial, while a massive hedge of American holly separates us from the corner store. You will immediately know that you have found us. Parking is plentiful but eccentric: immediately at the front of the house; at the right of the corner store's lot; and, turning right at the blinking light, along both sides of Woodville Road. There is no parking in the driveway of #495 itself, which is immediately north of the house. Access the garden by walking up the driveway.

Garden of Louis Raymond & Richard Ericson

DIGGING DEEPER
3:30 PM & 5 PM
Natural is for Wimps—Training Plants into Extraordinary Shapes
REGISTRATION: $30 Garden Conservancy Members / $35 general

Taking the lead with many of his garden's countless hundreds of plants, designer Louis Raymond collaborates with Nature to transform horticulture into "hortitecture"—striking shapes of simple architectural geometry that give the garden structure, mystery, whimsy, shelter, and astonishment. And that changes already marvelous plants into *coups de théâtre*. Drinks in hand, join Louis on a walk-and-talk from one such marvel to the next.

**Registration required — space limited
Go to opendaysprogram.org
or call 1 (888) 842-2442**

Charleston Gardens®
HOME AND GARDEN COLLECTION

Free Catalog 800-469-0118

www.CharlestonGardens.com

SOUTH CAROLINA
Charleston Open Days — Behind the Garden Gate

Saturday, May 26 — 10 to 4 — $75
Saturday, June 2 — 10 to 4 — $75

For the sixth year, we are partnering with Spoleto Festival USA and the Charleston Horticultural Society to present an extraordinary opportunity to visit the best of the Holy City's private gardens in conjunction with one of America's premier performing arts festivals.

Each weekend features eight different private gardens located within walking distance in the historic district, tours are self-guided.

Garden descriptions and more info at: gardenconservancy.org/open-days/charleston

TEXAS
Houston
Saturday, April 28

OUR PARTNER IN TEXAS

PECKERWOOD GARDEN CONSERVATION FOUNDATION

We are proud to partner with the Peckerwood Garden Conservation Foundation to bring you this Open Day. The foundation was established to preserve existing collections at Peckerwood, support continued plant explorations and trials, and develop, maintain, and preserve the land and facilities of Peckerwood Garden in Hempstead, Texas.

In 1998, Peckerwood Garden was designated a preservation garden of the Garden Conservancy. The garden has regular opportunities to visit and welcomes group tours. We hope you will make Peckerwood part of your garden-visiting plans this year.

Harris County
HOUSTON
HEIGHTS POLLINATOR CAFÉ AND SHADE GARDEN
414 West 13th Street, Houston
Hours: 10 a.m. to 4 p.m.
📷 | ♿ | NEW

The Dotys are longtime Heights residents who decided to update their garden in 2016. The front garden is shaded by several camphor trees, which made for poor lawn growing conditions. They sought help from a local design and landscaping company. The problem was overcome by designing a garden that was shade-tolerant, low-maintenance, and attractive. This was achieved by using several waves of ground covers (instead of lawn) and other adaptable plants along the house. A large ceramic vessel is placed under the "V" in the roofline to help divert water away from the house. Sarah wanted a garden along the side of their home that would attract birds and pollinators. Originally this side yard, which runs along the alley, was a long strip of lawn. The grass was removed and a winding path using decomposed granite edged with chop stone was put in. This space was turned into a "Pollinators Café." The majority of the beds are irrigated with drip tubing. The plants are mostly native, and something is meant to be in flower most of the year. ...[Read full description online]

DIRECTIONS—From I-10 you exit Heights Boulevard and head north. Go up to 14th

Street and turn left. At Rutland Street turn left again. Then turn right on 13th Street. The house is on the left. This is a residential neighborhood, and all parking is street parking.

ITCHY ACRES
405 Martin Street, Houston
Hours: 10 a.m. to 4 p.m.
📷 | **NEW** | 🏷️PECKERWOOD GARDEN PLANT SALE

Welcome to the Itchy Acres Artist Community, an informal, unofficial small neighborhood of artists, musicians, and other creative souls tucked into the northern edge of Independence Heights. Artists Paul Kittelson and Carter Ernst moved to their heavily wooded lot covered in giant ropes of poison ivy back in 1989. Over the years their artist friends joined them, drawn to the natural landscape despite the ivy! Their adjoining yards are filled with plants, wildlife, dogs, and sculpture—and a peacefulness only nature can bestow.

DIRECTIONS—Itchy Acres Artist Community is located just north of the Heights, about a mile from Loop 610 on Martin and Thornton streets between Yale and N. Shepherd. Travelling on Yale, turn left onto Martin Street. Number 405 is the entrance for this event, and parking is available on the street or at our nearby neighbor's, NSM Industries.

SELIA QYNN'S GARDEN HABITAT
10037 Hazelhurst Drive, Houston
Hours: 10 a.m. to 4 p.m.
📷 | ♿PARTIAL | **2017**

Selia Qynn's home is a backyard habitat certified by the National Wildlife Federation. It is located on a three-acre plot in Spring Branch. Her garden comprises three adjoining properties. It features a 12,000-gallon pond with bog, lily and koi areas divided by stepping-stones, and an island. Additionally, there are other water features throughout the garden, including fountains and waterfalls. Many sitting rocks, art installations, and animal habitats are woven together by lush plantings.

DIRECTIONS—From I-10 take the Gessner Road exit and head north. Cross Long Point Road to Hazelhurst Drive and turn right. The garden is on the right.

STEVE STELZER & KATHLEEN ENGLISH
2709 Albans Road, Houston
Hours: 10 a.m to 4 p.m
📷 | ♿PARTIAL | **NEW**

This lovely naturalized cottage garden contains many pollinator-friendly plants, special plant collections, and "green" and sustainable features on a standard-sized West University lot. Elements include a custom-designed green wall/fence, which adds approximately 135 square feet of vertical gardening with ornamental and edible vegetation; a 1,000-gallon above-ground, galvanized rainwater tank for roof-water collection; below-ground tanks for rainwater collection and storage through a porous driveway pavement system; water storage systems for plant watering; a concrete porch made with recycled glass; an exterior deck made of recycled plastic-bag/wood waste product boards; a naturalized dry creek that works as a detention swale for sixty to seventy percent of normal site runoff; and a rain garden created from porch roof runoff. Flowering, edible, and fruit-bearing plants are incorporated effortlessly into the landscape throughout the front and back.

DIRECTIONS—From US 59, take the Kirby

exit south. Albans Road is 2 blocks past Bissonnet Street. Head west on Albans Road to reach garden. Park along street.

PUBLIC GARDEN PARTNER

Waller County
HEMPSTEAD
PECKERWOOD GARDEN
20571 FM 359, Hempstead
(979) 826-3232
www.peckerwoodgarden.org

Hours: Guided garden tours on open days, the fourth Saturday of each month, plus the second Saturday of the month in spring and fall; check website for dates. Garden tours leave from the nursery approximately every half hour from 10 a.m. until 2 p.m.
Admission: $10 for garden tour. Call for private tour rates. Private tours and nursery visits available year round by appointment.

Peckerwood Garden is an artist's garden uniquely combining aesthetic experience and scientific exploration. It holds an unrivaled collection of plants from around the world with emphasis on plants collected in Mexico by its founder, John G. Fairey. Recently enlarged to thirty-nine acres, the cultivated garden occupies about ten acres and includes a woodland garden along the banks of a creek, a higher dry garden, and a meadow garden that is being developed into an arboretum. More than 3,000 species and cultivars can be found here.

DIRECTIONS—From Houston, take Highway 290 west past Prairie View. Before reaching Hempstead, take Exit FM359 towards Brookshire. Proceed through traffic light at intersection with Business 290.

Garden is located 1 mile past this intersection on right. Enter at sign for parking, nursery, and garden entry.

What our Garden Hosts recommend in Houston

Buchanan's Native Plants
611 E 11th St, Houston, TX 77008
(713) 861-5702
www.buchanansplants.com

Pampa Grill and Market
10111 Hammerly Blvd, Houston, TX 77080
(713) 722-0666

VERMONT
Upper Valley Area
Sunday, June 17

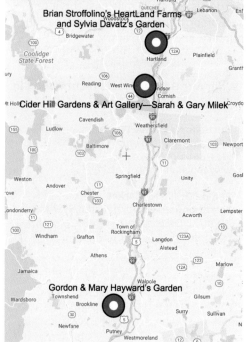

Brian Stroffolino's HeartLand Farms and Sylvia Davatz's Garden

Cider Hill Gardens & Art Gallery—Sarah & Gary Milek

Gordon & Mary Hayward's Garden

Windham County
WESTMINSTER WEST
GORDON & MARY HAYWARD'S GARDEN
508 McKinnon Road, Westminster West
Hours: 10 a.m. to 4 p.m.
📷 | ♿ | 2016

Gordon and Mary Hayward's one-and-one-half-acre garden surrounds their 220-year-old farmhouse in southeastern Vermont. Over the past thirty-four years they have developed a hybrid of Old England and New England gardens to reflect Gordon's growing up on an orchard in northwestern Connecticut and Mary's growing up on a farm outside Chipping Campden in the

North Cotswold Hills of England. The garden, the subject of their book *The Intimate Garden* (WW Norton, 2005), is comprised of fourteen garden rooms. One area includes a pair of ninety-foot perennial borders that terminates in a post-and-beam gazebo framing views of twenty acres of meadows. More than forty planted terra-cotta pots and many garden ornaments, several from England, figure into the mood of this garden. Go to their website, www.hayward-gardens.com, for photos.

DIRECTIONS—From I-91 north or south, take Exit 4/Putney. Take Route 5 north 0.5 mile into Putney Village center. Turn left onto Westminster Road and go 4 miles, making no turns, to the second entrance to McKinnon Road. That is, McKinnon is a "U"-shaped road that enters Westminster Road at two points. Pass the first and then take the second entrance to McKinnon and then immediately turn right into the field to park. (Please use zip code 05346 for GPS or mapping software).

Gordon & Mary Hayward's Garden
DIGGING DEEPER
4 PM
A Walking Design Workshop
REGISTRATION: $30 Garden Conservancy Members / $35 general

Gordon and Mary Hayward have been developing their Vermont garden, and their design skills, for more than thirty-five years. Gordon has written eleven books on how to design a garden and he lectures nationwide on the subject. In this one to one-and-one-half-hour walking design workshop, Gordon and Mary will follow the itinerary of their garden and highlight essential design elements they put into play to create their one-and-one-half-acre garden.

They will illustrate how they put universal elements of composition to work as they designed their garden: the role of paths to initiate a garden design which integrates house and garden, theme and variation, elements of coherence, positive and negative space, contrasting textures and forms, the many roles of itinerary, variations in mood, color contrast, scale and proportion. The Haywards will use their garden to illustrate universal design principles you can take home to put to work in your new or existing garden. At the very least, this workshop will enable you to see your garden and those of others in a new way.

Registration required — space limited
Go to opendaysprogram.org
or call 1 (888) 842-2442

Windsor County
HARTLAND
BRIAN STROFFOLINO'S HEARTLAND FARMS AND SYLVIA DAVATZ'S GARDEN
74 Gilson Road & 106 Gilson Road, Hartland
Hours: 10 a.m. to 4 p.m.
📷 | ♿PARTIAL | **2014**

Brian's HeartLand Farms is a small, diversified farm dedicated to producing the highest quality grain, herb, and vegetable seeds, while also producing market vegetables, fruit, berries, and meat. Brian farms using permaculture design principles and sustainable agricultural practices. The farm is on a gentle southwest-facing slope, contoured with terraces and swales, and planted with fruit and nut trees. Additionally, he now sells open-pollinated seeds under Solstice Seeds, continuing the catalogue previously offered by Sylvia. The visit continues to Sylvia's garden, right next door, where she grows seed of rare and endangered vegetable varieties, and continues to collaborate with Brian on growing seed for the catalogue. Sylvia's garden also includes many permaculture features and pollinator-supporting perennial beds. Both gardeners work closely together and are in multiple ways related. It is recommended that you begin your visit at Brian's farm, then continue to Sylvia's.

DIRECTIONS—From I-91 to Exit 9/Hartland/Windsor. Proceed north on Route 5 for 1 mile into Hartland Three Corners. Continue north on Route 5 for another 2.5 miles. As you approach the overpass you will see Gilson Road on left. Take Gilson Road for about 0.75 mile to #74 on right. This is Brian's HeartLand Farm, where the tour begins. After visiting Brian, go back to Gilson Road, turn right and continue to the very next driveway on the right, #106.

There is a small field on the left as you turn into the drive. House and garden are at the top. The driveway is steep and relatively long. Brian and I will both have signs at the end of our drives to help you find us.

WINDSOR
CIDER HILL GARDENS & ART GALLERY— SARAH & GARY MILEK
1747 Hunt Road, Windsor
Hours: 10 a.m. to 4 p.m.
📷 | ♿PARTIAL | **2014** | 🏷 PLANT SALES

Cider Hill, the ongoing creation and collaboration of artist and gardener, is set into the gentle hills of an ancient apple orchard and surrounded by stone walls. There are long beds of mature, stately perennials and shrubs with an overlook toward the mountains of New Hampshire. Rock gardens, woodland, and shade gardens are nestled into the landscape. An herb garden with peonies leads to the grape arbor, which in turn leads to the vegetable garden and daylily fields. Cider Hill is proud of its ecologically grown perennials, and extensive collections of daylilies, *Hosta*, and peonies, potted and field-dug. In the midst, the Art Gallery features Gary Milek's botanical and landscape paintings and works by other New England artists. Since 1974, Cider Hill has been inspiring artists and gardeners.

DIRECTIONS—There are two traffic lights in Windsor. At the northernmost traffic light (at State and Main streets), turn onto State Street. Cider Hill is 2.5 miles (though it will seem farther) due west. At the end of State Street, continue straight up the hill on Hunt Road. Do not bear right toward the hospital. Look for the Cider Hill sign on the left after a large open field. When you think you have gone too far you are almost there. Please park on lower level and walk up to the gardens. Or the driver may take people to the upper level and then park below. There will be a very few special-needs parking spaces on the upper level.

Manchester Area
Saturday, June 23, 2018

Bennington County
EAST ARLINGTON
ROGERLAND
1308 & 1268 East Arlington Road, East Arlington
Hours: 10 a.m. to 4 p.m.
📷 | ♿ | **2016**

When, in 1989, we purchased the two houses and twenty acres, the gardens were simple and overgrown with weeds. What is today the focal section was a hayfield. The challenge was to merge my desire for a symmetrical, structured, formal English garden around the 1830 farmhouse, fulfilling my enjoyment of golf, chess, and lawn bowls, while concurrently integrating my late wife's preference for a minimalist, locally traditional garden around the more modern ranch. A dry riv-erbed divides the two styles, and there are many water features, iron-fenced kitchen gardens, topiaries, and patios that round out the property. Key to the garden is the merging of the structured hardscape—stone walks and dry-laid walls, many sitting areas, extensive custom ironwork—with the softscape—thousands of peren-nials, annuals, trees, and shrubs. Among the garden's special areas are the putting green, lawn bowls, "Alice-in-Wonderland," alpine, a granite raised-bed vegetable garden, vineyard walk, hops production, and seven different water features. Several new features have been added since the last Open Day 2016. I recommend you plan to spend one and a half to two hours to enjoy the gardens. A brochure and map with suggested route will be provided at the entrance.

DIRECTIONS—From Bennington, go north on Route 7 toward Manchester. Take Exit 3 off Route 7/Route 313 West/Arlington. At the bottom of the ramp, turn left under the bridge onto Route 313 West. Take the first right (after the southbound exit ramp) onto South Road. Continue to end at "T" intersection and turn left onto Old Mill Road. Stay on Old Mill Road, staying right at all "Y" junctions through the Village of East Arlington. At the end of Old Mill Road, turn right onto East Arlington Road/Maple Street. The two houses are the 8th and 9th on the right from corner and just past the Arlington Antique Center. The mailboxes are #1268 and #1308 respectively, but look for Garden Conservancy signs.

—From Bennington or Manchester, take Route 7A and in the center of the Town of Arlington turn east onto East Arlington Road. Follow about 1 mile past the schools, library, and antiques center to the garden. Parking will be marked and is available in the empty lot opposite #1268.

—From Manchester, go south on Route 7 toward Bennington. Take Exit 3/Route 313 West/Arlington. At the bottom of the ramp, turn right and stay right on Route 313 West. Proceed as directed above. The distance from Bennington or Manchester to the garden is about 12 miles.

MANCHESTER
TURKEY HILL FARM
317 Silver Springs Lane, Manchester
Hours: 10 a.m. to 4 p.m.
📷 | ♿PARTIAL | **2016**

The gardens around the main house were designed during the 1930s and have been cared for since then by four generations of committed gardeners. The layout remains the same as the original's; the plantings have changed over the years. In 2004, we began a project to convert five acres of pasture into gardens.

Like most projects, this one took on a life of its own and is now a sculpture garden with a winding *arroyo*, a pergola, and mowed walking paths. More recently, we added a Japanese garden and a path through the woods featuring a boardwalk, a vine-covered arbor, and a gazebo. Across the road near the barn are the vegetable gardens; a small orchard of apple, cherry, and pear trees; a pond; a screen house; and a greenhouse. A converted corncrib is a one-room guest cottage. Turkey Hill Farm gets its name from the wild turkeys that graze in the apple orchard.

DIRECTIONS—Follow Route 7A south from Manchester. Turn right onto Silver Spring Lane (3 miles south of the Equinox Hotel). Turn right at the "T" intersection and follow road as it winds up hill to left. Turkey Hill Farm is first property up hill.

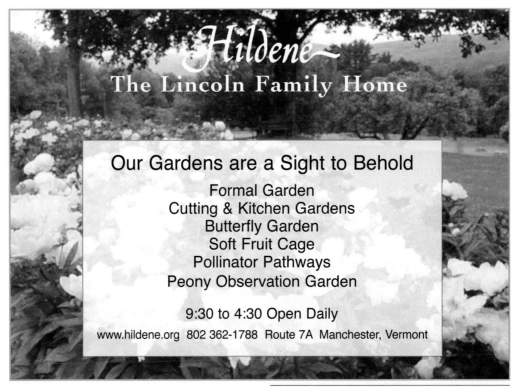

MANCHESTER VILLAGE
A COOK'S GARDEN
98 Franklin Avenue, Manchester Village
Hours: 10 a.m. to 4 p.m.
📷 | **2011**

My kitchen garden is hidden behind a green arborvitae located on the south side of the house. A true European potager based on a four-square organic rotation, it contains herbs, lettuce and other salad greens, and a few colorful vegetables. Edible flowers and vertical elements add visual interest and are planted in a way to create a tapestry of colors when seen from inside the house. When I moved to this one-quarter-acre set apart from a ten-acre farm, it seemed impossible to fit in a garden, but my kitchen garden is a good example of a classic garden design for a small space.

DIRECTIONS—From Manchester Center and the intersection of Routes 30 and 7A, turn left and go 1.5 miles. Before the Equinox Resort, turn right onto Seminary Avenue and then take the first right onto Franklin Avenue. Park in school parking lot on left, and walk down road to #98, fourth house on right.

WASHINGTON
Bainbridge Island
Saturday, June 16

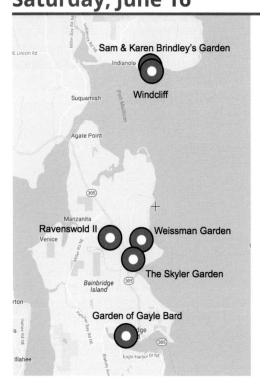

Sam & Karen Brindley's Garden
Indianola
Windcliff
Suquamish
Agate Point
Manzanita
Ravenswold II
Venice
Weissman Garden
The Skyler Garden
Bainbridge Island
Garden of Gayle Bard

Kitsap County
BAINBRIDGE ISLAND
GARDEN OF GAYLE BARD
257 Wood Avenue SW, Bainbridge Island
Hours: 10 a.m. to 4 p.m.
 | NEW

This small, in-town, front-yard garden combines formal structure, sculptural plant forms, and the illusion of greater space. For this artist/gardener it is painting with plants. Quickly providing privacy was the primary goal in its design, followed closely by being manageable for several years to come for its octogenarian creator. When

she downsized from previous large garden-tour installations, she brought along more than 100 plants to accompany her move to a small rented cottage; the transported plants left not the slightest dent in their original garden homes. One would be surprised to know this garden, save for the old cottage, was an empty lot only three years ago.

DIRECTIONS—From the ferry, turn left at intersection of Highway 305 and Winslow Way toward downtown. Proceed to 4-way stop (Madison and Winslow Way), go straight, then turn left at second street, Wood Avenue. Garden will be mid-block on your right behind a tall, undulating laurel hedge directly across from 3-story, light gray apartment building. If you must park there (and it is NOT advised), be SURE to park ONLY in spaces marked "VISITORS."

RAVENSWOLD II
11507 Chadwick Court N.E., Bainbridge Island
Hours: 10 a.m. to 4 p.m.
| 2011

The garden began about ten years ago as a "blank slate" with lawns and native plants (Salal, rhododendrons, and maple and cedar trees). It has developed into four areas: the entry path, the living area, the transition garden, and the large street-side section, which once was all lawn and is now a low-water, low-maintenance garden. Plants have been chosen for their year-round interest, variety of color, and texture. Most of the annuals and perennials are concentrated in the patio/living area. The property is surrounded by large maples and cedars, creating an interesting challenge in plant selection.

DIRECTIONS—From the Bainbridge Island ferry, follow the highway for about 3 miles. Watch for the sign "Meadowmeer Golf and Country Club, Bainbridge Athletic Club." Take the next left, Koura Road, and turn right at the club entrance. Follow the main road past the golf course and around the traffic island. Look for the parking signs. —From the west (Poulsbo area), follow the signs to Bainbridge and after the first traffic light look for the sign "Meadowmeer Golf and Country Club, Bainbridge Athletic Club." Take the next right, Koura Road, and turn right at the club entrance. Follow the main road past the golf course and around the traffic island. Look for the parking signs.

THE SKYLER GARDEN
9734 Manitou Place, Bainbridge Island
Hours: 10 a.m. to 4 p.m.
📷 | ♿PARTIAL | **2016**

Surrounded by waves of cedar pickets and an iron gate made by the owner, this private third-of-an-acre site sits at the end of a quiet cul-de-sac. Nestled among tall firs, vine maples, rhododendrons, azaleas, *Viburnum*, and magnolias, these gardens have been a work in progress for more than thirty years. Stroll the pathways, each leading to a different garden room, and you will discover seemingly endless groupings of *Hosta, Helleborus, Hebes*, barberries, *Spirea, Farfugium, Euphorbia*, and more than 100 varieties of ferns—the gardener's passion. These gardens have interest throughout the year with hardscape and water features. Enjoy the serenity of these gardens.

DIRECTIONS—From Seattle, take the Bainbridge Island ferry from the Coleman dock on the waterfront (a 30-minute crossing). On Bainbridge Island take Highway 305 to the fourth traffic light and turn right at the Manitou Beach sign. The road then forks—take an immediate left onto North Madison, going up the hill. After about 0.25 mile, turn right onto Beach Crest Drive. Turn left (3 houses down) onto Manitou Place, a private cul-de-sac where you may park, and then walk through the steel gates.

WEISSMAN GARDEN
10149 NE Roberts Road, Bainbridge Island
Hours: 10 a.m. to 4 p.m.
📷 | ♿PARTIAL | **2014**

Barbara and Eric began their stewardship of this beautifully laid-out garden six years ago and have enhanced it with many personal touches. Sunny borders and shady, fern-lined paths showcase Barbara's extensive plant collection. Last year's complete renovation of the water feature and removal of diseased ornamental cherries led to a rethinking of the northern half of the garden, including a seating area next to the pond, an extended birch grove, and a new collection of pines.

DIRECTIONS—From downtown and ferry, drive north on Highway 305 to Manitou Beach Road traffic light (signage for Municipal Court). Turn right, then follow the arterial left on Madison to Valley. Turn right on Valley to Kallgren, left on Kallgren to Roberts, right on Roberts. We are at the end of the third driveway on the right. —From the north, drive south on Highway 305. Turn left on Lovgreen. Follow Lovgreen, which becomes Winthers at Madison, to Kallgren. Turn right on Kallgren to Roberts, then left on Roberts. We are at the end of the third driveway on the right.

INDIANOLA
SAM & KAREN BRINDLEY'S GARDEN
10305 NE Shore Drive, Indianola
Hours: 10 a.m. to 4 p.m.
📷 | ♿PARTIAL | **2014**

Enter a cathedral of Douglas fir bordered by woodland plants in a rich variety of colors. Next a cut flower garden, where a spectral blend of pink, lavender, and blue paint a flowing canvas. The sandstone house entrance is terraced with a strong, evergreen palette. *Helleborus, Daphne*, and *Sarcococca* bring fragrance and color in the winter, yielding to *Abutilon*, roses, *Roscoea, Podophyllum, Beesia*, and *Arisaema* when summer arrives. Foodies might want to see the greenhouse area. Delicious! Meander to the tropics, where bananas, dates, bamboo, palms, and scrumptious vines weave together in lush, vibrant tones. Farther on, the panorama of Puget Sound comes into view and Mediterranean influences spring to life. Grasses, *Agapanthus, Echium, Eryngium*, lilies, and an immeasurable number of friends, both floral and structural, create waves of distinct color. A hardscape of bridges, a stone patio with a unique fire pit, and floating stones add clever whimsy. This garden, with its collection of rare and unusual varieties, is an Eden for all the senses.

DIRECTIONS—From the intersection of Route 104 & Miller Bay Road NE, go south on Miller Bay Road NE. In 2.7 miles, turn left onto Indianola Road NE. Go another 3.2 miles and turn left onto NE Shore Drive. Go 1 mile and the garden is on right. Follow church camp signs.
From the intersection of Route 305 and Suquamish Way NE, drive north on Suquamish Way NE. 4.9 miles. Turn right onto Indianola Road, go 3.2 miles, and turn left onto NE Shore Drive. Go 1 mile (follow church camp signs), and the garden is on right.

WINDCLIFF
10345 NE Shore Drive, Indianola
Hours: 10 a.m. to 4 p.m.
2015 | 🏷️PLANT SALES

Situated on six-and-one-half acres of south-facing high bluff overlooking Puget Sound, Windcliff is the home and garden of Dan Hinkley and Robert Jones, The house, designed by Jones, and garden are eleven years old. The garden is primarily plant-driven, showcasing Hinkley's collection work of twenty-five-plus years. The two-acre site south of the house is naturalistic in style with a large collection of xeric-minded grasses, perennials, shrubs, and small trees. Surrounding the greenhouse is a potager, and the area north of the house and along the drive is meant as an arboretum. A new experimental meadow, approximately one-half-acre in size, is approaching its third growing season. Collections of note here include *Acer, Sorbus, Mahonia, Magnolia*, and *Schefflera*, while one-offs, such as *Sinopanax formosanus*, are plentiful. No restroom facilities. Plants will be for sale from the small adjoining nursery.

DIRECTIONS—From the first traffic light just outside the Kingston ferry lot, move into left lane, go two blocks to Iowa, and turn left. Go through the first stop sign. At the second stop sign turn left onto South Kingston Road (25 mph). Continue on South Kingston about 4 miles (turning left at stop sign for Whitehorse, a housing development, to stay on South Kingston) to next stop sign (Indianola Road with wood-

en sign "Indianola" on stone pedestals opposite). Turn left onto Indianola Road and continue to stop sign at the Country Store (NE Shore Drive). Turn left onto NE Shore Drive, go to the end, and turn left onto the private one-lane road that goes up the hill (sometimes with sign to the Indianola Church Camp). Stay on road as it winds up the forested hill and changes from blacktop to gravel. At the top of the last rise, before going down to the Church Camp, you will break out of the forest and see a purple wood fence with a wavy line on your right. The wave leads to a gate where you will enter Windcliff at #10345.
—From Bainbridge Island, take the main highway (Highway 305) to north end of island, across Agate Pass bridge to first intersection. Move into right-turn lane and turn onto Suquamish-Hansville Highway/ Miller Bay Road. Go through Suquamish (25 mph) and continue a few miles to In- dianola Road (second light on the right) at the fish hatchery. Turn right onto Indianola Road and proceed as directed above.
—From Bremerton, Silverdale, Poulsbo, from Highway 3 take the Bainbridge, Poulsbo, Kingston exit onto Highway 305 (there is a traffic light at the end of the exit lane). Go through the next light and move into the left-turn lane to Highway 307 North/Kingston. On Highway 307 North, after about 3 miles and just before the traffic light, move into the right-turn lane to Gunderson Road. Stay on Gunderson Road to the traffic light at the end. Turn left onto Miller Bay Road NE. Go 0.5 mile to the next traffic light and turn right onto Indianola Road, then proceed as directed above. Park perpendicular to the fence on the grass strip outside the fence and gate. If the grass is wet and slick, park facing slightly downhill so that gravity will help move the car away from the fence.